Ancestry's
GUIDE TO RESEARCH
Case Studies in American Genealogy

Ancestry's
GUIDE TO
RESEARCH

Case Studies in American Genealogy

By Johni Cerny & Arlene Eakle

Ancestry Incorporated
Salt Lake City, Utah
1985

Library of Congress Catalog Number 84-72694
ISBN Number 0-916489-01-9

First Printing 1985
10 9 8 7 6

Printed in the United States of America

Contents

Preface vii

Introduction ix

Chapter 1. Elements of Genealogical Identification. 11

Chapter 2. Genealogy Yellow Pages 31

Chapter 3. On the Reference Shelf. 49

Chapter 4. Getting Started 61

Chapter 5. Organizing Yourself. 85

Chapter 6. Sources 105

Chapter 7. How Rules Apply to Genealogy 115

Chapter 8. Tracing an American Lineage 125

Chapter 9. Tracing Ancestors with Common Surnames . . . 239

Chapter 10. Ancestry by Occupation. 257

Chapter 11. Tracing a Lineage Through Burned Records . . 267

Chapter 12. Tracing the Women in Your Family. 275

Chapter 13. Military Ancestors 287

Chapter 14. Colonial Ancestors 297

Chapter 15. Ethnic Ancestors 323

Chapter 16. Immigrant Ancestors 339

Index. 355

IN MEMORY OF BERTHA RUTH SMITH
14 FEB 1889-28 AUG 1972

The Thomas Albert Smith Family
1897

Bertha Ruth

Thomas Albert   Mary Alice

Preface

Once again the would-be genealogist is indebted to the labors of Johni Cerny and Arlene Eakle, compilers of the invaluable research tool, *The Source*. Recognizing the bewilderment and frustration that often greet the beginning researcher, they have put together a most helpful compilation that takes the newcomer by the hand and leads him or her through some of the unusual paths, as well as the pitfalls, of research.

A perusal of the table of contents will show that they wisely begin with what you should know before launching into your search. Once you have started, they chart your course telling you not only how and where to search, but what to do with the data you accumulate. If one chapter leads to a dead end, the authors suggest other routes worth following. The upbeat enthusiasm that characterizes their writing is infectious.

Based as they are in Salt Lake City, they describe in detail some of the unusual resources, indexes, and other finding aids that characterize the unique collections of the Genealogical Library of the LDS Church, as well as some of the many new materials of value that have recently come off the press from other sources. All of it is beautifully clarified by numerous case histories interspersed with graphic illustrations of source material.

Are you ready for the great adventure of finding your roots? This *Guide to Research* will light and lighten your way.

Rabbi Malcolm H. Stern
New York, New York
January 1985

Introduction

Ancestry's *Guide to Research* was created as a companion to *The Source: A Guidebook of American Genealogy* after many would-be *Source* users said that it was too advanced for their skill level. With hundreds of genealogy how-to books already lining library and bookstore shelves, it was important to accomplish what most others did not do by going beyond presenting an overview of genealogical research and instructing novice and intermediate researchers how to trace American ancestry.

The first chapters of *The Guide* provide the basics to get started, analyze evidence, and plan successful research activities. The remaining chapters give research instruction through applying the basics in case studies and research cameos. Those methods used are not the only approaches to solving research problems. Other genealogists will use different methods and achieve the same results. Our goal was to present one approach to research that produced excellent results, involved using a variety of records, and was understandable to readers of any skill level. Like *The Source*, this book was designed with the user in mind.

Admittedly, there is an obvious emphasis on southern research problems and the use of census records. The southern emphasis came about accidentally while choosing research examples that would best instruct the reader in how to solve difficult problems. (More researchers are stuck on southern problems.) The census is a basic source in American research, especially in the absence of early vital records outside of New England. Thousands of lineages are built from census enumerations, and as the most widely used source in American research, we wanted to instruct the reader in how to use census material to its very best advantage.

Much of the information presented is based on firsthand experience. Special problem-solving sections such as "Tracing Common Surnames," "Tracing the Women in Your Lineage," "Ancestors on the Move," and "Immigrant Ancestors," include unique material designed to help those with similar problems formulate a sound research design of their own.

While the emphasis is on familiarizing the novice researcher with primary and original sources, printed sources should not be minimized. A full discussion of printed and secondary sources will appear in *The Second Source*, a future Ancestry project.

We deeply appreciate the participation of family members, close friends, and clients, who enthusiastically contributed materials for our use. We owe particular thanks to those who critiqued the final manuscript, including Rabbi Malcolm H. Stern, genealogist for the American Jewish Archives; Ralph Crandall, Director of the New England Historic Genealogical Society; and Jimmy D. Walker, former Director of Local and Family Services at the National Archives. Additionally, we sincerely thank the management and staff of the Genealogical Library of the LDS Church in Salt Lake City for years of assistance and use of their marvelous facility.

We also want to thank P. William Filby, Fellow of the Society of Genealogists, London (FGS); Dr. Donald J. Martin; William Thorndale, C.G.; Quincy Jones; John Coy Stewart; Harry L. Carle; McCown E. Hunt; Pingree Family Organization; Mrs. J. Harmon Carter; Vera P. Firebaugh; Afton J. Reintjes; Diane Dieterle, publisher and editor of *Genealogy Tomorrow*; and Gary Boyd Roberts, Research Director of the New England Historic Genealogical Society.

Those who particpated in project management and production contributed far more than they could ever be compensated for and they have our deepest gratitude, including Douglas J. Easton, who managed and edited the project; word processor Shirlene Franzen; typist Kathy Paraskeva; professional genealogists Kendall H. Williams (plantation owners research in Mississippi) and Loretto Dennis Szucs (eastern European ancestral research in Chicago); Robert Passey and Lisa Brashear of Newman Passey Design (Salt Lake City); and our patient staff members who survived another year of erratic schedules and preoccupation with publishing deadlines.

Johni Cerny
Arlene Eakle
Salt Lake City, Utah
January 1985

CHAPTER 1

Elements of Genealogical Identification

N ames, dates, relationships, and places are the four elements of genealogical identification. It is critically important to understand each element before researching in public and private records. Without a thorough understanding of these elements, compiling an accurate lineage is most difficult. Several years ago, I met an enthusiastic hobbyist who was thrilled to find an excellent published genealogy that extended his New England ancestry back to England and a well-proven royal connection. He carefully went through the book and extracted his lines onto a lineage chart, but suddenly he was confused when the author stopped using surnames for ancestors born prior to the thirteenth century. Instead of copying the material as it was presented, he added the seemingly appropriate surnames, creating an inaccurate lineage. When a royal lineage specialist reviewed his material, these surnames were spotted immediately and his entire work was suspect. He simply didn't know that surnames were not used in England prior to the thirteenth century.

NAMES

There are dozens of interesting and informative books about the history and origin of names. Most books begin with a discussion of Anglo-Saxon naming patterns whose roots reach back to about 3000 B.C. Anglo-Saxon names had simple meanings, such as Edward, meaning "rich guardian." Some had no known meaning, while others made no distinction between male and female names. You'll find Dragobert, Clovis, and Begga among those early names.

Not until after the Norman Conquest in 1066 did Anglo-Saxon naming patterns begin to fade and the people of Europe and Britain begin adopting popular Norman names. The Normans used surprisingly few names, the most popular being William, Richard, and Robert.

During the late Middle Ages there was such a scarcity of names—most adopted during the Norman period—that the church began to introduce biblical and nonbiblical saint's names, such as Stephen, John, Mary, Thomas, Elizabeth, James, and Katherine. These names were added to Norman names already in use. When it became necessary to distinguish one person from another with the same name, identifiers were added. Most denoted personal characteristics or a person's residence: "William—The Pious," "Thomas—The Bald," and "John de Sutton," John of Sutton Manor.

By 1200, it was common to find families with a mixture of Anglo-Saxon, Norman, and Christian names. The English Jocelyn family named their children Gilbert, Geoffrey, William, Ralph, Robert, John, Thomas, Elizabeth, and Jane between 1201 and 1275, illustrating a blend of names from all three eras.

It wasn't until the thirteenth century that surnames were adopted. By then Europe had outgrown its ability to identify people by just given names, yet it took nearly two centuries for surnames to become a standard practice. When people first chose surnames, they established a pattern that denoted places, occupations, characteristics, and relationships.

Place names indicated the town, region, or country from which a person originated. Richard lived on top of a hill and thus became Richard Hill. John lived in the west quarter of a village and became John West. Georg Jacob lived in the small Bavarian village of Wertheim and became Georg Jacob von Wertheim or Georg Jacob Wertheimer. French and Spanish names denoting place were prefaced by "de," Dutch by "van," and Polish place names suffixed by "ski." Eventually such prefixes or suffixes were dropped in most countries.

Occupational surnames—derived from a person's occupation—were some of the most common surnames. Smith (English), Schmidt (German), and Herrera (Spanish) denoted a blacksmith, silversmith, or goldsmith. Other English occupation surnames were Baker, Weaver, Taylor, Carpenter, and Mason. They were common because every village had one or more of each. Some occupational names, common during an early period, are no longer recognizable as occupations. However, a good surname guide will tell you the source of an occupational surname and its meaning.

Surnames were often descriptive of personal characteristics such as stature, coloring, emotional attributes, or the reverse of those characteristics. Names like Short and Longfellow denoted stature; Black, Gray, Brown, and White obviously denoted coloring; Moody, Sharp, Bright, and Dull referred to personal attributes. Other surnames reflected negative attributes, just as some nicknames do today.

Many countries adopted patronymics, the practice of giving a child the father's name as a surname. This was widely practiced in Scandinavia through the late nineteenth century and occurred in the British Isles and other parts of Europe in slightly different forms. Patronymics can be confusing, but are not difficult to understand if studied carefully. Let's say a Dane, Peder Olsen, had sons named Lars, Soren, and Jens. His sons would be known as Lars Pedersen, Soren Pedersen, and Jens Pedersen. All of Lars Pedersen's sons would have Larsen as a surname, while Soren Pedersen's sons would be Sorensen, and so on. Peder Olsen's female children, on the other hand, would have Pedersdatter as their surname, Peder's daughter.

English relationship surnames such as Thompson or Johnson denoted Thomas's son and John's son; however, the English did not change surnames with each new generation. The Irish "O" and Scottish "Mac" also mean "son of." Again, a good surname guide will list the origins and meanings of surnames denoting relationship.

NAMING PATTERNS

Naming patterns also deserve important consideration. Some immigrant groups named the first two males after their grandfathers and the first two females after their grandmothers. Quaker and Scots-Irish families favored naming children after parents, grandparents, aunts, and uncles. Matthew Karr, whose family will be studied in Chapter 8, named his sons James, Andrew, George, William, and John, names that were repeated in each son's family as first or middle names. This pattern often causes frustration in relating the right son with his father.

Middle names first appeared with frequency in the seventeenth century and grew in popularity until the turn of this century when they became standard. It isn't uncommon to find all of the children in one family with their mother's maiden name as a middle name. Giving male children their mother's maiden name as a first name was also popular. While this practice occurs extensively in affluent, upper-class families, don't conclude that a male with a surname as a given name carries his mother's or grandmother's surname. He may be named after a close friend, a prominent person, or no one in particular.

During the nineteenth century, southern families commonly gave children more than one middle name. American census records often show a child listed by four different names in successive enumerations, using different middle names at different times. Never reject a census entry, therefore, solely on the basis that some children's names appear differently than previously recorded.

NAME CHANGES AND SPELLING VARIANTS

Name changes and spelling variants can prove great sources of confusion for the genealogist. In most cases, a surname changed abruptly with the arrival of an ancestor in America; with others, the change took place over time. Some name changes were deliberate and voluntary, while others were the whims of immigration clerks. Most confusing of all, few of these name changes had any legal basis. Name changes were often matters of conscious choice. When Frank Carlsson emigrated to America in the nineteenth century and settled in Minnesota, there were hundreds of Carlssons and Carlsons already living there. To cut the confusion and to identify himself as an American, he shortened his surname to Carl. Some years later, his son Lloyd altered the spelling of the name to Carle (pronounced car-lee). Lloyd was an avid, self-taught journalist, and the leading writer with the *Minneapolis Tribune* at that time was Arthur Carle. One can speculate that Lloyd changed his name to associate himself with an idol. His children and grandchildren still use this spelling and pronunciation; his brothers, aunts, and nephews, however, are known as Carl.

Name changes frequently were made by association and then retained by conscious choice. Germans soon discovered that Americans had problems pronouncing their names correctly. Thus, ancestors such as Albrecht became Allbright, Dreisback became Treesebach, Emig became Amick, and Vogel became Fogel by pronunciation. Koch became Cook by translation because it looked and sounded more American.

Name changes made by local clerks were retained sometimes by unconscious choice. Jack Reilly, a devil-may-care Irishman, migrated to French Canada as a member of the Irish Brigade of the French Army. He served his regulation five years, married a French woman, and decided to stay. At the time of his marriage – performed by a French priest – his name was recorded in the church register as Jean Baptiste Reil Sansouci – Jack "Devil-may-care" Reilly. Jack really did not care. He spoke French, was married to a French woman, his children grew up French with French names, and he accepted his French disguise in good part.

Cerny, a Slovakian surname that is spelled Čierny, denotes the color black. Ján Čierny (pronounced chair-nee) had his name changed when he arrived in the United States to John Cerny (pronounced sir-nee) by Ellis Island processing clerks. His wife, Terézia Záhorcova, had her name changed to Theresa Zahorec. (Her father was Josef Záhorec and all of his female children carried the feminine ending "ova" in their surname.)

SEARCHING FOR ANCESTORS WITH CHANGED NAMES

As you search for these immigrant ancestors, you will discover them by their changed names first. Your family probably has some collective memory of how names were altered, though such traditions may be garbled. Sometimes clues can be found on tombstones or in statements by family members on death certificates.

A cemetery tombstone or a sexton's record may be the only American record where the original family name was recorded. This is especially true for those families who wanted to eradicate all traces of immigrant origins. If you walk through immigrant cemeteries today, you will discover that each is distinctive in its colors, its plantings, and its stones. Though living with Americanized names, some immigrants refused to be buried under these appellations. In other cases, their families made the choice for them after death, engraving original family names on their tombstones.

Occasionally, clues to the original family name come in the form of "errors" on death certificates. For example, you order death certificates on the children of the immigrant, upon which each informant has given the information he or she knows. You may find one in this family group with a foreign surname for the parents instead of the one they were known by. What appears to be an error in information might well be the family's pre-immigration name.

Variant spellings are especially troublesome in cities where people with these surnames converged from many parts of the United States and from foreign countries. On naturalization applications, for example, you will find these spellings for the surname Thom written by the immigrants themselves: Germans spelled it Thoma or Thumm, Greeks Toma, Italians Tomma, Austrians Tuma, and Welsh Thom. In the 1900 census schedule for New York City, some spellings match the country of origin; yet with others there is a commonality in spelling for the surname regardless of nationality. There are even some recorded as Thorn where scribes misread signatures.

Problems compounded when city officials and welfare agency personnel mispronounced, misspelled, and transposed characters in many of these names. Fortunately, a consortium of New York City welfare agencies established a list of variant spellings to help them with their work. The following examples from this list are the types of variation you may encounter.

Bailey	Frank	Madison	Meyer	Schaefer
Bailie	Franc	Maddison	Maier	Schafer
Bailly	Franck	Madsen	Mayer	Schaffer
Baillie	Francke	Matheson	Mayers	Scheaffer
Baily	Franke	Matison	Meier	Schiefer
Baley	Franks	Matsen	Meyers	Schiffer
Bayley		Matsin	Mier	Shaefer
Baylie	Kane	Matson	Miers	Shaffer
	Cain	Mattison	Myer	
Carl	Caine	Mattson	Myers	
Carle	Cane			
Carls	Canes			
Karl	Kain			
Karle	Kaine			
	Kanes			

Figure 1:1. Examples of spelling variants.

Searching records for altered names is a matter of common sense. If a name consistently carries the same initial letter in its variants, watch for this as you search survey sources like the International Genealogical Index (the IGI). Scan all the entries beginning with that initial letter, extracting all variants of the name. Keep pronunciation variants in mind as they will help you to find them all.

If the initial sound of the name, as it is pronounced, could be represented by more than one letter—Coons/Kuntz, Berriford/Perryfod—then you must anticipate those initial letters and watch for the name in other sections of the alphabet. Anticipate v/f, b/p, f/ph, l/s, j/n, m/n, v/w, j/y, variants that are the most common. Also anticipate that s/l, n/v, i/j may have been written so much alike by clerks that they are difficult to distinguish.

How do changes and variants influence your research? First, even though your ancestor consistently spelled the family name the same way, local clerks wrote down what they heard, spelling names the way they were used to writing them. Spelling is not a mark of national identity, although the way a name is spelled on specific documents can provide a clue to its origin. Remember

Jack Reilly/Jean Reil, the Irishman turned French, and realize that spelling is only a clue to nationality that must be corroborated by additional evidence.

If a formal change occurred, there may be a record of it. Before the Civil War, check court records as well as private legislative acts, as the authority to change names often stayed with the legislature. After the Civil War, consult courts that have divorce jurisdiction. They handled name changes as well.

DATES

Everyone knows that Christian nations begin a new year on 1 January. Fewer people realize that Jewish and Chinese new years fall on different days every year and fewer still know that the calendar as we know it has undergone many changes. New Year's Day, for example, used to fall on 25 March. The finest discussion of time in genealogical identification, "Dates and the Calendar," was written by Donald Lines Jacobus in *Genealogy as Pastime and Profession*, and an edited version of his work follows.[1]

Names, dates, and places are the working material of genealogy, and for ease and accuracy in handling dates, the genealogist should possess or develop a mathematical mind. He should see at a glance that a man born in 1738 was too young to marry in 1751 and that he probably did not marry a woman born in 1724. Experience teaches him to weigh problems of date and to draw conclusions from them almost instantaneously.

When very few positive dates are available and the genealogist desires to check the probability of an alleged pedigree or a series of relationships, it is helpful to assign guessed dates to births. If the children of given parents are known, but not their birth dates, these can be guessed from known dates. If the age at death of one of the children is found stated, then for this one we have an approximate date of birth, probably not more than a year away from fact in either direction. We thus can work from the known towards the unknown and group the other children about the one with the fixed date. The marriage dates of some of the children may be known, and birth dates may be guessed from these, on the basis that a man married from twenty-two to twenty-six and a woman from eighteen to twenty-four. When one of the women had recorded children born from 1721 to 1745, for example, then at a glance we can set down 1700 or 1701 almost with certainty as the approximate time of her birth because here we have the known limits of the period of childbearing to guide us.

Such guessed dates should be clearly marked in some way to avoid confusion with positive dates. They can be placed in brackets, thus: [abt.

---

1. Donald Lines Jacobus, *Genealogy as Pastime and Profession*, 2nd ed. (Baltimore: Genealogical Publishing Company, 1968), pp. 109-13. Our thanks to the Genealogical Publishing Company for allowing us to reproduce "Dates and the Calendar."

1701], or the date can be preceded by the word "circa," Latin meaning "about," or its abbreviation, "c."

When we have arrived at such approximate dates for the births of all the children, the advantage is the picture it gives us of the family as a whole. Perhaps our problem is the parentage of one Charles Evans, and we suspect that he belonged in the family whose approximate ages we have been working out. We know, let us say, from his age at death, that he was born about 1685. Let us suppose that the births of this group of children we worked out can be placed with extreme probability between 1698 and 1715. It then appears that our Charles, born about 1685, was more probably of the previous generation, possibly an uncle of the children whose ages we guessed.

For many reasons it is advantageous in doing genealogical research to consider the family group, not to look upon each ancestor as an isolated individual or as a mere link in the chain of descent. One of the most important reasons is that it enables us to check the chronology. Very often, the relation of dates determine or negate the possibility of an alleged line of descent or provide clues that might otherwise elude detection. It is a good idea to write out the full family history, or chart the relationships, while working, inclusive of guessed dates where positive dates are not known. It is a great aid to the memory, as well as to the imagination, if the eye can see the members of the family grouped together.

OLD STYLE/NEW STYLE

There is one technical matter that affects dates and needs to be studied in some detail if the genealogist is to understand and properly interpret the Old Style dates; this is the important calendar change of 1752. As few things are more confusing to the inexperienced searcher, a complete explanation of it will be given.

The Julian calendar was used throughout the Middle Ages in Europe. Its inaccuracy amounted to about three days in every four centuries. By the time the Gregorian calendar (named after Pope Gregory XIII) was adopted in 1582, calendar dates were ahead of actual time by ten days. Since actual time is the time it takes the earth for one complete revolution about the sun (a year), if the calendar had been left uncorrected, in the course of centuries the present summer months would have come in the winter, and vice versa.

Although the Roman Catholic countries adopted the Gregorian calendar in 1582, the conservatism of the English, and the fact that the new calendar was sponsored by a pope, delayed the acceptance of it in Great Britain and her colonies until after the passage of an Act of Parliament in 1751. By this time, the old calendar was eleven days ahead of sun time, so the act provided that in 1752, the second day of September should be followed by the fourteenth. In other words, what would have been September 3rd was called September 14th, exactly eleven days being thus dropped out of the year.

The cause of the error was the addition of a day to the calendar each fourth year (leap year). This very nearly made the average year correspond with sun time, but not quite. In every 400 years as stated above, the calendar went three days ahead of sun time. The dropping of eleven days in 1752 brought the calendar back into harmony with sun time, and to provide against a recurrence of the trouble, it was also provided that on the even century years, no leap year day should be added except in centuries divisable by 400. The century years 1800 and 1900 were not leap years, but 2000 will be. In this way, in the 400 years beginning with 1752, there will be three days less than there were in each 400 years preceding 1752, hence the old error will not be repeated.

So little did the people understand the need for the calendar revision that an angry mob gathered outside the Houses of Parliament, demanding that the eleven days filched out of their lives be restored to them. Actually, calling the third day of September the fourteenth did not deprive any person of eleven days of life any more than changing a man's name from Bill to Tom would make him a different person. The real effect was to make everyone born on or before 2 September 1752 eleven days older (by the new calendar) than the record of birth (in Old Style) would indicate. A child born on 2 September 1752 (the last day of Old Style) would be, by the calendar, twelve days old on the following day, 15 September 1752 (the first day of New Style).

People do not like to be considered older than they really are, not even eleven days older. It was natural that those living in 1752 should "rectify" their birth dates. George Washington was born 11 February 1731/2. In 1752 the calendar change automatically made him eleven days older, so like most men of his generation, he rectified his birth date, making it 22 February 1732. The latter is the date on which he would have been born if the New Style calendar had been in effect in 1732.

Although it was (and is) incorrect to change the dates prior to September 1752 into New Style, it was done to such an extent by those living in 1752 that the genealogist has to make allowances for it. Suppose, for example, that a group of brothers and sisters were born before the calendar change and in the town records the Old Style dates were used in entering their births. The first child was born, let us say, 25 May 1743. Now, after all the children had been born, the parents bought a Bible, say about 1765, and entered in it their own marriage and the births of the children, giving New Style dates for all the children, including those born before 1752 whose birthdays should properly have been entered Old Style. As a result, we find that the eldest child (whose birth in contemporary town records had been entered as 25 May 1743) was entered in the Bible as born 5 June 1743. Both dates are correct, but the former is the date that ought to be used, unless the latter has the words "New Style" added to indicate that it is a "rectified" date.

A further effect of this change must be mentioned. When a man died after 1752, assuming that he was born before September 1752 and his age at death was stated exactly in years, months, and days, the resultant date of birth (figured from the age at death) is the New Style date of birth, and therefore eleven days later against the recorded Old Style date of birth.

For example, Ephraim Burr, by his gravestone, died 29 April 1776, aged seventy-six years and thirteen days. Subtracting the age gives us 16 April 1700 for his birth, but of course to get the Old Style date then in use we must subtract eleven days more. His birth was not recorded, but he was baptized 14 April 1700, two days before his New Style date of birth. After subtracting the eleven days, we find that his real date of birth, in accordance with the Old Style calendar then in use, was 5 April 1700, which was nine days before he was baptized. Obviously he could not have been born two days after baptism, the result we get if we fail to make allowance for the calendar change.

It is very necessary that the genealogist, professional or amateur, should thoroughly understand this calendar change, or he will miss proofs of identity furnished by the comparison of birth records with stated ages at death. When a child was born before 1752 and the birth was recorded contemporaneously, add eleven days to the date to obtain the New Style equivalent. When a person born prior to September 1752 died after that date and the death record states that exact age, subtract the age from the date of death, and subtract eleven days more to obtain the Old Style equivalent.

Exact ages were not always stated, and unless the days are specified, the presumption is that the age is not exact. When the record states that a man died aged fifty years and eight months, he may have been that age to a day, but he may have been a few days over the fifty years and eight months. Recorders did not always bother to specify the age to a day, nor did those who had gravestones erected always so specify.

NEW YEAR'S CHANGE

One other change made in 1752 was the date of beginning the new year. It is understood by everyone that between one spring and the next a year has elapsed, similarly between one autumn and the next. But when we assign numbers to the years for convenience in referring to them, it is necessary to begin the new year on a particular day. The succession of seasons and years is entirely natural, caused by the orbit of the earth about the sun. But selecting one certain day on which to start a new year is an artificial and an arbitrary thing. Consequently, various peoples in various ages have celebrated different New Year's days. Some of the ancient races ended their year with a harvest festival, and the Jews still retain that

season. Others began the year with the vernal equinox, and since Easter
fell near that season, the date quite generally used for the religious New
Year's Day by Christians was 25 March. There was no uniformity in the
early centuries, and some began the year on 25 December, the traditional
birthday of Christ.

The only dates for New Year's Day which were in use in American
colonial days among English settlers were 25 March and 1 January. The
latter was the beginning of the legal year, while the former, as we have
seen, had more religious significance. The Act of Parliament in 1751 established 1 January as New Year's Day for 1752 and subsequent years. Thereafter, we are not bothered by the confusion that existed when the year
had two possible beginnings.

Now this change did not, like the dropping of eleven days, have any
effect on the ages of persons then living. This will be seen if we suppose
that it should be decided hereafter to celebrate the Fourth of July on
Armistice Day. A person born 4 May would still be born on 4 May, and
when New Year's Day was shifted from 25 March to 1 January, it did not
affect the birthday of a man born on 4 May.

Some have misunderstood the change in New Year's Day and have supposed that it caused a difference of nearly three months in people's ages.
When the names of the months of birth were entered, such a notion was
unthinkable. Before 1700, the early recorders sometimes used the number
of the month instead of its name. This was the practice of the Quakers,
and it occasionally survived until a later period. Of course, March was then
numbered as the first month, since New Year's Day fell in it, and dates
before the twenty-fifth were considered as belonging to the first month,
as well as dates after the twenty-fifth. April was the second month, and
May the third. The early Quaker records were often very precise, stating
that an event occurred "on the 10th of the 5th month which is called July."

When the number of the month was stated in any record prior to 1752,
the genealogist should reckon March as the first month and February as
the twelfth. If a record states that John Jones was born on the tenth of
the fifth month, 1710, this must be Old Style, and means that he was born
in July. After 1752, July became the seventh instead of the fifth month,
but this does not alter the fact that John Jones was born in July.

Before 1752, there is likely to be some confusion with regard to dates
between 1 January and 24 March, unless we know what New Year's Day
a particular recorder used. It is apparent that if the year began 25 March,
a man born on 20 February was born before the new year began, hence
a year earlier than it would be by New Style. If 1710 began on 25 March,
then a man born on 20 February following was born in 1710, since 1711 did
not begin until the next month. Dates between 1 January and 24 March
fell in the preceding year if Old Style was used; but if New Style was used,
this threw all dates after 1 January into the new year.

The only problem in this connection is the year in which a man was born, and we always run the chance of an error of exactly a year if we do not know which calendar the recorder used. Before 1700, we can usually assume that the year began on 25 March, and this is true of most church registers until 1752. But after 1700, the use of 1 January was gradually coming into favor, especially in legal documents and town records.

Careful recorders used a double date, and when this was done all confusion or uncertainty was eliminated. George Washington was born 11 February 1731/2, which means that the year was still 1731 if the new year was reckoned as not beginning until 25 March, but that the year was already 1732 if it had begun 1 January. That is, it was 1731 Old Style or 1732 New Style. Genealogists should always copy the double date when it is given in the records, for the single date is an uncertain one. The date 11 February 1731, Old Style, is identical with 22 February 1732, New Style.

Sometimes records in Old Style look peculiar to us. In Norwich, Connecticut vital records, we read that Robert Wade married 11 March 1691/2 and his eldest child was born 11 March 1691. We may assume that the marriage occurred 11 March 1690/1, this recorder happening to use the later year date here because he was thinking of March as the first month of the new year; the child was born January 1691/2, ten months later. It was still 1691, Old Style.

Remember that this confusion of year dates before 1752, applies only to dates between 1 January and 24 March, since all other dates belong to the same year regardless of when New Year's Day was celebrated.

Always remember to check the introduction to printed sources you use to determine whether adjustments have already been made to accomodate calendar changes. Many researchers believe that Quakers used the Julian calendar after 1752 and erroneously calculate dates into New Style. While the Quakers still refused to use the names of the months in their records, they did follow legislated changes in adjusting the calendar. Furthermore, Quaker recordkeepers sometimes noted the use of Old Style or New Style in post-1752 records.

RELATIONSHIPS

Relationships are significant elements in genealogical identification and every researcher must determine relationships between individuals to construct accurate genealogies. Most people understand their kinship to parents, grandparents, aunts, uncles, and cousins, but beyond that relationships can be confusing.

A few years ago I was contacted by John C. Stewart, who heard that I was tracing the Stewart family of Bourbon County, Kansas. He wanted to know what I had discovered about the family and how we were related. Stewart is a fairly common surname in this country, and there was more than one family with that surname in Bourbon County. Establishing a relationship between us required identifying a common ancestor and then calculating the degrees of our relationship to one another. Let's examine common ancestors more closely.

Common ancestors determine the degree of relationship between their descendants. Brothers and sisters are closely related because they share parents as common ancestors. Cousins are more distantly related because they share only two of four grandparents as common ancestors. Those close relationships are easily determined. But what about more distant ones?

First we must distinguish between direct ancestors and collateral relatives. A direct ancestor is someone listed on your lineage chart, namely your father, mother, grandfathers, grandmothers, great-grandfathers, great-grandmothers, and so on. A collateral relative is not listed on your lineage chart, but would appear on family group records as brothers and sisters of your direct ancestors. Collateral relatives also include the descendants of your aunts and uncles.

A common ancestor will appear on the lineage charts of two individuals who are related. We'll look at the Stewart family to illustrate common ancestry. The following chart shows two lines of descent from John Stewart and illustrates how John Coy Stewart and I are related.

John Stewart

William Stewart	brothers	Allen Stewart
Andrew Beecher Stewart	cousins	Laura Stewart
John Coy Stewart	2nd cousins	Grover Cleveland West
John Coy Stewart	3rd cousins	Vivian Elaine West
		Jonnette Elaine Cerny

John Coy Stewart and I are not of the same generation. Our relationship as cousins is determined by his relationship to my mother and the one generation that we are removed from each other: John is a third cousin once removed (3clr). Those ancestors listed in my line of descent with the exception of John Stewart, the common ancestor, are John Coy Stewart's collateral relatives and, in reverse, all of his direct ancestors are my collateral relatives. Let's study a second example using President Herbert Hoover's ancestry as it relates to my grandmother's adoptive lines.

Andreas Hüber/Andrew Hoover

John Hoover	brothers	Jonas Hoover
Jesse Hoover	cousins	Rachel Hoover
Eli Hoover	2nd cousins	Alice Davis
Jesse Clark Hoover	3rd cousins	Martha P. Huffman
Herbert Clark Hoover	4th cousins	Mary Alice Karr
	4c1r	Bertha Ruth Smith
	4c2r	Vivian Elaine West
	4c3r	Jonnette Elaine Cerny

Determining how a number of individuals descend from a common ancestor can be confusing. Edward I, King of England, is a common ancestor of a large number of notable people. Let's examine the relationships between a few famous people who descend from Edward I through his son Edward II and grandson Edward III using Charles, Prince of Wales, as the person to whom the others are related. Charles and Princess Diana's common ancestor is James I, King of England (James VI, King of Scotland). The number of generations between King James and Diana is twelve and the number of generations between Charles and King James is thirteen. The first generation after James is a brother-sister relationship followed by eleven generations to Diana and twelve generations to Charles. Thus, Diana is an eleventh cousin once removed (11c1r) of her husband.

Edward III is the common ancestor of Prince Charles, Princess Diana, Thomas Jefferson, James Madison, and Gerald R. Ford when determining the relationship between the royal couple and the presidents.

Prince Charles—Thomas Jefferson 13c8r
Prince Charles—James Madison 17c4r
Prince Charles—Gerald R. Ford 19c2r
Princess Diana—Thomas Jefferson 13c7r
Princess Diana—James Madison 17c3r
Princess Diana—Gerald R. Ford 19c1r

As descendants of the three Edwards, Thomas Jefferson, James Madison, and Gerald R. Ford are also cousins:

```
                              Edward I
                           King of England
                               |
                             Edward II
                           King of England
                               |
                             Edward III
                           King of England
        ┌──────────────────────┴─────────────────┐
   John of Gaunt              Lionel                        (brothers)
  Prince of England      Prince of England
        |                      |
   Joan Beaufort        Philipa Plantagenet                 (cousins)
        |               Countess of March
        |                      |
   13 Generations      Elizabeth De Mortimer
       from              ┌──────────┴──────────────────┐
   Joan Beaufort       Elizabeth Percy        Richard Camoys (bro-sis)
       to                     |                        |
  Thomas Jefferson      Mary Clifford          Eleanor Camoys (cousins)
                               |                        |
                        19 Generations          17 Generations
                            from                    from
                        Philipa Plantagenet     Philipa Plantagenet
                            to                      to
                        Gerald R. Ford          James Madison
                            and                     and
                        16 Generations          14 Generations
                            from                    from
                        Mary Clifford cou       Eleanor Camoys
                            to                      to
                        Gerald R. Ford          James Madison
```

Thomas Jefferson—James Madison 13c4r
Thomas Jefferson—Gerald R. Ford 13c6r
James Madison—Gerald R. Ford 14c2r

Direct ancestors begin with your parents and continue on to grandparents, great-grandparents, great-great-grandparents, great-great-great-grandparents, etc. The number of greats becomes unmanageable beyond a generation of great-grandparents. Genealogists simplify identification by referring to them as great-grandfather, 2nd great-grandfather, 3rd great-grandfather, and so on with each succeeding generation. The same numbering system applies to grandsons. Let's determine the relationship between Edward I and his five descendants shown in the chart:

Prince Charles — 22nd great-grandson (22 ggson)
Princess Diana — 21st great-granddaughter (21 ggdau)
Thomas Jefferson — 14th great-grandson (14 ggson)
James Madison — 19th great-grandson (19 ggson)
Gerald R. Ford — 20th great-grandson (20 ggson)

There are other relationships to be considered, including in-law, step, and adoptive relationships. In-laws are the ancestors and relatives of a spouse and stepchildren the offspring of a spouse while married to another husband or wife. Your wife's father is your father-in-law, her uncle is your uncle-in-law, her cousin is your cousin-in-law, and so on. If your father married a second time, his wife becomes your children's step-grandmother. There are also half relationships to consider. Your grandfather's children by his second wife (not your grandmother) would be your half aunts and uncles. Legally, an adopted child becomes the rightful heir and descendant of the parents who adopt them. Many people choose to be genealogically identified with their adoptive parents, others prefer to be identified with their natural parents, and still others choose to trace both lines. Some hereditary and lineage societies will not accept nonblood descendants as members, despite their legal rights of heirship.

Determining relationships can be confusing to the beginner, and it is helpful to have a guide to work with until calculating relationships becomes second nature. The relationship chart illustrated in Figure 1:2 is included to help you calculate accurate relationships from the start.

PLACES

A little geographical knowledge about the places where your ancestors lived can be important in effective ancestor tracking. Knowledge about a particular region can furnish clues to their lives not found in genealogical record sources. You may encounter a situation sometime when all of your sources are inconclusive and only a geographical clue will help determine who an ancestor is. Few beginning genealogists know enough about geography to ask questions about an ancestor's life from the perspective of place. Yet posing questions from this angle is often what it takes to solve tough genealogical problems.

Knowing the lay of the land will help you determine which trails or rivers your ancestors used for migration, how and where they marketed their crops, and even where they attended church or laid their dead to rest. Geography can distinguish between two or more persons of the same name, enabling you to identify the correct person as your ancestor. For example, in a letter dated 31 January 1911, William Johnson's family was outlined, as were a few of its geographical locations:

Our great grandfather was born in Penn. His name was William. His father came from Ireland. His son our grandfather was the first white child born in Augusta County, Va. He married Miss Marry Berry. They had five

Figure 1:2.
RELATIONSHIP CHART

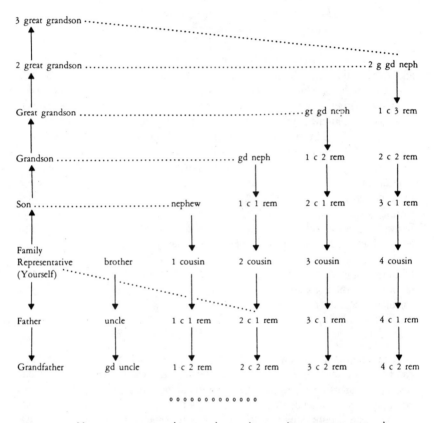

Note: g = great   gd = grand   neph = nephew   rem = removed

Example: "2 c 1 rem" means a second cousin one generation removed from yourself. See text for additional explanation of this chart.

sons and three daughters. Their names were Francis (father), William, John, Charles, and Josiah. Father married Miss Mary Jane Hall. Josiah married Agnes Harmon, daughter of Tamon [?]. Thomas Harmon of Kanhwa, W. Va. John died while on the Island of Jamaica. William died of Diptheria. Charles also died; none of them were married. Father's sisters were, Rebecca who died single. Jane, married a Mr. Barker, Isabelle married a Mr. Cummings.

A family tradition handed down through another branch stated:

> The Johnson home was on Brushy Neck, on Middle River near Laurel Hill. Grandfather John Johnson's grave is under the northeast corner of Laurel Hill Baptist Church. At his death, he left his wife with many small children to care for. The only help was an elderly colored man, who froze to death one night while he was drunk.

Still another family member contributed a sketch of Brushy Neck made in February 1884. A sixteen-year-old descendant of William, Lee Johnson, went on a trip to Augusta County, Virginia to visit his father's family, taking along a sketch pad and a diary. On this trip, he sketched Brushy Neck where his cousins resided, located the grave of his grandfather, Francis Johnson, and described the problem of getting to church in New Hope when the river was high: "It had been raining steadily for several days, the river is very full and is still rising. Almost over its banks. The mud is knee deep. Unable to attend church."

Research into the records of Augusta County, Virginia turned up too many Johnsons, including six Williams and four Johns. One essential clue, however, emerged from a printed church history: On the inside back cover of Howard M. Wilson's *Tinkling Spring: Headwater of Freedom: A Study of the Church and Her People, 1732-1952* is a map of the original patentees in the Beverley Patent from 1736 to 1815. This map shows a William Johnston with 100 acres and a Jno. Johnston adjoining with 65 acres. These two pieces of land are on a neck of the Middle River of the Shenandoah.

In *Tinkling Spring* are many entries referring to William Johnston/Johnson, including a footnote to the list of baptisms performed by the Reverend John Craig: "There seem to be two fathers by this name. When there appears sufficient reason to do so, one family is indicated by asterisks." A careful study of these entries shows that there is a William Johnson living on Brushy Neck and another living on Lower Quarter Christian's Creek. Their lives are reviewed in this volume, but there is no way to determine from the given data alone which is the William of Brushy Neck and which the William of Christian's Creek.

These sources gave many place clues to go on. The tie to the right William Johnson is Brushy Neck. From this point it had to be determined by geographical clues which of the necks on the river is Brushy Neck. Three different relatives visited the area at different times and each identified a different

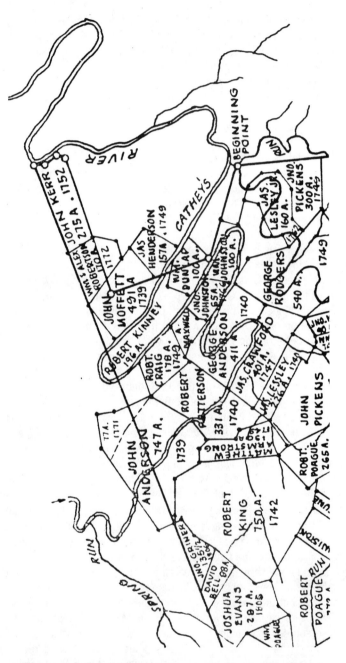

Figure 1:3. Detail from patentee map in Howard M. Wilson's *Tinkling Spring*.

spot; however, only one spot matched the patentee map printed in *Tinkling Spring*.

Paul Shirey, a retired postman familiar with the area, was hired and given instructions to interview the residents on each of the necks and to examine their property documents. A copy of an 1884 map drawn by Jed Hotchkiss and a photocopy of the patentee map from *Tinkling Spring* were sent to him. The following are his reports, and though difficult to decipher, they contain valuable information about the area in question.

REPORT: Field Trip, Apr. 19, 1964.
Laurel Hill Section: Paul C. Shirey and D. Moody Yeago.

Visited the Cline or Kline Place and examined a number of old deeds, the oldest April 5, 1858 transferring 284 acres. People mentioned in the deeds:

Wm. Pague	Frank McCue	A. D. Trotter, surveyor
James M. Stout	J. Cyrus McCue	Wm. A. Burnett, clerk
Wm. I. Stout		Robert J. Bickle, J.P.
J. M. Quarles		
Cornelia Quarles		
D. Glenn Ruckman	W. W. King for Mary Baldwin	

Many of the roads have been changed in this section. Middle River, meanders back and fourth [sic] many times between these bluffs. Many of the roads are now dead ends, in bad repair, semi-private. Where they once forded the river with horses, they now go miles around with cars.

I have not found anybody that ever heard of Brushy Neck, but a Miss McCue said one of these isolated sections they knew as Bald Rock.

Mr. Yeago is an old timer at the real estate business. He knows most every piece of property in the county, and many many people, but he said this section was too much for him, and was surprised to find how far one had to travel to get to a place that was only a few hundred yards away. It is a minature [sic] Grand Canyon. There is a good bit of good land along the river on one side, but the farmers have moved out nearer a good road, and they discourage town fishermen from running over their crops and leaving gates open and tearing down fences.

You may understand the situation better from the map I am sending you. Northeast of Verona you will note Isaac Keister. His son Guy an old man sold out a few days ago and moved to Charlottesville. Guy was a good historian. Most of the road east of his place has been closed, where it once crossed the river to the Jas. Stout, or Cline farm.

You will note there is no road from Rt. 11, to the point Ashby. That might be your point of interest. You can see there are no roads and no houses by Ashby. I would guess this might be Bushy Neck [sic]. It is a very good section along Rt. 788. But the people there are isolated from the bluff across the river. The road north of the John Kenney place is also closed at the river. North and east of the above point is sparcely [sic] settled only a few dirt and semi-private roads, and dead ends.

Apr. 21, 1964, Field Trip No. 2

Went east on Rt. 781, from Rt. 11 to the dead end 3.20 Mi. This would be the spot, "Ashby" on Jed Hotchkiss Map. Your No. 1. A family by the name of Alexander lives there now, but the house is not exactly the same spot as the old one. This is evidently the Johnston land marked on your map No. 2.

This is a large area of fairly flat good farm land now owned by only a few people. Several people told me they had heard the area called "Brushy Neck", but the name is not used much today. The old road into "Ashby" came off Rt. 788 and crossed the river into the point where Rt. 781, now ends. The whole area along the river between your black X and green X is still a brushy area and it was correctly named "Brushy Neck". I find there are other areas along Middle River that were also known as Brushy Neck. Laurel Hill is just across the river to the southeast from the Alexander home, some ¼ mile, but one has to travel now in a car about 8 or 10 miles between the two places.

The Jno. Stout property, now Cline is evidently not Brushy Neck, but Ashby, (now Alexander) as shown on your Map No. 1. When Lee Johnson visited this area in 1884 it would have been only a ride of a few minutes horseback between the two places. The Alexanders (an old couple) said they had heard a man was buried under the old church. The new church is in sight of the Alexander home. The home of Henry Borden is shown in this neck on Hotchkiss' map but I found no public road to this place. The land was likely also Johnston land 1740.

From Mr. Shirey's notes, the patentee map, and the 1884 diary entry, the location of Brushy Neck was established and thus which of the William Johnstons belonged to the family. The old ford over the river would be impassable when the river was at flood stage in the early spring, and thus the family would have to attend church on the same side of the river or else stay at home. They elected to stay home the Sunday Lee Johnson wrote about.

Familiarity with geography is also important to understanding migration routes and patterns. Chapter 14 discusses families on the move and presents a series of maps to help the beginner gain a rudimentary understanding of the geographical obstacles encountered during the push west. Whether your interest is in pinpointing the exact residence of your ancestors for personal satisfaction, following their paths as they moved from place to place, or establishing a place of residence to enable you to search records that will add to your knowledge of a family, geographical clues are often key tools.

CHAPTER 2

Genealogy Yellow Pages

G enealogists today have many options for access to genealogical data, options made available the last ten years by rapid strides not only in technology but through the dedicated efforts of other genealogists who saw specific needs and developed aids, indexes, and tools to fill them. Using the detailed directions which follow, genealogical materials can be located with a minimum of frustration.

TELEPHONE GENEALOGY

The telephone is the closest, most direct link to those who can help document your lineage. You can ask questions of relatives over the phone and get quick answers when writing takes too much time. Your personal call can be especially effective with relatives living in rural areas and outside the continental U.S. In many cases, you'll be calling distant cousins whose names and locations you'll know, but not necessarily their numbers. You can locate them through these sources:

1. Directory Assistance will have current directories for many locations in the U.S. and Canada. They can also supply copies of any directory you wish for a nominal charge.

2. Directory Assistance will supply business and personal phone numbers and addresses and will *verify* personal addresses. By law, they cannot give out personal addresses. In case relatives have moved, Directory Assistance can track your relatives with their extended-area, computerized number databases, some of which cover areas crossing state lines.

3. Long Distance Information will check two numbers at a time in the same directory. As well, you can submit a list of names and numbers and an operator will verify them or supply missing information for a small fee.

4. You can also check phone-fiche, telephone directories for some 700 American cities put on microfiche by Bell and Howell. Copies can

be found at public or university libraries or by contacting Orphan Voyage, 13906 Pepperell Drive, Tampa, FL 33624. For a fee, Orphan Voyage will check their telephone database for persons in the continental U.S. carrying your surname of interest.

5. Local communities publish directories, similar to city directories, with telephone numbers included. Sometimes even unlisted numbers are given. Write the chamber of commerce or the mayor's office for a copy or the address of the publisher/printer.

6. Many public and university libraries will have telephone directories on their shelves. These collections are a valuable information source, although they can be random and dated.

Telephone contacts must be well planned to be effective, especially if you are calling someone you don't know. Introduce yourself and give your reason for calling. Outline your questions carefully, keeping them brief and to the point. As you gain experience in telephone interviews, you will become more successful in drawing out the information you need most. (For sample questions, see the oral interviews section in Chapter 4.) When interviewing in person, ask open-ended questions; however, when interviewing by telephone, begin by asking questions that are focused and solicit specific responses.

INTERNATIONAL CALLS

The telephone is an effective way for contacting foreign relatives. International calls have the benefit of surprise that someone in the U.S. cared enough to call, an element which is a door-opener for asking questions about the family. International Information Service will supply numbers for direct dialing if you don't have them already.

In the urban areas of Europe, many people between fifteen and forty-five have studied English as a second language, so you can speak English with them—schoolbook English free of slang and colorful phrases. Write your questions out and read them over several times before dialing to ensure that they will be understood.

For relatives in rural areas, write your questions out first in their native language. Have someone familiar with the language review them for correct usage. Foreign language professors or students at your nearest college can be consulted for a nominal fee. Major American cities often have translation services advertised in the phone book. The *Genealogical Helper* also carries ads for translators in every issue.

CORRESPONDENCE

CORRESPONDENCE WITH RELATIVES

Genealogical correspondence seeks personal information about a person's life. If you expect accurate answers from your relatives, create a trusting, comfortable atmosphere in your letters in which sharing can take place.

1. Introduce yourself first: your name, what you do, where you live, and how you are related if you are writing for the first time. Reference to a shared memory or event is appropriate if your relative is known to you.

2. Use informal language as if you are speaking across the dinner table to your correspondent. Friendly conversation invites sharing while book phrases sound artificial and suspect.

3. Keep your requests for information brief. You can always write again.

4. Make your questions easy to answer by including a partially filled-in family chart, a photocopy of a photograph with unidentified persons circled, or a questionnaire with an invitation to fill in the blanks. Offer a copy of the family photograph with faces identified or an interesting document from your family research as an incentive to respond. An offer to share what you discover carries credibility.

5. Personalize your correspondence to relatives. If you send a questionnaire, a family record, or a checklist of questions, be sure to write a personal cover letter.

6. Keep copies of your letters to evaluate responses and stimulate further questions. The information you get back will be based on what you asked. A follow-up question phrased differently may trigger a different answer, especially from elderly relatives.

7. Send a self-addressed, stamped envelope (SASE) with every request for information and your response rate will be higher.

CORRESPONDENCE WITH PUBLIC OFFICIALS

Correspondence with public officials requires a different approach. They are not interested in your family history nor the documents you have discovered. Clerks beseiged with genealogy requests will eventually get to yours. Some agencies have a six- to eight-month backlog of unanswered requests. They respond to the simple requests first and set aside more complex queries for later. In order to hasten responses:

1. Keep your letters brief and to the point.

2. Use correct addresses. A valuable aid for addresses is *Where to Write for Vital Records: Births, Deaths, Marriages, and Divorces* available from the U.S. Government Printing Office, Washington, DC 20402. *Names and Numbers* (New York: John Wiley & Sons, 1978 and later editions) is available at most public libraries and includes county and state record officials.

3. Address officials by their correct title. *The Handbook for Genealogical Correspondence* (Logan, Utah: Everton Publishers, 1974) includes the most-used titles for church and civil officials and military personnel.

4. Leave space between questions for the clerk to write in the answers. Even when you have requested only a certificate, the clerk may want to write comments directly on your letter.

2 March 1984

Mr. Donald A. Schuder
818 East Courtland Place
San Gabriel, California 91778

Dear Donald,

At last we are about ready to write a family history on the Eakles in

America. Your data has been very helpful in identifying the family

branch that settled in California. As nearly as I can fit the pieces

together at this time, this is how we are related:

John Harmon Eakle=Anna Margaretha Ohrendorff		
Henry Eakle=Mary Poffenberger	brothers	Christian Eakle=Maria Elisabetha [Baker?]
Christian Eakle=Anna Hibbitts	1st c.	John Baker Eakle=Catherine Kennedy
Mary Eakle=Joseph Reid Schuder	2nd c.	Henry Kennedy Eakle=Mary Jane Johnson
William C. Schuder=Florence C. Peake	3rd c.	Millard Fillmore Eakle=Miriam Adams
Paul S. Schuder=Martha E. Hucke	4th c.	Alma D. Eakle=Mary Alice Rodgers
Donald A. Schuder	5th c.	Alam D. Eakle Jr.=Arlene Haslam

Will you take a few minutes from your busy day to fill in the following

document inventory? If we can identify some of the original documents

of our family, the history will be more interesting and better docu-

mented.

Return the completed inventory to us in the envelope provided and we'll

send you photocopies of the oath of allegiance signed by John Harmon

Eakle in 1741 and his marriage in 1743 to Anna Margaretha Ohrendorff as

a preview of the book to come. These documents are new to our family

and we'd like to share them with you.

Thank you for your help.

More later,

Arlene.

Figure 2:1. Sample correspondence.

EAKLE FAMILY DOCUMENT INVENTORY, 1984

Check those items that apply, fill in the blanks where you can, and mail
to Arlene H. Eakle, 57 West South Temple, Salt Lake City, Utah 84150
and we'll send you photocopies of John Herman Eakle's Oath of Allegiance
in 1741 (with his signature) and his marriage to Anna Margaretha
Ohrendorff in 1743.

I have the originals or copies of the following records:

___Bible. Dated_____.

___Letters written by_____

_____.

___Diary of_____.

___Photographs of_____.

___Unidentified photographs_____.

I have done research on_____who lived in

_____about_____. I will be pleased to

share the information.

Please list the names and addresses of other family members who might
have records to share. If you don't know addresses, give the last known
places of residence.

_____

_____

_____

Thank you for your help. We will pay for all copies and photos to be
reproduced.

Figure 2:2. Sample family document inventory.

5. Always include your return address on your letter in case your SASE gets separated from it.

6. If your first letter does not get a reply, send a second. Refer to the letter you sent, give the date and the check number (if you enclosed money), briefly restate your request, and enclose another SASE.

7. If you receive an answer from a clerk who claims there is no entry, wait a couple of weeks and try again. It may take more than one letter to get the response you want. One patient genealogist wrote the same county twenty-two times before he got the death date of his great-grandmother.

8. Request a photostat of the original record, not a certified extract. The cost is usually the same but you get all the information the record contains, not just what the records clerk enters in the blanks of a standard form.

9. Calculate search dates carefully if you lack specific dates. It is a good idea to ask for a five-year search. Records clerks vary in their policy, some searching only for the date you specify, some for twelve months, and some for a five-year period.

10. When you ask for records for a common surname, supply as many specific references as you can. Some clerks will not search for a common name without more detail.

11. When you request copies of a case file or a packet of documents, ask for a cost estimate first. Some packets may be lengthy and photocopy costs run surprisingly high.

RECORDS BY MAIL

Many records on microfilm are available for purchase, rental, or loan, including records from the National Archives, printed books and periodicals, and the vast collection of original materials filmed by the Genealogical Library of the LDS Church. Figure 2:3 lists the vendors of these resources, costs, and how to order.

INTERLIBRARY LOAN

Many public, research, and university libraries also loan printed books and microfilmed records. For example, the University of Virginia in Charlottesville loaned me microfilmed church registers, county histories, newspapers, and special indexes through a public library in Utah. No single library has all the materials needed for genealogical research. Through interlibrary loans, however, a local library can borrow records from other libraries across the country or around the world. It is the most frequently used and least expensive way of obtaining books, microfilms, theses, and even manuscripts. Requests for loans must be handled through local libraries; patrons are not allowed to borrow books on their own behalf.

Figure 2:3.

TABLE OF MICROFILM VENDORS

Vendor	Records Available	Cost	Time Limit	Requirements/Comments
American Genealogical Lending Library Box 244 Bountiful, UT 84010 801-298-5358	1790-1910 Censuses, Mortality schedules, Some state censuses and tax rolls Ships Passenger Lists Revolutionary War Pension and Bounty Land Applications General Index to Compiled Military Service Records for Revolutionary War	$2.50/roll (rental) $9.00/roll (purchase)	14 days	Membership required, $30.00 (includes 745-page catalog of film available) initially; $15.00 renewal. Films loaned or sold directly to members. Microfilm readers also available.
Microfilm Rental Program Box 2490 Hyattsville, MD 20784	1790-1910 Censuses Revolutionary War Pension and Bounty Land Applications Compiled Service Records of Revolutionary War Soldiers	$3.25/roll (rental only)	7 days	Must order through public or university library, genealogical or historical societies, educational institutions. Ask your librarian for order forms.
Genealogical Library of the LDS Church 35 North West Temple Salt Lake City, UT 84150 801-531-2531	Microfilmed records from most countries of the world—almost 1.5 million reels	$2.50/roll (loan)	30 days, can be extended to 6 months	Must order through and use film at branch library. Write for name and address of branch nearest you or check pp. 696-701 of *The Source.* Microfilm catalogs of holdings available at branches.

TABLE OF MICROFILM VENDORS (CONT.)

Vendor	Records Available	Cost	Time Limit	Requirements/Comments
Genealogical Center 2815 Clearview Place #400 Atlanta, GA 30340 404-457-7801	Microfiche copies of printed books	varies	14 days	Send SASE for complete catalog.
Genealogy Unlimited Rental Library Rt. 8 Box 702 Tucson, AZ 85748	Printed histories, source abstracts	varies	14 days	July 1984 catalog, $2.00.
Mid-Continent Public Library N. Independence Branch Independence, MO 64501 Martha L. Meyers, Librarian	Selected reels of U.S. Censuses (1790-1900), Passenger Lists, State and Indian Censuses, Military Records, Newspapers	varies	2-3 weeks	Must be ordered through public or university library. Send SASE and $1.00 for list of reels available.
National Archives and Record Services Washington, DC 20408	Microfilmed federal and territorial records on almost 500,000 reels	$15.00/roll (purchase only)	3-4 weeks	Order catalogs from NARS Trust Fund, Washington, DC 20408: 1. National Archives Microfilm Publications (free) 2. 1900 Census (free) 3. 1910 Census (free) 4. Specialty Catalogs ($2.00 each) Genealogical and Biographical Research Immigrant and Passenger Arrivals Black Studies American Indians Military Service Records Diplomatic Records

	Photocopies of selected files or pages	$5.00 minimum or cost estimate	varies	For military service and pension files (NATF Form #180); for passenger lists (NATF Form #181); order from Reference Service Branch (NNIR), NARS, Washington, DC 20408.
New England Historic Genealogical Society 101 Newbury Street Boston, MA 02116	Printed genealogies, local histories, source abstracts, general histories	$5.00 per order	3 weeks	Direct loan of 3 books per order. Membership required, $40.00, 4-volume catalog, $20.00.
Rental Library 5300 S.E. 1st Street Ct. Des Moines, IA 50315	Books by mail	varies	3 weeks	Long SASE for catalog and details. Direct loan.
Stagecoach Library 1840 S. Wolcott Ct. Denver, CO 80219	Books by mail	varies	3 weeks	Catalog $5.25. Membership required, $15.00. Direct loan.
University Microfilms International 300 N. Zeeb Road Ann Arbor, MI 48106 800-521-0600 or Canada 800-261-6090	Books on demand: genealogies, family histories, local histories	c. 25¢/page	30 days	Xerox copies of out-of-print books are available on request. Send title, facts of publication to UMI. They will locate, copy, bind, and ship book to you. Microform books also available. Catalogs: 1. Genealogies & Family Histories 2. Local Histories of the States 3. Genealogy & Local History, parts 1-4

Place your request through your local public library, giving the complete bibliographic data needed to identify the books or records you want. You will be notified when the records arrive and will be required to use them under whatever provisions the lending library stipulates. The only charge is usually the postage to and from the home library. If you know the name and address of the library which has the record, give that information to the librarian also. If the record does not circulate, the home librarian can obtain a cost estimate for microfilm or photocopies.

If you are unable to locate the book you need, there are bibliographic centers to assist in locating and borrowing copies of individual titles. Regional centers in Denver, Seattle, and Philadelphia have union catalogs of books, microfilms, manuscripts, and newspapers. Through these, copies of most books can be located within the region. If they cannot be found there, contact the Library of Congress. Its *National Union Catalog* covers book titles held by libraries nationwide. The *Union List of Serials, Union List of Microfilms*, and *Union List of Newspapers* are also available. Copies of these can be found in most large libraries.

RESEARCH SERVICES

A wide variety of low-cost search services exist to help you search or obtain the documents you need to trace your family. Most are reasonably priced, usually costing less than requesting official or certified copies from county offices.

EXCHANGING RESEARCH

There are 550,000 genealogists who belong to genealogical societies in the U.S. and Canada. Most of them are eager to exchange research favors. They search records in their area for you and you perform like searches for them. In actual cash, you pay only for photocopy charges and some out-of-pocket travel and postage costs. Consult these directories and lists to find a genealogist with whom to exchange research.

1. *Genealogical Research Directory,* Library of Australian History, 17 Mitchell Street, North Sydney, NSW 2060, Australia. This annual directory includes ancestor interests primarily from the United Kingdom, origins shared by Australians, Canadians, and Americans. Entries are included for societies in twenty-five countries. Since 1981, 10,000 contributors have submitted more than 150,000 surname entries. $15.

2. Genealogical Time Sharing, 1822 Harding Avenue, Abington, PA 19001. Free research assistance is offered by exchange. Write for details.

3. *National Directory of Local Researchers,* The Family Tree, 450 Potter Street, Wauseon, OH 43567. This semiannual directory listing 300 genealogists is divided in two parts: Section I includes descriptive list-

ings in random alphabetical sequence, while Section II includes the name, address, and area researched arranged by state of residence. $5.

4. *National Genealogical Directory*, Michael J. Burchall, Editor, 3/33 Sussex Square, Brighton BN2 5AB, Sussex, England. First issued in March 1979 and annually since, this international directory lists 130,000 surnames being researched by family historians worldwide. $12.50.

If none of these directories list genealogists in the area where you need research, consult Mary K. Meyer's *Directory of Genealogical Societies in the USA and Canada*, 5th edition (1984), available from Libra Publications, 5179 Perry Road, Mt. Airy, MD 21771 for a genealogical society in that area and write requesting the name and address of a member willing to exchange research with you.

GENEALOGICAL SOCIETY RESEARCH SERVICES

Sixty-five percent of American genealogical societies offer research services for their members as a membership benefit. Society quarterlies publish how-to articles, queries from genealogists seeking information on common lines of interest, and local sources for particular areas. You should join a genealogical society; actually it is suggested that you belong to at least two. First, join a local society near your residence where you can share findings and increase expertise in using sources and fitting data together correctly. Then join a society located in the area where your search is currently focused.

For example, if your ancestor settled west of Milwaukee, Wisconsin, join the Milwaukee County Genealogical Society. With your membership, you can get certificates sent from the county courthouse or city hall, indexes checked at the Milwaukee Public Library, and searches done at the local historical society by researchers who have a vested interest in your success. When your research shifts to New York, then select another society to join there.

LIBRARY RESEARCH SERVICES

Reference librarians at the library nearest where your ancestor resided will perform a variety of services by phone or letter. They can recommend local or family histories and reference books and specific manuscript collections pertinent to your research. They will often check printed or card-file indexes to cemetery inscriptions, obituaries, and family and local histories. As well, they can supply bibliographic citations and help locate old maps and pictures of places and the people who lived there.

Letters to local archives, historical societies, and museums requesting inventories of holdings, citations to printed materials, searches of indexes, lists of local researchers for hire, and other general reference information will usually receive good results. Some offer free search services in indexes, reference guides, or card files. With their help, you can sit in the comfort of your own home and plan an effective research program. Periodically send a gift volume for their collection if you do a lot of research through their facility. If you have original documents on residents in their area, make copies and send them along. When research is complete, send a letter thanking them for their help and never (unless they ask) entertain them with tales about your ancestry.

Many libraries and archives will share the cost of purchasing books, microfilmed records, and other materials within their acquisition guidelines. If you pay half, they'll pay half. You get to read or search the record and they get to keep it for their collection. Inquire about such acquisition purchasing at the libraries and archives you use regularly.

PROFESSIONAL SEARCH SERVICES

Specific searches are offered by several professional organizations. Determine what information you seek and they will search for it for you. Most of these are clustered in Utah; however, there are a substantial number across the country which deal with specific types of records such as passenger lists and printed biographies. Check the pages of the current *Genealogical Helper* for ads as you need them, as there is a steady attrition rate in genealogical vendors. The vendors in Figure 2:4 are survivors, those who have been in business more than two years.

PUBLIC AGENCY SEARCH SERVICES

If you don't know the address, but you know of an institution with which relatives were or are affiliated, send an unsealed letter with a cover letter to the agency describing why you need to make contact through them. If your relative is still living or has an address on file, the agency will usually forward it, since this approach does not violate a person's privacy. For example, if Uncle Robert is the only person who can tell you the specific things about your mother's family and you have lost track of him in the last few years, try the Social Security Administration. Write a letter to Uncle Robert, leaving it unsealed, and add a cover letter asking the Social Security Administration to forward it to his last known address. Supply as much information about him as you can. If they are unable to forward the letter, they will return it to you with the reason: dead, could not identify such a person in their files, etc. You will get better results if you know the Social Security number of the person for whom you are looking.

HIRING A PROFESSIONAL GENEALOGIST

If you are too busy to do all the research yourself or if you are stuck with a problem you cannot solve, hire a professional genealogist to help. Even the most avid researcher will one day need professional assistance, and the Association of Professional Genealogists has published a pamphlet, "How to Hire a Professional Genealogist" (APG, Box 11601, Salt Lake City, UT 84147) to help you with your choice.

DECIDING WHAT YOU WANT

Once you have the names of some professionals (see the professional directories listed below), contact several. Ask them for their credentials: experience, geographical areas of expertise, education, professional affiliations, publications, foreign language skills (where applicable), and their access to records. If special skills are needed, ask if they have those skills. For instance, if you want a written family history, your genealogist will need writing experience. If you wish on-site photographs or oral interviews with family members, your genealogist will need skills in photography and interviewing. If your research involves adoption or ethnic origins, ask what experience the professional has had in these areas and what success you can expect.

WHAT TO EXPECT FROM PROFESSIONAL RESEARCH

Many people who hire a genealogist have no idea what to expect for their research fee. Commonly, someone with no knowledge of the research process believes that his fee can extend a family line as far back as possible. Many believe that doing genealogical research is as simple as pushing a button on a computer, which will then print out all the information needed.

Genealogical research is a time-consuming process, requiring special knowledge and skills that few people have developed. Searches in several different records are difficult and costly. Even searches that are not so involved take time. Computers are just beginning to be used for storing genealogical information, and it is doubtful that the lineages of all mankind will ever be stored for easy access. However, research alone is only part of the genealogical project. "What to Expect from Professional Research" is a pamphlet Lineages, Inc., a Salt Lake City research firm, sends to its clients. The following points extracted from it will give you an idea how involved professional research can be.

1. *Analyzing data received from the client.* The information that accompanies a research request must be carefully sifted in order to understand the research problem, ancestors of interest, reliability of the information provided, and areas where the ancestors lived to ensure that prior research is not duplicated. It is important that the client furnish the genealogist with copies of *all* data previously acquired by the family or other genealogists. This way, the client can avoid the disappointment of being told what he already knew about his ancestors.

2. *Determining the research objectives.* This important step, done with the client's assistance, ensures that the professional does not focus on a portion of his ancestry that is not of interest.

3. *Surveying the types of records sources available.* The Genealogical Library of the LDS Church has the largest collection of records in the world. However, that repository does not hold everything that might be needed to solve a research problem or to extend the ancestry of a

Figure 2:4.

TABLE OF PROFESSIONAL SEARCH SERVICES

Vendor	Search Service	Cost	Time Limits	Comments
Name Search BYU Genalogical Library Room 4385, Lee Library Provo, UT 84602	1790-1900 Censuses State Censuses Southern DAR records Other Sources	varies	3 weeks	Long SASE for list of charges.
Quick-Search Box 11911 Salt Lake City, UT 84147 801-532-3327	1790-1910 Censuses International Genealogical Index Vital Records of New York City, Philadelphia County Records	$8.00/search	7 days	Search includes index, records, photocopies of entries.
Genealogical Helper Box 368 Logan, UT 84321 801-752-6022	"Free Help" section in every issue	SASE	varies	Searches other genealogists will make for you.
Max Kade German-American Document & Research Center 2080 Wescoe Hall University of Kansas Lawrence, KS 66045 913-864-4657	German-American Ancestry	SASE	3-4 weeks	Search services include: 1. Contact church or state archives in German areas where ancestors lived. 2. Translate documents, letters. 3. Advise on steps to take to research ancestors. 4. Search documents, books on file at Center.
George F. Schweitzer 7914 Gleason Knoxville, TN 37919	Revolutionary War Ancestors	$2.00 per name and SASE	2 weeks	Check of indexes to 275,000 names.

Econ-Fast-Search Box 1115 Chester, CA 96020	Passenger-Immigration Research	$10.00 first 200 sheets, 5¢ per sheet and SASE	2-3 weeks	Full passenger list supplied when available. Refund if name not found.
Ancestry, Inc. Box 476 Salt Lake City, UT 84110	Time-Saving Searches	$5.00 to $20.00 per search	2-3 weeks	Membership provides substantial discount from search costs: **United States** U.S. Census Records Probate Records Military Records City Directories Passenger Lists Surveys Vital Records Local and Family Histories International Genealogical Index (IGI) Lineage Society Applications **British Isles** Marriage Indexes Civil Registration Indexes Parish Register Printouts **Ireland and Scotland** Marriage Indexes Civil Registration Indexes **Germany** Hamburg Passenger Lists Parish Registers Other source searches available upon request. Catalogs ($4.00 each): 1. U.S. Vital Records 2. U.S. Census Records: Federal, State, Local.

client. An analysis of what can and should be done in the library's collection is essential—along with an analysis of the records maintained in other libraries or public records offices.

4. *Reviewing information submitted by the client.* When the client presents the genealogist with a large amount of previously extracted information, it takes time to examine, evaluate, and commit it to memory. If the material is voluminous, it could take an entire research period. It is crucial that the genealogist see that evidence and evaluate it in order to avoid duplication.

5. *Choosing the research strategy.* Next, the genealogist constructs a research strategy which outlines the search of the most pertinent records available to meet the client's objectives. Those records that should contain the most valuable information are top priority.

6. *Searching the records.* The genealogist will locate and obtain the record, then search it for mention of the ancestor of interest and take notes or photocopy that document. If records are not available in the local repository, letters will be written to the appropriate person or agency requesting needed information.

7. *Evaluating the records.* Each piece of evidence found in a document must be carefully examined to determine its value, the leads it provides in identifying additional ancestors, and its accuracy. It must be determined whether it agrees or conflicts with information already known and proven.

8. *Compiling family group records and lineage charts.* Although simple on the surface, this time-consuming process consolidates a great deal of information into a manageable, understandable format. Each document extracted from the records must be culled for information to appear on these forms.

9. *Reporting on research.* As important a part of the project as quality research, the research report tells the client exactly what was done and how, and the conclusions reached. Every report is accompanied by photocopies of the documents to which it refers. It also tells the client what more can be realistically done to extend the lineages during future projects.

DIRECTORIES OF PROFESSIONAL GENEALOGISTS

Who's Who in Genealogy and Heraldry, Mary K. Meyer, P. William Filby, 8944 Madison Street, Savage, MD 20863, (301) 255-9229 or (301) 792-7051. Volume I was published by Gale Research Company in 1982. $45. Volume II is in preparation.

Directory of Professional Genealogists and Related Services, Association of Professional Genealogists, P.O. Box 11601, Salt Lake City, UT 84147, (801) 532-3327. Biannual. Listings restricted to APG members. $6.

Genealogists in the United States and Canada, Dr. William D. Andersen & Associates, 2935 Cordell Street, Memphis, TN 38118. The names and addresses of 1,600 professional genealogists with their specialties and qualifications. Entries arranged under the state in which the genealogist lives. $10.

"Directory of Genealogical Societies, Libraries, Periodicals, and Professionals," July-August issue of *Genealogical Helper,* Everton Publishers, Box 368, Logan, UT 84321, (801) 752-6022. Annual. Available by subscription, $15.50 per year for six issues.

Directory of Independent Search Consultants, ISC, P.O. Box 10192, Costa Mesa, CA 92627. Annual. Persons certified to aid adoptees in their search for natural parents, siblings, and ancestors. $10.

In summation, decide what research you want done. Obtain the names of several professionals who seem to fit your needs. Give the chosen researcher clear instructions and comprehensive information. When your project is complete, evaluate it for accuracy and quality. If you are uncertain about the results, contact the researcher for clarification. If you have an unresolved grievance with a professional genealogist, write to the Association of Professional Genealogists, Box 11601, Salt Lake City, UT 84101. Their review board offers free, confidential arbitration for professionals and clients.

FIELD RESEARCH

Perhaps the most personally rewarding of all the search approaches is field research where you visit the locales of your ancestors and search the records firsthand. You can walk the cemeteries and copy the inscriptions, interview local residents who may be related, and stop by the county courthouse to handle original documents produced by your ancestors.

If you are to get the most out of your research trip, you need to plan carefully. Search everything available at home before leaving on your trip, as there is little sense in paying motel bills while searching items you can find at home. Determine what records are available in the area where your ancestor lived and the procedures to be followed in acquiring them in person. Write the county courthouse, give the dates you will be there, and ask whether any holidays (local or federal) will close the courthouse during your visit. In some states, government agencies choose which days they are open, so be sure to inquire into this as well. You should also find out whether the courthouse has a copier and what the charge is for its use. Some counties require that records be ordered in advance, while others require a genealogical society membership card and notarized letters of release from living family members to comply with privacy laws.

Write the public library, the state archives, and other libraries you plan to visit and ask for printed guides or inventories of their record holdings to facilitate planning. As with courthouses, ask about copies, costs, restrictions, etc. Order any printed guides or inventories in advance and study them carefully for the sources you wish to consult. Afterwards send a letter telling the librarian or archivist the specific collections that you want to see. Advanced preparation insures smooth, efficient, and productive research.

When you return home, send thank-yous to those archives and libraries who went out of their way to make your visit productive. If this seems like a lot of extra work, it is. But the benefits are worth the effort. The agencies you visit will be expecting you, will be prepared to assist in your research, and may make allowances for your limited stay. Archivists and librarians will go out of their way to help when you take the time to consider their position and show appreciation for their efforts.

SPECIAL AIDS

Regardless of where you may travel to do research, two important aids are now available. *The Early American Historian's Travel Guide* is designed specifically for the historical researcher on the road, providing a lot of practical information. Written for historians and genealogists studying pre-1820 America, the *Guide* includes major repositories in the thirteen original states as well as selected research institutions in other parts of the country. The *Guide* briefly describes each of the forty-nine towns and cities covered and lists specific information on the following: (1) how to get there, (2) how to get around by car or public transportation, (3) addresses, hours, and fees of major libraries, (4) where to eat and sleep, (5) location of universities and historic sites, and (6) tips on neighborhoods and recreation. You can order the *Guide* from the Institute of Early American History and Culture, Box 220, Williamsburg, VA 23187.

With a membership in Visiting Friends ($15 lifetime fee) and an exchange fee of $20 for one to six nights lodging ($30 for seven or more nights), you can stay in a private home carefully matched to your needs near state archives, county courthouses, and other research facilities. Accomodations are now available in thirty-four states. Write to Visiting Friends, Inc., Box 231, Lake Jackson, TX 77566, or call Mrs. Laura LaGess at (409) 297-7367 for details.

CHAPTER 3

On the Reference Shelf

On the reference shelves of many libraries are books, periodicals, pamphlets, and card files—materials of importance to genealogists. These items can save hours of research time and enable concentration on the analysis of data. The purpose of this chapter is to alert you to some principal resources and their general availability as well as ways to use them. The resources selected for study include many that have revolutionized genealogy and the way we trace ancestors. Some are finding tools enabling you to locate ancestors when you have no idea where they went or why. Others supply facts for evidence analysis, allowing you to fit the pieces of the puzzle together more easily.

FINDING TOOLS

THE *GENEALOGICAL HELPER*

The *Genealogical Helper* should be on every genealogist's reference shelf. First published in 1947, it is dedicated to "helping more people find more genealogy." Its pages are filled with titles of new books and reprints, genealogists seeking cousins to share data, and search services offered by professional genealogists. Each issue also has a computerized "Roots Cellar," the Bureau of Missing Persons (genealogists seeking living relatives), questions and answers where problems get specialized help for free, and classified ads for every conceivable genealogical product and service. It is available annually for $15.50 from Everton Publishers, Inc., Box 368, Logan, UT 84321.

INTERNATIONAL GENEALOGICAL INDEX

The International Genealogical Index (IGI), maintained by the Genealogical Library of the LDS Church, is a computer file estimated to include more than eighty million births and marriages (1984 edition) taken from church and vital records throughout the world. Seven to ten million names are added annually. The IGI is especially rich in U.S. church records: Pennsylvania German, New York and New Jersey Dutch, and New England Congregational. The file will eventually include the 1880 U.S. Census and other important American sources. Still, the IGI is truly an international source, as only twenty percent of the collection relates to the U.S. and Canada.

The IGI is organized by country and then by state or province within that country. Each state or province contains an alphabetical list of the names submitted and the birth and marriage information about each individual. The original source documents submitted to the Genealogical Library are on microfilm and include the name and address of the person submitting the information, as well as the source of that information.

You can consult this index yourself at the Genealogical Library of the LDS Church in Salt Lake City or at any of its branches throughout the country. Copies can also be found in many research libraries. Write to the Genealogical Library, 35 North West Temple, Salt Lake City, UT 84150 for the name of the branch library nearest you. You can also send $1 per name to the same address and library personnel will check the file for you, supplying photocopies of any entries found.

FAMILY GROUP RECORDS ARCHIVES

The forerunner of the IGI was the Family Group Records Archives (FGRA). It was compiled from 1924 to 1978 and consists of nearly eight million family group records submitted by members of the LDS Church. There are over forty million people listed in the collection. The name and address of the person submitting the record is listed on each sheet. Again, those sharing common ancestry are encouraged to contact the submitter to exchange research.

FAMILY HISTORY COLLECTIONS

Thousands of family histories and genealogies are in print with the number increasing each year. Excellent printed genealogies are also included in genealogical journals, such as the *New England Historical and Genealogical Register* and the *American Genealogist,* to name only two. The Genealogical Library of the LDS Church has an excellent collection of family histories, genealogies, and journals. Other libraries also have excellent collections, particularly the Library of Congress, the New York Public Library, and Newberry Library in Chicago.

USING THE IGI

The IGI serves a variety of purposes. In addition to being a source of information about a particular ancestor, it also serves as an index to research completed by other genealogists. Updated versions of the IGI appear about every three years, the most recent edition dated April 1984. Figure 3:1 is a sample page from the new edition.

Let's examine the IGI more closely and apply it to a specific research problem. The Eakle family roots in America begin in Pennsylvania in the early 1740s. After several years of research, the immigrant ancestor, Johann Herman

THE INTERNATIONAL GENEALOGICAL INDEX (IGI)

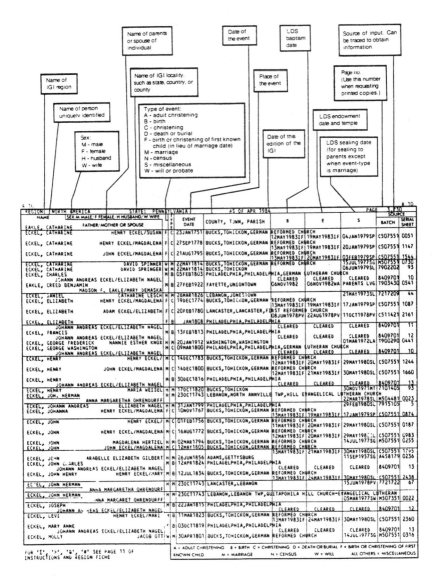

Figure 3:1. Sample page from the International Genealogical Index.

Eckel, was discovered. From the new IGI, it was learned that he married Anna Margaretha Ohrendurff at Hill Church, Lebanon County on 23 October 1743. There are three entries for John Herman Eckel (Harmon Eakle) that are obviously for the same person. They are entered separately by the computer because each entry differs slightly. The entries also come from different sources, none of which are the same as the sources of previous information.

These entries corroborate the sources already examined; alone, however, they do not prove that John Herman Eckel is the ancestor sought. Previously established facts combined with IGI data prove the relationship. The Eakle family moved from Pennsylvania to Maryland, where Harmon established his home. The IGI for Maryland contains entries for many family members, including his second marriage to Regina Salady. Find the entry in Figure 3:2 and examine the source section. The batch number begins with a "7," an indication that it was submitted by another genealogist, perhaps a descendant. Batch numbers refer to a specific type of source or submission to the index. See Figure 3:3 for an explanation of batch numbers.

The entry for Harmon's son, Christian, is an entry prefaced with a "C," a code letter referring to a christening extracted directly from church records. Though the IGI has the information you want, it is wise to check the submission forms. These often contain more information than is found in the index. Send a SASE for a free leaflet, "Tracing the Original Source of an IGI Batch Number," from the Genealogical Library, 35 North West Temple, Salt Lake City, UT 84150.

If you do not find an entry for your family, refer to the *Parish and Vital Records Listings* to determine what sources have been entered. Since the Eakle family settled in Washington County, Maryland, we can check the *Listings* page for Maryland. The records of five churches have been entered thus far, the *Listings* being updated every month. The type of record, the dates covered, and the GS (Genealogical Society) call number of the source from which the entries were taken are given for each church record.

All entries in each record type are entered for the time period stated. If your ancestor does not appear in the index, you can bypass searching these records. For church records, however, note that deaths are not entered into the database. It is recommended that you search the registers themselves for deaths and for other records that go beyond the dates included in the database. Search for all possible spelling variations of your surname in alphabetical sequence. In some cases, there will be several possible surname variants.

Arranged alphabetically by state, the IGI is a finding tool in which you can locate specific life events—births and marriages for the most part, although some wills, census entries, and other sources are included. You can locate a county or city of residence as well as spot clusters of families in specific localities, all of whom may be related. A search of each state in which your ancestor lived should yield entries for that surname and its variants. Using those entries submitted by other researchers, additional family members—

N 12 — PAGE 1,763

REGION: NORTH AMERICA STATE: MARYLAND AS OF APR 1984

NAME	SEX	E	FATHER/MOTHER OR SPOUSE	COUNTY, TOWN, PARISH	EVENT DATE	B	E	S	BATCH	SERIAL SHEET
EAKLE, ANNA MARIA	F	C	PHILIP ECKEL/CATHARINA	WASHINGTON,MAGERSTOWN REFORMED CONGREGATION	02AUG1771				C507741	0042
ECKEL, BUCKKWARD	M	C	PHILIP ECKEL/	BALTIMORE,BALTIMORE,GAY STREET AND COURT HOUSE	25FEB1805	26APR1978OK	11JUL1978OK	09AUG1978OK PLAZA IION	GERMAN LUTHE	2020
EAKLE, CATHARINE	M		JOHN HOFFMAN/	WASHINGTON	17OCT1800	30MAR1978MA	02JUN1978MA	23JUN1978MA PLAZA IION	7032405	55
EAKLE, CATHERINE	M		JOHN HAYS	WASHINGTON	03JAN1825			08SEP1977IF 06APR1976MT	7516316	60
ECHEL, CHAS. FRIED.	M	C	PHILIP ECHEL/	BALTIMORE,BALTIMORE,GAY STREET AND COURT HOUSE	19APR1799	29MAR1978MA	01JUN1978MA	28JUN1978MA PLAZA IION	GERMAN LUTHE	1152
ECKEL, ELISABETH	F	C	ANDREAS ECKEL/	BALTIMORE,BALTIMORE,GAY STREET AND COURT HOUSE	24JUL1800	22MAR1978MA	25APR1978MA	22JUN1978MA PLAZA IION	C507641	1329
EAKLE, MARMANN	M		REGINA SALADY	WASHINGTON	26MAY1784			04AUG1972PV	7120205	79
EAKLE, HENRY	M		FRANEY FUNK	WASHINGTON	09OCT1810			23JUL1975LG	7630401	83
EAKLE, JOHANES	M	C	PHILIP ECKEL/	BALTIMORE,BALTIMORE	05OCT1794	29MAR1978MA	31MAY1978MA	24JUN1978MA PLAZA IION	C507641	0668
ECKEL, JOHANN	M	B	JOHANN ANDREAS ECKEL/MARGARETHA GERTRUDE PRIESTENBACH		09JAN1785		26OCT1979SL	24JAN1980SL 09APR1980SL	7915221	87
EAKLE, LEAH S.	W		ALEXANDER SHAFFER	WASHINGTON,MAGERSTOWN,ZION REFORMED CHURCH	10SEP1834			17MAY1978AL	M507751	0122
EAKLE, MAGDALINA	W		DAVID GROVE	WASHINGTON	25OCT1816			28OCT1947SL	A186790	4596
ECKEL, MARIA HAYNES	F	C	PHILIP ECKEL/	BALTIMORE,BALTIMORE,GAY STREET AND COURT HOUSE	13MAY1802	29MAR1978MA	31MAY1978MA	22JUN1978MA PLAZA IION	GERMAN LUTHE	1619
EAKLE, MARY	W		SAMUEL MILL	WASHINGTON	15MAY1809	INFANT		06APR1976MT	7516316	49
EAKLE, MARY ANN	W		JOHN PETRY OR PETRIE	WASHINGTON	02JAN1849	INFANT		04FEB1964AZ	A456431	0046
ECKEL, PHILIPP PETER	M		MARY TINGES	BALTIMORE,BALTIMORE	19OCT1781			J4APR1980SL	7915221	88
EAKLE, SARAH	M		MARY HAYS	WASHINGTON	23JAN1832			06APR1976MT	7516316	68
EAKLE, SARAH	W		BENJAMIN LONG	WASHINGTON	20OCT1842			17OCT1951AZ	A456259	0240
ECHEL, THEODORE	M	C	PHILIP ECHEL/	BALTIMORE,BALTIMORE,GAY STREET AND COURT HOUSE	19APR1799	29MAR1978MA	01JUN1978MA	28JUN1978MA PLAZA IION	GERMAN LUTHE	1153
ECKEL, WILHELM	M	C	PHILIP ECKEL/	BALTIMORE,BALTIMORE,GAY STREET AND COURT HOUSE	24APR1793	29MAR1978MA	01JUN1978MA	24JUN1978MA PLAZA IION	C507641	0507
EAKLE, WILLIAM HENRY	M		MARY C BIZER	WASHINGTON	19MAR1884			29NOV1946AZ	A170725	0877

Figure 3:2. Eakle entries for Maryland.

Figure 3:3.

EXPLANATION OF BATCH CODES

Batch Code	Batch Type
A------	Archive sealing record, extracted from Family Group Records Collection Archive Section or other Temple records.
C------	Christening or birth record extraction project. Names came originally from lists of christenings or births.
D------	Deceased Members or 110-Year Suspended File.
E------	Early marriage record extraction project used for proxy baptisms and endowments.
F------	Family entry patron submitted Family Group Record. Some IGI event dates or places are estimates.
H------	Deceased Members File LDS record at a time of person's death. IGI ordinance data may be misleading.
J------	Extraction project.
K------	Extraction project.
M------	Marriage record extraction project.
M17------	Marriage extraction project of LDS sealings to spouse.
P------	Christening/birth record extraction project.
T000001 to T000010	Manual 110-Year file from Family Group Records Collection Archive Section.
T000011 to T000136	Temple Index Bureau (TIB) conversion.
T9------	Temple submitted Family Group Records taken directly to Temple by living child, sibling or parent of person on entry.
T990001 to T990075	Either royalty, nobility, peerage, or medieval (pre-1501) families, or special handling.
T998-----	For persons who previously had some LDS ordinances completed, or were entered on the same entry form as such persons.
T9991----	Special Services cases.
0------	Temple Service Center originated entry, usually in the native language.
694----	Early LDS membership records.
6940405 to 6940426	Minnie Marget's Membership Card Index.
69407----	Scandinavian LDS Branch Card Index.
69409----	Archive Section entry lacking ordinances.
696----	Special Services.
725----	Gibson's Marriage Index.
744----	Nordic and others.
745----	Vermont/Connecticut extraction project.
754----	New Hampshire.
766----	Special Services project.

perhaps unknown to this point – can be contacted and invited to assist in some future research.

SUGGESTED READING

For a more complete description of the IGI and its uses consult these references:

The International Genealogical Index, Research Paper Series F, No. 6, 1973, $2.50. Order from the Genealogical Library, 35 North West Temple, Salt Lake City, UT 84150.

Jacob, Lance J., "The International Genealogical Index: A Tool to be Used with Understanding," *Genealogist's Magazine* (June and September 1983). A British perspective.

Nichols, Elizabeth L., "The International Genealogical Index," *New England Historical and Genealogical Register* (July 1983). Official information from a person directly connected with the IGI.

ACCELERATED INDEXING SYSTEMS INDEX

A new and valuable research tool is now available. This is the Accelerated Indexing Systems (AIS) Index also found in the Genealogical Library. The index is a merging of the state census indexes, some tax rolls, and other miscellaneous sources as well. A separate guide has been prepared by Genealogical Library personnel describing various parts of the AIS Index, listing abbreviations for places and sources used, explaining how to locate an individual in the indexes, what to do if you do not find an entry for your ancestor, and where to go for further help.

The AIS Index is the first nationwide surname index. Americans have been on the move since early times, some families moving every three to ten years. Tracking these moves is difficult without indexes covering interstate areas. Because the AIS Index includes all of the census records before 1850, many state and local censuses, and a smattering of tax rolls and church and military lists, ancestors you might not find in other sources can be found listed in this index. You can use the index to determine how common a surname is in a given area for a specific time period, spot family naming patterns, discover migration routes, and identify spelling variants of your surname before searching various records.

The AIS Index is produced from statewide census indexes you may have used already *and* contains the same errors, a weakness to be considered before use. Extensive studies have demonstrated a twenty percent error rate in the AIS Index – names misspelled, entries omitted even though they are in the original censuses, typographical errors, and more.

The AIS Index is not a bypass source. If your ancestor is not in the index, do not overlook searching the original record, as your ancestor may have been omitted or his name incorrectly printed in another part of the index. Even with these problems, the AIS Index is a valuable research tool that may save time and solve problems.

PASSENGER LIST INDEXES

Another genealogical milestone is the *Passenger and Immigration Lists Index* compiled by P. William Filby, Mary K. Meyer, and numerous contributing genealogists. Mr. Filby receives about 2,000 names per week from books and articles. To date, five volumes have appeared, giving us indexed access to more than a million immigrants who came to America between 1538 and 1900. Accompanying these volumes are two more with annotated bibliographic citations to the sources from which the names were taken.

Using the *Passenger and Immigration Lists Index* is not difficult. The entries are easy to scan. Each immigrant is identified by name (spelled as it appears in the sources), age (if given), place of arrival, year of arrival, source code, and page number. All persons traveling together are listed with the head of household; cross-references make it possible to locate family members who immigrated together.

The *Passenger and Immigration Lists Index* includes all of the entries in the Harold Lancour and Richard Wolfe *Bibliography of Ship's Passenger Lists* found in many library reference sections. In the late 1930s, Harold Lancour published a bibliography of passenger lists for the New York Public Library from printed sources where the place of origin for an American family was supplied. His work was subsequently revised and enlarged by Richard Wolfe in 1963.

Included in the items found in Filby and Meyer are emigrant lists recorded at the port of embarkation, passenger lists recorded at the port of arrival, occupation lists, shipboard lists, and sundry items from church records, convict and pauper lists, naturalizations, customs lists, legal papers and petitions, county histories, oaths of allegiance, and other records – all under the heading of "passenger lists."

STATEWIDE INDEXES

Statewide indexes where several sources are indexed together can prove beneficial. If you are uncertain where your ancestor resided, a statewide index can provide the answer. If you do not know the specific place where your ancestor married, a statewide index could save untold hours of searching.

Carol Willsey Bell, using a corps of local genealogical society volunteers, compiled *Ohio Wills and Estates to 1850: An Index* (available from the author, 4649 Yarmouth Lane, Youngstown, OH 44512). Bell includes a county-by-county breakdown of the records available, shows where information gaps exist, and gives references to entries for which there are no supporting documents or original papers surviving.

Another significant resource made available within the last few years are abstracted collections of state and local records. One of the most significant projects is the work of Brent H. Holcomb for the Carolinas before 1850. He has copied and indexed marriage and death notices from all South Carolina newspapers through 1850 with the exception of Charleston, which goes only to 1830. He has also transcribed all pre-1800 county court minutes providing everyname indexes. These records include jury lists, persons required by law to build and maintain local roads, small court actions like trespass or libel, tavern licenses, bastardy bonds (one of the few sources that identify reputed fathers of illegitimate children), and some marriage bonds or licenses. Many people who were residents of the counties appear only in these minutes — some are not even recorded in the 1790 census. His volumes are also bypass sources. If you find no entry for your ancestor, you can bypass searching the original sources.

WPA INDEXES

During the 1930s, make-work projects for unemployed professionals made a substantial contribution to genealogy, although very few of the indexers were genealogists. The WPA compiled an everyname index to court records for Tennessee, an index of immigrants in naturalization records, a passenger lists index for New York and New England ports, and a cemetery inscriptions index for North Carolina. The *WPA Historical Records Survey: A Guide to the Unpublished Inventories, Indexes, and Transcripts* (Chicago: Society of American Archivists, 1980) describes these projects and where they can be searched.

CENSUS MAPS

For several years, genealogists have depended upon Everton's *The Handy Book for Genealogists* as the principal source for county maps and for dates of county formation. The maps in the *Handy Book*, however, are current county outline maps and do not demonstrate boundary changes that radically effect where to look for an ancestor in the corresponding census year.

Two professional genealogists facing this problem over and over decided it was time to draft a new series of maps showing the historical county boundaries for each census year. Thus, one of the most significant genealogical reference aids came into existence: *Map Guide to the U.S. Federal Censuses, 1790-1920* available from Dollarhide Systems, Box 5282, Bellingham, WA 98227. Where previous census maps relied on old atlases and contemporary maps, these maps are based on actual state laws. William Thorndale researched county boundaries and redrew them to reflect the original lines. William Dollarhide drafted and published the maps using the U.S. Geological Survey Base Map of the United States. Together they have created a highly accurate set showing census boundaries and modern county lines.

While these maps will be used most often to gain a general sense of where county boundaries were positioned each census year, they can also help identify "gores" where the change in boundary lines resulted in a no-man's land. Sometimes the census entries for gores will be found recorded in one county, sometimes in an adjoining one, and sometimes records will be taken separately. Where the census is indexed on a statewide basis this will not create a major search difficulty, as the index will show where the family is recorded.

The maps can be used to track other county and local records also separately entered for the gore. Portions of two maps reproduced here – New York in 1790 and 1800 – show the gore created by surveys of what became the western boundary line of Seneca County. Note the differences between 1790 and 1800. This gore, while rather small on the maps, represents a substantial area, and a substantial number of persons living within who can be difficult to identify.

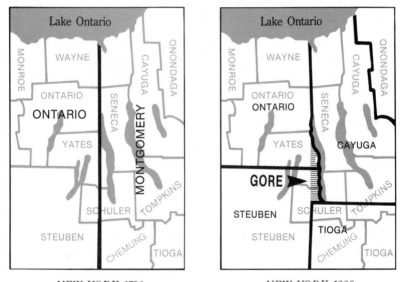

NEW YORK 1790

White = Modern Boundaries
Black = 1790 Boundaries

NEW YORK 1800

White = Modern Boundaries
Black = 1800 Boundaries

Figure 3:4. Example of a gore on the western Seneca County, New York boundary, 1790 and 1800.

SOURCE GUIDES AND HOW-TO BOOKS

Available on reference shelves are a selection from more than 2,000 how-to books and source guides. Genealogists keep buying them and publishers keep bringing them out to fill various needs. Some are general in nature, covering a broad variety of sources with tips on where to find them and how to use them. Others are narrowly defined, covering a county or a particular source. Good examples you may want to review are *Family History for Fun and Profit* (Salt Lake City: Genealogical Institute, 1972), *Genealogical Research Methods and Sources*, available in two updated volumes (Washington, D.C.: American Society of Genealogists, 1980, 1983), and Val Greenwood's *The Researcher's Guide to American Genealogy* (Baltimore: Genealogical Publishing Co., 1973).

The Source: A Guidebook of American Genealogy (Salt Lake City, Utah: Ancestry, Inc., 1984) is a source book discussing a large number of genealogical sources you can expect to encounter. It suggests alternative sources to replace burned or pilfered records, and it identifies both those sources that are more effective for solving specific problems and those that can be found most easily, noting limitations and giving cautions in the use of the evidence the records yield. Finally, *The Source* describes sources that cover large geographic areas crossing county and state lines.

What makes *The Source* something out of the ordinary is the practical approach it takes to hundreds of possible genealogical sources – so many that even professional genealogists are often intimidated by the information available. How does a genealogist deal with such a body of potential data? How is a collection ten to twenty years in the making searched? *The Source* suggests searching one source at a time, one family at a time, one generation at a time, and one step at a time.

RESEARCH BY FOOTNOTE

Historians and genealogists use the same sources for their research. They often seek the same answers, though asking different questions. Professional genealogists keep abreast of what is available by reading historical journals on a consistent basis. Select an historical journal yourself that covers the area where your ancestors lived or the subject matter you are currently searching. For example, if you are searching the colonial period, a good journal to consult is the *William and Mary Quarterly*. It carries documented articles and book reviews spanning all thirteen colonies. Articles often contain facts that help make sense of the time period in which your ancestor lived. More significant will be footnote identification of sources that can make your own research more thorough and effective. This approach is called research by footnote.

A genealogist wrote some time ago seeking a guide to Barbados research. At that time, there was very little. A recent survey article in *William and Mary Quarterly*, "Guide to British-American History," 41 (April 1984):227-95, included a lengthy footnote on resources in Barbados mentioning Jerome S. Handler's *Guide to Source Materials for the Study of Barbados History, 1627-1834* (Carbondale, Ill.: Southern Illinois University Press, 1971) and updates for subsequent materials issued from 1980 to 1983 in the *Journal of the Barbados Museum and Historical Society*.

Book reviews in these journals can also be highly important for your research. An essay on three books dealing with Washington's Army during the Revolutionary War appeared in *William and Mary Quarterly* 40 (April 1983): 327-30. The writer asked this question:

Although Gillett's research is extensive – the bibliography contains dozens of obscure primary and secondary sources – she adds little to what is already known about the Hospital Department from the studies of other historians . . . .

Do we need to know the exact number of patients in every hospital in Philadelphia during the winter of 1777-78?

Historians most likely do not, but genealogists need to know every patient. What sources are included in Mary C. Gillett's *The Army Medical Department, 1775-1818* (Washington, D.C.: Center for Military History, United States Army, 1981)? Where are they located? How can the genealogist search the same sources? These questions are answered in Gillett's book, so kindly footnoted by the reviewer.

In a review of David W. Galenson, *White Servitude in Colonial America: An Economic Analysis* (New York: Cambridge University Press, 1982) in *William and Mary Quarterly*, 40 (April 1983):132-34, the author describes the contracts for indentured servants. By studying these contracts as a group, Galenson discovered that seventy-seven percent of the servants who came to America in the seventeenth century were male and sixty-six percent were under twenty-five. This means one can expect the average indentured servant to come without parents and to marry in America. In the eighteenth century, ninety percent of indentured servants were male and fifty percent were skilled laborers. This means you should watch carefully for an occupation. As males in this century too will come without parents and marry in America, your best chance of locating them in their place of origin in Europe will be through occupation. Such indirect clues and guidelines are the result of research by footnote.

There are thousands of reference materials in addition to those discussed here. Many researchers are reluctant to investigate some reference works because of the small number of people listed in comparison to the total population of a given period. Don't be lazy in your approach to research. Most reference works are well indexed and require only minutes to review, and those few minutes invested could save months or years of searching.

CHAPTER 4

Getting Started

One day I was having lunch with an old friend and the conversation turned to family. My friend had lost her parents to cancer within the five years that had passed since our high school graduation. After the initial shock was over, she began to feel at loose ends, needing contact with some family members. She realized that after her parents moved from New York to Los Angeles when she was an infant, there had been no contact with family members in the East. As months passed, she became obsessed with knowing as much as possible about her family, to establish some sense of heritage.

Then she began to relate fascinating stories about her ancestors who settled New Amsterdam in 1635. Before lunch was over I was wondering about my own past and asked the single question that started a life-long quest beginning as a hobby and leading to a satisfying career as a professional genealogist: "Where do I begin?" And the answer she gave me was quite simple: "Begin with yourself and your immediate family." My friend gave me a few lineage charts and family group records and I was on my way.

There are a number of family and home sources. Figure 4:1 shows a complete checklist of all the records and documents that might exist in your home or in your relatives' homes that might contain valuable genealogical information. My mother only had records pertaining to our immediate family, such as birth and baptism certificates, my father's military discharge papers, and immunization records. We sat down and began recording the names, dates, and places of birth, marriage, and death on the forms. When we finished, the family group record for our family was complete, but the lineage chart was still nearly blank. Figures 4:2 and 4:3 illustrate those charts when we were finished.

Three of my grandparents were living in 1966 when I started tracing my ancestry and they were logically the next people to contact. Unfortunately, they lived half a continent away and phone calls had to be made. Getting information by phone is expedient, but it isn't the best approach as it doesn't allow people time to rummage through old papers and family memorabilia. When you phone for information it's a good idea to list the questions you want to

FAMILY AND HOME SOURCES CHECKLIST

HOME SOURCES

This checklist is a guide to the records you should find in the homes of your relatives. Check each record you search.

Personal Records

____Journal
____Diary
____Biography
____Patriarchal Blessing
____Letters
____Seal
____Photographs
____Autograph Album
____Personal Knowledge
____Baby Book
____Wedding Book
____Scrapbooks
____Funeral Book
____Guest Register
____Travel Account
____Treasures of Truth
____Book Plates

Legal Papers

____Will
____Deeds
____Land Grants
____Water Rights
____Mortgages
____Leases
____Bonds
____Loans
____Contracts
____Summons
____Subpoena
____Tax Notices
____Guardian Papers
____Abstracts of Title

Certificates

____Birth
____Marriage
____Death
____Divorce
____Adoption
____Graduation
____Christening
____Blessing
____Baptism
____Confirmation
____Ordination
____Transfer
____Ministerial
____Mission Release
____Membership
____Apprenticeship
____Achievement
____Award

Military Records

____Service
____Pension
____Disability
____Discharge
____National Guard
____Selective Service
____Bounty Award
____Service Medals
____Ribbons
____Sword
____Firearms
____Uniform
____Citations
____Separation Papers

Citizenship Papers

____Naturalization
____Denization
____Alien Registration
____Deportment
____Passport
____Visa
____Vaccination

School Records

____Diplomas
____Report Cards
____Honor Roll
____Awards
____Transcripts
____Yearbooks
____Publications

Employment Records

____Apprenticeship
____Awards
____Graduation
____Citations
____Severence Papers
____Social Security
____Retirement Papers
____Pension
____Union
____Income Tax

Family Records

____Bible
____Books of Remembrance
____Family Group Records
____Lineages
____Genealogies
____Family Bulletins
____Family Histories
____Printed Histories
____MS Histories
____Local Histories
____Family Traditions
____"Birth Briefs"

Newspaper Clippings

____Announcements
____Obituaries
____Special Events
____Vital Statistics
____Home Town Papers
____Professional
____Trade

Figure 4:1. Family and Home Sources Checklist. Courtesy of the Genealogical Institute, Salt Lake City.

Announcements

___Wedding
___Birth
___Death
___Funeral
___Graduation
___Divorce
___Anniversary
___Memorial Cards
___New Job
___Travel
___New Home
___Birthday
___Professional
___Engagement

Membership Records

___Cards
___Publications
___Programs
___Uniforms
___Awards
___Certificates

Financial Records

___Accounts
___Bills
___Receipts
___Check Stubs
___Estate Records

Health Records

___Xrays
___Insurance Papers
___Hospital Records
___Medical Records
___Immunizations

Licenses

___Business
___Occupation
___Professional
___Hunting
___Firearms
___Drivers
___Motor Vehicle

Household Items

___Silverware
___Needlework
___Sampler
___Tapestries
___Dishes
___Friendship Quilt
___Coat of Arms
___Insignias
___Souvenirs
___Clothing
___Tools
___Memorial Rings
___Engraved Jewelry

Books

___Atlases
___Yearbooks
___Textbooks
___Prizes
___Treasured Volumes
___Vocational
___Foreign Language

INSTITUTIONAL SOURCES

This checklist is a guide to the records you should find in institutional libraries.
Check each record you search.

Composite Records

___Special Indexes
___Family Histories
___Local Histories
___MS Histories
___Printed Histories
___Genealogies
___Pedigrees
___Biographies
___Heraldry Collections
___Coats of Arms
___Personal Papers
___MS Collections
___Printed Collections
___Oral History Files
___Periodicals
___Journals
___Proceedings
___Transactions

Membership Records

___Lists
___Enrollment Books
___Admissions
___Transfers
___Removals
___Terminations
___Disciplinary
   Proceedings
___Biographies
___Bequests
___Yearbooks
___Bulletins
___Newspapers
___Directories
___Memorials
___Alumni

Administrative Records

___Minutes
___Histories
___Donations
___Disbursements
___Accounts
___Correspondence
___Charitable Funds
___Insurance Funds
___Scholarship Funds
___Migrations Funds
___Refugee Records
___Immigrant Files
___Displaced Persons

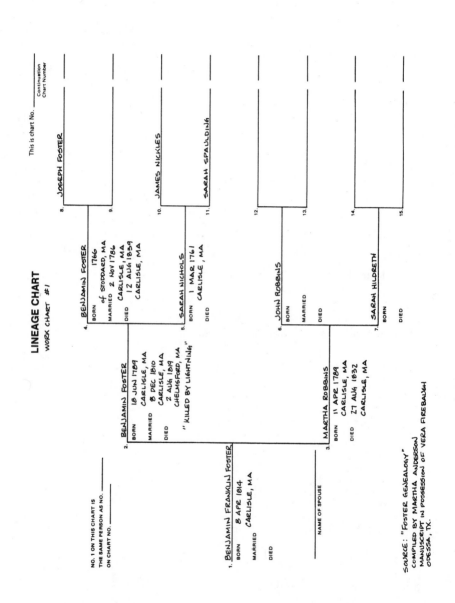

Figure 4:2. Lineage Chart 1, Jonnette Elaine Cerny.

FAMILY GROUP SHEET

HUS. JOHN STEVE CERNY — OCCUPATION(S)

BORN	2 JAN 1916	PLACE	Chicago, Cook, Illinois
CHR		PLACE	
MARR	20 MAR 1943	PLACE	Kansas City, Jackson, Missouri
DIED	9 SEP 1982	PLACE	Yuma, Yuma, Arizona
BUR	15 SEP 1982	PLACE	Cave Creek Cemetery, Phoenix, Maricopa, AZ
FATHER	JOHN CERNY / JAN ČERNY		
MOTHER	THERESA ZAHOREC / TEREZIA ZÁHORECOVA	OTHER WIVES	

WIFE VIVIAN ELAINE WEST

BORN	24 DEC 1922	PLACE	La Harpe, Allen, Kansas
CHR		PLACE	
DIED		PLACE	
BUR		PLACE	
FATHER	GROVER CLEVELAND WEST		
MOTHER	BERTHA RUTH SMITH	OTHER HUSBANDS	

SEX	CHILDREN		DATE BORN / PLACE BORN	DATE MARRIED / TO	PLACE	DATE DIED / PLACE DIED
X 1 F	JONNETTE ELAINE	CERNY	27 AUG 1943 / Kansas City, Jackson, Missouri	20 FEB 1970 / KENNETH GREENSTONE	Reno, Carson City, NV	
2 F	ANTOINETTE IRENE	CERNY	4 DEC 1946 / Kansas City, Jackson, Missouri	24 MAY 1969 / JERRY ELMORE SHINKLE	Los Angeles, Los Angeles, CA	
3 F	STEVETTE MARIE	CERNY	12 JAN 1948 / Kansas City, Jackson, Missouri	10 APR 1982 / CINDY PADGETT	Coolidge, Pinal, AZ	
4 M	JOHN JOSEPH	CERNY	23 SEP 1951 / Kansas City, Jackson, Missouri			
5 F	NANETTE THERESA	CERNY	14 APR 1956 / Encino, Los Angeles, California	4 MAR 1981 / PETER OSWALD MARIN	Las Vegas, Clark, NV	
6						
7						
8						
9						
10						

OTHER MARRIAGES

SOURCES OF INFORMATION

Family Records of Vivian West Cerny, 527 N. Topping, Kansas City, Missouri 64123
Photocopies in possession of the author, P.O. Box 417, Salt Lake City, Utah 84110

RESEARCH NOTES

Figure 4:3. Family Group Record, John Steve Cerny and Vivian Elaine West.

ask. Refer to the oral interview section of this chapter to get ideas on how to adapt interviews for use over the telephone.

Within a few days after conversations with each grandparent, letters arrived giving more information that had been located in desk drawers, boxes in the attic, and from other family members living in the Midwest. They also sent addresses of other family members who might contribute more information. Eventually, each family member was contacted and his or her contributions were added to the charts.

Unless the information recorded on the charts is taken directly from documents made at the time an event occurred or shortly afterward, it is considered indirect or circumstantial evidence. Verbal accounts of events taking place in the lives of early ancestors are considered family tradition. Everything but information taken from documents made at the time of an event or shortly afterward must be verified by searching records which would attest to the validity of a purported fact. Chapter 8, "Tracing an American Lineage," presents a step-by-step approach to verifying circumstantial evidence obtained in an oral interview.

Searching family and home sources is an important step that gives you a base from which to plan research strategies in public and private records. Records found in the home often provide details of a person's life that may not be elaborated upon in public records. This is particularly true of personal journals, diaries, and autobiographies.

One example of the valuable history in these types of records was found while searching a client's ancestry. Some of his ancestors were Mississippi slaves just prior to the Civil War, and—as is typical of almost all slave ancestors—their lives were nondescript. There were no family histories or public records to attest directly to their lives. However, they were last owned by a man who didn't fit the stereotypical description of the unfeeling and uncaring slave owner. He kept a plantation diary recording the events which affected the lives of his family and his slave families: the plantation rules, accounts of what was grown and how much it brought at market, the birth and death dates of his slaves, and many other interesting anecdotes about life as a slave and a plantation owner in the South. Without that plantation diary, the lives of my client's ancestors would have been imagined much the same as the slave characterizations in some of the many novels and motion pictures depicting life during that period. The journal made his ancestors come alive and placed them in an exact setting with real-life dramas which were very different from the experiences of slaves owned by insensitive masters just a plantation away.

The degree of future research success can depend significantly upon how thoroughly family and home sources are searched. Study the checklist shown in Figure 4:1 and then contact family members who might have one of those documents or records in their possession.

ORAL INTERVIEWS IN GENEALOGY AND FAMILY HISTORY

I don't know of a single researcher who has not conducted a personal interview to obtain information about his or her ancestors. I remember the first interview I conducted and grimace over the many questions I didn't think of asking. Sometimes there's only one chance to interview a relative or someone who knew family members, and if the right questions aren't asked, key information may not surface elsewhere.

Oral history has become a major field of study for historians, and there are a number of manuals in print giving instructions in conducting an interview. (See the list of suggested readings at the end of this section.) While those manuals are useful guides for compiling a personal history, few focus on family history or genealogy.

After seventeen years of research, I decided that it was time to write a history of the Cerny family. I chose a family history over a genealogy because a history includes much more biographical and narrative information than is found in a genealogy. One important feature of the proposed book was the inclusion of personal histories of living family members. I was also eager to interview them for anecdotes about our ancestors that I hadn't recorded earlier when I was more interested in compiling names, dates, places, and relationships. It isn't always possible to tape oral interviews, especially now when family members are spread across the country. Often a questionnaire adapted from oral interview questions can be substituted.

Preparation is the key element in every good oral interview. It's a good idea to allow the person you're interviewing to prepare in advance by giving them a list of the questions you plan to ask. Some people are afraid of tape recorders and, in their nervousness, unable to think clearly. Always remember to take writing materials with you to take down important facts and phrases that will help you recall the interview on tape after you get home. Taped interviews are preferable because they capture the feelings as well as the memories of the person you're interviewing. That tape also becomes a family heirloom that can be handed down through future generations, just as the family Bible was by earlier generations.

It's difficult to compile a list of standard questions to ask in an interview. Questions will vary depending upon the purpose of the interview and the background of the individual you're interviewing. The following list of questions is a basic guideline for conducting your interview. As the interview proceeds you will want to ask other questions to clarify something said in the interview. However, jot down those questions and ask them later rather than interrupt the flow.

1. What is the name you were given at birth?
2. Were you named after a relative or friend of the family?
3. Where were you born?

4. Were you born in a hospital or at home?

5. What is your nationality?

6. Did your family change their name when they arrived in America?

7. Do you know the names of your family members who first came to this country?

8. Do you know why they left their homeland to come to America?

9. Where did they settle when they arrived here?

10. Where did they live prior to coming to this country? Do you know the name of the town or village they lived in there?

11. Do you know any stories they told about what life was like before they came here?

12. How did they earn their living?

13. What are your parent's names? When and where were they born?

14. How many children did your parents have?

15. What were your brothers and sisters named?

16. When and where were your brothers and sisters born?

17. What are the names of your brothers' and sisters' spouses?

18. When and where were they married?

19. Which of your parents, brothers, or sisters are deceased?

20. When and where did they die?

21. Where are they buried?

22. Where did your parents live during their lifetime?

23. Do you remember any stories your parents told you about their childhood and their parents?

24. What did your parents do for a living?

25. What were your grandparents' names?

26. Do you remember when and where they were born?

27. Can you tell stories your grandparents told you about their childhood, where they grew up, and what life was like for them when they were young?

28. Do you recall when and where your grandparents died?

29. Where are they buried?

30. What were your parents like?

31. Did you have any aunts and uncles? What do you remember most about them?

32. Where did you grow up? What do you remember about the places where you lived as a child? What were the houses like?

33. When did you get married and to whom? Where did you marry?

34. What do you remember about your courtship? Where did you go on dates in those days?

35. What religion did your parents and grandparents practice?

36. Where did you go to school?

37. Did you/your husband/wife serve in the military? Did you/your husband/wife serve during wartime?

38. Did you ever hear of anyone in your family serving in the Civil War or the Revolutionary War? What were those soldiers' names?

39. What were your in-laws names? Where did they live?

40. What did you look like as a child?

41. What are your children's names? When and where were they born?

42. Describe some of your family's customs and traditions.

43. Did you ever hear that you were related to anyone famous?

44. What were some of the memorable or historical events that touched your life or the lives of your parents?

45. Who do you admire the most?

46. Have you ever been involved in politics?

47. What are your deepest values?

48. Can you share the most important moment in your life?

49. Do you know anyone who has a written history of your family?

50. Do you know of any family Bibles handed down from earlier generations?

There are dozens of other questions that could be asked. You should choose the questions that will provide information to fit the purpose of your interview. If you want to focus upon the more personal aspects of a person's life, you will want to include questions about their hopes, fears, personal views, philosophies of life, and on a larger number of life events.

Some interviews will have a special purpose, such as seeking information from someone who has conducted research into or knows about your immigrant ancestors. The following questions will help you get the information you need:

1. Where were the immigrants born and where did they reside before coming to this country?

2. Describe their hometown.

3. Why did they decide to leave their homeland and come to America?

4. Who did they leave behind?

5. What port did they sail from?

6. How did they describe their departure?

7. Who did they travel with?

8. Were there any births, marriages, or deaths en route to America?

9. Did they stop anywhere along the way?

10. What was their voyage to America like?

11. At which port did they arrive?

12. Where did they first settle once they were in America?

13. What stories did they tell about life in their homeland?

14. What customs and traditions did they bring to America?

15. Did they become naturalized citizens? If so, when and where?

16. Did they practice the same religion after they settled in America? What was that religion?

17. Did any family members follow them to America at a later date?
18. Did they already have relatives in America when they arrived?

Many people discover an interest in tracing their ancestry long after grandparents or more contemporary relatives have passed away. If that's the case, interview close friends or associates of those deceased relatives who might recall some moments they shared with members of your family. Professional genealogists often go on research field trips to interview residents of an area who share the surname of a family that lived there several generations earlier. Rarely do they come away empty handed. One genealogist was seeking information on a man who grew up in Little Falls, Minnesota. She knew the general part of town where he had lived, so she interviewed several people who lived there. She called the local grocery, which was clearly built before his birth, and asked the owner, "Do you recall him?" The grocer's response was surprising, "The only kid I knew by that name was the meanest kid in this neighborhood. He could always be counted on to raise hell." "That's him!" she cried, "May I come and talk to you about the family?" In the end, he gave her many details about a family who had moved away many years earlier.

Oral accounts of events, dates, and names of people involved cannot stand alone when compiling a family history or genealogy. The farther back one's memory reaches, the greater the chances that what is recalled may be in error. Memory fades with time and facts get confused. For this reason, one needs to compare the information given in an oral interview with facts included in records created at the time of the event.

You might construct a chronology of the life of an ancestor or relative to see if documented events agree with what you have been told. If the majority of events told to you agree with documented evidence, the accuracy of the person you interviewed is excellent and information that cannot be verified in records is likely to be true. If only fifty percent of the events told to you agree with documented evidence, the accuracy of the person interviewed is average and information that cannot be verified in records is likely to contain some truth. Where the majority of events told to you disagree with documented evidence, oral information that cannot be verified in records should be used with caution.

There is no substitute for personal interviews with those who can supply detailed information about your family's past. Always ask for as many facts as possible, but don't ever overlook the opportunity to collect those wonderful details about your family's lives that add substance and meaning to your family history.

SUGGESTED READING

Allen, Barbara and Montell, Lynwood. *From Memory to History: Using Sources in Local Historical Research*. Nashville: American Association for State and Local History, 1981. Excellent sections on testing oral sources for truth and producing a written manuscript from oral sources.

Epstein, Ellen R. and Mendelsohn, Rona. *Record and Remember: Tracing Your Roots Through Oral History*. New York: Monarch, 1978. Includes a chapter on preparing a family history questionnaire for immigrant ancestors.

Jolly, Brad. *Videotaping Local History*. Nashville: American Association for State and Local History, 1982. Discussions of equipment, interpretation, and storage of tapes with a separate chapter on videotaping oral interviews.

Zimmerman, William. *How to Tape Instant Oral Biographies*. New York: Guarionex Press, 1981. An outstanding instructional manual containing sections on tape recording and videotaping oral histories. This valuable guide lists dozens of questions you may want to use in oral interviews.

WHAT YOUR COUSINS HAVE ALREADY DISCOVERED

Once you have contacted your immediate circle of relatives—parents, aunts, uncles, grandparents, and cousins—you can begin searching for distant cousins, ones you have never met but who might share a keen interest in your family. You may find distant relatives who have had professional research done or have traveled extensively in search of their (your) ancestors. Some 550,000 Americans belong to genealogical societies; millions more work independently. Among them all are your cousins, and finding one of them can be almost as exciting as finding a common ancestor. The following section will tell you where you can look for them.

SURNAME REGISTRIES

There are several surname registries where genealogists have registered the ancestors they are seeking. These are listed with access details in Figure 4:4. Since they are inexpensive to consult (some even refund your money if there is no data), you may wish to check your surname interests with them all. This is one of the quickest ways to find cousins.

QUERIES

An effective way of finding others searching your name is to run queries in genealogical publications. A query is a paragraph-style advertisement for ancestors and for cousins searching for them. The *Genealogical Helper* (Box 368, Logan, UT 84321) has the largest circulation, an estimated readership of 200,000, many of whom read it solely for the queries. If you have unknown cousins searching for your surname, you will get responses from a query in the *Helper*. Similar queries appear in *Genealogy Tomorrow* (P.O. Box 88100, Atlanta, GA 30356), an estimated readership of 10,000, and the *Tri-State Trader* (Box 90, Knightstown, IN 46148), with more than 20,000 subscribers in the Midwest.

All states and many counties have local genealogical societies that publish queries in their quarterlies or newsletters. Most genealogical publications carry queries, some free to subscribers, some charging per word or per name.

Figure 4:4.

TABLE OF SURNAME REGISTRIES

Registry	Address	Cost	SASE	Free Registration	Refund if Nil	Queries Accepted	Display Ads Accepted	Write for Details	Membership Required	Computer Data Available
Ancestral Charts	Berry Hill Plantation Gifts 13473 Old Dairy Dr. Herndon, VA 22071	$2	●							
Appalachian Roots	Appalachian Roots Box 4004 Parkersburg, WV 26104					●	●		●	
Computer Ancestors	Compu-Gen Box 864 Dover, OH 44622		●	●				●		
Computerized Genealogy Library (310,000 names)	United Ancestries 2530 W. 4700 S. Taylor's Landing Taylorsville, UT 84119		●					●		●
Conneticut Headstone Photos	Yvonne Pitts RR 4 Olney, IL 62450		●					●		
"Dead End" Surname Exchange	NC Genealogical Exchange Service G. P. Stout 1209 Hill St. Greensboro, NC 27408		●					●		
Directory of Texas Genealogists	Ericson Books 1614 Redbud St. Nacogdoches, TX 75961					●		●		
Early Ontario Settlers	Joan Abele Griffin 45541 Denise Dr. Plymouth, MI 48170					●	●	●		
Family Data Exchange	Family Data Exchange 314 W. Center #134 Bountiful, UT 84010								●	●
Family Exchange Service	Family Exchange Box 2 Carmichael, CA 95608	$1	●	●	●					
Family Group Sheet Exchange	Yates Publishing FGSE Box 237 Ozark, MO 65721								●	
Family Organization Registry	AFRA 311 E. 12th St. Kansas City, MO 64106		●	●				●		

Registry	Address	Cost	SASE	Free Registration	Refund if Nil	Queries Accepted	Display Ads Accepted	Write for Details	Membership Required	Computer Data Available
Family Registry	Genealogical Library 35 North West Temple Salt Lake City, UT 84150			•				•		•
First Families of America	Lineages Box 417 Salt Lake City, UT 84110							•	•	•
Free Help	*Genealogical Helper* Box 368 Logan, UT 84321		•					•		
Genealogists Exchange	G-TR & E 1021 Market St. Sainte Genevieve, MO 63670					•			•	
Gen/Fo Registration	Gen/Fo International Box 342 Grimsby, Ontario Canada L3M 4H8		•					•		
Genealogical Research Directory	Library of Australian History 17 Mitchell St. North Sydney 2060 Australia		•				•			•
Genealogy Tomorrow	*Genealogy Tomorrow* 2815 Clearview Place #400 Atlanta, GA 30340		•					•		
General Surname Index	Western Heraldry Organization Box 9225 Denver, CO 80209	50¢	•		•			•		
German Genealogical Index	GGI Box 10155 Minneapolis, MN 55440		•	•				•		
German Surnames	Karen Boerboom 8354 Richfield Dr. Marshfield, WI 54449	$5	•		•			•		
International Genealogical Directory	International Genealogical Directory P.O. Box 20425 Cleveland, OH 44120		•					•		
International Tracing Service (39,700,000 names)	International Tracing Service Arolsen D-3548 Federal Republic of Germany							•		•

TABLE OF SURNAME REGISTRIES (CONT.)

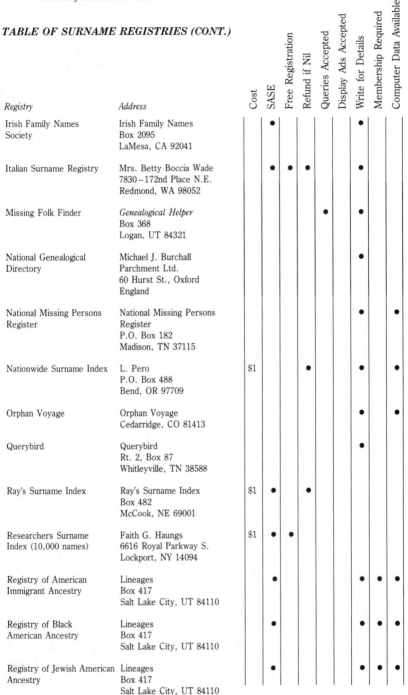

Registry	Address	Cost	SASE	Free Registration	Refund if Nil	Queries Accepted	Display Ads Accepted	Write for Details	Membership Required	Computer Data Available
Irish Family Names Society	Irish Family Names Box 2095 LaMesa, CA 92041		•					•		
Italian Surname Registry	Mrs. Betty Boccia Wade 7830–172nd Place N.E. Redmond, WA 98052		•	•	•			•		
Missing Folk Finder	*Genealogical Helper* Box 368 Logan, UT 84321						•	•		
National Genealogical Directory	Michael J. Burchall Parchment Ltd. 60 Hurst St., Oxford England							•		
National Missing Persons Register	National Missing Persons Register P.O. Box 182 Madison, TN 37115							•		•
Nationwide Surname Index	L. Pero P.O. Box 488 Bend, OR 97709	$1				•		•		•
Orphan Voyage	Orphan Voyage Cedarridge, CO 81413							•		•
Querybird	Querybird Rt. 2, Box 87 Whitleyville, TN 38588							•		
Ray's Surname Index	Ray's Surname Index Box 482 McCook, NE 69001	$1	•			•				
Researchers Surname Index (10,000 names)	Faith G. Haungs 6616 Royal Parkway S. Lockport, NY 14094	$1	•	•						
Registry of American Immigrant Ancestry	Lineages Box 417 Salt Lake City, UT 84110		•					•	•	•
Registry of Black American Ancestry	Lineages Box 417 Salt Lake City, UT 84110		•					•	•	•
Registry of Jewish American Ancestry	Lineages Box 417 Salt Lake City, UT 84110		•					•	•	•

Registry	Address	Cost	SASE	Free Registration	Refund if Nil	Queries Accepted	Display Ads Accepted	Write for Details	Membership Required	Computer Data Available
Roots Cellar (250,000 entries)	Genealogical Helper Box 368 Logan, UT 84321							•		•
Searchers	The Searchers Box 1305 Elgin, IL 60120	$1	•					•		
Surname Exchange	Compu-Gen Box 684 Dover, OH 44622	$1	•	•						•
Surname File	Snow-Data-SFI Box 1173 Snowflake, AZ 85937	$1	•	•	•					
Surname Heritage	Surname Heritage 3569 Ledyard Way Aptos, CA 95003	$1	•	•						
Surname Index	International Surname Index 215 H St. Chula Vista, CA 92010		•					•		
Surname Register	Marilee Hageness Rt. 1 Qtrs. 42 IAAP Middletown, IA 52638		•					•		
Surname Registry	AFRA 311 E. 12th St. Kansas City, MO 64106		•	•				•		•
Surname Registry	Carol Christiansen Box 471 Astoria, OR 97103	$1	•							
Surname Registry	W.A. McCormick 38623 Lancaster Livonia, MI 48154		•	•						
Surname Research	Dorothy Swearingen Rt. 1 Box 359 Mounds, OK 74047	$1	•	•						
Surn-Reach	Surn-Reach Box 25545 Milwaukee, WI 53222	$1	•	•						
Surname Searchers Quarterly	Stone Computer Service Box 251 Bartley, NE 69020			•					•	

TABLE OF SURNAME REGISTRIES (CONT.)

Registry	Address	Cost	SASE	Free Registration	Refund if Nil	Queries Accepted	Display Ads Accepted	Write for Details	Membership Required	Computer Data Available
Treeline Surname Exchange	Treeline 8266 Warbler Way #B5 Liverpool, NY 13088	$1	•		•					
Trace-Dex, Inc. AIS Computer Searchers	Trace-Dex, Inc. Box 0824 Salt Lake City, UT 84151							•		•
Triadoption	Triadoption Library Box 638 Westminister, CA 92683								•	•
Ultimate Index	Ultimate Index Box 612 West Jordan, UT 84048								•	

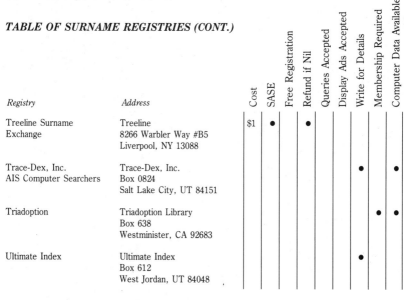

WOOD —Need parents of Rev. Jesse L. Wood, b. either Duck Hill, Mississippi or Tennessee in 1840. He was a Methodist Episcopal minister and dentist. Married four times: (1) M._____ca. 1858; (2) Nancy Evelener Hall at Carroll County, Tenn.,15 Dec. 1866; (3) Ada M. Dabbs at Greene County, Missouri,6 May 1877; (4) Mrs. Mary Fuson neé Hathaway at Dekalb County, Tenn., 2 Aug 1877. Jesse died 16 Dec. 1896 at Ardmore, Indian Territory. Anyone having information, please write: Johni Cerny, P.O. Box 2607, Salt Lake City, Utah 84110.

$500 REWARD
For first proof parents of
Fielding Ethington
of Henry, Owen, and other
nearby Kentucky counties
b. 1790 in Kentucky or Virginia
Johni Cerny
P.O. Box 2607
Salt Lake City, Utah 84110

Figure 4:5. Example of a query and an advertisement.

To write an effective query, keep in mind that the more information you include the more likely you are to get a response. Obtain a copy of the publication you want to use and follow their format. Always include the dimensions you have set for your ancestors: complete name, dates of birth, marriage, and death, places where your ancestor lived, and the names of his spouse and children if you know them. Occupation and religion are also helpful.

ALPHABETICAL INDEXES
Genealogists and genealogical societies across the country are compiling indexes to specific family surnames. Many indexes are advertised in the *Genealogical Helper* and other publications already discussed. Some are noted in news columns in periodicals, while others are deposited in public libraries where the family originally lived. Watch for these. The Allen County Library in Fort Wayne, Indiana, for example, has a massive index to biographies in county and town histories for Ohio, Indiana, Kentucky, Illinois, and other states. In just a few minutes you can search a large number of volumes for your surname.

Many new regional indexes and specialized finding aids are available. The Michigan Genealogical Council has just published the *Michigan Surname Index* (1984) with some 52,000 entries from contributing genealogists across Michigan. This hardcover volume sells for $30 from the MGC at 735 E. Michigan, Lansing, MI 48909. The index includes birth, marriage, and death dates and places, and spouse or other relatives' names.

Seventeen California genealogical societies have published the *"Gone West" Index: California's Major Gold Region, 1840-1940.* This regional surname index is taken from the "surnames members are researching" card files of these genealogical societies. Revisions are published at regular intervals. The current edition can be ordered from Tuolumne County Genealogical Society, Box 3956, Sonora, CA 95370.

Donald O. Virdin and Raymond B. Clark Jr. have published *Maryland Family Genealogies and Family Histories: A Bibliography*, with a separate index to authors and allied families, and *Delaware Family Histories: A Bibliography.* Both of these can be ordered from Mr. Clark at Box 352, St. Michaels, MD 21663.

An ambitious, but little-known project was begun several years ago by Michel L. Call who established the Mormon Pioneer Genealogy Library, linking a large number of the 8.5 million family group records in the Genealogical Library of the LDS Church. Two indexes are available to determine if your ancestry is recorded here: (1) The *Index to Mormon Pioneer Genealogy Library* includes the names of more than 10,000 Mormon pioneers born between 1776 and 1850 with their birthdates and spouses, (2) The *Index to the Colonial American Genealogy Library*, selling for $125, includes 40,000 American ancestors born between 1500 and 1776. These are ancestors not only of Mormon pioneers, they are also ancestors of millions of Catholic, Congregational, Presbyterian, Methodist, Baptist, and Unitarian pioneers who settled in all parts of the U.S. Membership, indexes, and copies of lineage charts and family group records can be obtained from the Mormon Pioneer Genealogy Society, Box 98, Grover, WY 83122.

If you assume that because your ancestor did not live in Michigan or that none of your families were Mormon and thus do not check these indexes, you are making a serious error. The largest number of early Mormon converts were made in New York, Ohio, Indiana, Kentucky, and other parts of the South, and they share the same ancestry as many other Americans whose families lived there for a period of time whether they ever became converts to the Mormon faith. Persons who moved to Michigan from New York, Pennsylvania, Connecticut, Canada, and dozens of other places also share their heritage with many Americans. Be sure to check these sources.

PERIODICALS

Periodicals published by genealogical or historical societies, family organizations, and lineage societies are often overlooked as resources. Many hundreds of well-documented genealogies compiled by professional genealogists working for their clients or by hobbyists working on their own families are available in periodical articles, some with corrections and updates after review by other genealogists. You can find these works, saving research hours and dollars, by consulting finding aids and indexes to genealogical perodicals.

FINDING AIDS

Cappon, Lester J. *American Genealogical Periodicals: A Bibliography with a Chronological Finding-List*. Bowie, Md.: Heritage Books, 1962.

Konrad, J. *Directory of Genealogical Periodicals*. Munroe Falls, Ohio: Summit Publications, 1980.

Meyer, Mary K. *Directory of Genealogical Societies in the U.S.A. and Canada*. Mt. Airy, Md.: Libra Publications, 1984.

INDEXES TO GENEALOGICAL PERIODICALS

Jacobus, Donald L. *Index to Genealogical Periodicals, 1870-1952*. 3 vols. Reprint. Baltimore: Genealogical Publishing Co., 1978.

Milner, Anita C. *Newspaper Genealogy Columns*. Metuchen, N.J.: Scarecrow Press, 1979.

————. *Newspaper Indexes, 1977-1982*. 3 vols. Metuchen, N.J.: Scarecrow Press, 1977.

Munsell, Joel. *Index to American Genealogies to 1900*. 5th ed. Supplement, 1900-1908. Reprint. Baltimore: Genealogical Publishing Co., 1979.

Quigley, Maud. *Index to Family Names in Genealogical Periodicals, 1937-1980*. Grand Rapids, Mich.: Western Michigan Genealogical Society, 1981.

————. *Index to Hard-to-Find Information in Genealogical Periodicals, 1937-1980*. Grand Rapids, Mich.: Western Michigan Genealogical Society, 1981.

Rogers, Ellen S. *Genealogical Periodical Annual Index, 1961-1965.* Vols. 1-4. Bowie, Md.: Heritage Books, 1963-67.*
Russell, George E. *Genealogical Periodical Annual Index 1967-1970.* Vols. 5-8. Bowie, Md.: Heritage Books, 1967-73.*
Sperry, Kip. *Index to Genealogical Periodical Literature, 1960-1977.* Detroit: Gale Research Co., 1979.
Towle, Laird C. *Genealogical Periodical Annual Index, 1974-1982.* Vols. 13-18. Bowie, Md.: Heritage Books, 1974-present.*
Waldenmaier, Inez B. *Annual Index to Genealogical Periodicals and Family Histories, 1956-1962.* 8 vols. Washington, D.C.: by the author, 1956-63.

---

*Note: Volumes 9-12 of *Genealogical Periodical Annual Index, 1970-1973* have not yet been published.

Each of these indexes includes varying numbers of periodicals. Earlier indexes omit short articles, notes, and book reviews, and entries indexed in other publications. In recent years a partial listing of surname periodicals has been included. With a specific citation from one of these indexes, the genealogist can order photocopies of articles through interlibrary loan from larger genealogical libraries such as the New York Public Library, the Cleveland Public Library, the Los Angeles Public Library, or the National Genealogical Society Library.

FAMILY TRADITIONS

Family traditions are stories about ancestors that have been handed down from generation to generation. You'll find family traditions published in genealogies and family histories and hear them discussed at the dinner table. No matter what form family traditions take, they are held sacred. After all, dear Aunt Millie, who at seventy years old is saintly in every way imaginable, would never pass on a tradition that wasn't absolutely true. Aunt Millie wouldn't do that— even if she remotely suspected that the story was partially or totally false. The problem with traditions is that they often reach so far back that it's hard to pinpoint where they originated or when parts were deleted or enhanced by fertile imaginations. After passing through several generations, traditions become treasured fact.

While most family traditions are positive, such as those attesting to a family's origins, the valiant efforts of a Revolutionary War ancestor, or the family's link to someone with royal blood lines, there are also negative traditions that reflect poorly on a "black sheep" of the family. Regardless of the type, all family traditions must be verified for accuracy.

Professional genealogists must be sensitive to a family's feelings about their traditions and try to educate their clients before research begins, explaining that family tradition, like every other piece of genealogical information, must be proven by examining records that offer greater detail about an event and an individual's involvement. Some segments of a family tradition will be accurate, but once research is completed a tradition rarely resembles its original form.

A few years ago I worked on a very difficult research problem. The first piece of information offered by the client was a family tradition that explained why he wasn't interested in his paternal grandfather's history. He wanted me to skip that generation and trace the rest of his family line. According to tradition, Jesse L. Wood was a convicted murderer. He sued his first wife for divorce to marry the client's grandmother, Ada Dabbs, a younger woman. After Jesse married Ada, his first wife traveled from Tennessee to Springfield, Missouri, to sue him for fraudulent divorce and won. Enraged, Jesse went back to Tennessee seeking revenge. He set fire to her house and she died in the holocaust. Arrested, tried, and convicted of arson and murder, Jesse was then sentenced to a federal penitentiary, leaving young Ada to fend for herself and their two young sons. I informed the client that Jesse's life would have to be examined to link him with his parents, but once they were identified, research would focus on earlier generations.

As it turned out, Jesse's parents were never located even though every aspect of Jesse's life was probed in an effort to establish his parentage. Simultaneously, family tradition was closely examined, and the following account shows how the Wood family tradition was verified—and where it proved erroneous.

When the 1860 census enumerator made his rounds of rural Dyer County, Tennessee, he stopped at a small farm house and found a young man, Jesse Wood, who had recently taken a wife. They owned only $100 in personal property, about average for a couple barely into their twenties. His wife was expecting their first child later in the year and Jesse was working as a farm laborer. The census enumerator was in a hurry and didn't take the time to spell out the wife's full name. She is known only as "M. Wood."

Nothing further is known about Jesse until 27 December 1863 when he enlisted into Company I of the 7th Tennessee Cavalry Regiment, United States Army. He enlisted for three years and participated in only a few skirmishes not far from his home in Huntingdon, Tennessee, before being captured. Wounded in the leg before capture, Jesse was taken to Andersonville Prison near Americus, Georgia.

Jesse only spent a few months as a prisoner of war. He escaped from Andersonville and worked his way north at night on foot, avoiding bloodhounds and soldiers, but further injuring his leg. He reached his regiment at Paducah, Kentucky, in September 1864 and spent several months in the hospital before receiving a disability discharge.

Jesse's war injury allowed him to apply for a disability pension and it was his pension file that unraveled family tradition. Jesse returned to Carroll County, Tennessee, after the war where he did a little farming. Nothing is known of the circumstances of his first wife's death, except that after Jesse died, his widow and fourth wife, Mary Fuson Wood, stated that she had died during the war. Jesse married his second wife, Nancy Evelener Hall, in Carroll County, Tennessee, on 15 December 1865. Nancy is buried in a cemetery near McLemoresville, Tennessee, with her parents, her tombstone reading: Evelener Wood, wife of Rev. J. L. Wood, 23 April 1848 – 2 November 1881.

Jesse took up two occupations after the war, neither requiring hard labor. He first established himself as an Evangelical Methodist minister and then as a dentist. His ministerial duties took him all over Tennessee and eventually to Iowa's Des Moines Conference. While there, his marriage to Evelener became strained and she, according to Jesse, began seeing another man. She left him and returned to Carroll County taking their three sons with her. He maintained custody of the daughter born to his first wife. The 1880 census shows Evelener living with her boys next door to her mother in Carroll County.

After his family left Iowa, Jesse moved south to Christian and Greene counties, Missouri, where he met nineteen-year-old Ada M. Dabbs. He married for a third time on 6 May 1877 at Springfield, Missouri, after divorcing Evelener. That Jesse was sued by his second wife for fraudulent divorce was true according to an article that appeared in the *Springfield Patriot-Advertiser* on 25 October 1877:

A MAN WITH TWO WIVES

A divorce suit of more than ordinary interest was heard at a special session of the Christian County Circuit Court last week. One Doctor J. L. Wood had obtained a divorce from his wife at the spring term, and immediately afterwards married Miss Ada Brown, of Christian County, to whom he had previously been engaged. The former Mrs. Wood still resided in Tennessee, and was not informed of her husband's second marriage, although a letter, purported to be from her was read at the spring term, and was made the basis for granting the divorce. Counsel for Mrs. Wood, No. 1, proved the letter to be a forgery, and asked that the divorce be set aside on that ground. Judge Geiger, while of the opinion that the preponderance of testimony was largely in favor of Mrs. Wood, No. 1, and that her husband had doubtless obtained his divorce through fraud, did not consider that the law would permit him to set the decree aside. The attorneys for Mrs. Wood, No. 1, Messrs. Boyd and Vaughn, have taken an appeal to the Supreme Court. Messrs. Patterson and Barker are attorneys for Wood. The public will await with interest the decision of the higher court.

No follow-up articles appeared in the newspaper, but other documents showed that Evelener's appeals to the higher courts were turned down.

Jesse was listed as a forty-year-old dentist in the 1880 census of Springfield, Missouri. His household consisted of Ada, two young sons, and his oldest daughter, Anna Wood. Shortly after the 1880 census was taken, Jesse moved to Cherryvale, Montgomery County, Kansas, a move that would have devastating consequences for his future.

Jesse Wood arrived in Cherryvale with his wife and children to establish a dental practice and to continue his ministry. He was a staunch prohibitionist and, as such, quickly made many close friends — and bitter enemies. A few of those enemies proved powerful enough to cause his imprisonment.

According to affidavits filed in a plea for Jesse's pardon, these are the events that led to his arrest and conviction:

A Mrs. Titus told her husband that their house was broken into between 10:30 p.m. and 12:30 a.m. one night in August 1883. The house was torched in several places and $900 stolen. Mr. Titus offered a $450 reward for the return of the money and the conviction of the thief.

Shortly thereafter, Mrs. Titus changed her story and told her husband that she had given the money to Jesse Wood with the understanding that they would run off together. When Jesse reportedly backed out of the arrangement, Mrs. Titus told her husband, who filed a complaint against him. Ten days later, en route to Springfield, Missouri, Jesse was arrested and returned to Cherryvale.

While Jesse was under guard at a hotel, Mrs. Titus was being held at his dental office. She told authorities that Jesse hid the money in a quinine bottle buried in the town's ash pile. An unknown individual confessed, however, that on the night Mrs. Titus told of the money's whereabouts, it had been hidden in the ash pile. This was also the same night Jesse had been arrested. The sheriff went directly to the spot indicated by Mrs. Titus and found the money under an inch of ashes. Of greater bearing is that prior to leaving for Springfield, Jesse made arrangements for the ash pile to be cleared while away. It is unlikely that he would have left $900 to be hauled away.

Jesse's activities on the night of the arson and theft were well established between early evening and 1:00 a.m. He was in the company of several individuals, including the marshall. Despite this evidence and that Mrs. Titus was a known prostitute, the jury found Jesse guilty of grand larceny and the judge sentenced him to four years in the Kansas State Penitentiary at Lansing.

Three jurors later confessed that they didn't think Jesse was guilty of the charges. One convicted him based on the rumor that he was involved with other women and, as a minister, he should not have been so. The judge later concluded that Jesse was framed by Mr. Titus and others, but he refused to put his opinion into writing. Those who prepared the petitions to the governor for Jesse's pardon stated that Jesse was convicted because of his strong stand against alcohol. He was president of the Temperance Convention of Tennessee and the leader of the Cherryvale group for temperance.

Jesse was also tried, as was the custom, by the Methodist Episcopal Church and was acquitted. A conservative group, they usually judged more harshly than civil authorities. If there was the slightest indication of guilt, Jesse would have been immediately excommunicated. Additionally, the majority of Cherryvale's citizens signed a petition certifying their belief that he was innocent.

While others were fighting for Jesse's release, he remained in prison, convinced that so long as the judge and the Montgomery County attorney would not come to his assistance, he would remain there. The events in Cherryvale had other devastating effects on Jesse's life. The clerk of the district court in Montgomery County stated that on 3 November 1883, just two weeks before the first petition for clemency was filed, Ada M. Wood sued for divorce. The summons was served in Leavenworth County, site of the Kansas State Penetentiary. Ada took the children to Arkansas and married a Mr. Guffy, reportedly dying in 1892.

The prison ledger of the Kansas State Penitentiary records that Jesse L. Wood was convicted on 22 September 1883 of grand larceny in Montgomery County and received a four-year sentence. He was forty-four years old when sent to the prison on 24 September 1883. His conduct was good while there and 238 days were commuted from his sentence. He was released on 18 January 1887.

Of the hundreds of records searched while looking for Jesse's parents, relatively few were needed to untangle the family tradition including: census enumerations, marriage records, church historical records, newspaper articles, military pension files, prison records, and clemency petitions. Let's list the parts of the family tradition and see which ones held up under verification:

1. Jesse divorced his first wife to marry Ada Dabbs.

Analysis: He didn't divorce his first wife; she reportedly died during the Civil War.

2. The former Mrs. Wood sued Jesse for fraudulent divorce and won her suit at Springfield, Missouri.

Analysis: Evelener Wood did sue Jesse for fraudulent divorce; however, the court did not find in her favor. Appeals made to higher courts also found in Jesse's favor, but only because there were two infants born to his third wife by that time.

3. Angered over his former wife's suit, Jesse returned to Tennessee to set fire to her home, causing her death.

Analysis: There is no indication in any record that Jesse returned to Tennessee. One of Evelener's sons testified in a pension file document that she died at her home in 1881 and made no mention of arson or murder. Her death date is also noted on her tombstone. One can only speculate about how the story telling of arson and murder evolved. Perhaps bits of several incidents were tied together in a distorted fashion. Family members think that Ada Dabbs started the story in her anger over her divorce suit and Jesse's alleged involvement with other women in Cherryvale.

4. Jesse was convicted of arson and murder and sentenced to a federal penitentiary.

Analysis: As already discussed, Jesse was tried for arson and grand larceny and convicted only for the latter. He was sentenced to the Kansas State Penitentiary at Lansing and never served time in a federal prison. The fact that Lansing is in Leavenworth County where Leavenworth Federal Penitentiary is located may have caused this confusion.

As you can see, some parts of the tradition were partially true, as is the case with most family traditions. The most important result of verifying the Wood family tradition was the family's warmer feelings toward Jesse. Getting skeletons out of the closet and putting the flesh back on them is usually the best approach to putting a family's history in true perspective.

If you don't take time to verify family traditions, you run the risk of building a faulty lineage and further perpetuating erroneous information. Many people who are new to research get excited about traditions and legends found in printed family histories. They take the information as gospel and begin to extend the lineage in their eagerness to reach that ever-sought immigrant ancestor. Hundreds of research hours and many dollars later something surfaces that completely destroys the work they accepted as true. Had they taken the time to verify each tradition as it surfaced, they would never have been sidetracked.

CHAPTER 5

Organizing Yourself

A s a professional genealogist, I've been asked to work on research problems that have stymied experienced hobbyists. Many had worked on problems for close to twenty years and had amassed a file drawer full of information. Before I could begin work I had to study and evaluate their material to understand the problem and avoid duplicating their research. When one client's records arrived I took one look and cringed, realizing it would take close to one hundred hours to organize, evaluate, and analyze what he had accomplished in fifteen years. When I finished going through everything, it wasn't surprising to discover he had the answers to his problem all along but was too unorganized to know what he did and didn't have.

Organize your research from day one or you're going to create problems that will take twice as long to deal with later on when documents, lineage charts, and family group records have become numerous and unmanageable. There are hundreds of ways to organize your material and the method offered here may not be exactly the one you want to use. It's a method developed and refined over a ten-year period by a number of professional research firms in Salt Lake City. It includes forms and a filing system that are complementary and easy to use. Furthermore, it can be adapted for use with other systems.

MATERIALS

You're going to need some materials commonly used by genealogists. If you don't live near a commercial outlet that sells genealogical materials, you'll have to order most of the forms by mail. The forms used for demonstration in this chapter can be ordered from Ancestry, Inc., P.O. Box 476, Salt Lake City, UT 84110. Here's a list of what you will need to get started:

1. Lineage Charts
2. Family Group Records
3. Research Calendars
4. Research Extracts
5. Source Checklist
6. Correspondence Logs
7. Legal-Size File Folders
8. File Tabs

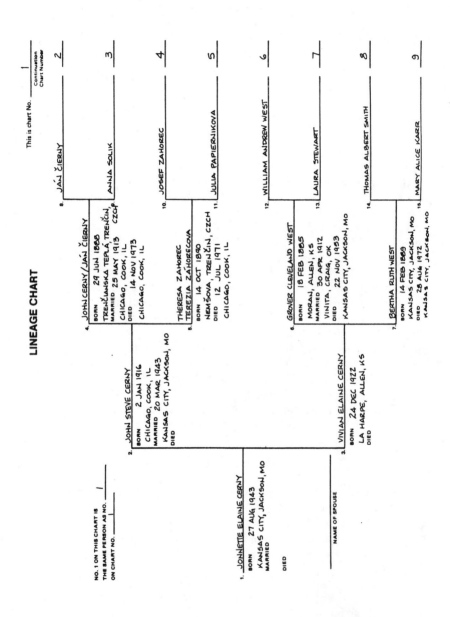

Figure 5:1. Example of a completed lineage chart.

LINEAGE CHARTS

Lineage charts (also called pedigree charts) are forms used in genealogical research to illustrate graphically the direct ancestors of the person in the number 1 position on the first chart. Direct ancestors are parents, grandparents, great-grandparents, etc. They represent your blood line. Figure 5:1 is an illustration of a completed lineage chart. There are many styles of lineage charts on the market and you should choose one that best suits your needs. Most are 8½ by 11 inches in size and provide space enough to record four or five generations of your ancestry. Larger charts that are 11 by 14 inches have space to record five generations.

Lineage charts are not designed to record all the known information about a family. They are used along with family group records as synopses of the information found in the records you've searched. Lineage charts should be filled out exactly as the sample charts in the numbering system. Let's work through that process using the chart shown in Figure 5:1.

This is the first lineage chart and the block in the upper right-hand corner of the chart should read "This is chart no. 1." The blocks on the left-hand side should read "No. 1 on this chart is the same person as no. 1 on chart no. 1." Ján Čierny is person no. 8 on the chart. There isn't enough space to enter his identifying information on this chart so he is continued over to chart no. 2–"This is chart no. 2" and "No. 1 on this chart is the same person as no. 8 on chart no. 1." Anna Solik is continued on chart no. 3, Josef Záhorec on chart no. 4, and so on until we reach Mary Alice Karr who is continued on chart no. 9. Figure 5:2 is a handy guide to numbering lineage charts.

FAMILY GROUP RECORDS

Family group records (also called group sheets) are genealogical forms designed to help organize your research findings. They illustrate the information you already have and also show what remains to be added to complete the family group. A family group record includes information about a husband and wife and their children. You should prepare family group records for each couple on your lineage chart. Researchers interested in compiling extended genealogies should compile group records for all the married children of each husband and wife. Children on a family group record are listed in order of birth with the eldest child in the number one position. An "x" is placed above the sex designation of the child through whom you descend. Figure 5:3 illustrates a completed family group record.

Like lineage charts, there are also many family group record formats. Select a chart style that permits you to record as much information as possible. The chart illustrated is used by a number of professional research firms because it provides space to record the children's places of marriage and death. It facilitates easy reading and prevents confusing birth and death dates by listing them in separate columns.

Figure 5:2.
GUIDE TO NUMBERING LINEAGE CHARTS

Chart Number	Beginning No.	Ending No.	Chart Number	Beginning No.	Ending No.	Chart Number	Beginning No.	Ending No.
1	2	9	51	402	409	101	802	809
2	10	17	52	410	417	102	810	817
3	18	25	53	418	425	103	818	825
4	26	33	54	426	433	104	826	833
5	34	41	55	434	441	105	834	841
6	42	49	56	442	449	106	842	849
7	50	57	57	450	457	107	850	857
8	58	65	58	458	465	108	858	865
9	66	73	59	466	473	109	866	873
10	74	81	60	474	481	110	874	881
11	82	89	61	482	489	111	882	889
12	90	97	62	490	497	112	890	897
13	98	105	63	498	505	113	898	905
14	106	113	64	506	513	114	906	913
15	114	121	65	514	521	115	914	921
16	122	129	66	522	529	116	922	929
17	130	137	67	530	537	117	930	937
18	138	145	68	538	545	118	938	945
19	146	153	69	546	553	119	946	953
20	154	161	70	554	561	120	954	961
21	162	169	71	562	569	121	962	969
22	170	177	72	570	577	122	970	977
23	178	185	73	578	585	123	978	985
24	186	193	74	586	593	124	986	993
25	194	201	75	594	601	125	994	1001
26	202	209	76	602	609	126	1002	1009
27	210	217	77	610	617	127	1010	1017
28	218	225	78	618	625	128	1018	1025
29	226	233	79	626	633	129	1026	1033
30	234	241	80	634	641	130	1034	1041
31	242	249	81	642	649	131	1042	1049
32	250	257	82	650	657	132	1050	1057
33	258	265	83	658	665	133	1058	1065
34	266	273	84	666	673	134	1066	1073
35	274	281	85	674	681	135	1074	1081
36	282	289	86	682	689	136	1082	1089
37	290	297	87	690	697	137	1090	1097
38	298	305	88	698	705	138	1098	1105
39	306	313	89	706	713	139	1106	1113
40	314	321	90	714	721	140	1114	1121
41	322	329	91	722	729	141	1122	1129
42	330	337	92	730	737	142	1130	1137
43	338	345	93	738	745	143	1138	1145
44	346	353	94	746	753	144	1146	1153
45	354	361	95	754	761	145	1154	1161
46	362	369	96	762	769	146	1162	1169
47	370	377	97	770	777	147	1170	1177
48	378	385	98	778	785	148	1178	1185
49	386	393	99	786	793	149	1186	1193
50	394	401	100	794	801	150	1194	1201

FORMULA: Lineage # x 8 minus 14 plus the person # = continuing chart #

FAMILY GROUP SHEET

HUS. THOMAS ALBERT SMITH   OCCUPATION(S) BAPTIST MINISTER AND FARMER

BORN	20 FEB 1862	PLACE New Lancaster, Miami, Kansas
CHR		PLACE
MARR	30 APR 1884	PLACE New Lancaster, Miami, Kansas
DIED	16 JUN 1924	PLACE Xenia, Bourbon, Kansas
BUR	18 JUN 1924	PLACE Bronson Cemetery, Bronson, Bourbon, Kansas
FATHER	JOHN SMITH	OTHER WIVES
MOTHER	MARY JANE PLEDGER	

WIFE MARY ALICE KARR

BORN	5 OCT 1864	PLACE New Lancaster, Miami, Kansas
CHR		PLACE
DIED	3 AUG 1947	PLACE Fort Scott, Bourbon, Kansas
BUR	6 AUG 1947	PLACE Bronson Cemetery, Bronson, Bourbon, Kansas
FATHER	AMBROSE N. KARR	OTHER HUSBANDS
MOTHER	MARTHA P. HUFFMAN	

SEX	CHILDREN	DATE BORN / PLACE BORN	DATE MARRIED / TO	PLACE	DATE DIED / PLACE DIED
X F	1 BERTHA RUTH SMITH	14 FEB 1889 / Kansas City, Jackson, Missouri	30 APR 1912 / GROVER CLEVELAND WEST	Vinita, Craig, Oklahoma	28 AUG 1972 / Kansas City, Jackson, MO
	2				
	3				
	4				
	5				
	6				
	7				
	8				

OTHER MARRIAGES

SOURCES OF INFORMATION
1. Death Certificate, Dept. of Vital Statistics, State of Kansas.
2. Marriage Record, Marriage Book F, Miami County, Kansas, p. 80.
3. Marriage Record, Vinita, Craig County, Oklahoma.
4. 1900 U.S. Census, Blue Mound, Linn County, Kansas.
5. Family Bible Record, Rev. John Smith, Miami County, Kansas.
6. Obituary of Bertha Ruth Smith West, Kansas City Star, 30 August 1972.

Figure 5:3. Example of a completed family group record.

Follow the example in Figure 5:3 to fill out your family group records. Always record each individual's full name and list the town, county, and state of birth, marriage, and death whenever possible. As many of your ancestors will have lived in rural locations, there won't be a town to record. If your ancestors were born in foreign countries, add the name of the country after the town, county, and state or province. Finally, each family group record should list the sources of information used to compile the record. A discussion of how to document your sources follows later in this chapter.

RESEARCH CALENDARS

Research calendars are employed to record the sources you've searched and the results of each search. They are an important part of every research file because they prevent you from duplicating searches, enable you to relocate sources if you have to refer to them again, and enable you to locate a document or extract in a file. If someone else picks up your research files, he or she will know immediately what you've searched, when you made the search, who you were looking for, and the results of each search.

A separate research calendar is created for each person on a lineage chart and they are identified by name and file number on the form. Let's examine the various headings on the research calendar.

File Name: Enter the name of the person you are researching.

Researcher: Enter your name here.

File Number: File numbers correspond to an ancestor's position on a lineage chart. Figure 5:1 shows John Cerny on lineage chart no. 1 in position 4. His file number would be 1:4, the first number representing the lineage chart number and the second the individual's position on that lineage chart. Mary Alice Karr's grandmother was Amanda P. Hopkins. She is recorded on lineage chart no. 9 in position 5. Her file number would be 9:5.

Date: Enter at least the month and year the search was conducted.

Repository: Enter the library, archive, courthouse, etc. where you conducted the search.

Call Number: Always enter the complete call number of the record you're searching. It will be used later when you cite your sources on the family group record. You may also refer to the source again and having it handy will save looking it up again.

RESEARCH CALENDAR

SUBJECT:	RESEARCHER:	FILE NUMBER:
WILLIAM A. KARR AMANDA P. HOPKINS	JOHNI CERNY	6:1

Date	Repository Call No.	Description of Source	Ind Cond	Search Objective	Time Period Searched	Comments	Doc. No.
MAR 1967	GS FGRA	FAMILY GROUP RECORDS ARCHIVES MAIN SECTION	✓ EXC	WILLIAM KARR			NIL
MAR 1967	GS	1860 U.S. CENSUS LYKINS COUNTY, KANSAS	NO POOR	"	1860	ALSO AMBROSE KARR	1
MAR 1967	GS	1870 U.S. CENSUS MIAMI COUNTY, KANSAS (FORMERLY LYKINS COUNTY)	NO GOOD	"	1870		2
MAR 1967	GS	1880 U.S. CENSUS MIAMI COUNTY, KANSAS	NO FAIR	"	1880		3
MAR 1967	GS 58039 pt. 1-5	1850 U.S. CENSUS OF IOWA COUNTIES A-L	NO GOOD	"	1850		NIL
MAR 1967	GS 58039 pt 6	1850 U.S. CENSUS MARION COUNTY, IOWA	NO GOOD	"	1850		4
MAR 1967	GS 977.783 H2	HISTORY OF MARION COUNTY, IOWA VOL. I - II PP. 304, 696, 752	YES EXC	"			5
MAR 1967	GS Q977.7 H2b	IOWA, ITS HISTORY AND ITS FOREMOST PEOPLE	NO EXC	"			NIL
MAR 1967	GS 977.7 D2c	CHARTS AND GENEALOGIES OF PIONEER FAMILIES OF IOWA	YES EXC	"			NIL
MAR 1967	NEW LANCASTER CEMETERY CORRESPONDENCE	NEW LANCASTER CEMETERY TOMBSTONE INSCRIPTIONS	NO —	WILLIAM & AMANDA KARR		AMBROSE & MARTHA ONLY	NIL

Figure 5:4. Example of a completed research calendar.

Description
of Source:

Enter a complete bibliographic citation of each source searched, including the author's name, title of the record, the place it was published, name of publisher, date published, volume number, and page number if it's a printed source.

Ind.:

Ind. is a space for entering whether a source is indexed. It is easy to check that block to indicate that a record or book is indexed, but you'll find that inadequate when you want to review your work. Fill the blank in with a helpful key word. For example, most marriage records are indexed only by male names. If so, enter "males only" in that space. Some census records are soundexed and if that's the case enter "sndx." When records are only partially indexed, "part" should be entered.

Cond.:

Cond. is a space for noting the condition of the record. Records that are in excellent condition with legible handwriting are deemed to be in excellent condition and "exc." should be entered. Many microfilm copies of records are difficult to read and some originals are water damaged or torn. They would be listed as in "poor" condition.

Search
Objective:

Enter the name(s) of the individual(s) you are looking for in the record.

Time Period
Searched:

Many records cover extended periods of time but you may only search the records covering a few years. Enter only the years you searched in this space. The entire period covered by the record should be entered in the "description of source" column.

Comments:

You will often search a record for someone and not find him or her listed, but there will be others of the same name or surname who may be related to that person. It's a good idea to jot their names down in the space for comments. This space can also be used to note when a record was too poor to read.

Doc. No.:

If you search a record and do not find any mention of the person you're looking for, enter "nil" in this space. If you locate the person you're looking for, make a photocopy of the record or document and number each consecutively. When a record cannot be photocopied make an extract and give it a document number. Let's assume that you make ten searches and are fortunate enough to find your ancestor in each record searched. You would number each document consecutively from 1 to 10, then start a second research calendar. The first document produced in the next series of searches would be number 11. When you start work on another ancestor the first document or record you photocopy would again be number 1, the rest numbered consecutively thereafter.

RESEARCH EXTRACTS

Research extracts are used to record information that cannot be photocopied. Some records are restricted from photocopying and others are too poor to reproduce. When that's the case, you should use an extract. The same information listed on the research calendar is entered at the top of the research extract to identify the source. The document number is entered in the box in the lower left-hand corner. Figure 5:5 illustrates how a research extract should be filled out.

Research extracts become abstracts of records and knowing what information to abstract from a record is learned through experience. The best rule to follow is to take the time to copy all pertinent information. The more complete your extract is, the better your chance will be in locating ancestors. One of the most common blocks in tracing a lineage is failure to extract all of the information needed from the source.

SOURCE CHECKLISTS

Source checklists are optional research forms. They are used as reminders of the records that might be searched for information as well as what sources you have already looked at. It's a good idea to include one in each research file.

CORRESPONDENCE LOGS

You're going to do a lot of letter writing, and you'll need to keep correspondence logs of the letters sent out and responses received. It's also an excellent way to keep track of the money you've sent with each request for a record. Figure 5:6 illustrates how a correspondence log should be completed.

LEGAL-SIZE FILE FOLDERS

Legal-size file folders are used to store your research files. One folder is used for each husband and wife on your lineage chart. Color-coded file tabs should be filled out with the following information and placed on the file tab:

RESEARCH EXTRACT

File Number 1:6	Repository KANSAS STATE HISTORICAL LIBRARY	Call Number

Description of Source _____ 1865 KANSAS STATE CENSUS - MIAMI COUNTY KANSAS

Indexed NO	Condition FAIR	Time Period 1865	Date 28 DEC 1967

Search Objective AMBROSE KARR

MIAMI COUNTY, MIAMI TWP   4 AUG 1865

#438	AMBROSE CARR		26 M W	FARMER	$2000/$1200	INDIANA
	M.A.	"	24 F W			INDIANA
	J.M.	"	1 M W			KANSAS
	ALICE	"	3/12 F W			KANSAS

#452	WILLIAM CARR		52 M W	FARMER	$3400/$2100	PENNSYLVANIA
	A.P.	"	50 F W			KENTUCKY
	ELIHU	"	19 M W			INDIANA
	W.H.	"	15 M W			IOWA
	S.A.	"	17 F W			IOWA
	E.M.	"	13 M W			IOWA

8

Figure 5:5. Example of a completed research extract.

CORRESPONDENCE RECORD

Name ___KARR___

DATE SENT	ADDRESSEE/ADDRESS	PURPOSE	DATE REPLIED	RESULTS
6/18/66	SEXTON, NEW LANCASTER CEMETERY, NEW LANCASTER, KS	TOMBSTONE INSCRIPTION AND BURIAL RECORD OF AMBROSE N. AND M	6/28/66	DOCUMENT 4 FILE 9:2
6/18/66	KANSAS STATE DEPARTMENT OF HEALTH- DIV. OF VITAL RECORDS, TOPEKA, KANSAS	DEATH CERTIFICATE OF MARY ALICE KARR AND THOMAS ALBERT SMITH	6/25/66	DOCUMENT 11 FILE 8:1
2/28/67	PROBATE CLERK, MIAMI COUNTY, KANSAS, PAOLA, KS	PROBATE PACKET OF AMBROSE N. KARR	3/11/66	DOCUMENT 5 FILE 9:2
2/28/67	RECORDER OF DEEDS, MIAMI COUNTY COURT HOUSE, PAOLA, KS	SEARCH GRANTEE AND GRANTOR INDEXES FOR AMBROSE, WILLIAM, MARTHA, AND AMANDA KARR	4/27/67	DOCUMENT 6 FILE 9:2
2/28/67	PROBATE COURT, MIAMI COUNTY, PAOLA, KS	MARRIAGE RECORD OF AMBROSE AND MARTHA P. KARR	4/20/66	NOT ON FILE (RECHECK)

Figure 5:6. Example of a completed correspondence log.

CERNY, JOHN STEVE	1:2	(green tab)
WEST, VIVIAN ELAINE	PARENTS	

WEST, GROVER CLEVELAND	1:6	(green tab)
SMITH, BERTHA RUTH	GRANDPARENTS	

ZAHOREC, JOSEF	4:1	(green tab)
PAPIERNIKOVA, JULIA	G-GRANDPARENTS	

KARR, AMBROSE N.	9:2	(green tab)
HUFFMAN, MARTHA P.	2ND GGPARENTS	

You will also need a master file to store your lineage charts. Use one color file tab for the master file and another for research files to distinguish them from one another. You may also want to create a correspondence file for each surname on your lineage chart and that file should be labeled with a third color tab.

MASTER FILE #1	(red tab)
CERNY CORRESPONDENCE FILE	(blue tab)

As your research progresses you will need more than one master file to hold all of your lineage charts, especially if one of your lines descends from royalty.

Using this system lets you know exactly where to look for information pertaining to every person on your lineage charts. You may want to choose an entirely different method. This one is a simple system that can be easily modified to conform to your preferred style. The key point to remember is that a good notekeeping system makes preserving and analyzing information easier. How you keep your notes is not important as long as the material found is preserved in an efficient and careful way, easily understandable to you and to others.

Every genealogist should develop a comfortable notekeeping system. Just remember that no one system is correct and experts differ widely on how to keep notes. Don't be intimidated into using a system you don't like. The following bibliography lists books with sections on notekeeping systems. Review a few of them before you decide to establish your system.

SUGGESTED READING

Doane, Gilbert H. and Bell, James C. *Searching for Your Ancestors*. 5th ed. Minneapolis: University of Minnesota Press, 1980.

Jones, Vincent L.; Eakle, Arlene H.; and Christensen, Mildred H. *Family History for Fun and Profit*. Salt Lake City: The Genealogical Institute, 1972.

Linder, Bill R. *How to Trace Your Family History: A Basic Guide to Geneal-
ogy.* New York: Everest House, 1978.
Stryker-Rodda, Harriett. *How to Climb Your Family Tree: Genealogy for Begin-
ners.* Baltimore: Genealogical Publishing Co., 1983.
Wright, Norman E. *Preserving Your American Heritage: A Guide to Family
and Local History.* Provo, Utah: Brigham Young University Press, 1981.
Zabriski, George O. *Climbing Our Family Tree Systematically.* Salt Lake City:
Parliament Press, 1969.

DOCUMENTING YOUR WORK

The only acceptable genealogy is a documented genealogy. Without proper
documentation, the validity of your research is questionable. There are many
ways to document your research and the method used is dependent upon the
form in which it's presented. Family group records provide only a small space
for listing the sources of your information, necessitating brief but adequate
citations such as those shown below:

1. Family records in possession of Mrs. Vivian E. Cerny, 527 N. Topping, Kansas City, Missouri 64123.
2. 1870 U.S. Census – Miami Twp., Miami Co., Kansas, p. 11, (GS#
545939).[1]
3. Kansas Historical Collections, Vol. X, 1907-1908, p. 273, (GS#
977.8/H22b).
4. Tombstone Inscriptions – New Lancaster Cemetery, Miami Co.,
Kansas. Transcribed on location.

You will probably need to cite more sources than space on a family group record
allows. Continue to list your sources on the back of the group record, listing
only those that provided information. Negative searches are recorded on the
research calendar.

Many genealogists spend years collecting information to extend their lineages but only a few ever bother to publish their research findings. As a result
the same research is duplicated over and over again. You don't have to spend
large sums of money to publish your family history. The important thing is
to get it into library collections where it will be accessible to others as soon
as you have enough material to make it worth the effort.

There are good published histories and then there are very poor ones.
A good family history is well documented and contains a complete name index
of everyone mentioned in the book. An unindexed volume will hardly receive
notice while an undocumented work lacks credibility and reflects negatively

1. GS # represents the collection call numbers at the Genealogical Library of
the LDS Church.

upon your competence. Others will have to check your research extensively before accepting its validity.

The Source: A Guidebook of American Genealogy contains an excellent commentary on documenting your research. Here is an excerpt:

> Yet probably ninety percent of all family histories published in book form in the United States today have few or no citations. Whatever proof lies behind all the information in these books, neither the present reader nor future genealogists will be able to determine from the books themselves. Some have a page or two in the back listing some books and articles checked and even some document collections, but they do not give specific citations for specific statements. If X was born and died at a stated time and place, it does little good to give a page or two in the back on general sources. The user deserves the specific source or sources concerning when X was born and died, and authors ought to be proud to show where they were so industrious as to find these facts. Further, if the author gives specific citations, the user can evaluate such sources and better correspond with the author, thus improving what is known about these people.
>
> Experts debate just how extensive source citations should be. A thorough citing of sources and discussing of conjectures would take more pages than the lineages, so efforts should be taken to keep citations as few and short as good scholarship allows. To see how the experts handle citations, look at some lineage articles in the major genealogical journals. Three of the best are the *National Genealogical Society Quarterly,* the *New England Historical and Genealogical Register,* and *The Genealogist.*[2]

Specific footnote style used is up to the author. Unless you are meeting the requirements of a publisher, it is far more important to be consistent, complete, and efficient than it is to use any given style. Many genealogists use the *Chicago Manual of Style* 13th ed. (Chicago: University of Chicago Press, 1983) as a style guide and supplement it on particular genealogical points with Richard S. Lackey's *Cite Your Sources: A Manual for Documenting Family Histories and Genealogical Records* (New Orleans, La.: Polyanthos, 1980). The important point is to give sources in an economical yet complete way so other researchers can judge the quality of the proof and know where to find the cited sources. If the source is a "personal interview, 12 Feb. 1978, with Mable Ann (Alton) Jones, Upper Fairfax, Pierce Co., Wash.," say so. If the information is from a will not seen but given in a published abstract of probates, say that.

---

2. Arlene H. Eakle and Johni Cerny, eds., *The Source: A Guidebook of American Genealogy* (Salt Lake City: Ancestry Publishing, 1984), p. 24.

CREDIT WHERE CREDIT IS DUE

If you make the decision to print a family history, an index to marriage records, a family newletter, or any other publication, you place yourself in a vulnerable position, for what you write – and claim as your own – is now open to public view. When you begin your project, you often do not know whether you will publish it, so it is suggested you review your writing with a critical eye *before* sending it off to the printer.

This is especially important when giving credit to others whose works you have quoted in your own project. Plagiarism is an easy pit to fall into. Sometimes you borrow without being fully aware to what extent you have used someone else's work and labeled it as your own. The discerning reader, however, will spot this immediately and your credibility as a writer will be undermined.

You should always make a citation when quoting from another's work. Regardless of whether you paraphrase, reword, or make a full quotation, document your source with a full citation. If the ideas are not your own, acknowledge the author. The notes you make should be precise, including the author's name, the title, the publisher and publisher's location (and address if possible), the date of publication, and the page or pages from which you have quoted. If you have the library call number, note that, too, so that others may use your source.

When quoting from another's work, make sure you are not using more than ten percent of the original piece. Anything beyond ten percent breaks the bounds of "reasonable use," and in such cases you must write to the copyright holder (usually the publisher) for permission to quote extensive amounts. Often permission will require a user's fee, the size of which depends on the extent of quotation and the number of copies you intend to publish.

WHO OWNS WHAT IN YOUR RESEARCH FILES?

Ownership of only *part* of the materials in your research file may be yours, even though you have purchased the research for your own use. Some items can be used over and over again without any further permission, while others require permission in writing if you plan to print and share them with others:

Research Materials	Ownership
1. Documents, photos, genealogies, lineages from family members.	Original compiler retains ownership.
2. Printed materials (usually photocopies): maps, census indexes, marriage or will abstracts, immigration and passenger list indexes, etc.	Compiler or publisher retains ownership.

3. Unpublished materials:

Public documents like birth and death records, deeds, wills, military pensions from state or federal archives or county clerks' offices.	In public domain. These are subject to rights of privacy laws, state and federal.
Private archives such as letters, diaries, family papers deposited in historical societies or university libraries.	Archive or donor retains ownership.

From a research report compiled by a professional genealogist, the genealogist retains ownership of the following:

1. Research strategies, including written descriptions of the research process, search order, and suggestions for follow-up.
2. Analysis forms, family sheets and lineage charts, and checklists.
3. Format, layout of pages, and design and packaging of the report.
4. Original artwork and maps.

As a protection for yourself and your work, sign a letter of agreement with family members allowing you to share their materials with others, with professional genealogists, and with libraries and archives so you can reproduce documents and photographs from their collections.

PLANNING FOR RESEARCH SUCCESS

Achieving success in genealogical research is never an accident. Successful research is the result of a thorough knowledge of record sources, an ability to identify, analyze, and interpret the facts found in each record, and a careful construction of a research plan based on what is known and what is found in the records searched.

The scientific method of research suggests that all available records should be searched, beginning with a survey of published and unpublished records pertaining to the ancestor of interest and by contacting his or her relatives and descendants to obtain information they may possess. Searching all available sources does not imply searching records with no bearing on the research problem. For example, let's say that you want to obtain the marriage records of ten siblings enumerated in the 1850 census of Marion County, Iowa. The oldest child of each sibling is listed born in Indiana. While marriage records exist for Marion County, searching those records would not produce evidence of their marriages because the census clearly suggests that they married in Indiana before migrating to Iowa. The marriage records of those Indiana counties in which the families resided should be searched.

Planning for successful research requires a thorough knowledge of record sources. The most comprehensive volume on American genealogical records is *The Source: A Guidebook of American Genealogy*. It reviews every major and many minor record sources and explains their content, use, availability, and location. It also illustrates how to overcome special problems encountered when searching for and using more obscure sources.

Once you have a working knowledge of record sources, a research plan must be devised. This consists of a list of records to be searched to obtain specific results. Start with the known and move to the unknown, searching those records most likely to produce the needed facts. For example, William Andrew West was born in 1849 in Vermilion County, Illinois, and had moved to Bourbon County, Kansas by 1859. Nothing is known of his parents, brothers, or sisters. Which records would most likely produce information about his parent's family?

1. William's death certificate would list his parent's names and birth-places providing the informant had knowledge of those facts.
2. Bourbon County census records compiled after William's arrival may list other West families to whom he might be related.
3. The 1850 census of Vermilion County would include William's family if they remained there through the census taking.
4. Family Bible records maintained by William's parents would produce the needed information, providing such can be found.
5. William's obituary notice may name his living family members and his descendants.

It is important to organize searches with the record most likely to produce the needed information listed first. In this case, the 1850 census of Vermilion County is most likely to solve the research problem. Letters should be sent to obtain William's death certificate, to request a copy of his obituary notice from the newspaper serving the area where he died, and to query family members about the existence and whereabouts of a family Bible record. The last search listed should be a study of the Bourbon County census records.

One pitfall for many beginning genealogists is name gathering. They search records randomly and compile information about everyone listed by the surname of interest. The names they gather are often individuals who never lived in the areas where their ancestors resided or who were alive when their ancestors were not living. Competent researchers learn the importance of time and place and restrict their searches according to the time period and areas in which their ancestor lived. Researchers must learn to identify items essential to genealogical identification and carefully abstract them. It is costly and time consuming to search documents repeatedly because important information was overlooked. Each abstract you make should be checked against the source to insure against copying errors. Be sure that dates and names are copied exactly with no change of spelling or meaning.

An abstract should contain:

1. All names including neighbors, witnesses, clerks, and bondsmen.
2. All places, dates, and relationships.
3. All references to other documents.
4. All property descriptions such as land, personal property, chattels, and shares.
5. All considerations such as money, affection, produce, exchanges, agreements, and contracts.
6. All signatures or marks exactly as they appear.
7. All historical information that may serve as clues to other sources such as occupation, religion, military service, nationality, membership in organizations, involvement in migrations, and acts of God.
8. All biographical descriptions.

Remember, photocopies are preferable. Make abstracts or extracts only when it is impossible to obtain a clear copy.

Many novices fail to understand the importance of working from the known to the unknown. One hobbyist had a female ancestor with the Stowe surname and hoped to prove that she was related to Harriet Beecher Stowe. Disregarding that Stowe was Harriet's married surname and that if she was related to her through the Stowe family it would be as an in-law, the hobbyist began searching Ohio records where Harriet lived while her husband, Calvin Stowe, was a professor of religion. She should have focused on her family in Illinois and worked toward extending the Stowe line based on information she knew about her ancestor. It is entirely possible that she descended from an ancestor commonly shared by Calvin Stowe, but that relationship would not be established without working from the known to the unknown with each new generation identified.

Making a research outline and then following through by searching the records listed is not the only ingredient of successful research. You'll also need to know how to evaluate the evidence in each record and how to calculate relationships based on facts found in those records. Every possible clue in each record must be recognized and then followed up in other record sources. Every conceivable avenue to identification of each ancestor must be considered and taken. As there is no lack of source material in American genealogical research, the challenge comes in determining which sources apply to your research problem, then searching them systematically.

Thorough searches are important to successful research. But what constitutes a thorough search? Let's say family tradition states John Harrison arrived in Virginia from England in 1756 and immediately settled in Surry County. A search of county land records shows that John purchased land there in 1756. An inexperienced genealogist would conclude that family tradition was accurate. Does that deed prove that John *arrived* in Virginia in 1756? No, it only proves that he *purchased land there* at that time. A study of the 1756 deed discloses that John was of Sussex County, Virginia and that information suggests searching Sussex County records. Further research revealed that John Harrison was born in Sussex County. He is mentioned in his father's and grandfather's wills, and the earliest Sussex County record for his family involved his great-grandfather. If research had stopped with the 1756 deed and that deed had been accepted as proof of John's arrival from England, the family's lineage would have ended with him.

Many faulty lineages exist as a result of incomplete research. Overly eager researchers have been known to accept the first entry of the name they are searching for as the person being sought. Lackadaisical ones will justify not digging any further by claiming the surname is uncommon or that only a few insignificant facts don't fit. Search records thoroughly to make sure there are no other entries for the same name. If there are other entries, check the records to determine which one is the person you are seeking. Remember to plan for research success by learning as much as possible about record sources and always work from the known to the unknown.

CHAPTER 6

Sources

Hundreds of records and documents contain genealogical information. The source list shown in Figure 6:1 contains only a few of the more commonly used and accessible record sources. There are eight major and many minor sources used to document American lineages. Since the nation's recordkeeping system was developed by English and European immigrants, many records found in the United States also exist in other countries. While major record sources are original records, printed secondary sources consist of information compiled from a variety of sources, some citing original sources and others containing hearsay.

Original sources generally contain the best evidence, but in some instances they can be inaccurate. Each record is only as precise as the knowledge of its compiler. A single piece of evidence produced in an original record source should be supported by evidence in a second record. There are instances when no other records or evidence exist, and what is found in a record will have to stand unsupported.

Printed secondary sources consist of biographies, histories, family group records, lineage charts, county histories, and genealogies published individually or as articles in periodicals. The accuracy of printed sources is questionable and must be evaluated by comparing their content with facts found in original records. Most printed genealogies are the result of years of research. Documenting every fact is unnecessary. The links between early generations are usually the most difficult to prove and are the weakest links in a genealogy. Verifying the strength of those early relationships will indicate the reliability of the remainder of the genealogy. If a printed secondary source lacks documentation or contains obvious discrepancies, it is unacceptable and should be used only for clues toward finding the original records.

Novice researchers are urged to acquire a broad and comprehensive knowledge of each major record source, including their social and historical roots, content, availability, location, the time period they cover, and how they are used in genealogical research. *The Source: A Guidebook of American Genealogy* was created to help genealogists of every skill level acquire record knowledge. Its size and scope immediately explain why original record sources are

SOURCE CHECKLIST

Family name _____

Residence _____

Check √ each item as you search it.
Although these sources have American titles, most countries keep similar records.

1. FAMILY RECORDS

Personal/family records
____ Family Bibles
____ Oral traditions
____ Journals, diaries
____ Letters
____ Memorial cards
____ Scrapbooks
____ Photographs
____ Heirlooms
____ Farm records
____ Health/medical
     records
____ Military files
____ Citizenship papers
____ Social Security cards
____ Account books
____ Employment records

Certificates
____ Birth
____ Marriage
____ Death
____ Adoption
____ Baptism
____ Confirmation
____ Blessing
____ Graduation
____ Fraktur
____ Ahnentafel
____ Manumission
____ Divorce

School Records
____ Elementary
____ Secondary
____ Vocational
____ Trade
____ College
____ University
____ Private
____ Ladies Finishing
____ Arts

Insurance
____ Life
____ Marine
____ Fire
____ Automobile
____ Accident
____ Health

2. VITAL STATISTICS

Vital records
____ Births
____ Deaths
____ Marriages
____ Divorces
____ Adoptions

Marriage records
____ Indexes
____ Banns
____ Bonds, Applications
____ Licenses
____ Contracts
____ Returns

3. COMPILED SOURCES

Genealogical Society of Utah Indexes
____ Family Group Records
     Archives (FGRA)
____ Temple Index
     Bureau (TIB)
____ International
     Genealogical Index
     (IGI)
____ Ancestral File
____ Family Register

Printed sources
____ Family histories
____ Genealogies
____ Biographies
____ Pedigrees
____ County, local histories
____ City directories

Genealogical periodicals
____ Indexes
____ Queries
____ Genealogies
____ Source extracts
____ Historical articles

Genealogical directories
____
____

4. PUBLIC SOURCES

U.S. Federal censuses
____ Indexes
____ 1790   ____ 1850
____ 1800   ____ 1860
____ 1810   ____ 1870
____ 1820   ____ 1880
____ 1830   ____ 1900
____ 1840   ____ 1910
____ Mortality schedules
____ Agriculture
____ Revolutionary War
____ Union Army survivors

State/local censuses
____
____

Land records
____ Grantee index
____ Grantor index
____ Deeds
____ Mortgages
____ Surveys
____ Patents, grants

Probate records
____ Indexes
____ Wills
____ Administrations
____ Inventories
____ Bonds
____ Settlements
____ Packets
____ Guardianships

Court records
____ Dockets
____ Minutes
____ Orders, decrees
____ Judgments
____ Case Files
____ Indexes

Court related records
____ Sheriff
____ Police
____ Jail
____ Jury
____ Lawyers Briefs
____ Justice of Peace

Tax records
_____ Poll tax
_____ Personal property
_____ Real estate
_____ School
_____ Poor rate
_____ Tax exemptions

Military records
_____ Service files
_____ Pensions
_____ Bounty awards
_____ Discharges
_____ Muster rolls

Immigrant records
_____ Passenger lists
_____ Passports
_____ Vaccination
        certificates
_____ Alien registration
        cards
_____ Change of name
_____ Oaths of allegiance
_____ Register of voters
_____ Logbooks
_____ Naturalization
_____ Citizenship papers
_____ Customs records
_____ Immigrant Aid
        Societies

Cemetery records
_____ Sextons
_____ Monuments
_____ Plats
_____ Deeds
_____ Perpetual Care
_____ Fund
_____ Tombstones
_____ Memorials
_____ Gifts

5. PRIVATE SOURCES

Church records
_____ Birth
_____ Christening
_____ Baptism
_____ Confirmation
_____ Ordination
_____ Marriage
_____ Banns
_____ Divorce
_____ Annulment
_____ Death
_____ Burial
_____ Circumcision
_____ Admissions
_____ Removals
_____ Disciplinary
        proceedings
_____ Subscription lists
_____ Membership lists
_____ Ministers' records
_____ Minutes
_____ Mission reports

Newspapers
_____ Indexes
_____ Births
_____ Deaths
_____ Marriages
_____ Anniversaries
_____ Obituaries
_____ Advertisements
_____ Local news
_____ Unclaimed mail

Legal notices
_____ Probates
_____ Auctions
_____ Forced sales
_____ Divorces
_____ Bankruptcies
_____ Court claims
_____ Convictions

Employment records
_____ Indentures
_____ Apprenticeships
_____ Licenses
_____ Pensions
_____ Service awards
_____ Personnel files
_____ Account books

Mortuary records
_____ Burial registers
_____ Funeral cards
_____ Funeral books

Institutional records
_____ Charities
_____ Hospitals
_____ Convents
_____ Seminaries
_____ Libraries
_____ Historical societies
_____ Genealogical societies
_____ Mission societies
_____ Orphan agencies
_____ Reunion registries

Collections
_____ Indexes
_____ Personal papers
_____ Correspondence
_____ Surname files
_____ Biographies
_____ Inscriptions
_____ DAR
_____ Business records
_____ Oral histories
_____ WPA projects

Figure 6:1. Source Checklist. Courtesy of the Genealogical Institute, Salt Lake City.

not discussed in depth here. The following discussion is simply an introduction to the eight major record sources used to trace American ancestry.

VITAL RECORDS

Vital records consist of documents attesting to the central life events: birth, marriage, and death. Maintained by civil authorities, they are prime sources of genealogical information. While many British and European countries began keeping birth and death records nationally in the nineteenth century, the United States elected to leave vital registration under state jurisdiction. The majority of the states did not implement registration until the first quarter of the twentieth century. Every state required marriage registration in some form at the time the state was created, with New York, Pennsylvania, and South Carolina the exceptions.

Towns and counties compiled early marriage records in most states. Registration usually dated from the time the town or county was organized. The type of marriage record required differed from place to place and included:

Applications	Consents	Licenses
Bonds	Contracts	Registers
Certificates	Intentions	Returns

Birth and death registration existed in New England, metropolitan cities, and a few other states before the twentieth century. The U.S. Department of Health and Human Services periodically compiles "Where to Write for Vital Records – Births, Deaths, Marriages and Divorces," DHHS Publication No. (PHS) 82-1142, listing state-by-state, the dates the records began, the type of records kept, the cost of certified copies, and the address of the records custodian in each state.

Enforcement of early registration was haphazard, particularly in rural and frontier areas, and not everyone who was born or died during the initial registration period is included. Early records offer considerably less information than a modern birth or death record, but are still considered the best evidence for those events. Researchers are encouraged to obtain vital records whenever possible.

CHURCH RECORDS

Prior to state registration of vital life events, churches were the sole keepers of vital records in the form of births, christenings, marriages, deaths and burials, and other ecclesiastical records. Unlike other countries, the United States has no state church. The country's guarantee of freedom of religion drew people of every faith and with each faith came a different approach to maintaining records.

Puritans and Separatists founded New England, Maryland became a haven for Catholics, and Scots and Scots-Irish Presbyterians settled predominantly in Pennsylvania and Virginia during the early colonial period. Pennsylvania had a mixture of religions practiced by people of every nationality, including Quakers, Lutherans, Huguenots, Dunkards, and others.

An ancestral family's religious preference must be determined before church records can be used effectively. If an ancestor came from Scotland or Northern Ireland, he or she most likely practiced Presbyterianism. Thus, an ancestral family's country of origin can be an excellent clue to the church attended.

Each religious group maintained a variety of records. Congregational, Anglican, Dutch Reformed, Lutheran, and Catholic churches kept birth, christening, marriage, death, and burial records. The form and content of each record varied from group to group. Quakers kept excellent records, including entire family groups with complete birth, marriage, and death information. Religions with American roots, such as the Baptist, Methodist, and United Brethren churches rarely recorded births, christenings, deaths, or burials. Some kept marriage records, but on the whole only membership rolls were compiled. Vital events may appear as well in a minister's diary or journal.

Church records are excellent substitutes for vital records and, like vital records, should be consulted whenever possible. Keep in mind that America experienced a number of evangelistic periods resulting in mass conversions from the religion a family embraced for generations to one or more religions born in the United States. A German pioneer family attending a Baptist church in Kentucky probably belonged to the Evangelical Lutheran or Dutch Reformed church in Pennsylvania.

CENSUS RECORDS

Mention of the word census immediately brings the United States federal population schedules to mind. State, local, school, slave, and other types of census enumerations exist as well. Federal censuses are used most extensively because they exist for the entire nation and are available nationwide.

America first enumerated its population in 1790 and subsequent censuses were taken every ten years thereafter on a county-by-county basis within each state. The 1790 to 1840 enumerations list the head of each household and the number of males and females living in that household according to age groups. Beginning in 1850, census schedules list each household member by name and, minimally, each member's age and birthplace. The 1880 census includes each person's relationship to the head of the household. Only the 1900 census states the month and year each person was born. Census enumerations from 1880 list the state or country in which the mother and father of each person was born. The 1900 and 1910 schedules list the year an immigrant arrived in the United States, their citizenship status, the number of years a couple was married, the number of children born to a mother, and the number of children still living.

Portions of the 1890 census were destroyed by fire and later Congress passed a law authorizing the destruction of what remained. Only the 1890 Veteran's Schedule and a few fragments of the original census exist today.

At present, U.S. Census records through 1910 are available to the public. Microfilm copies of the enumerations are located at the Genealogical Library of the LDS Church in Salt Lake City and its branches, Regional Federal Archives and Records Centers, and other state, local, and university libraries. State indexes exist for enumerations taken between 1790 and 1870 for some states. Soundexes (phonetic indexes) exist for the 1880 census (a partial index to families with children under eleven years old) and the 1900 census (complete). The 1910 census is partially indexed.

Census records are an excellent source for getting a picture of family groups and tracking pioneer families. Many census records list faulty information, especially incorrect ages and birthplaces and misspelled names. They should always be supported with evidence in other records. State, local, and other census enumerations should be consulted when possible because they frequently contain information not included in federal schedules and list children who died between federal censuses.

ESTATE RECORDS

Estate records are produced by civil courts, such as county, circuit, orphans, and other courts. Wills, administrations, guardianships, and settlements are some of the records related to a person's estate or probate record.

When someone dies, his real and personal property is often disposed of in a legal manner. Many ancestors had the foresight to write wills directing the distribution of their estates. Those who died without leaving a will died intestate, and the court directed the estate settlement by appointing an administrator. The property left by the deceased was inventoried and if assets were insufficient to meet the claims against the estate, all or part of the real and personal property was sold. A bill of sale was then filed with the court, listing the property sold and naming those who made purchases. The court often appointed guardians to manage the estates of minor heirs and/or to raise them in their father's absence even if their mother was still living. Probate records may include one or more of the following documents:

Accounts and Settlements	Divisions	Returns
Appointments	Guardianships	Sales
Bonds	Inventories	Settlements
Codicils	Letters	Support Bills
Distributions	Petitions	Wills

Identifying family groups before 1850 is difficult due to the absence of everyname census enumerations. Probate and estate records, especially wills, are excellent substitutes for census records in compiling early family groups. They are frequently the only means of identifying married daughters during that early period.

Probate and estate records are located in the lower court having probate jurisdiction. Many court records have been microfilmed by the Genealogical Library of the LDS Church and are available in Salt Lake City or through its branch libraries. Records can also be obtained by writing the clerk of the probate court of the county where an ancestor's estate was probated.

LAND RECORDS

Land records are also major sources of genealogical information. They frequently include an ancestor's prior county of residence, the names of his wife, children, grandchildren, parents, brothers, sisters, and other relatives, when he arrived in a particular county, and when he left that area.

Using land and property records effectively requires thorough knowledge of the nation's land development and those records produced to document land ownership, such as:

Abstracts	Lotteries
Applications (Homestead)	Mortgages
Bounty Land Warrants	Patents
Contracts	Plat Books
Deeds	Quitrent Rolls
Entry Books	Slaves
Grants	Surveys
Indentures	Tax Lists
Land Claims	Warrants
Leases	

Most land and property records are filed on the town and county level. Many county and property records were microfilmed by the Genealogical Library of the LDS Church and are available in Salt Lake City or at its branch libraries. Indexes to grantors (sellers) and grantees (buyers) exist for most counties. Searches of the indexes and copies of records can be obtained by correspondence.

MILITARY RECORDS

The United States has been involved in at least eleven major wars, numerous Indian wars, and two conflicts since colonial times. Military records provide both historical and genealogical information about direct ancestors and their fathers, brothers, uncles, and cousins. Military service records and records of veteran's benefits are the two principal categories of military records useful in genealogical research. Service records generally contain more historical than genealogical information. They include enlistment records, muster rolls, orders, reports, and commendations.

Veteran's records are excellent sources of genealogical information, especially pension application files—the most widely used military record. Pension files also provide details of enlistment and discharge to prove eligibility. Revolutionary and Civil War pension application files contain different documents and information. Revolutionary War veterans applied for pensions between 1776 and 1853, with all veterans eligible to apply in 1832. Applications were made to the United States Government, but they were initiated in the courts of the counties and towns in which the veteran lived. They contain affidavits made by the veteran and his neighbors or associates to support his claim, summaries of his service, the military organization in which he served, the dates of his service, his date and place of birth, names of heirs, relationship to others who served with him, his movements after the war, and information from family Bible records. Sometimes the Bible pages, torn out of the book, are enclosed as evidence. Each application may include all or part of the above information.

Revolutionary War pensions are indexed in the National Genealogical Society's Special Publication No. 40, *Index of Revolutionary War Pension Applications in the National Archives* (Washington, D.C.: National Genealogical Society, 1976). Pension application files were microfilmed and are available at the Genealogical Library of the LDS Church, its branches, Regional Federal Archives and Records Centers, and other repositories.

Civil War pension applications of veterans and their widows or minor children contain significantly more information than those earlier pension applications. They are the best of the early military documents in terms of the genealogical information they contain. These files do not all contain the same amount of information, but one can expect to find the name of the veteran, the military or naval unit in which he served, the date and place of his enlistment, his birthdate and place (in some files only), the date and place of his marriage, the names and birthdates of his children, the maiden name of his wife, information about subsequent marriages, the date and place of his discharge, the physical disabilities connected with service-related injuries, and his residences since his discharge. There will also be general affidavits of individuals who could attest to his disabilities and copies of the findings of examining physicians. Other types of military records include: soldier burial records, veteran's home records, military censuses, selective service registrations, bounty land warrants, and military hospital records.

Indexes to Civil War pension application files are microfilmed and available in the same repositories as Revolutionary War pension applications. Civil War pension applications are available through the National Archives in Washington, D.C., along with most of the other military records listed above, except bounty land warrant applications which are included with Revolutionary War pension applications.

Military pension files are some of the most interesting records you will encounter. They offer colorful historical information and document an important period of an ancestor's life. If an ancestor or one of his close relatives was of prime military service age during one of America's major wars, get a copy of his military records whenever possible. They may contain the answers to difficult research problems.

COURT RECORDS

American court records are a mystery to most researchers. Many early lower court records are unindexed and some researchers, both professional and hobbyist, do not invest the time required to search these records thoroughly. Unfortunately, many researchers leave problems unsolved because they resist digging into court records; however, it is there that the solutions usually are found.

There are two classifications of courts, the state court system and the federal court system. Records maintained by the various courts within these systems offer a variety of personal and genealogical information about a family. Chapter 6, "American Court Records" in *The Source: A Guidebook of American Genealogy*, is the most comprehensive treatment of this major record source. Once researchers understand the ins and outs of searching court records, they will no longer fear using them. Rather than give an inadequate summary of a complex subject and further compound hesitancy to use court records, the chapter cited above is highly recommended.

CEMETERY RECORDS

Most hobbyists think only of cemetery records and printed volumes of tombstone inscriptions. While such publications are worthwhile to a genealogist, they represent only one of several available cemetery records.

A sexton oversees cemetery operations, maintains interment, plot ownership, and financial records, and works with funeral directors. The absence of a tombstone does not mean that there are no facts available about a relative's death. A sexton's record often contains the information needed from a tombstone and sometimes more, such as who purchased the burial plots, who owns the unused plot, and specific places of origin for immigrant ancestors.

Cemetery records can be obtained by correspondence; however, it is best to search the cemetery in person or hire an agent to search it for you. The graves surrounding your ancestor's burial site may be those of other relatives disclosing missing maiden surnames, and a sexton or clerk may not make the connection. Not all cemeteries maintain records, something particularly true of small rural cemeteries and family burial grounds.

CHAPTER 7

How Rules Apply To Genealogy

When students of genealogy first learn that it is impossible to prove a lineage absolutely, they resist that fact. They live in an era when advanced technology demands absolutes, the products of societies driven to achieve perfection. Neither resistance, technology, nor the pursuit of perfection will alter reality; at best, a lineage can be proven only beyond a reasonable doubt, just as guilt or innocence is proven in a court of law. Lineages, like court cases, are built upon available evidence.

Compiling accurate lineages requires evidence. Genealogical evidence is the information gathered primarily from documents and records. Some records, such as a birth certificate with the date a person was born, clearly state genealogical fact. Other records are not as specific, such as an 1850 census record noting that William Huffman was thirty-five years old. While the entry does not clearly date his birth, it implies that he was born in 1815. Both records are genealogically valuable. One states a fact and the other provides information from which a fact must be deduced. The first, a record that states a fact, provides direct evidence, while the second, offering information from which a fact must be inferred or deduced, provides circumstantial or indirect evidence.

USES OF GENEALOGICAL EVIDENCE

Evidence is used in genealogical research to establish names, dates, places of events, and relationships. Let's assume that Mary Alice Karr is your great-grandmother, and you want to prove that Ambrose and Martha Karr are her parents, as family tradition states. Mary Alice Karr was born before birth records were issued. Ambrose Karr died in 1867 and his estate was administered by the probate court that same year. The following information was included in his probate packet:

1. Martha P. Karr was the widow of Ambrose N. Karr.
2. Ambrose N. Karr died 13 August 1867 at Miami County, Kansas.
3. James Karr (age four), Alice Karr (age two), and Sarah Karr (age two months) were the minor heirs of Ambrose N. Karr.

A record providing direct evidence that a person is your ancestor must specifically state the name and relationship of a spouse or one of the children you have already determined to be your ancestor. In this instance, you have already proven that Mary Alice Karr was your great-grandmother and you know she was known as Alice during her lifetime. The probate record provides direct evidence that she was the daughter of Ambrose N. and Martha P. Karr. It also provides direct evidence of her father's date and place of death and the names of her brother and sister. The indirect evidence stated is related to the birthdates of the children. James Karr was four years old, and you can deduce that he was born about 1862-63, based on the 3 September 1867 date of the document. The daughters' birth years can be similarly calculated from their ages at this time.

Some records contain only indirect or circumstantial evidence. Let's try to prove Martha P. Karr's parentage. She died in 1871, prior to the registering of deaths in Kansas. She was known as Patsy Karr during her life, Patsy a derivative form of Martha. Her marriage record clearly states that Ambrose Carr [sic] married Patsy Huffman on 26 May 1859. There is only one Huffman family living near her in the 1860 census, the William Huffman family. According to that census, one of William's children was born in Illinois in 1850. Since Martha was already married in 1860 and living with her husband, she was not listed in William's household. It was necessary to attempt to link Martha to William Huffman by searching the 1850 census of Illinois. William Huffman was a resident of Fulton County when the 1850 census was taken. He had a female child, Patsy, age eleven, born in Illinois living in his household. The names of the other children listed in his 1850 household matched those living with him in 1860 in Kansas, proving that the two entries were for the same William Huffman.

The 1850 census does not give relationships to the head of the household. Thus, finding Patsy Huffman in William's household does not prove that she was his daughter. The 1850 census enumerations rarely provide direct evidence to support relationships; but, a study of that census shows that entries generally represent family groups with the father listed first, followed by his spouse and then by his children in order of age. Nevertheless, direct evidence of relationship is absent. The fact that Patsy Huffman is listed in William's household in 1850 only circumstantially suggests that she is his daughter. Other indirect evidence allows the deduction that Patsy was born in 1839 in Illinois and that she was the sister of the other children listed in the census.

Evidence must always be evaluated for its potential accuracy. Direct evidence can be worthless, just as circumstantial evidence can be completely accurate. How is evidence evaluated? Since there are definite criteria for evaluating evidence, ask yourself the following questions:

1. Was the record made at the time or shortly after the event?
2. Was the person providing the information an eyewitness?
3. Is the document the original or a microfilmed copy?

4. Is the record a printed, typewritten, or manuscript copy of the document?

Primary sources are those records, documents, or statements made at the time of the event or shortly thereafter by eyewitnesses or persons directly related to the event. Records not meeting these criteria are secondary sources. It is also important to examine the record for originality. Records that have been transcribed into printed or handwritten form could contain errors. They are subject to handwriting interpretation and typewriting and typesetting errors. It would be ideal to compile all genealogies and family histories from original, primary sources. Unfortunately, that is impossible. Whenever faced with a choice of records, choose original, primary sources, but bear in mind that even they can contain errors.

For example, Mary Lee Huffaker was born 3 July 1942 to John Huffaker and Valerie Kellar in New Haven, Connecticut. Her birth certificate is a primary source which attests to her name, birthdate, birthplace, and parentage. But does it? Thirty years after Mary's birth, her aunt disclosed that Valerie Kellar met and married John Huffaker after she conceived her daughter. Mary's birth certificate only provides direct evidence of her relationship to her mother, her birthdate, and birthplace. Only Valerie Kellar Huffaker can provide direct evidence to identify Mary's biological father, evidence that would be oral testimony. Unless a person or another document surfaces to correct primary records containing false information, little can be done to compile Mary Lee Huffaker's lineage.

TYPES OF GENEALOGICAL RECORDS

Let's take a closer look at the three types of genealogical records. The records to be evaluated will fall into one of three categories: (1) personal knowledge and family tradition, (2) public records, and (3) printed sources, including copies of original records and compiled family histories and genealogies. You'll need a good understanding of each to evaluate their evidence properly.

The value of personal knowledge and family tradition depends entirely upon the quality of the memory of the person recalling the information as well as the time that elapsed between the event and recall. You grew up, for example, living with your immediate family. You know your parents, brothers, sisters, aunts, and uncles. Personal knowledge of these relationships is acceptable as primary evidence. You were also present at family gatherings to hear your grandmother talk about her great-great-grandfather, Matthew Karr, who arrived in America from northern Ireland when he was eight years old and the Revolutionary War was nearly over. She heard this story from her mother who in turn heard it from her grandfather. This story is family tradition—not acceptable as primary evidence. None of those passing the story possessed direct personal knowledge of the event of their timing. Their statements are secondary and must be corroborated before they are acceptable as evidence.

Family traditions are rarely without substance, yet each statement of fact requires additional proof in the form of recorded evidence, as does all other secondary evidence.

Memory is not infallible as everyone knows. Busy lives are not uniquely a twentieth-century phenomenon, and older family members have decades of events stored in their memories. The further back one's memory reaches the fewer details it will recall. Things get fuzzy and dates are often mixed up. Some seniors have remarkable recall, as you'll see later on in the case study of Bertha Ruth Smith's lineage. Her memory of events, dates, and places is excellent; nevertheless, each fact she stated had to be documented to verify accuracy.

Family records are also grouped with personal knowledge and family tradition even though they are not oral testimony. Family records come in many forms, such as Bibles, journals, and diaries. The value of these records is determined by the time at which the entries were made. Let's say, for example, that your great-grandparents received a Bible as a wedding present. They immediately recorded their names and the date of their marriage in the family record section. Then, as each child was born, they recorded the child's name and birthdate. They also recorded names and deathdates of family members. When entries into family Bibles are made immediately following an event, they are likely to be accurate and are considered direct evidence. But what if the family didn't acquire their Bible until most of their children were born? Entries made after considerable time has elapsed are subject to error. Remember, time's passage often muddles the memory, especially concerning dates. The names will probably be accurate, but you'll need additional evidence to prove the accuracy of the dates. How do you determine when the entries were made? You simply check the date the Bible was printed. If the printing date is later than the dates of recorded events, then the record was made after the events took place. The time difference between publication and the events listed will tell you how much time elapsed and allow you to determine the credibility of the evidence.

There are hundreds of public records containing genealogical information. Genealogists use them all to resolve one problem or another. Vital records — records attesting to birth, marriage, or death — are considered the most valuable by genealogists. However, they are not always primary sources of evidence nor are they without their unique qualifications.

You've already seen how the birth records can be inaccurate. While Valerie Kellar was the legal wife of John Huffaker at the time of her daughter's birth and the birth certificate legally accurate, it was erroneous in terms of genealogical accuracy. There are other instances when people intentionally gave false information to records clerks. This is particularly true when someone underage applied for a marriage license without parental consent. Many birth records were made years after a person's birth, delayed birth records that were instituted when people had to have proof of age to receive social security benefits. While applicants for these documents had to provide material proof of the facts recorded on the delayed certificate, proof was sometimes contrived. If you note discrepancies between a birth record and other evidence, keep this in mind and search for additional evidence to clarify them. Birth and marriage records are primary sources only if they were created at the time of the event.

Death records pose even greater problems. While they are compiled immediately following death, accuracy is not ensured. Let's say that your great-uncle moved away from the nucleus of his family as a young man and died without any close relatives living nearby. His neighbor provided authorities with the information recorded on his death certificate. That neighbor did not have direct knowledge of most of the facts stated on the death certificate. With the exception of the information pertaining to the death itself, burial data, and the name of the deceased, the facts on a death certificate are the personal knowledge of the informant. As such, they are in need of further proof and verification. Death records are both primary and secondary in nature.

Census records are essential to tracing American lineages, especially those taken prior to the advent of vital records. Most genealogists are aware that census records are riddled with errors, the most common being misspelled names, incorrect ages, and incorrect birthplaces. While census data is a valuable research tool, it cannot stand alone. Census information is a secondary source and must be supported by other evidence whenever possible.

The same criteria are applied to other record sources to determine their value, reliability, and acceptability as genealogical evidence. If the record or document was created at the time of or immediately after an event, that document is a primary source. Its value is lessened only when it is a transcribed copy taken from the original.

Printed sources, such as compiled family histories and genealogies, transcribed records, biographical sketches in county histories, and biographies are secondary sources. Many printed sources contain citations referring to primary sources; however, they are still considered secondary sources. All printed sources must be checked for accuracy.

CORROBORATION

Some research problems will be tough to solve. Fewer records are available for the colonial period, and they will quite often produce only circumstantial evidence. More relationships are built on circumstantial evidence than direct evidence. There are also times when circumstantial evidence is more accurate than some direct evidence. How does one build a lineage on circumstantial evidence?

Let's return to the Huffman family. Hundreds of research hours were devoted to detailing the life of William Huffman and his children. In the course of documenting his life, the researcher focused on his parents. William's obituary notice and several other documents showed that he was born 1 July 1815 at Butler County, Ohio and moved to Parke County, Indiana with his father in 1831. He married Alice Davis there 15 January 1835 and began his work as a United Brethren minister in Parke County before moving west to build the church in the role of a missionary. He took his family to Fulton County, Illinois and then Benton County, Iowa. He finally established his church in Miami County, Kansas, where he lived out his life.

With those residences in mind, the search began for his parents. Four Huffman families were listed in the 1820 U.S. Census of St. Clair Township, Butler County, Ohio with male children under ten years of age: Gabriel Huffman, Sampson Huffman, John Huffman, and Jacob Huffman. Since young William Huffman would have been five years old when the census was taken, he would have been the son of one of these men.

The Huffman family had moved to Parke County, Indiana by 1830 when William Huffman was fifteen. Only one Parke County family had a male that age in its household. Henry Huffman headed that household, but he was not a resident of Butler County, Ohio in 1820. Moving to the 1840 U.S. Census of Parke County, Indiana, we find William Huffman living in a dwelling next to John Huffman. That John Huffman is twenty years older than the John Huffman located in the 1820 census of Butler County, Ohio. Both John and William Huffman are living near Edmond Davis, the twin brother of William's wife, Alice.

By 1850, William Huffman was in Fulton County, Illinois and so were John Huffman and Edmond Davis. John Huffman was a seventy-five-year-old native of Virginia according to the census. His wife Mary, English born, was seventy-three.

John Huffman's probate records were not on file in Fulton County, Illinois, nor could he be located in Benton County, Iowa, William's residence after leaving Illinois. All of the evidence linking William Huffman to John Huffman is circumstantial. Proximity between two individuals in a single census may suggest a relationship, but it does not prove one. There must be corroboration of circumstantial evidence to establish a relationship. In the case cited above, the continual presence of John and William Huffman in the same locations as William moved across the nation constitutes corroboration. Always strengthen circumstantial evidence with other records until the accumulation of evidence allows inferrence of a relationship.

Lineages are constructed from a combination of direct and circumstantial evidence intricately woven together through careful and skillful evaluation and analysis. The next chapter takes you through a generation-by-generation process of searching record sources and evaluating them to construct an accurate lineage.

PREPONDERANCE OF EVIDENCE

A preponderance of evidence literally means that some pieces of information, some record sources, some facts carry more weight than others. These "weightier" pieces add strength to your conclusions. For example, a professional genealogist documenting the marriage of his own grandmother, located five different "primary" sources detailing that event:

1. Marriage certificate issued by Episcopal parish where marriage occurred, 26 June 1888, St. Ann's Church, Dorchester, MA.
2. Another marriage certificate issued by the *same church*, 27 June 1888, St. Ann's Church, Dorchester, MA.
3. Marriage certificate issued by Commonwealth of Massachusetts, 28 August 1969, and certified to be correct, 28 June 1888, Revere, MA.
4. Family Bible entry, 27 June 1888, St. Ann's Church, Roxbury, MA.
5. Diary entry written after 28 April 1915 by the grandmother herself, 27 June 1888: "As we lived in Revere and St. Ann's was in Dorchester the preparations of the day and the family supper were to be at my sister Nell's [in Roxbury]."

Documents 1 through 3 were official or certified copies reportedly made from original entries. Document 4 was created at the time of the event from personal knowledge by the mother of the bride. Document 5 was made years later by the principal eyewitness—the bride herself. Which one is the weightier piece?

The preponderant record is the diary entry. Although it is a recall of the event, the bride provides specific details that resolve the seemingly conflicting evidence in the other four documents.

The most important element in compiling your lineage is the degree to which you can match one piece of data to another. Compatibility is the key to proof. How well do the pieces go together? In the discussions that follow, the emphasis will be to show you how to fit evidence together—how to corroborate what you already know with additional details, and how to fit new information into the picture.

DEALING WITH DISCREPANCIES

Discrepancies are a frustrating fact of genealogical research. The best method of research demands that every possible source of genealogical information be searched in compiling a lineage, and as you search each record you're going to discover that "facts" in one record don't agree with "facts" stated in others. The question then arises: "How do I resolve discrepancies?"

Let's first examine how discrepancies come to exist. There are instances when only one piece of evidence pertaining to an individual can be found. There can be no dissimilarities because there is nothing else available for fact comparison. When only one record exists, you are forced to evaluate the evidence in that record by subjecting it to a credibility test. Is it a primary source? How much of the evidence found in the source is direct or circumstantial? Is the record source an original or a transcribed copy? Was the information recorded on the document given by an eyewitness to the event?

When more than one piece of evidence pertaining to an individual exists, each fact contained in each piece of evidence must be compared for conflicting information. Differences appear in names, dates, places, relationships, and historical details, a number of factors seen as the cause of discrepancies. Early marriage records were compiled from minister's returns given to county record-keepers. The clerk would take the returns and enter them into marriage books. While some clerks were meticulous in their transcriptions, others were sloppy, carelessness accounting for a number of discrepancies. Census enumerators and other record compilers recorded names and places as they heard them pronounced instead of asking how they were spelled. The results were phonetic spelling variations. The Reynolds family in Georgia, for example, moved to Arkansas just prior to the 1870 census. They were listed in earlier census records with their surname spelled "Reynolds," and when attempts were made to locate them in Arkansas they couldn't be found. A closer examination of each entry in the Arkansas census revealed a family from Georgia with the exact same given names and approximate ages of the Reynolds family being sought. The surname, however, was Runnells. The census enumerator, probably unfamiliar with the Georgia dialect of the Reynolds family, recorded the surname as he heard it pronounced—"Runnells."

Other discrepancies evolve from faulty memories, changes in geographical boundaries, generalities, deception, and ignorance. Some people have poor memories for dates, and rather than not respond to a question posed by a census enumerator, they will estimate or guess at the facts to satisfy the need for an answer. Others simply have no interest in remembering names, dates, and places and give indifferent answers. Professional genealogists are often faced with compiling lineages for people who can't remember their parent's birthdates or their grandparent's names, much less where they were born or died.

America has experienced many geographic boundary changes. Large tracts of land were carved into relatively large counties, and as the population grew, those jurisdictions were unable to administer effectively to a larger number of people. The problem was solved by creating new counties out of old ones. A classic example of confusion over a change in boundaries is seen in an entry in a family history. John Ball's 1768 birthplace was given as Surry County, North Carolina, when in fact that county was not created until 1770 out of Rowan County. Another example is seen in Washington County, Tennessee which was created in 1777, nineteen years before Tennessee became a state. People born in Washington County before Tennessee statehood were citizens of several North Carolina counties. Most genealogists list the geographic area as it was known at the time of an event and note the present-day location in parentheses.

Generalities are the most difficult discrepancies to deal with in research. The generality seen most often deals with location. While most Americans lived in rural areas during the nineteenth century, chances of one knowing where some small, midwestern farm town was located were slim. Thus when asked where they were from, ruralites not too distant from a big city would respond that they were from that city. Another example is seen in the millions of records that list the country of an immigrant's birth rather than the specific town or village. Occasionally, you'll see a German province such as Württemburg or Hesse-Darmstadt listed but rarely any jurisdiction smaller than that. Generalities contribute little to research knowledge and create a need for ingenious planning to get around them.

Deception ranks almost as high as generalities as the most difficult research discrepancy. People deceived recordkeepers for a number of reasons, most of which can only be speculated upon. Marriage age requirements were quite low in frontier America, and it's common to find girls marrying at fourteen or fifteen. Males were required to be slightly older. An eighteen-year-old male could marry without parental consent, but a young girl usually had to have parental consent to marry underage. Many young couples lied about age then, just as they do now, and the records reflect deception.

Another interesting example of deceit comes from a client's research. The client's father stated that he was born 1 August 1900 in Charleston, South Carolina and that his father died when he was eight years old. A research plan was designed around that information. Every record in existence for his father supported the date and place of birth he gave, but none of the searches conducted in an effort to find him with his parents were successful. Professional experience proved in the past that when nothing surfaces from the known facts, those facts may be in error. Eventually the client's father—eight years old—was found living with his widowed mother in a rural South Carolina county in the 1900 census. Why had he lied about his birthdate and birthplace? Perhaps he did so to avoid conscription during World War I.

Ignorance is also a cause of dissimilarities. Most of the nation bordered on illiteracy before this century, and this lack of education is often seen in records of genealogical interest. While many recordkeepers did not ask how to spell a surname, just as many people had no idea how their name was spelled anyway. It's impossible to estimate how many people had no knowledge of their birthdate. Countless Revolutionary War pension applications prove that point by including affidavits that a person was approximately so many years old or was believed to have been born in a particular year.

Whatever the causes of discrepancies between records, they must be dealt with to ensure the most accurate lineage possible. The first step in dealing with discrepancies is to list them. I've chosen to use a discrepancy chart to simplify the process. Let's list the discrepancies found in records pertaining to William Karr.

	1860 Census	1870 Census	1st Marriage	2nd Marriage	Bio. Sketch
Name	William Karr	William Karr	William Carr	William Karr	William Karr
Date of Birth	Cal. 1814	Cal. 1813		Cal. 1815	24 Mar 1813
Place of Birth	Indiana	Pennsyl-vania			Washington Co., Penn.
Date of Marriage			19 Feb 1833	21 Aug 1871	19 Feb 1833
Place of Marriage			Decatur Co., Ind.	Miami Co., Kansas	Indiana
Father					Matthew Karr
Mother					Hannah Pease

William Karr's name is spelled the same in four out of the five records. Carr is a phonetic variation of Karr and in view of that there is no unresolved discrepancy. Both census records offer direct evidence of his name and residence and circumstantial evidence of his age and birthplace. The 1860 census states he was born in Indiana and the 1870 reports that he was born in Pennsylvania, the first major difference. William Karr surely knew where he was born and would not state an incorrect birthplace. Thus it is likely that someone other than William provided the information in one of the enumerations. His biographical sketch states that he was born in Washington County, Pennsylvania. The number of details in that sketch suggest he was personally interviewed before it was written. While the sketch would be classed as a secondary source providing circumstantial evidence of the events in his life and family relationship, it has greater credibility and thus carries more weight than the census enumerations in this case. The biographical sketch supports all of the information listed on the chart except his second marriage, which isn't mentioned at all, and his Indiana birthplace given in 1860.

When attempting to resolve discrepancies, accept the facts provided by the record containing the preponderant evidence. Solve them by evaluating the credibility of the sources. Favor primary over secondary sources and direct over circumstantial evidence. Primary sources containing direct evidence of a name, date, place, event, or relationship are the best forms of evidence. Primary sources containing circumstantial evidence are less credible. Least acceptable are secondary sources providing only circumstantial evidence.

CHAPTER 8

Tracing an American Lineage

T racing an American lineage isn't easy, but it can be challenging and fun. You begin with yourself and the information in your home and the homes of your relatives. Start by filling out from your memory a lineage chart of names, dates, places, and relationships. Then dig through drawers, boxes in the attic, garage, and basement, looking for old letters, documents, diaries, yearbooks, and anything else that will contain genealogical information or bits of family history. Before long you'll be amazed at the volume of information accumulated over a short period of time. Once you've exhausted your own resources, start contacting relatives and compare your information with theirs. What follows then is the question, "Where do I go from here?"

There are no simple answers to that question. If no one is available to respond, most people will try to locate an instructional manual for direction. While the information found in how-to books is valuable, only rarely will you find a step-by-step approach to doing research. The following series of case studies is designed to instruct the novice researcher in the art and science of genealogical research. The methods used in each case study are not the only approaches that could be used; they were chosen because they produced excellent results and included a variety of record sources. Other genealogists may approach the same problem differently and achieve the same results. The scope of this book did not permit discussing every record source available. Only those most pertinent were included in the study.

The first case study concerns a basic research problem, beginning with family and home sources, then moving into original research in public and private records. The study is designed to give the beginner some understanding of basic research methods employed throughout the research process.

THE ANCESTRY OF BERTHA RUTH SMITH

Bertha Ruth Smith, my maternal grandmother, was seventy-eight years old when I first became interested in tracing my ancestry. She was visiting our home in Los Angeles in the spring of 1966 when we sat down with a lineage chart and some family group records that had been partially completed with the help of my mother. They looked like this when the interview began:

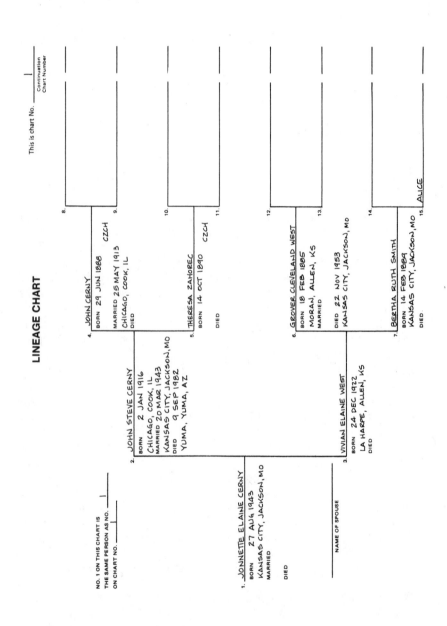

Figure 8:1. Lineage Work Chart 1, Jonnette Elaine Cerny.

FAMILY GROUP SHEET

HUS. JOHN STEVE CERNY — OCCUPATION(S) HEATING AND AIR CONDITIONING TECHNICIAN

BORN	2 JAN 1916	PLACE Chicago, Cook, Illinois
CHR.		PLACE
MARR.	20 MAR 1943	PLACE Kansas City, Jackson, Missouri
DIED		PLACE
BUR.		PLACE

FATHER JOHN CERNY

MOTHER THERESA ZAHOREC

OTHER WIVES

WIFE VIVIAN ELAINE WEST

BORN	24 DEC 1922	PLACE La Harpe, Allen, Kansas
CHR.		PLACE
DIED		PLACE
BUR.		PLACE

FATHER GROVER CLEVELAND WEST

MOTHER BERTHA RUTH SMITH

OTHER HUSBANDS

SEX	CHILDREN		DATE BORN / PLACE BORN	DATE MARRIED / TO	PLACE	DATE DIED / PLACE DIED
X F	1	JONNETTE ELAINE CERNY	27 AUG 1943 / Kansas City, Jackson, Missouri			
F	2	ANTOINETTE IRENE CERNY	4 DEC 1946 / Kansas City, Jackson, Missouri			
F	3	STEVETTE MARIE CERNY	12 JAN 1948 / Kansas City, Jackson, Missouri			
M	4	JOHN JOSEPH CERNY	23 SEP 1951 / Kansas City, Jackson, Missouri			
F	5	NANETTE THERESA CERNY	14 APR 1956 / Encino, Los Angeles, California			
	6					
	7					
	8					
	9					
	10					

OTHER MARRIAGES

SOURCES OF INFORMATION
1. Birth Certificate of each family member in possession of Vivian West Cerny
   527 N. Topping, Kansas City, Missouri 64123
2. Marriage Certificate of Husband and Wife, in possession of Vivian West Cerny, address above.
RESEARCH NOTES

Figure 8:2. Family Group Work Record, John Steve Cerny and
Vivian Elaine West.

My mother didn't possess any family records other than those pertaining to our immediate family members. She remembered her maternal grandmother, who she knew only as Alice Smith. However, she thought Bertha Ruth was adopted because of a family story that said her older sister, Greta Carroll West, was given Bertha's father's surname as a middle name. My mother also said that she couldn't remember her maternal grandfather because he died either before she was born or when she was very young. She did recall hearing that he was a Baptist minister.

Bertha Ruth Smith's memory was remarkably accurate for her age. During our interview, she provided the following information:

I was born 14 February 1889 in Kansas City, Missouri. My mother's name was Kate Carroll and I was told that she was a widow at the time of my birth. I was also told that my father's name was John Carroll and that he died in a mining accident in or near Rosedale, Kansas. He worked at the Argentine Mine in that area. My mother had tuberculosis and died shortly after my birth. She placed me in an orphanage before she died, a Catholic orphanage I think it was. A Mrs. Moore took me out of the orphanage shortly afterwards and gave me to the Smiths to raise.

I don't remember exactly how old I was when I went to live with the Smiths. It was probably 1890 or 1891. My adoptive parents were Thomas Albert Smith and Mary Alice Karr. Father was a Baptist minister and a farmer. He attended a theological seminary in Osawatomie, Kansas. I was never legally adopted, but they called me their adopted daughter.

Thomas Albert Smith, known as Albert most of his life, was born in New Lancaster, Kansas on 20 February 1862. His mother died when he was an infant and his father married her sister. I think dad's mother was Jane Pledger, but I'm not sure. His father was born in England and was also a minister. He died young. Dad had an older brother, George Andrew Smith, who I don't know much about. He also had a number of half-brothers and sisters, including Florence, Oscar, and Lizzie Smith. Dad died on 16 June 1924 at Xenia, Kansas.

Mary Alice Karr was called Alice. I named your Aunt Laura Alice after her and your grandfather's mother, Laura Stewart. Mother was born 5 October 1864 at New Lancaster, Kansas to Ambrose and Patsy Karr. My grandmother Patsy was a Huffman. Mother said Ambrose served in the Civil War and died in a logging accident when she was about three years old. Mary Alice had an older brother, James Marion, who was born the same day she was, only a year or two earlier. She also had a younger sister, Sadie, who married Ulysses S. Grant Prowell, a minister. Mother died 3 August 1947 at Fort Scott, Kansas and was buried with dad in the Bronson, Kansas cemetery not far from your grandfather's grave site.

After Ambrose died, my grandmother married her first husband's cousin whose name was Hopkins. They weren't married too many years when Patsy died. I don't recall who raised the children after that. James was sent to work on a cattle ranch in Texas, but he ran away and returned to New Lancaster. He married Emma Lane Smith, the ex-wife of George Andrew Smith, my father's brother. James and Emma had three sons, including one set of twins.

I married your grandfather on 30 April 1912 in Vinita, Oklahoma. My parents were opposed to the marriage so we eloped. Your grandfather was the son of William Andrew West and Laura Stewart. They had fifteen children, but four boys died at birth. Your Aunt Ida was the first child to survive. They had three other children who died in childhood, including Elmer and Emma, who were twins.

The information Bertha Ruth provided was transcribed onto the working lineage chart, and family group records were compiled. Since she was close to her adoptive parents, she asked that their ancestry be traced first. With my then limited research skills, that was an excellent choice. Tracing her natural parents during the period in which she was born required professional experience I didn't have. The working lineage chart and family group records are illustrated below with the information added from the interview with Bertha Ruth highlighted.

While the information given by Bertha Ruth Smith was detailed and plentiful, it couldn't stand alone. Given her age and the number of years that elapsed between the events and the date of the interview, the chance of error was great. Simply gathering names, dates, places, relationships, and events was not enough. Each piece of information she offered had to be verified in existing records.

SURVEY PHASE

Before launching into research, it is advisable to conduct a preliminary survey. Someone may have already accomplished research on the same lines you are trying to extend. It would be time consuming, costly, and perhaps unnecessary to reconstruct their research, especially if it was well documented.

The Genealogical Library of the LDS Church has compiled three major record collections: the International Genealogical Index (IGI), the Family Group Records Archives, and the Family History Collection. Each contains millions of names submitted by members of the Church of Jesus Christ of Latter-day Saints (Mormons). These collections are located in Salt Lake City and available on microfilm through their branch libraries.[1] (For a full description of these collections, see Chapter 3.)

Using these collections is often impossible if if you do not live near a major

---

1. Kory L. Meyerink provides an excellent chapter on these collections in Arlene Eakle and Johni Cerny, eds., *The Source: A Guidebook of American Genealogy* (Salt Lake City: Ancestry Publishing, 1984).

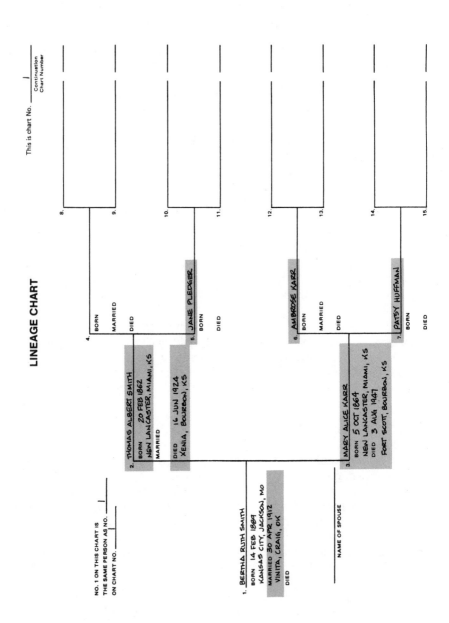

Figure 8:3. Lineage Work Chart 1, Bertha Ruth Smith.

FAMILY GROUP SHEET

HUS. THOMAS ALBERT SMITH — OCCUPATION(S)

- BORN 20 FEB 1862 — PLACE New Lancaster, Miami, Kansas
- CHR. — PLACE
- MARR.
- DIED 16 JUN 1924 — PLACE Xenia, Bourbon, Kansas
- BUR. — PLACE
- FATHER JANE PLEDGER — OTHER WIVES
- MOTHER

WIFE MARY ALICE KARR

- BORN 5 OCT 1864 — PLACE New Lancaster, Miami, Kansas
- CHR. — PLACE
- DIED 3 AUG 1947 — PLACE Fort Scott, Bourbon, Kansas
- BUR. — PLACE
- FATHER AMBROSE KARR — OTHER HUSBANDS
- MOTHER PATSY HUFFMAN

SEX	CHILDREN	DATE BORN / PLACE BORN	DATE MARRIED / TO	PLACE	DATE DIED / PLACE DIED
X F	1 BERTHA RUTH SMITH	14 FEB 1889 / Kansas City, Jackson, Missouri	30 APR 1912 / GROVER CLEVELAND WEST	Vinita, Craig, Oklahoma	
	2				
	3				
	4				
	5				
	6				
	7				
	8				
	9				
	10				

OTHER MARRIAGES

SOURCES OF INFORMATION
Oral interview with Bertha Ruth Smith West, 1966.

RESEARCH NOTES

Figure 8:4. Family Group Work Record, Thomas Albert Smith and Mary Alice Karr.

library or a branch of the Genealogical Library. There are firms which provide survey services in Salt Lake City for a fee of $10 to $25 per name and will usually fill your request within four to six weeks. Only ten to fifteen percent of those surveys completed have positive results, but if one of your ancestors is found, you could save years of research. It is well worth the fee in those instances. Many of the family group records and some of the IGI entries contain erroneous information, as do the family histories and genealogies. You should attempt to verify the poorly documented submissions and minimally spot check to determine the quality of the information. These records are excellent finding tools that will lead to previously unexplored areas of research.

When these major record collections were surveyed in 1966, there were no entries for the Smith or Karr ancestors of Bertha Ruth Smith. The bulk of information in these collections pertains to people born prior to 1850. It is a good practice to check these collections again once you have identified earlier generations of your family—especially if you have colonial New England ancestry.

THE FIRST GENERATION

BERTHA RUTH SMITH (1:1)

Not everyone will choose to conduct a survey and will instead begin original research into public and private records as soon as family and home sources have been searched. Original research into Bertha Ruth Smith's ancestry began after a careful study of the working lineage chart, family group record, and the contents of the oral interview. Each piece of information she gave and the different approaches to verifying each fact are listed.

Facts attesting to Bertha Ruth Smith's birth and marriage:

1. Name: Bertha Ruth Smith
2. Birthdate: 14 February 1889
3. Birthplace: Kansas City, Jackson County, Missouri
4. Marriage Date: 30 April 1912
5. Marriage Place: Vinita, Craig County, Oklahoma
6. Spouse: Grover Cleveland West

Records that could verify the facts attesting to Bertha Ruth Smith's birth and marriage:

1. Birth: Kansas City, Missouri registered births at the time Bertha Ruth was born. These early records are incomplete in that they do not always list the child's name. Since birth records are made at the time of the event, they are primary sources and should be obtained in every instance where they exist.

You will occasionally meet with resistance on the part of recordkeepers. This is particularly true when requesting records that are restricted under the provisions of the Privacy Act. As well, each state or city may have its own set of laws governing accessibility. Some jurisdictions will release information only to the person about whom it pertains if that person is still living. A notarized release from Bertha Ruth permitted me access to her birth record.

There was a birth record on file for an unnamed female child born 14 February 1889 in Kansas City, Jackson County, Missouri. While the father's name was not listed, the mother's name was Kate Carroll. This is not direct evidence that Bertha Ruth was the daughter of Kate Carroll; however, it is excellent circumstantial evidence when remembered that she was told her mother's name was Kate Carroll and that she was born 14 February 1889. Further, there was no other female child born on that date whose mother was identified as Kate Carroll. The circumstantial evidence is strong enough to support Bertha's birthdate, birthplace, and the identity of her natural mother.

2. Marriage: Proof of Bertha's marriage to Grover Cleveland West could be obtained in one of three ways: (1) locate her original marriage certificate among her personal papers, (2) visit the courthouse in Vinita, Craig County, Oklahoma, or (3) send a written request for a certified copy of their marriage record to the county clerk in Craig County, Oklahoma.

The original marriage certificate had been misplaced or lost many years earlier. Since I did not live near Craig County, it was impractical to request the document personally. (If you live close enough to visit a record repository, take advantage of your proximity, as most interested parties search the records more thoroughly and effectively than record clerks.) Therefore, a written request was sent to obtain a certified copy of the needed document. (See Chapter 2 for detailed instructions about preparing genealogical correspondence.)

The marriage record is direct evidence attesting to their identities, age at the time of their marriage, marriage date, and place of marriage. If their birthdates were unknown, the year of their birth could be inferred from their ages at the time the document was made. Bertha's marriage record offered the following facts: "Grover Cleveland West, age 27, married Bertha Ruth Smith, age 23, 30 April 1912 at Vinita, Craig County, Oklahoma."

At this point, attention is turned to Bertha's adoptive parents. While not legally adopted, she was raised by Thomas Albert Smith and Mary Alice Karr. If a legal adoption had taken place, it would be necessary to obtain court records attesting to adoption. Adoption records usually contain the identity of the child's natural parents. Bertha surely knew who raised her, so it was not necessary to document that fact. If Bertha had died and someone else had given the information, verification would be required. Her relationship to Albert and Alice Smith was verified in the 1900 U.S. Census of Blue Mound, Linn County, Kansas:

Name		Relationship	Birthdate	Birthplace
Smith,	Thomas A.	Head	Feb 1862	Kansas
	Mary A.	Wife	Oct 1864	Kansas
	Bertha R.	Adopted Dau	Feb 1889	Missouri

In the absence of court records attesting to Bertha's adoption, her relationship to Thomas A. and Mary A. Smith is corroborated by her presence in their 1900 household as an adopted daughter, lending further support to family tradition.

THE SECOND GENERATION

THOMAS ALBERT SMITH (1:2)
MARY ALICE KARR (1:3)

Let's return to verifying the oral interview. Focusing on Thomas Albert Smith and Mary Alice Karr, the following facts attesting to their identities and the events of their lives are given:

Thomas Albert Smith—aka Albert

1. Birthdate: 20 February 1862
2. Birthplace: New Lancaster, Miami County, Kansas
3. Deathdate: 16 June 1924
4. Deathplace: Xenia, Bourbon County, Kansas
5. Spouse: Mary Alice Karr
6. Mother: Jane Pledger
7. Father's Birthplace: England
8. Brother: George Andrew Smith
9. Half Brother and Sisters: Florence, Oscar, and Lizzie Smith
10. Occupation: Baptist Minister and Farmer
11. Buried: Bronson Cemetery, Bronson, Bourbon County, Kansas

Mary Alice Karr—aka Alice

1. Birthdate: 5 October 1864
2. Birthplace: New Lancaster, Miami County, Kansas
3. Deathdate: 3 August 1947
4. Deathplace: Fort Scott, Bourbon County, Kansas
5. Spouse: Thomas Albert Smith
6. Father: Ambrose Karr
7. Mother: Patsy Huffman
8. Brother: James Marion Karr
9. Sister: Sarah Jane Karr
10. Buried: Bronson Cemetery, Bronson, Bourbon County, Kansas

Records that could verify the information given about Thomas Albert Smith and Mary Alice Karr are: (1) death certificates, (2) marriage license, (3) census records, and (4) family Bible records.

Kansas did not register births when Albert and Alice were born. Their death records, then, would offer the most detailed genealogical information to verify the facts given by their daughter. Death records are maintained by states, counties, or towns/cities. Sometimes they can be found in more than one jurisdiction. Death records are maintained only by the state in Kansas. Certified copies of their death records were requested by correspondence. There is a fee which should be included with each request. (For a complete list of where to write for birth, marriage, and death records, see Appendix F of *The Source: A Guidebook of American Genealogy* or write to the Government Printing Office for a copy of *Where to Write for Vital Records,* U.S. Department of Health and Human Services Publication No. [PHS] 82-1142, 1984, price: $3. Record fees continually change and the prices listed in Publication No. [PHS] 82-1142 may be outdated. If you send the incorrect amount, you will be advised of the new fee.)

Death Certificate Information

Full Name:	Thomas Albert Smith	Mary Alice Smith
Place of Death:	Xenia, Bourbon County, Kansas	Fort Scott, Kansas
Date of Death:	16 June 1924	3 August 1947
Usual residence:	———	Bronson, Kansas
Sex:	Male	Female
Race:	White	White
Marital Status:	Married	Widowed
Name of Spouse:	M. A. Smith	Thomas A. Smith
Date of Birth:	20 February 1862	5 October 1864
Age:	62 yrs., 3 mos., 24 days	82 yrs., 10 mos., 28 days
Occupation:	Ministry	Housewife
Birthplace:	Kansas	New Lancaster, Kansas
Father:	John Smith	Ambrose Karr
Father's Birthplace:	England	Unknown
Mother:	Jane Pledger	Pattie Huffman
Mother's Birthplace:	Illinois	Unknown
Informant:	M. A. Smith	Bertha West
Informant's Address:	Xenia, Kansas	Kansas City, Missouri
Cause of Death:	Valvular Heart Disease	Intestinal Obstruction
Date of Burial:	18 June 1924	5 August 1947
Place of Burial:	Bronson Cemetery	Bronson Cemetery
Undertaker:	W. D. Viles, Bronson, Kansas	E. G. Daniel, Blue Mound, Kansas

Analysis: Information found recorded on the death certificates exactly matched the facts Bertha gave in the oral interview, a rare occurrence. Albert's death record provided new genealogical information—his father's name, John Smith, and his mother's birthplace, Illinois.

While no marriage date is stated, the document verifies that Albert and Alice were husband and wife. Death records contain both direct and circumstantial evidence. The following facts are direct evidence: name, place of death, sex, race, marital status, name of spouse, occupation, cause of death, place of burial, and date of burial. The remaining information is circumstantial, though Mary Alice and Bertha, as informants, lend greater credibility to its accuracy. If someone not closely related had provided the information, it would lessen that credibility.

There was no mention of Albert and Alice's marriage date or place in the oral interview. They were both reportedly born in New Lancaster, Miami County, Kansas. They lived in Bourbon, Allen, Linn, and possibly Wyandotte counties. If they did not marry in Miami County, then the other counties would have to be considered in tracking down their marriage record. Correspondence with the probate judge of Miami County, Kansas yielded this entry from *Marriage Record F*, page 80: "Thomas A. Smith and Alice M. Karr [sic] were joined in marriage the 30th day of April 1884 at New Lancaster, Kansas by C. F. Tracy, Justice of the Peace."

Only the death records attested Albert and Alice's birthdates. Other types of records can be searched for direct evidence to substantiate the circumstantial evidence in those death records, such as employment, insurance, driver's license, and pension records. They are excellent sources for birth information, especially if your ancestors lived well into the twentieth century. Alice and Albert were not found in any of those records. Their birth month and year were given only in the 1900 U.S. Census cited earlier, information that matched what was stated in their death records. Additional circumstantial evidence can be found in earlier census records.

Another source of early birth information is the family Bible. Thomas Albert Smith's father was a minister and kept a record of births, marriages, and deaths in his Bible:

> John Smith married Mary Jane Pledger May 6th 1856
> George Andrew Smith Born April 25 1857
> Thomas Albert Smith Born Feb 20 1862
> Mary Jane Smith died March 18 1862
> John Smith married Sarah Catherine Pledger March 26th 1865
> Florence Cecelia born Nov 26 1866
> Frances Wayland Smith born Dec 30th 1869
> Elizabeth Sarah Lucetta Smith born Dec 21 1871
> Martha May born May 23 1874
> David Oscar born 21 Oct 1876
> Sarah Catherine Smith Jones May 18 1887 age 38 yrs 9 mos 10 days

Analysis: It can be assumed this record was made as the events took place, as the Bible was published in 1850, prior to the first entry. Entries were made by at least three different people, the last of which was one of the children who recorded the death of Sarah Catherine Smith Jones, an entry that indicates she married a second time after her husband's death. The Bible record is a primary source that provides direct evidence of Thomas Albert Smith's birthdate and parentage. His wife's birthdate is supported only by the circumstantial evidence in her death certificate and the 1900 U.S. Census enumeration.

All new information taken from the death records, marriage record, census enumeration, and family Bible is added to the working lineage chart and family group records. Updated versions are shown below with additions in italics.

THE THIRD GENERATION

AMBROSE N. KARR (1:6)
MARTHA P. HUFFMAN (1:7)

From here we go on to search information about Mary Alice Karr's ancestry. Since this case study was designed to trace an American lineage, only her ancestry will be studied, leaving her husband's English ancestry for another publication.

Mary Alice Karr was the daughter of Ambrose Karr and Patsy Huffman. At this point only their names and possible birthplaces have been determined. According to Bertha's oral interview, her maternal grandparents died prior to death registration in Kansas, a point at which census records play an important part in compiling an American lineage.

The American population has been enumerated every ten years since 1790. Census records for the years 1790 to 1910 are available on microfilm at libraries all over the country and at Regional Federal Archives and Records Centers located in major cities. (The 1890 U.S. Census was destroyed and only fragments for a few locations exist.) Early census records contain only the names of heads of households and unnamed members of the household grouped according to age and sex. Beginning in 1850, census records list all members of a household by name, age, sex, race, and occupation. Relationship to the head of each household was included from 1880 to 1910. Census records from 1790 to 1850 have been indexed by Accelerated Indexing Systems, and while these indexes are useful in pinpointing the county of residence within each state for most of the country's early population, there is a perplexing error rate in each. (See Chapter 3 for an in-depth discussion of the AIS Index.) Some entries were missed during indexing and others incorrectly identifed when handwriting was misinterpreted or the entry too faded to read. When you do not find a person listed in a census index, do not assume they were not in the state or county where they were reportedly living. If you know

FAMILY GROUP SHEET

HUS. THOMAS ALBERT SMITH   OCCUPATION(S) BAPTIST MINISTER AND FARMER

BORN	20 FEB 1862	PLACE New Lancaster, Miami, Kansas
CHR.		PLACE
MARR.	30 APR 1884	PLACE New Lancaster, Miami, Kansas
DIED	16 JUN 1924	PLACE Xenia, Bourbon, Kansas
BUR.	18 JUN 1924	PLACE Bronson Cemetery, Bronson, Bourbon, Kansas
FATHER	JOHN SMITH	
MOTHER	MARY JANE PLEDGER	OTHER WIVES

WIFE MARY ALICE KARR

BORN	5 OCT 1864	PLACE New Lancaster, Miami, Kansas
CHR.		PLACE
DIED	3 AUG 1947	PLACE Fort Scott, Bourbon, Kansas
BUR.	6 AUG 1947	PLACE Bronson Cemetery, Bronson, Bourbon, Kansas
FATHER	AMBROSE N. KARR	
MOTHER	MARTHA P. HUFFMAN	OTHER HUSBANDS

SEX	CHILDREN	DATE BORN / PLACE BORN	DATE MARRIED / TO	PLACE	DATE DIED / PLACE DIED
1 X F	BERTHA RUTH SMITH	14 FEB 1889 / Kansas City, Jackson, Missouri	30 APR 1912 / GROVER CLEVELAND WEST	Vinita, Craig, Oklahoma	28 AUG 1972 / Kansas City, Jackson, MO
2					
3					
4					
5					
6					
7					
8					

OTHER MARRIAGES

SOURCES OF INFORMATION
1. Death Certificates, Dept. of Vital Statistics, State of Kansas.
2. Marriage Record, Marriage Book F, Miami County, Kansas, p. 80.
3. Marriage Record, Vinita, Craig County, Oklahoma.
4. 1900 U.S. Census, Blue Mound, Linn County, Kansas.
5. Family Bible Record, Rev. John Smith, Miami County, Kansas.
6. Obituary of Bertha Ruth Smith West, Kansas City Star, 30 August 1972.

Figure 8:5. Final Family Group Record, Thomas Albert Smith and Mary Alice Karr.

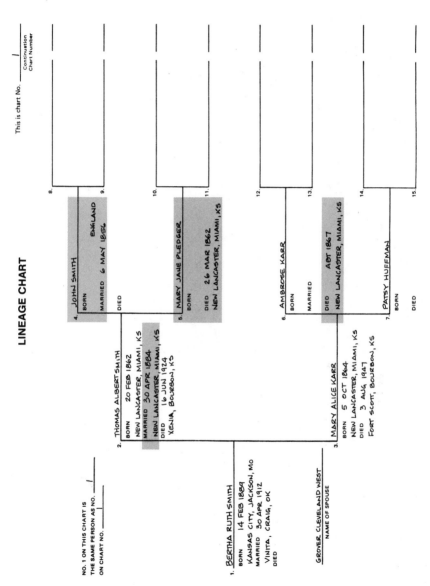

Figure 8:6. Lineage Work Chart 1, Bertha Ruth Smith.

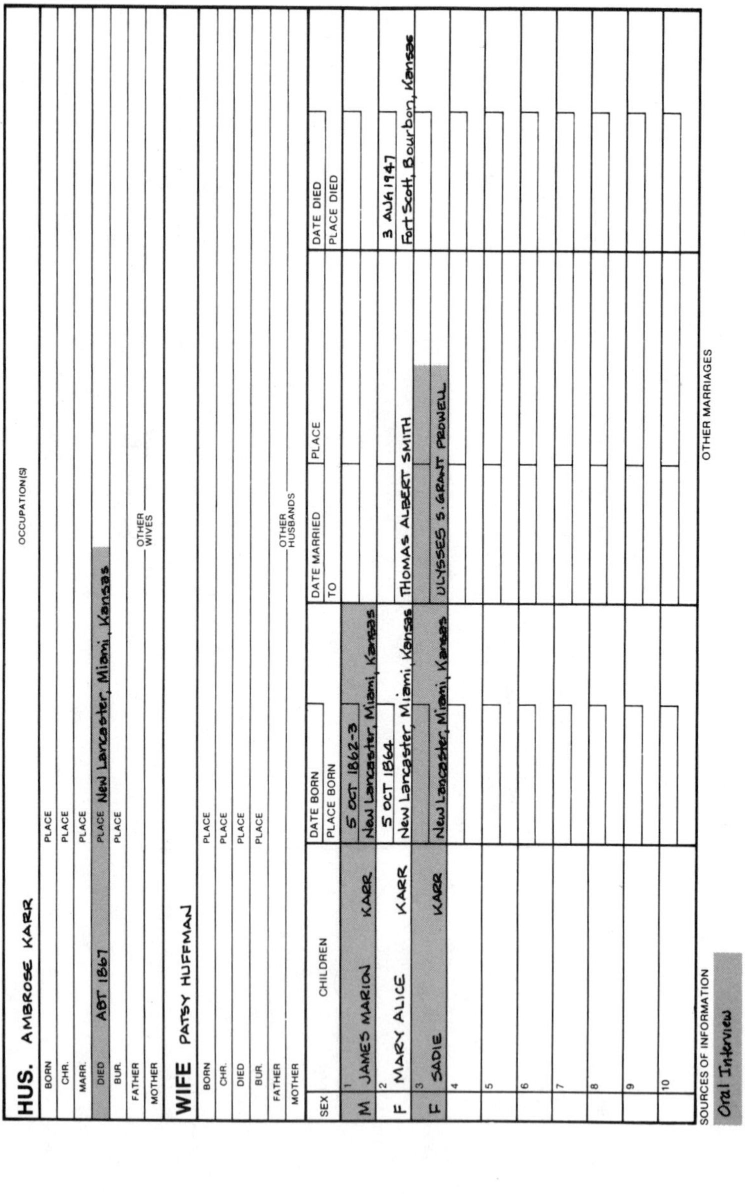

FAMILY GROUP SHEET

HUS.	AMBROSE KARR	OCCUPATION(S)
BORN		PLACE
CHR.		PLACE
MARR.		PLACE
DIED	ABT 1867	PLACE New Lancaster, Miami, Kansas
BUR.		PLACE
FATHER		OTHER WIVES
MOTHER		
WIFE	PATSY HUFFMAN	
BORN		PLACE
CHR.		PLACE
DIED		PLACE
BUR.		PLACE
FATHER		OTHER HUSBANDS
MOTHER		

SEX	CHILDREN	DATE BORN / PLACE BORN	DATE MARRIED / TO	PLACE	DATE DIED / PLACE DIED
M	1 JAMES MARION KARR	5 OCT 1862-3 New Lancaster, Miami, Kansas			
F	2 MARY ALICE KARR	5 OCT 1864 New Lancaster, Miami, Kansas	THOMAS ALBERT SMITH		3 AUG 1947 Fort Scott, Bourbon, Kansas
F	3 SADIE KARR	New Lancaster, Miami, Kansas	ULYSSES S. GRANT PROWELL		
	4				
	5				
	6				
	7				
	8				
	9				
	10				

SOURCES OF INFORMATION: Oral Interview

OTHER MARRIAGES

RESEARCH NOTES

Figure 8:7. Family Group Work Record, Ambrose N. Karr and Martha P. Huffman.

the county they were living in when the census was taken, conduct a house-by-house search of that county before abandoning that locality. This approach is useful in rural counties, but can rarely be employed in metropolitan areas. Before starting a house-by-house search of a city the size of New York, use city directories to find an address and narrow the search to a smaller area.

Professional genealogists usually conduct census studies of a family or a surname in a given area. At this point in research, for example, the known facts about Mary Alice Karr's parents are meager. She was the daughter of Ambrose Karr and Patsy Huffman, both of whom died while she was a child. How many Karr and Huffman families lived in Miami County, Kansas and how were they related to her parents? Were any of those families headed by couples old enough to have been their parents? The answer to these questions is obtainable in census records. A census study will provide a wealth of information about everyone in Miami County with the Karr and Huffman surnames. Census studies usually begin with the most recent census available and move back to earlier enumerations, extracting each entry listed for the surnames of interest. Mary Alice had already been located in the 1900 census that reported she was born in October 1864 in Kansas and her parents were born in Iowa. When the 1880 census was taken she was fifteen years old and an orphan. The 1880 census soundex (index) lists only those families with children under eleven years of age. On the chance that she was living in a household with younger children, the 1880 soundex was searched for all Karr families living in Kansas. Mary Alice was listed neither under her full name nor as Alice Karr.

Ambrose and Patsy Karr may have lived in Miami County when the 1860 U.S. Census was taken. They may have been married or they may have been living in their parents' homes. Miami County was formerly Lykins County, and it was under this name that Miami County was included in the 1860 census of Kansas:

Dwelling Number	Name	Age	Sex	Color	Occupation	Birthplace
#703	Ambrose Karr	23	M	W	Farmer	Indiana
	Martha Karr	20	F	W		Indiana

The only other Karr family living in Miami Township, Lykins County, Kansas in 1860 was located one dwelling away from Ambrose and Martha Karr:

#701	William Karr	46	M	W	Farmer	Indiana
	Amanda Karr	44	F	W		Kentucky
	James Karr	17	M	W		Indiana
	Elihu Karr	16	M	W		Indiana
	Sarah Karr	12	F	W		Iowa
	Henry Karr	10	M	W		Iowa
	William Karr	8	M	W		Iowa

1860 CENSUS – UNITED STATES

State: KANSAS County: LYKINS Township/Town, etc.: MIAMI Post Office: PAOLA

Page	Dwelling number	Family number	The Name of every person whose usual place of abode on the first day of June, 1860 was in this family.	Age	Sex	Color	Profession, Occupation or Trade	Real Estate	Personal Estate	Place of birth	Married within year	Attended school	Persons 20 or older who cannot read or write	Whether deaf and dumb, insane, idiotic, pauper or convict
	1	2	3	4	5	6	7	8	9	10	11	12	13	14
92	703	703	AMBROSE KARR	23	M	W	FARMER	400	250	INDIANA				
			MARTHA "	20	F					INDIANA				
91	701	701	WILLIAM KARR	46	M	W	FARMER	1600	600	INDIANA				
			AMANDA "	44	F	W				KENTUCKY				
			JAMES "	17	M	W				INDIANA		✓		
			ELIHU "	16	M	W				INDIANA		✓		
			SARAH "	12	F	W				IOWA		✓		
			HENRY "	10	M	W				IOWA		✓		
			WILLIAM "	8	M	W				IOWA				

Figure 8:8. 1860 U.S. Census, Miami Township, Lykins County, Kansas.

Ambrose Karr's real estate was valued at $400 and William's at $1600.

Analysis: William and Amanda Karr were old enough to have a twenty-three-year-old son in 1860. They were also past residents of Indiana where Ambrose was born. They were one-time residents of Iowa, the state in which Mary Alice believed her father was born when the 1900 census was taken. The Karr family's migration pattern is also established in the census entries: Indiana, 1814-1844; Iowa, 1848-1858; and Kansas, 1860.

There were only two Huffman families living in the same area when the 1860 census was taken:

Dwelling Number	Name	Age	Sex	Color	Occupation	Birthplace
#671	William Huffman	45	M	W	UBN	Ohio
	Lewvisa Huffman	19	F	W		Indiana
	Gabriel M. Huffman	17	M	W		Indiana
	Franklin H. Huffman	15	M	W		Indiana
	Angeline Huffman	10	F	W		Illinois
	Jonas Huffman	6	M	W		Iowa
	Charles L. Huffman	4	M	W		Iowa
	Elam S. Huffman	2	M	W		Kansas Terr.
	Susan D. Huffman	1/12	F	W		Kansas Terr.
	Alice Huffman	44	F	W		N. Carolina
#680	Andrew J. Huffman	24	M	W		Indiana
	Margaret I. Huffman	20	F	W		Pennsylvania
	Mortimer G. Huffman	6/12	M	W		Kansas Terr.

William Huffman owned property valued at $600.

William Huffman's census entry departs from the norm. Ordinarily, the husband's entry is followed directly by his wife's and then the children are listed by descending age. Alice Huffman, in whose memory Mary Alice Karr was named, is listed last. As later research showed, Alice Huffman died a few days prior to the census enumerator's arrival. Census schedules were supposed to record only living household members. Those who died during the census year were recorded in mortality schedules. There are also instances when families list all of their children, even those no longer living at home. In those cases you will find two entries for the same person.

Looking closely at the Karr and Huffman families in the census entries, you will note that there are significant gaps in the ages of the children. Women living in the nineteenth century gave birth, on the average, every twenty-four months. When there are greater time periods between the birth of two children, it is possible that a child is living outside the home or that a child died at birth or between census enumerations. Missing children may be found in earlier enumerations.

William and Alice Huffman were old enough to be the parents of both Andrew J. Huffman and Martha P. Karr. They were also past residents of Indiana, where both Andrew and Martha were born. They were also residents of Iowa, the state in which Mary Alice believed her mother was born. The Huffman family's migration pattern is also established by the census entries: Ohio, 1815-?; Indiana, 1836-1845; Illinois, 1850; and Iowa, 1854-1856.

Based on the 1860 census entries for the Karr and Huffman families William and Amanda Karr are the primary candidates for Ambrose Karr's parents, while William and Alice Huffman are the primary candidates for Martha P. Huffman's parents. Those relationships must be proven by evidence from other records, however.

Census records often contain errors and should be used primarily as leads to further research. There are instances when a census record is the only one that can be found for a person or family. In that case, your family record will be based on purely circumstantial evidence. Census information should always be supported by other evidence whenever other records exist.

Moving to the 1870 U.S. Census of Miami County, Kansas, Ambrose Karr's family was located in Miami Township:

Dwelling Number	Name	Age	Sex	Occupation	Birthplace
#72	Martha P. Karr	30	F	Keeping House	Indiana
	James Karr	8	M		Kansas
	Alice Karr	6	F		Kansas
	Sarah Karr	2	F		Kansas

The census suggests that Martha P. Karr was widowed between 1867 and 1870 which agrees with Bertha's oral interview statement that Mary Alice's father died when she was about three years old.

By 1880, the Karr children were obviously orphans. They were all too old to be listed in the 1880 census soundex if they were not living in households with younger children. A house-by-house search of the 1880 U.S. Census of Miami County found the girls living in separate households. Alice Karr was listed with William Karr in Osage Township as his fifteen-year-old granddaughter. Sadie Carr [sic] was living with David and Susannah Smith as their fourteen-year-old adopted daughter in Louisberg, Miami County, Kansas. James Marion Karr was not living in Miami County when the 1880 census was taken and may have been in Texas as Bertha stated in her oral interview.

This concluded the census study for Ambrose and Martha Karr's family. The study continues with the fourth generation, following the William Huffman and William Karr families in each census from 1840 to 1900 when they moved west from Indiana to Iowa and Kansas.

Now that there are circumstantial facts to work with, research begins in earnest to find as much as possible about Ambrose Karr and Martha P. Huffman, including birthdates, places of birth, date and place of marriage, children's birth data, and any historical facts available.

The Genealogical Library of the LDS Church has ambitiously filmed county records all over the United States, especially those in states east of the Mississippi River. Some filming has been done in western states and the Genealogical Library has camera crews in several locations at this time. They film birth, marriage, death, probate, and land records, and special record collections are sometimes included. Microfilm copies of these records are available in Salt Lake City and through branch libraries.

The Genealogical Library has yet to film Kansas county records. This case study was chosen specifically to illustrate how research is accomplished without needed records at your fingertips. Once the families are moved out of Kansas, the Genealogical Library's microfilm collection of county records will play an important role in research.

Unless you happen to live in the same place your ancestors lived for generations, you will not be able to trace your ancestry without writing letters. Corresponding with county clerks, probate judges, and clergymen will grow more important as oral tradition diminishes. Care must be taken in letter writing. (See the section on genealogical correspondence in Chapter 2 for helpful ideas.)

Once the initial part of the census study was completed, several letters were dispatched to Miami County, Kansas to obtain more information and records. As they were answered, the information received had to be analyzed for content and accuracy.

The first response was to a request for a search of the New Lancaster Cemetery and of the inscriptions on those tombstones belonging to the Karr and Huffman families. A later trip to Miami County permitted photographing the tombstones. Photographs are always preferable to copying the information on a tombstone; however, some stones are worn and cannot be read in a photograph. For those badly weathered, rubbings can be made by placing newsprint against the inscription and rubbing charcoal or some other soft substance over the paper, outlining the engraving.

Ambrose and Martha Karr's tombstone in the New Lancaster Cemetery was not placed there at the time of their death. The stone was marble and stood out from older ones made of a softer, sandstone-like substance. Their tombstone gave the family name, Karr, and given names and dates: Ambrose N., 1838-1867 and Martha P., 1839-1877.

The second response came from the probate judge of Miami County and included a copy of Ambrose Karr's probate packet. A probate record can consist of several types of documents, such as letters of administration, bonds, inventories, bills of sale, periodic accountings made by the administrator, and court actions involving the care of a widow and minor children, such as guard-

ianship papers. Most of the documents in a probate packet contain little genealogical information yet they still have historical value and, like census records,
often contain important clues to research elsewhere. You must be specific when
requesting probate records, stating exactly those records you desire. If there
are numerous documents in a file, obtaining the entire packet will be costly.
When your budget is limited, request a description of the documents in the
file and the cost of a photocopy of each document, then choose only those
documents containing the information you need. Professional genealogists
prefer to review all documents and court entries involved in administering an
estate because court clerks are not always able to determine what is or is
not of importance to a genealogical research problem.

Ambrose Karr's probate record was requested to obtain additional facts
about his death. Rarely will a probate record attest to a deceased person's
birth, but it may list birth information about minor heirs. His probate record
provided the following important information:

1. William Karr was made administrator of Ambrose Karr's estate
on 3 September 1867 by the probate court of Miami County, Kansas.

2. Ambrose left as his heirs, Pattie Karr, widow, and James Karr,
age four years, Alice Karr, age two years, and Sarah Karr, age nine months,
residing in Miami County at the time of his death in or about August 1867
at New Lancaster.

3. Martha P. Hopkins petitioned the court on 10 March 1872 for
her third of her late husband's estate. The petition states that Ambrose
died on 13 August 1867, leaving as his heirs, the petitioner, his widow,
and the following minor heirs: James, Mary Alice, and Sarah Jane, each
under age fourteen.

The remaining documents in the packet refer to payment of Ambrose's
debts, an inventory of his estate, and William Karr's reports to the court.
Ambrose's property was not sold to satisfy his debts, but some of his personal property was sold at a public sale. The personal property of deceased
ancestors is often purchased by family members. It is a good practice to review
carefully bills of sale to note the names of those who puchased items belonging to the estate. Then look into other records to determine the relationship
of the buyers to the deceased. Many difficult research problems have been
solved in this manner. It is also important to scrutinize the administrators of
an estate carefully because they are usually related to the deceased or close
personal friends who may have migrated from one place to another with the
deceased.

Let's examine each piece of information of genealogical interest in the probate record. First, William Karr is the administrator of the estate. There were
two William Karrs living in Miami County in 1860: William Karr, grandfather
of Alice Karr in the 1880 census and thus Ambrose Karr's father, and Wil-

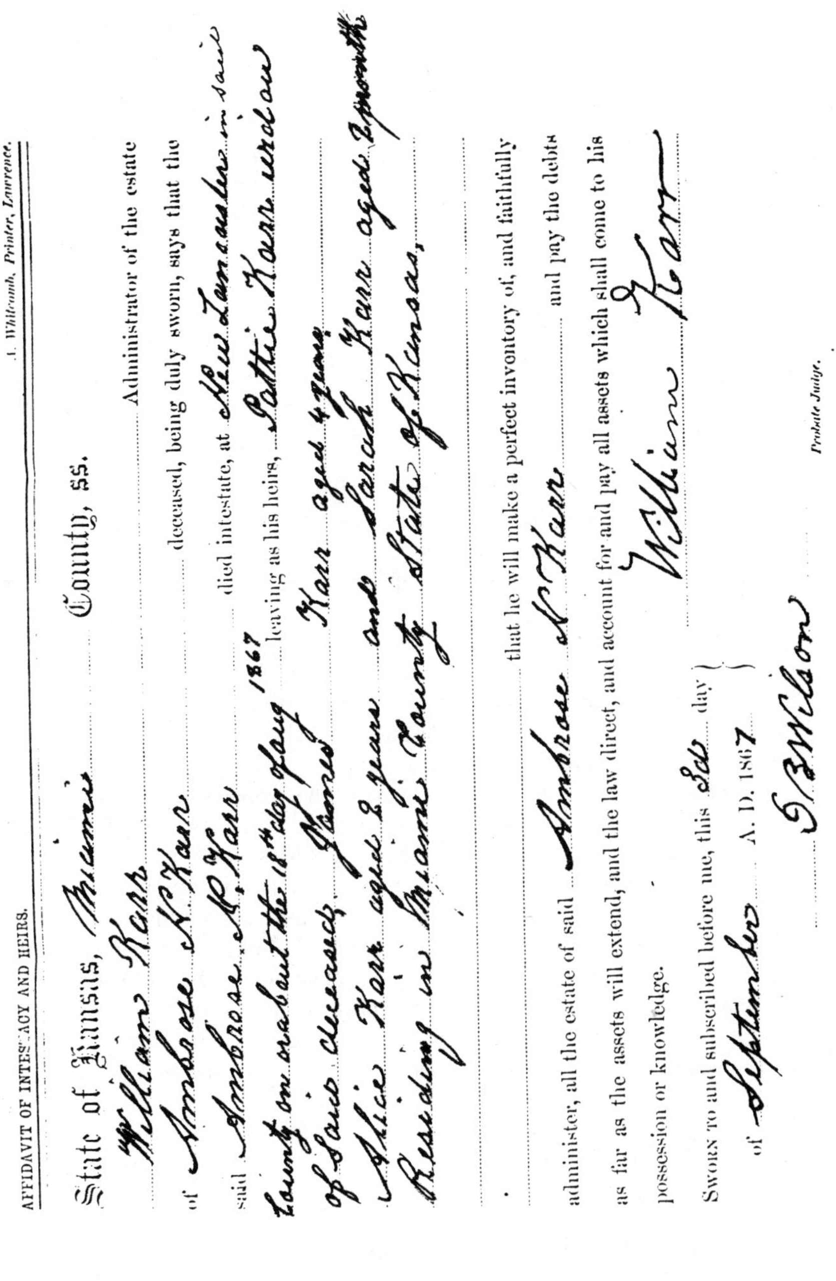

AFFIDAVIT OF INTESTACY AND HEIRS.

A. Whitcomb, Printer, Lawrence.

State of Kansas, Miami .... County, ss.

William Karr .... Administrator of the estate

of .... Ambrose N. Karr .... deceased, being duly sworn, says that the

said .... Ambrose N. Karr .... died intestate, at New Lancaster in said

County on or about the 18th day of Aug. *1867*

.... leaving as his heirs, ... Pattie Karr widow

of said deceased. James .... Karr aged 4 years,

Alice Karr aged 2 years and .... Sarah .... Karr aged 2 months

Residing in Miami County, State of Kansas,

.... that he will make a perfect inventory of, and faithfully

administer, all the estate of said .... Ambrose N Karr .... and pay the debts

as far as the assets will extend, and the law direct, and account for and pay all assets which shall come to his

possession or knowledge.

William Karr

Sworn to and subscribed before me, this 3d day

of ..... September .... A. D. 1867

G B Wilson

Probate Judge.

Figure 8:9. Affidavit of Intestacy and Heirs, Estate of Ambrose N. Karr, dated 3 September 1867, Miami County, Kansas.

liam's eight-year-old son William. The court would not permit a fifteen-year-old to administer an estate, leaving only William Karr Sr., father of the deceased, as administrator of his son's estate.

The record lists Ambrose Karr's death date in two separate documents as 13 August 1867. One document states that he died at New Lancaster. Two documents identify his children by name and one includes their ages at the time of his death. Each piece of information about the children agrees with oral testimony of Bertha Ruth Smith.

The petition tells us indirectly that Martha P. Karr remarried before 10 March 1872. She is identified in the document made that day as Martha P. Hopkins. Bertha Ruth stated that her grandmother married her husband's cousin, a Hopkins, after Ambrose died. This important clue suggests that Amanda Karr's maiden name may have been Hopkins. If not, then one of William's or Amanda's sisters married a Hopkins, important information in either case.

Guardianship papers are maintained as separate records in Miami County. Other locations include them with the probate packet or among the daily court actions recorded in probate journals. There were several entries in the probate journals of Miami County pertaining to the guardianship of the Karr children.

The first entry, dated 23 March 1871, stated that Mrs. Patsy Hopkins, mother of James, Mary Alice, and Sarah Karr, asked the court to appoint William Hopkins, her husband, guardian of the children and their estate. The next, dated 5 August 1878, stated that William Karr asked the court to revoke the guardianship granted to William Hopkins who apparently moved out of Kansas. William Karr thus became the legal guardian of his grandchildren. A final entry, dated 7 May 1883, stated that W. H. Ellis was appointed guardian of the three children. Could William Karr have died around this time?

One primary reason for searching the guardianship papers was to see if they mentioned William Huffman as the children's grandfather. While they did not mention him, interesting facts are learned. First, William Hopkins was named as Martha's second husband. The second entry was dated after Martha's death in 1877 (recorded on her tombstone) and suggests that William Hopkins abandoned the children after his wife's death. Then there is the 1883 entry making W. H. Ellis the guardian of all three children just a few months prior to James Karr's twenty-first birthday. William Karr was only sixty-nine when the document was written and may have died, but no reason was stated for the change in guardianship. Later research revealed that he had moved to Wichita, where his daughter, Sarah, was living.

The last census in which Martha P. Karr appeared was the 1875 Kansas State Census. Many states compiled census information for their own purpose halfway between the federal census enumerations. Kansas took its own census every ten years from 1855 to 1895. These records were only available at the Kansas State Historical Library in Topeka when research into the Karr

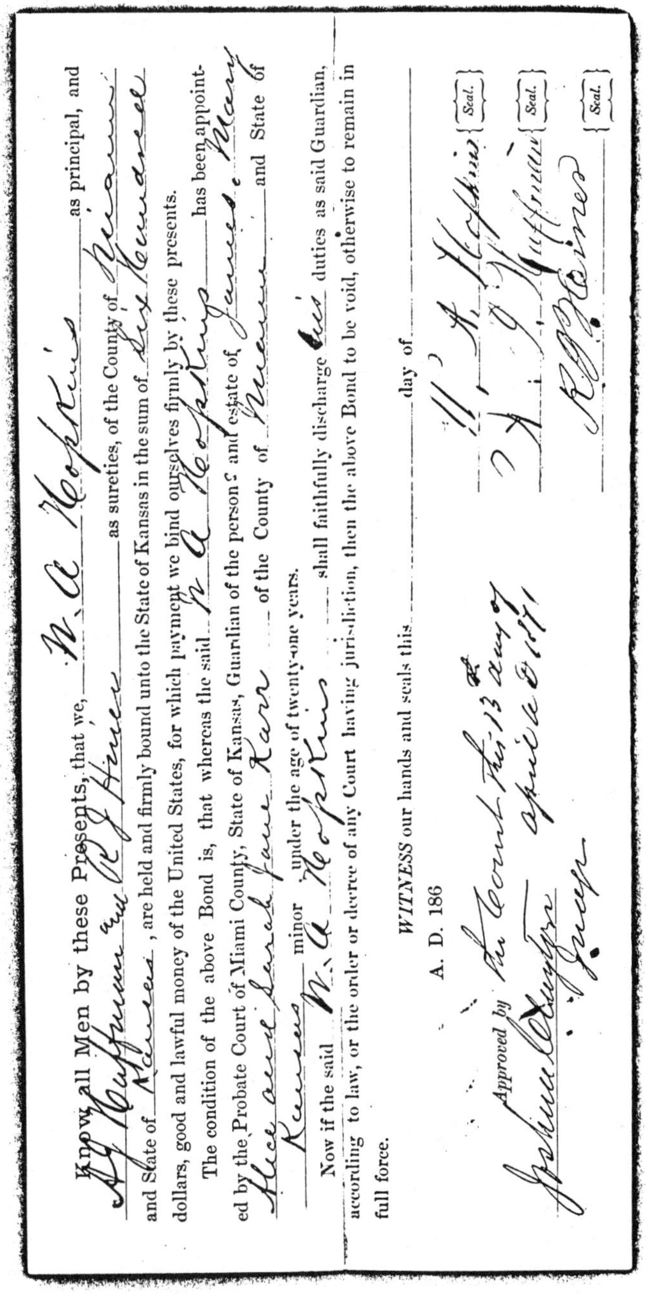
Know all Men by these Presents, that we, W. A. Hopkins as principal, and A J Huffman and R J Hines as sureties, of the County of Miami and State of Kansas, are held and firmly bound unto the State of Kansas in the sum of Six Hundred dollars, good and lawful money of the United States, for which payment we bind ourselves firmly by these presents.

The condition of the above Bond is, that whereas the said W A Hopkins has been appointed by the Probate Court of Miami County, State of Kansas, Guardian of the persons and estate of James, Mary Alice and Sarah Jane Karr of the County of Miami and State of Kansas minor under the age of twenty-one years.

Now if the said W. A Hopkins shall faithfully discharge his duties as said Guardian, according to law, or the order or decree of any Court having jurisdiction, then the above Bond to be void, otherwise to remain in full force.

WITNESS our hands and seals this day of A. D. 186

W. A. Hopkins {Seal.}
A. J. Huffman {Seal.}
R J Hines {Seal.}

Approved by the Court this 13th day of April AD 1871
Joshua Clayton
Judge

Figure 8:10. Guardianship Bond, Minor Heirs of Ambrose N. Karr, dated 13 April 1871, Miami County, Kansas.

family was being conducted. They have since been microfilmed and are available through the Genealogical Library of the LDS Church. Since Bertha Ruth was still living in Kansas City, Missouri, I spent Christmas there in 1967 and used some of that visit to travel to Miami County and to the Kansas State Historical Library. Further research could have been accomplished by correspondence, but that can be time consuming, and record collections exist that one wouldn't know about without visiting the repository or courthouse.

The probate judge of Miami County is responsible for probate and marriage records. The clerk of the court permitted me to examine the records at my leisure without charge, except for photocopying. According to *Marriage Book A*, page 216 of the Miami County, Kansas marriage records, Ambrose Carr [sic] and Patsie Huffman were married 26 May 1859 by William Huffman, father of the bride and minister of the gospel in New Lancaster. Her second marriage was recorded on page 385 of *Marriage Book B*, stating that William Hopkins, age twenty-two, married Patsie Karr, age thirty, on 4 March 1871 in New Lancaster. Other marriage records pertaining to the Karr and Huffman families were also extracted during the search of original records and will be discussed in the study of the fourth generation of Bertha Ruth Smith's ancestry.

The last census enumerating Ambrose Karr was the 1865 Kansas State Census of Miami Township, Miami County, taken 4 August 1865. That census was searched in its original form at the Kansas State Historical Library:

Dwelling Number	Name	Age	Sex	Occupation	Birthplace
#438	Ambrose Carr	26	M	Farmer	Indiana
	M. A. Carr	24	F		Indiana
	J. M. Carr	1	M		Kansas
	Alice Carr	3/12	F		Kansas

The only discrepancy in the census is Alice's age. She was born in October 1864 and was nine or ten months old when the census was taken. The enumeration further supports earlier entries stating that Ambrose and Martha were born in Indiana instead of Iowa as their daughter stated in the 1900 census.

The last census enumerating Martha P. Karr was taken by the State of Kansas in 1875 in Miami Township, Miami County:

Dwelling Number	Name	Age	Sex	Birthplace	Residence Prior to Kansas
#2	W. A. Hopkins	26	M	Iowa	Iowa
	Martha P. Hopkins	35	F	Indiana	Iowa
	James Marion Karr	12	M	Kansas	Kansas
	Mary A. Karr	10	F	Kansas	Kansas

| Sarah Jane Karr | 7 | F | Kansas | Kansas |
| J. M. Martin | 23 | M | Illinois | Missouri |

While these enumerations provide no new information, they do offer additional circumstantial evidence to support the lineage. If the Huffman family's residence prior to living in Kansas was unknown, this census enumeration is invaluable in directing research to Iowa.

Newspapers are also an important source of genealogical information. While early obituary notices are not as detailed as those written today, they do offer important details about the lives of deceased ancestors. The existing issues of the *Miami Republican* were searched for reference to Ambrose Karr and Martha P. Karr Hopkins. The following notice appeared on page 3 of the 30 June 1877 edition:

> Hopkins, Martha P. – died on Friday the 15th [June], the wife of W. A. Hopkins.

Another source of primary importance is property records. At this point, one must move the Karr family out of Kansas and into Iowa and Indiana to at least establish the Indiana county in which Ambrose Karr was born. Prior to census indexes, land records were heavily used to show family movement from one place back to an earlier residence. Using land records to establish a prior residence is still necessary in time periods prior to the advent of the census in 1790.

William Thorndale's chapter "Land and Tax Records" in *The Source: A Guidebook of American Genealogy* opens stating:

> Land records provide two types of important evidence for the genealogist. First, they often state kinship ties, especially when a group of heirs jointly sell some inherited land. Second, they place individuals in a specific time and place, allowing the researcher to sort people and families into neighborhoods and closely related groups.[2]

There were only two Karr families in Miami County and they were easily identified in other record sources. Property records were not needed to sort out families in this instance. They were consulted, rather, in an attempt to determine where the Karr family lived in Iowa prior to 1860.

The first deed recorded in Miami County by Ambrose Karr was dated 12 May 1865, several years after his family arrived in the area. The deed, however, was interesting: Kishecoquah, a member of the reserve of the Miami Indians of Kansas, sold Ambrose a piece of land for $200. This is slightly con-

---

2. Arlene Eakle and Johni Cerny, eds., *The Source: A Guidebook of American Genealogy* (Salt Lake City: Ancestry Publishing, 1984), p. 217.

fusing because Ambrose Karr stated that he owned $400 worth of property in the 1860 census. There should have been an earlier deed.

The source of his initial land acquisition was found in a later property record: United States to Martha P. Karr, Patent; Homestead Certificate No. 107, Application 41 which explained that she received a patent showing ownership of land in the public domain for having met homestead requirements. The patent was dated 5 January 1869 and was recorded in the District Land Office in Topeka, Kansas. The property Ambrose Karr "owned" probably represented the land he was homesteading. He had no legal title to it in 1860.

Homestead application files contain information of greater genealogical value than the average deed or patent, including the homestead application, proof of homesteading, and other documents. The final-proof documents give the claimant's name, age, and post office address, description of the tract and the house, the date the claimant took up residence, the number and relationship of the members of the family, and note citizenship, crops, acres under cultivation, and testimony of witnesses. These files are in the custody of the National Archives or one of the Regional Federal Archives and Records Centers. If you need to locate a homestead file, check the summary for the state at the end of William Thorndale's chapter in *The Source* to determine where that state's records have been deposited.

Miami County property records did not disclose where Ambrose Karr lived prior to his residence there, nor did the deeds filed for his father. Moving a family from one state to another is challenging, especially in a period for which census indexes do not exist. There were no 1850 census indexes when this research was conducted and no clues in Miami County records to the Karr family's residence in Iowa, nor to the family's residence in Indiana where Ambrose was born. It was necessary to determine their residence in Iowa in order to search records that might lead to their Indiana home.

One approach to finding out where they were from would be to trace William Karr's children to determine where they died and then request their death certificates. Those children, however, left the Miami County area without leaving a trail. The approach taken to finding the Karr family in Iowa, then, was to search each county systematically in the 1850 census, a time-consuming and tedious search that should not be considered until all other avenues have been closed. That search takes us to the study of the fourth generation of Bertha Ruth Smith's ancestry.

THE FOURTH GENERATION

WILLIAM A. KARR (6:1)

Before continuing research into William A. Karr's family, let's study the work lineage chart and family group record to see exactly what is known and then construct a research design.

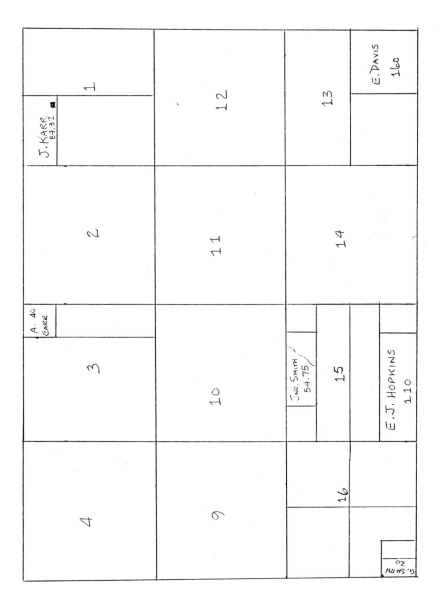

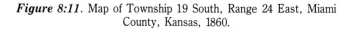

Figure 8:11. Map of Township 19 South, Range 24 East, Miami County, Kansas, 1860.

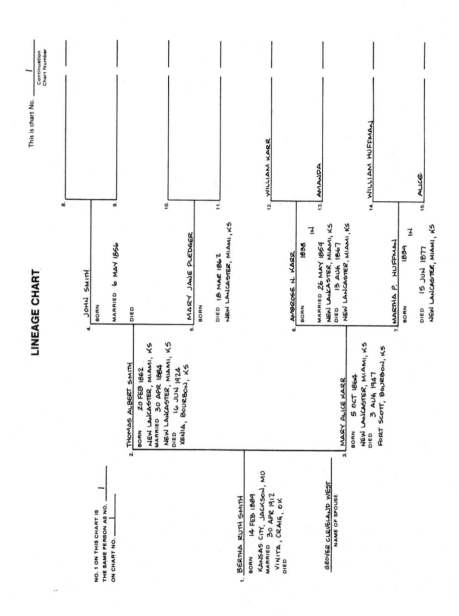

Figure 8:12. Lineage Work Chart 1, Bertha Ruth Smith.

FAMILY GROUP SHEET

HUS. AMBROSE N. KARR   **OCCUPATION(S)** FARMER

	DATE	PLACE
BORN	1838	Indiana
CHR		
MARR	26 May 1859	New Lancaster, Miami, Kansas
DIED	13 Aug 1867	New Lancaster Cemetery, New Lancaster, Miami, Kansas
BUR		

FATHER WILLIAM KARR
MOTHER AMANDA
OTHER WIVES

WIFE MARTHA P. HUFFMAN

	DATE	PLACE
BORN	1839	Indiana
CHR		
DIED	15 JUN 1877	New Lancaster, Miami, Kansas
BUR		New Lancaster Cemetery, New Lancaster, Miami, Kansas

FATHER WILLIAM HUFFMAN
MOTHER ALICE
OTHER HUSBANDS

SEX	CHILDREN	DATE BORN / PLACE BORN	DATE MARRIED / TO	PLACE	DATE DIED / PLACE DIED
1 M	JAMES MARION KARR	5 OCT 1862, New Lancaster, Miami, Kansas	30 APR 1884 EMMA JANE SMITH	New Lancaster, Miami, KS	28 AUG 1941, New Lancaster, Miami, Kansas
x 2 F	MARY ALICE KARR	5 OCT 1864, New Lancaster, Miami, Kansas	THOMAS ALBERT SMITH	New Lancaster, Miami, KS	3 AUG 1947, Fort Scott, Bourbon, Kansas
3 F	SARAH JANE KARR	31 DEC 1866, New Lancaster, Miami, Kansas	24 APR 1888 ULYSSES S. GRANT PREWELL		12 MAR 1966, Louisburg, Miami, Kansas
4					
5					
6					
7					
8					

SOURCES OF INFORMATION

1. Death Records of children, State of Kansas.
2. Marriage Records, Miami County, Kansas.
3. Tombstone Inscriptions, New Lancaster Cemetery, Miami County, Kansas.
4. Probate Records of Ambrose N. Karr, Miami County, Kansas.
5. Guardianship Records, Probate Court, Miami County, Kansas.
6. Death Notice, Miami Republican, 22 JUNE 1877.
7. 1880 U.S. Census, Miami County, Kansas

8. 1870 U.S. Census, Miami Twp., Miami County, Kansas.
9. 1860 U.S. Census, Miami Twp., Lykins County, Kansas.
10. 1865 Kansas State Census, Miami County, Kansas.
11. 1875 Kansas State Census, Miami County, Kansas.

Figure 8:13. Family Group Work Record, Ambrose N. Karr and Martha P. Huffman.

Available Information

1. 1860 U.S. Census of Lykins, Miami County, Kansas: a. William Karr was born about 1814 in Indiana. b. Amanda Karr was born about 1816 in Kentucky. c. Ambrose, James, and Elihu Karr were born in Indiana between 1838 and 1844. d. William's family moved to Iowa between 1844 and 1848, a fact deduced from Sarah Karr's 1848 birth in Iowa. e. Henry and Eldridge Karr were born in Iowa between 1850 and 1852. f. William's family moved to Miami County, Kansas after 1852.

2. Ambrose N. Karr's marriage record states that he married on 26 May 1859, implying that the family moved to Miami County between 1852 and 1859.

3. 1880 U.S. Census of Miami County, Kansas: a. William Karr was born about 1814 in Pennsylvania. b. William's wife is Margaret Karr, who was born about 1826 in Virginia, indicating that Amanda Karr had died and he married a second time. c. William Karr's father was born in Ireland and his mother in Pennsylvania.

RESEARCH PLAN

1. Locate William Karr's family in the 1850 U.S. Census of Iowa to determine a county of residence in that state. County histories and other public records may lead to identifying the family's residence in Indiana and details about William Karr's family.

2. While research continues on any family line it is always wise to recheck the International Genealogical Index and Family Group Records Archives (FGRA) to see if they mention newly identified ancestors. It is also a good practice to check regularly some of the many surname registries where genealogists have registered the ancestors they are seeking. (See Chapter 4 for a list of known registries.) Recheck the IGI and FGRA and begin checking registries for the Karr surname.

3. Attempt to locate living descendants of William Karr who might have information about his family and their early origins.

Searching Iowa's 1850 census on a house-by-house basis for William Karr's family was not a pleasant task. This search took place before the research trip to the Kansas State Historical Library. Had it been delayed until later, it would have been unnecessary. Five full rolls of microfilm were searched before William's family was found in Summit Township, Marion County, Iowa:

Dwelling Number	Name	Age	Sex	Occupation	Birthplace
#649	William Karr	37	M	Farmer	Indiana
	Amanda P. Karr	36	F		Kentucky
	Ambrose Karr	12	M		Indiana

Matthew Karr	11	M	Indiana
James W. Karr	6	M	Indiana
Elihu A. Karr	4	M	Indiana
Sarah A. Karr	3	F	Iowa
William H. Karr	4/12	M	Iowa

Other information included William's ownership of real estate valued at $2000.

Analysis: William Karr was born about 1813 in Indiana and Amanda about 1814 in Kentucky. Matthew Karr was not listed in the 1860 U.S. Census of Miami County, Kansas. He either married and lived elsewhere or he died prior to that census year. There is a five-year span between Matthew and James W. Karr, indicating that a child may have died in infancy or early childhood. The youngest child, William H. Karr, was listed in the 1860 census as Henry Karr and was followed by a William Karr. It appears that the 1860 enumerator was confused and entered the first and middle names of one child as two separate people. This discrepancy, however, needs clarification in other records. Lastly, the Karr family migrated from Indiana to Iowa between 1846 and 1847. This is supported by Elihu's birth in 1846 in Indiana and Sarah's birth in 1847 in Iowa.

William Karr wasn't the only person of that surname in Marion County, Iowa in 1850. George W., James, and Andrew P. Karr were also living there and were prior residents of Indiana. Their census entries will be examined later. Keep in mind that it was quite common for extended families and neighbors to migrate together. The lone pioneer, while not unheard of, was definitely in the minority.

The International Genealogical Index did not exist in 1967, but if it had, it would have been searched a second time for Ambrose and William Karr in the Indiana entries. The Family Group Records Archives was extant, consisting of two sections, the Main Section and the Patron's Section. The latter consists of sheets representing direct ancestors within the first four generations of individuals submitting these sheets to the Genealogical Library of the LDS Church.

During the recheck of the Patron's Section, a family group record was found for a John Karr who died in Dunreath, Marion County, Iowa. He was born in Franklin County, Indiana in 1818 and had children named Sarah and William, names held in common with William Karr's children. The person submitting this record lived in Orem, Utah and was listed in the telephone directory. Whenever you find information that leads to others working on the same line, you should make every effort to contact them. They may save you the frustration of unproductive searches and add historical and biographical information you'll never find in public records.

An interview with Mrs. Cleota Karr was very productive. She had very little genealogical information about my ancestors, but did know of others

1850 CENSUS – UNITED STATES

State IOWA | County MARION | Township/Town SUMMIT | Enumeration Date 23 SEP 1850 | Census film number

Page	Dwelling number	Family number	The name of every person whose usual place of abode on the first day of June 1850, was in this family.	Age	Sex	Color	Occupation, etc.	Value of Real Estate owned	Place of Birth	Married within year	School within year	20 years of age cannot read or write	Whether deaf, dumb, blind, insane, idiotic, pauper or convict.
1		2	3	4	5	6	7	8	9	10	11	12	13
649	603		WILLIAM KAER	37	M		FARMER	2000	INDIANA				
			AMANDA P. "	36	F				KENTUCKY				
			AMBROSE "	12	M				INDIANA		✓		
			MATTHEW "	11	M				INDIANA		✓		
			JAMES W. "	6	M				INDIANA				
			ELIHU A. "	4	M				INDIANA				
			SARAH A. "	3	F				IOWA				
			WILLIAM H. "	4/12	M				IOWA				

Figure 8:14. 1850 U.S. Census, Summit Township, Marion County, Iowa.

actively involved in tracing the Karr family in Iowa, Indiana, and Pennsylvania. She was certain that John Karr had a brother William who moved to Kansas from Marion County, Iowa; however, she had no proof of relationship. She offered the following information about John Karr:

> John Karr left Indiana 24 November 1859 and arrived in Iowa 24 March 1860 to settle in Marion County. He was born 14 November 1818 at Franklin County, Indiana and died 9 October 1903 at Dunreath, Marion County, Iowa where he is also buried. He married Caroline Jones 28 November 1839 in Shelby County, Indiana. She was the daughter of Samuel and Rebecca Jones. After her death, he married a woman named Anna in Marion County, Indiana. He and Caroline had three children: Alexander Campbell, Sarah Jane, and William Edward.

While the information concerning John Karr did not directly help in the search for details of William Karr's life, it is important to completing the fifth generation if William and John Karr were brothers. Such information should be recorded on a research extract and filed with other materials until needed. It is also important to remember that all of the information about John Karr is circumstantial in nature because it was handed down to Mrs. Karr from other relatives.

Letters asking for more detailed information about William Karr and his relationship to other Karr families in Marion County, Iowa were sent to the same individuals Mrs. Karr had corresponded with about John Karr. Over the next several months hundreds of pages were written to several people who descended from the Karrs of Marion County, Iowa. The information contained in those letters is voluminous and cannot be discussed in detail here. The important parts will be analyzed, along with some of the erroneous information which led many people astray for several years.

While awaiting responses to the inquiries sent out, the material already gathered in Kansas was carefully reviewed and recorded onto the working charts. A summary of the contents of those records and an analysis of each one follows:

1870 U.S. Census, Miami County, Kansas

Page	Name	Age	Sex	Occupation	Birthplace
100	William Karr	57	M	Farmer	Pennsylvania
	Amanda Karr	55	F	Keeping House	Kentucky
	Wm. Henry Karr	20	M	Farmer	Indiana
	Eldridge Karr	17	M	Farmer	Iowa

William Karr's real estate holdings were valued at $7000 and his personal property at $500. His father was listed as foreign born.

Analysis: William's birthplace is recorded as Pennsylvania instead of Indiana as in the 1850 and 1860 enumerations. This entry agrees with the 1880 census. The son born in 1850 was William Henry Karr and the son mistakenly identified as William Karr in 1860 was actually Eldridge Karr. There are slight age discrepancies between this and the 1860 census for both William and Amanda Karr. This is not unusual and could be the result of when the census was taken. The discrepancies are not significant enough to cause serious concern.

Miami County, Kansas marriage records showed that William Karr, age fifty-six, married Mrs. Margaret Abrogast, age forty-two, on 21 September 1871 in New Lancaster, Kansas. The only other marriage recorded in Miami County for a member of William's family was for Elihu A. Karr to Hannah Jane Steward on 22 January 1867 by F. H. Dunbarld, Justice of the Peace.

Analysis: Based on the marriage date, it appears that Amanda Karr died between 1 July 1870 when the census was taken and 21 September 1871 when William married his second wife.

William's family was enumerated in the 1865 and 1875 Kansas State censuses. The information in those enumerations did not differ significantly from any other enumerations, nor did they add any new information of importance. Both of those records gave William's birthplace as Pennsylvania.

The Kansas State Adjutant General's Enrollment of Soldiers Act of 1883 required all Civil War veterans to register with the state. William Karr was listed with Miami County veterans as a first lieutenant in Company A, 5th Kansas Militia Cavalry, enrolled at Fontana, Miami County, Kansas. None of his sons were listed.

Analysis: William Karr may have lived long enough to receive a pension for his war services. If he applied for a pension, he would be listed in the Civil War Pension Application File Index. That none of his sons were listed with the Miami County veterans in 1883 does not mean they did not serve in the Civil War. They may have been living elsewhere in Kansas or in another state when the enrollment was compiled. Their names may also be found in the pension application file.

Many state historical libraries maintain card index files of early residents mentioned in county histories or other collections found in their library. The Kansas State Historical Society card file listed several entries for William Karr.

Summary of entries in the *Kansas State Historical Collections*: William Karr ran for the office of representative to the Kansas State Legislature several times and was elected twice. During all of the research done in Miami County records it was interesting to note that William Karr and William Huffman were never linked in any way. It almost appeared as though they didn't know one another even though they were related by marriage. That peculiar situation was explained in the *Annals of Kansas* which disclosed that they ran against one another for several county offices and in elections for state representative. William Karr was the first representative to sign Resolution No. 42, ratify-

RESEARCH EXTRACT

File Number 6:1	Repository PROBATE COURT - MIAMI COUNTY, KANSAS	Call Number NONE

Description of Source MARRIAGE RECORDS - MARRIAGE BOOK A
MIAMI COUNTY, KANSAS

Indexed MALES ONLY	Condition GOOD	Time Period 1857-1871	Date 26 DEC 1967

Search Objective WILLIAM KARR FAMILY

MARRIAGE BOOK A

1. AMBROSE CARR AND PATSIE HUFFMAN   26 MAY 1859

2. ELIHU A. KARR AND HANNAH JANE STEWARD   22 JAN 1867

   BY F.H. DUNBARLD, J.P.

3. WILLIAM KARR AND MRS. MARGARET ABROGAST   21 SEP 1871

   AGE 56   AGE 42

Figure 8:15. Research Extract, *Marriage Book A*, 1857-1871, Miami County, Kansas.

ing the amendment to the Constitution abolishing slavery on 7 February 1865. The *Portrait and Biographical Album of Sedgwick County, Kansas* (Chicago: Chapman Brothers, 1888) contains a biographical sketch of William Karr:

> Hon. William Karr. The intelligence and education of the citizens of Wichita have in this gentleman a worthy representative – one who keeps himself well posted upon matters of general interest, and has served in many positions of trust and responsibility. The later years of his life, until 1887, were occupied in mercantile pursuits. In December of that year he retired from business, and in a tasteful and comfortable home now spends his time largely in reading and study, and in the enjoyment of the society of his many friends.
>
> Our subject, a native of Washington County, Pa., was born on the 24th of March 1813, and is the son of Matthew and Hannah (Pease) Karr, the father a native of Ireland and the mother of Washington County, Pa.
>
> Matthew Karr was born in Ireland, and came to this country with his parents when a lad eight years of age. They were among the earliest settlers of Washington County, Pa., where they followed farming, and became the parents of a fine family of sons and daughters. Matthew, in 1814, early in life, removed to Franklin County, Ind., where he spent the remainder of his days. He had been educated for a Presbyterian minister, but preferred agricultural pursuits, and never entered upon the course which had been marked out for him by his parents.
>
> Our subject was but one year old when his parents removed from Pennsylvania to Indiana. Their household included ten children, most of whom were natives of the Keystone State. They all lived to years of maturity. Only six are now living, and residents mostly of Iowa and Kansas. William was one of the younger members of the family, and like the others, was reared to farming pursuits. He continued with his parents until 1846, and then made his way westward to Marion County, Iowa, where he engaged in merchandising and remained ten years. He next located in Miami County, this State, where he operated a 200 acre farm, and made a specialty of blooded stock. He lived there until 1883, a period of eleven years then abandoned agriculture, and took up his residence in the city of Wichita.
>
> Mr. Karr, in 1844, was elected Justice of the Peace, which office he held during his entire residence in Indiana. In 1862-64 he was chosen also to represent Miami County, Kan., in the State Legislature, and after serving his term resumed the duties of Police Justice. For a short time after coming to Wichita he engaged in merchandising, but sold out in December, 1887, since which time he has lived retired from active business.
>
> The marriage of our subject took place in Indiana, on the 19th of February, 1833, the lady of his choice being Miss Amanda Hopkins, of

Kentucky. They commenced life together in a modest home in Bartholomew County, Ind., and after a lapse of years found themselves the parents of ten children, of whom but four are now living. Of the latter, Elihu A. married Miss Hannah J. Stewart, of Miami County, this State, and is engaged in the real estate business at Wichita; Sarah A., Mrs. H. Brown, the wife of a Wichita merchant, is the mother of three children – Ida, Carrie and Cora; William H. and Milton remain with their parents in Wichita. The mother departed this life Nov. 22, 1871, and her remains were laid to rest in the cemetery at New Lancaster, Miami Co., Kan.

Hon. William Karr was the second man who signed his name to the Fifteenth Amendment, in 1864, while a member of the Kansas Legislature, and following his were eighty-four names of members. Early in life he affiliated with the Whig party, and subsequently entered the Republican ranks. During the late war he was First Lieutenant in Company A, in the State Militia, which was instituted and maintained for the protection of the frontier. A well-informed man and a fluent speaker, he was often called upon to address political or other meetings. He was President of the Union League during the war, and materially assisted in diffusing Union sentiments. Early in life he identified himself with the Baptist Church, with which he has been connected now for a period of over forty years. He has always taken an active interest in the establishment and maintenance of religious institutions, believing that the sentiments taught in these are the surest weapons against anarchy and misrule. The family residence is pleasantly located at No. 204 Locust Street.

Analysis: Biographical sketches in county histories are secondary sources of information providing circumstantial evidence. It is likely that the person writing the sketch personally interviewed William Karr given the number of details included about his life and movements. Let's cull the genealogical information that can be used to further support other circumstantial evidence about the life of William Karr:

1. William Karr was born 24 March 1813 in Washington County, Pennsylvania.

2. William Karr's parents were Matthew Karr and Hannah Pease.

3. Matthew Karr moved his family to Franklin County, Indiana in 1814 when William was a year old.

4. William Karr remained in Indiana until 1846 and then moved to Marion County, Iowa.

5. He remained in Marion County for ten years and then moved to Miami County, Kansas in 1857.

6. William Karr married Amanda Hopkins of Kentucky on 19 February 1833 in Indiana and they resided in Bartholomew County after their marriage.

7. William and Amanda Karr were the parents of ten children, four of whom were still living in 1888: Elihu A., Sarah A., William H., and Milton.

8. Amanda Karr died 22 November 1871 and was buried in New Lancaster, Miami County, Kansas.

9. William Karr was living at 204 Locust Street, Wichita in 1888.

The only discrepancy of genealogical importance noted in the sketch is Amanda Karr's death date. William Karr married his second wife on 21 September 1871 which would have been two months prior to Amanda's death. Assuming the month and day are correct, she most likely died in 1870.

The biographical sketch also provided circumstantial information about William's parents that was valuable in directing future research. The following must be subjected to further proof by searching other records:

1. Matthew Karr arrived in the United States from Ireland with his parents when he was eight years old.

2. Matthew Karr married Hannah Pease who was born in Washington County, Pennsylvania.

3. Matthew's father was a farmer, indicating he probably owned land.

4. Matthew Karr was trained to be a Presbyterian minister, indicating his religious preference.

5. Matthew Karr died in Franklin County, Indiana.

6. Matthew and Hannah Karr were the parents of ten children all of whom lived to maturity.

7. Six of Matthew and Hannah Karr's children were still living in 1888, residing in Kansas and Iowa.

While biographical sketches in county histories and biographies provide useful genealogical information, they are excellent sources of historical color and substance to the routine compiling of names, dates, and places. Additionally, they provide excellent clues to a family's movements, leading you to locations where other records should be searched.

The *History of Marion County, Indiana* contains several references to the Karr family. "William, Andrew, and George Karr were among the settlers who located along the river in the Whitebreast Settlement and between there and Coalport."

Additionally,

John Marion Karr-Otley, ... His grandfather was born and raised in Ireland, and in early manhood came to America, and settled in Pennsylvania, where he married Miss Hannah Pease, a lady of American parentage. Their son, George W., was born in Pennsylvania in 1812. He was a farmer and married Eliza Dickey, a lady of American birth, who bore him ten children, one of whom was John, who was born September 9, 1837, in Bartholomew County, Indiana. When ten years old his father emigrated to this county, landing at Red Rock, in September 1847. . . .

Analysis: This entry indicates that George W. Karr and William Karr were brothers and further links the family to Bartholomew County, Indiana before their move to Iowa.

The first response to the letters sent after the interview with Cleota Karr came from Des Moines, Iowa. It stated that William Karr was known as "Heineke Bill" and that he hauled freight from Keokuk to Des Moines. His brothers and sisters were James, Eliza, Andrew P., George W., John, Mariah, and Catherine.

A second letter included photocopies of correspondence exchanged between "cousins" over a period of months. The most valuable information in these letters explained that Hannah Karr's grave was in Davis County, Iowa. Her tombstone reads: Hannah Karr, wife of M. Karr. She is buried with two of William Karr's children.

Analysis: William Karr lived in Davis County as well as Marion County, Iowa. A search of the Karr family cemetery located on a farm owned by William Karr showed that Hannah Pees Karr died 9 May 1855 near Pulaski, Davis County, Iowa. William's son, Matthew, was buried there following his death on 11 February 1857. His daughter, Elmyra J., also rests there. She died 28 November 1856. Hannah's grave is decorated with a marker placed there by the Daughters of the American Revolution, as her father, Nicholas Pees, served in that war.

A third letter provided marriage records for a number of the Karr family members, including William Karr of Decatur County, Indiana. *Marriage Record C,* page 104 states that William Carr [sic] married Amanda P. Hopkins on 19 February 1835. Records of the marriage of other children of Matthew and Hannah Karr will be discussed in the section on the fifth generation.

William Karr is known to have resided in Marion and Davis counties in Iowa, Bartholomew and Franklin counties in Indiana, and Washington County, Pennsylvania. A thorough search of the deeds recorded in these locations identified the property William Karr owned in Indiana, Iowa, and Kansas. None of those deeds provided any genealogical information, but they were helpful in showing when he was in a particular area and when he left. One deed of interest involved land granted to William Karr by the United States. This instrument would be helpful to genealogists tracing the ancestry of Othineil Preston. He was a private in the New York State Militia during the War of 1812 and applied for a Bounty Land Warrant in payment for his service. He assigned his warrant for land in Miami County, Kansas to William Karr. This type of entry is valuable for its reference to Mr. Preston's service and his presence in New York in 1812. Bounty land applications often contain useful genealogical information and should always be obtained for evaluation of evidence.

One last document found in Miami County pertained to James W. Karr, one of William's sons. James died prior to 8 November 1865 at New Lancaster. William Karr was his administrator and the only heir listed in the probate records. James probably served in the Civil War, the date of his probate records suggesting he may have died of wounds received while fighting. There are no records to verify that supposition.

The Civil War Pension Application File listed only one of William Karr's sons, Elihu A., who served in Company D, 15th Kansas Cavalry and applied for a pension 7 March 1879. After his death, his wife, Alma applied for a widow's pension on 24 August 1908. Elihu's pension application file was requested and received from the National Archives. The contents of that pension file provided the following genealogical information:

1. Elihu A. Karr died on 15 June 1908 at Rolla, Missouri.

2. He married Hannah J. Stewart, 22 January 1867, at Miami County, Kansas. She was living when he applied for his supplemental information for his pension file on 4 May 1898.

3. Elihu and Hannah had no children.

4. Hannah died prior to November 1903.

5. Elihu married Alma Poynter at Yellville, Marion County, Arkansas on 15 November 1903. He was fifty-seven years old and she was twenty years old.

6. Elihu and Alma had no children.

William Karr was enumerated in the 1840 U.S. Census of Bartholomew County, Indiana as a resident of the Haw Creek Township:

William Karr	2 males under 5	[Ambrose and Matthew]
	1 male 15-20	[Andrew J. Hopkins – his brother-in-law]
	1 male 20-30	[William Karr]
	1 female 15-20	[Martha Jane Karr – his sister]
	1 female 20-30	[Amanda P. Karr]
	1 female 60-70	[Hannah Karr – his mother]

William's brothers, George, James, and Andrew P. were also listed in that census.

The 1830 census of Bartholomew County, Indiana listed only Hannah Karr. A discussion of that census will be found in the section on the fifth generation.

AMANDA P. HOPKINS (7:1)

The last task to complete the fourth generation of the Karr family is to identify Amanda P. Hopkins's parents. According to family tradition, Amanda's family lived in Decatur and Bartholomew counties, Indiana before migrating

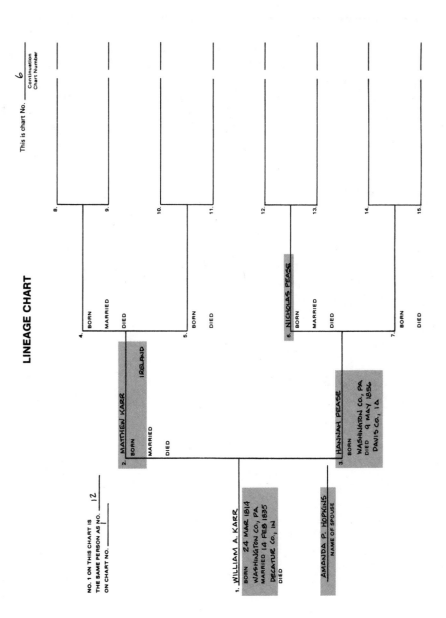

Figure 8:16. Lineage Work Chart 6, William A. Karr.

to Davis County, Iowa. Research in Miami County, Kansas revealed that Amanda was born about 1815 in Kentucky and that Eldridge and William W. Hopkins followed the same migration pattern as the Karr family.

RESEARCH PLAN

1. Correspond with Jeanette Woodruff, a descendant of both the Hopkins and Karr families, who has researched them extensively.

2. Search the 1850 census of Davis County, Iowa, and the 1830 and 1840 census enumerations of Bartholomew and Decatur counties, Indiana.

3. Search Davis County, Iowa wills and probate records for Hopkins wills mentioning Amanda P. Hopkins Karr.

4. Correspond for Davis County, Iowa cemetery searches to locate the tombstones of Hopkins family members.

While awaiting an answer from Mrs. Woodruff, the 1850 U.S. Census of Davis County, Iowa was searched to identify those couples old enough to have been Amanda's parents. Only one living in Prairie Township qualified as potential parents, and they lived next door to what appeared to be two of their younger sons:

Dwelling Number	Name	Age	Occupation	Birthplace
#11	William Hopkins	68	Farmer	Virginia
	Sarah Hopkins	62		Virginia
	Abner Hiner	13		Indiana
#10	Andrew Hopkins	25	Farmer	Kentucky
	Martha J. Hopkins	25		Indiana
	Elizabeth Hopkins	4		Iowa
	Sarah Hopkins	10/12		Iowa
#9	William W. Hopkins	27	Farmer	Kentucky
	Caroline P. Hopkins	24		Indiana
	Artemecia Hopkins	7		Indiana
	Alden J. Hopkins	6		Iowa
	Amanda J. Hopkins	3		Iowa
	William A. Hopkins	1		Iowa

These entries are another classic example of group migration patterns, in this case from Virginia to Kentucky to Indiana to Iowa and then later to Kansas where Amanda and some of her brothers lived out their lives.

Mrs. Woodruff's response was a gold mine of information. She had spent forty years tracing the Hopkins family, mainly through exhaustive correspondence and hiring research agents in the areas where the family lived. Her research notes were complete with citations that documented the sources of her conclusions.

According to her research, Amanda Peace Hopkins was the daughter of William Hopkins Jr. and Sarah Smathers and she was born in Nicholas County, Kentucky. Her birthplace was deduced from the fact that the family lived in that county between 1814 and 1826. Her relationship to William and Sarah is documented in two records:

1. William Hopkins left a will dated 1 July 1856 that was proven in court at Davis County, Iowa, 6 October 1856. He names the following heirs in his will:

Temperence Ann—wife	Mary Ann Myers—dau
Joseph S. Hopkins—son	Eldridge Hopkins—son
William W. Hopkins—son	Martha J. Hopkins—dau in law
Andrew J. Hopkins—son	Elizabeth Shelton—dau
Amanda P. Karr—dau	Abiah Hiner's heirs—dau
	Ambrose J. Hopkins's heirs—son

2. William Hopkins and his first wife, Sarah, were buried near Bloomfield, Davis County, Iowa and their tombstone reads: William Hopkins, d. 5 August, 1856; Sarah Smathers, wife of William, d. 9 May 1854, age 66 years.

Analysis: William Hopkins's will states that his wife is Temperence Ann Hopkins, a fact that contradicts Mrs. Woodruff's research. His tombstone clears up the discrepancy by disclosing that Sarah Smathers Hopkins died prior to the writing of his will. He obviously married a second time between 9 May 1854 and 5 August 1856.

Abner Hiner, recorded living with William and Sarah Hopkins in the 1850 census, is most likely their grandson, based on the mention of Abiah Hiner's heirs in William's will. Abiah was William's oldest child and she married Joseph Hiner on 26 May 1824 in Nicholas County, Kentucky, according to Mrs. Woodruff's research notes.

Based on the contents of four record sources, Amanda P. Hopkins's parentage was proven. Countless other records were searched to complete the family group of William and Sarah Smathers Hopkins, research that will be discussed in the section on the fifth generation.

WILLIAM ROLLEN HUFFMAN (8:1)

Martha P. Huffman's marriage record clearly states that she was married in New Lancaster by her father, William Huffman, and she was listed in William's 1850 household in Fulton County, Illinois. The marriage record is direct

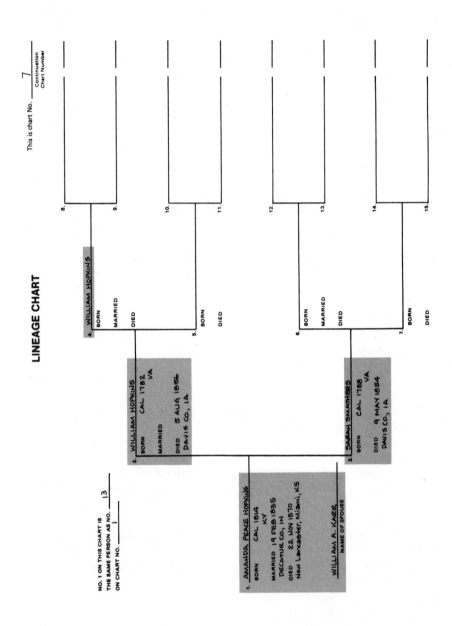

Figure 8:17. Lineage Work Chart 7, Amanda Peace Hopkins.

FAMILY GROUP SHEET

HUS. WILLIAM A. KARR		OCCUPATION(S) KANSAS STATE LEGISLATOR AND FARMER
BORN	14 MAR 1814	PLACE Washington County, Pennsylvania
CHR		PLACE
MARR	19 FEB 1833	PLACE Decatur County, Indiana
DIED	AFTER 1869	PLACE
BUR		PLACE
FATHER	MATTHEW KARR	
MOTHER	HANNAH PEASE	
		OTHER WIVES (2) MRS. MARGARET ABROGAST 21 SEP 1871

WIFE AMANDA PEACE HOPKINS		
BORN	CAL 1814	PLACE Kentucky
CHR		PLACE
DIED	22 NOV 1870	PLACE New Lancaster, Miami, Kansas
BUR		PLACE
FATHER	WILLIAM HOPKINS	
MOTHER	SARAH SMATHERS	
		OTHER HUSBANDS

SEX	CHILDREN	DATE BORN / PLACE BORN	DATE MARRIED / TO	PLACE	DATE DIED / PLACE DIED
1 M	AMBROSE N. KARR	1828 / Bartholomew County, Indiana	26 MAY 1859 / MARTHA P. HUFFMAN	New Lancaster, Miami, KS	13 AUG 1867 / New Lancaster, Miami, Kansas
2 M	MATTHEW KARR	CAL 1839 / Bartholomew County, Indiana			before 8 NOV 1865 / New Lancaster, Miami, Kansas
3 M	JAMES W. KARR	CAL 1843 / Bartholomew County, Indiana			15 JUN 1908 / Rolla, Phelps, Missouri
4 M	ELIHU A. KARR	CAL 1847 / Bartholomew County, Indiana	22 JAN 1867 / HANNAH J. STEWART	Miami County, Kansas	
5 F	SARAH A. KARR	1850 / Marion County, Iowa	H. BROWN		
6 M	WILLIAM HENRY KARR	1853 / Marion County, Iowa			
7 M	ELDRIDGE MILTON KARR	1855 / Marion County, Iowa			
8 F	ELMYRA J. KARR	Marion County, Iowa			28 NOV 1856 / Davis County, Iowa

OTHER MARRIAGES   #4 md (2) ALMA POYNTER, 15 NOV 1903

SOURCES OF INFORMATION
1. 1850 U.S. Census - Marion County, Iowa
2. Portrait and Biographical Album of Sedgewick County, Kansas
3. 1860 U.S. Census - Lykins County, Kansas
4. Marriage Records - Miami County, Kansas and Decatur County, Indiana
5. Probate Records - Miami County, Kansas
6. Tombstone Inscriptions - New Lancaster Cemetery, Miami County, Kansas
7. Tombstone Inscriptions - Karr Family Cemetery, Davis County, Iowa

Figure 8:18. Family Group Work Record, William A. Karr and Amanda P. Hopkins.

evidence of her relationship to William Huffman, and the census record is circumstantial evidence that supports the marriage record.

Now that Martha's relationship to her father is established, it's time to search records that will genealogically identify William Huffman's entire family. Let's study the working family group record to see what is already known about William Huffman's family.

The first step in identifying William Huffman's family was a census study of Miami County, Kansas enumerations between 1860 and 1900:

1860 U.S. Census, Miami Township, Lykins (Miami) County, Kansas

Dwelling Number	Name	Age	Sex	Race	Occupation	Birthplace
#671	William Huffman	45	M	W	UBN	Ohio
	Lewvisa Huffman	19	F	W		Indiana
	Gabriel M. Huffman	17	M	W		Indiana
	Franklin H. Huffman	15	M	W		Indiana
	Angeline Huffman	10	F	W		Illinois
	Jonas Huffman	6	M	W		Iowa
	Charles L. Huffman	4	M	W		Iowa
	Elam S. Huffman	2	F	W		Kansas Terr
	Susan D. Huffman	1/12	F	W		Kansas
	Alice Huffman	44	F	W		N. Carolina

1870 U.S. Census, Miami Township, Miami County, Kansas

Dwelling Number	Name	Age	Sex	Race	Occupation	Birthplace
#82	William Huffman	55	M	W	Ret Grocer	Ohio
	Lucy Huffman	38	F	W		Kentucky
	Jonas Huffman	18	M	W		Iowa
	Elam Huffman	14	M	W		Iowa

1880 U.S. Census, Miami Township, Miami County, Kansas

Dwelling Number	Name	Age	Birthplace	Father's Birthplace	Mother's Birthplace
#5	William Huffman	65	Ohio	Pennsylvania	———
	Lucy E. Huffman	46	Kentucky	Alabama	Virginia
	Elam Huffman	21	Iowa	Ohio	N. Car

FAMILY GROUP SHEET

HUS. WILLIAM HUFFMAN		OCCUPATION(S): UNITED BRETHREN MINISTER
BORN	CAL 1815	PLACE Ohio
CHR.		PLACE
MARR.		PLACE
DIED		PLACE
BUR.		PLACE
FATHER		
MOTHER		OTHER WIVES

WIFE ALICE		
BORN	CAL 1816	PLACE North Carolina
CHR.		PLACE
DIED		PLACE
BUR.		PLACE
FATHER		
MOTHER		OTHER HUSBANDS

SEX	CHILDREN	DATE BORN / PLACE BORN	DATE MARRIED / TO	PLACE	DATE DIED / PLACE DIED
M	1 ANDREW J. HUFFMAN	CAL 1836 / Indiana			
F	2 MARTHA P. HUFFMAN	1839 / Indiana	26 MAY 1859 / AMBROSE N. KAER	New Lancaster, Miami, KS	15 JUN 1877 / New Lancaster, Miami, Kansas
F	3 LEWVISA HUFFMAN	CAL 1841 / Indiana			
M	4 GABRIEL M. HUFFMAN	CAL 1843 / Indiana			
M	5 FRANKLIN H. HUFFMAN	CAL 1844 / Indiana			
F	6 ANGELINE HUFFMAN	CAL 1850 / Illinois			
M	7 JONAS HUFFMAN	CAL 1854 / Iowa			
M	8 CHARLES L. HUFFMAN	CAL 1856 / Iowa			
M	9 ELAM S. HUFFMAN	CAL 1858 / Kansas			
F	10 SUSAN D. HUFFMAN	1860 / Kansas			OTHER MARRIAGES

SOURCES OF INFORMATION
1. 1860 U.S. Census, Miami Twp, Lykins County, Kansas.
2. Marriage Records, Miami County, Kansas.
3. Tombstone Inscriptions, New Lancaster Cemetery, Miami County, Kansas.

Figure 8:19. Family Group Work Record, William Huffman.

1900 U.S. Census, Miami Township, Miami County, Kansas

Dwelling Number	Name	Birth Mo	Birth Year	Birthplace	Father's B'place	Mother's B'place
#109	William Huffman	Jul	1815	Ohio	Virginia	Virginia
	Lucie Huffman	Oct	1827	Kent	Georgia	Georgia
	R.A. Nichols	Jan	1857	Missouri	Kent	Kent
#129	C. F. Tracy	Sep	1839	Ind	Kent	Kent
	Lewvisa Tracy	Jan	1841	Ind	Ohio	Ohio
	5 children					
#90	Elam Huffman	Jul	1858	Kansas	Penn	Ind
	Francis Huffman	Dec	1863	Kansas	Kansas	Kansas
#326	David S. Huffman	May	1854	Iowa	No. Car	No. Car
	Emma E. Huffman	Mar	1870	Kansas	Maryland	Tenn
	2 children					

1900 U.S. Census, Lecompton Township, Douglas County, Kansas

#76	G. M. Huffman	Feb	1843	Ind	Ind	Ind
	Sue Huffman	Jul	1841	Penn	Penn	Penn
	1 child					

1900 U.S. Census, Washington Township, Anderson County, Kansas

#16	Frank H. Huffman	Sep	1844	Ind	Ohio	So. Car
	Martha P. Huffman	Mar	1848	Ohio	Penn	Virginia

1900 U.S. Census, Union Township, Lincoln County, Oklahoma Terr.

#94	Chas. S. Huffman	Feb	1856	Iowa	Ohio	Ohio
	Martha	May	1871	Kans	Iowa	Missouri
	5 children					

1900 U.S. Census, Liberty Township, Clay County, Missouri

#114	Jonas D. Huffman	May	1853	Iowa	Penn	Ohio
	Frances Huffman	Dec	1857	Wisconsin	New York	Unknown
	3 children					

Analysis: The 1900 census listings for William's children provided a month and year of birth, information that was not available in other records and which supports the circumstantial evidence in attesting to their birth year in other census records. You will note that there are discrepancies in the entries pertaining to William Huffman's birthplace and that of his wife. At this point William's birthplace is most frequently cited as Ohio and his wife's as North Carolina. Not mentioned in the census summary is the number of years each couple has been married, the number of children born to each wife, and the number of those children still living in 1900. Once you know the number of years a couple has been married, you are able to calculate their marriage year, thus limiting the number of years to search in the marriage records if they are unindexed. Additionally, if a wife gave birth to five children and only two are still living, you know that the deceased children, if unidentified previously, may be identified in earlier census enumerations or in cemetery records for the area in which the family lived. If one of your ancestors was an immigrant, the 1900 census also lists the year of arrival in the United States and citizenship status. These are excellent clues to follow in searching ship's passenger lists and naturalization records.

Aside from the birthplace and birthdate discrepancies, the census information is acceptable as circumstantial evidence in support of the lineage. William Huffman's family is well sorted out to facilitate identifying them in Miami County, Kansas records. When you are dealing with a large family you will save considerable research time and avoid making incorrect connections by conducting a thorough census study.

Correspondence was sent to New Lancaster, Kansas to request that the information recorded on the tombstones of the Huffman family be forwarded. A later trip to New Lancaster permitted photographing the tombstones. The following information was found on them:

Alice Huffman wife of Wm Huffman Mar 15, 1816 Jun 28, 1860 44 yrs, 3 mos, 23 days William Huffman July 15, 1815 Sept 16, 1900	Father David S. Huffman 1854-1927 Mother Emma E. Huffman 1870-1952

Mother
Lucy E. Huffman
1827-1913

Tracy
C. F. Tracy
1839-1911
Lewvisa, his wife
1841-1935

Analysis: Tombstone inscriptions contain circumstantial and direct evidence. The person giving the information on a tombstone—as with death certificates—is usually directly related to the deceased. He or she would certainly know the relationships between the family members buried in the cemetery plot. If the tombstone was carved immediately following death, the death date on the tombstone is most likely accurate, but the birthdate could be incorrect if birth took place many years before. The tombstone inscription of a child is less likely to contain incorrect birth information. As with other records containing circumstantial evidence, tombstone inscriptions must also be supported by other evidence. Death records were requested for each person whose passing occurred after death registration was required in Kansas. They will be discussed later.

Returning to the 1860 U.S. Census record of William Huffman's family, you will remember that Alice Huffman was listed at the end of the family's enumeration. The census was taken four days after her death. You will rarely find deceased family members listed in a census, as their names usually appear in mortality schedules. Note that Alice gave birth to Susan D. Huffman shortly before she died. Susan was not found in any other record. A small, unmarked grave next to Alice Huffman's grave suggests she died in infancy after her mother.

William Huffman was identified as a United Brethren minister in his daughter's marriage record. Most protestant church records in America contain scant genealogical information. Only a few denominations kept birth/baptism, marriage, and death/burial records. Most New England churches kept excellent records, and Quaker records are also extensive and well maintained. Churches whose growth took place along the frontier, such as the Baptists and Methodists, have membership records and little more. Most denominations have a headquarters with historical departments. Since William Huffman was an ordained minister, it was likely that the United Brethren Church had some valuable information about his life and family in their files.

A letter was sent to the Historical Society of the Evangelical United Brethren Church in Dayton, Ohio requesting a search of their files for information about William Huffman. Their historical division consisted of one individual who could not afford the time to do any in-depth research, but he was willing to send some easily photocopied materials.

William Huffman was not the only member of his family to enter the United Brethren ministry. His son, Gabriel M. Huffman, was also an ordained minister for that sect. Gabriel completed a biographical sketch for the church's files on 30 September 1898 that included the following information:

1. Give the names of your parents, with their nationality, date and place of birth:

Father—William Huffman, born 1815 Butler Co., Ohio

Mother—Alice Davis, born 1815 Randolph Co., North Carolina of English Quaker stock.

1860 CENSUS – UNITED STATES

State: KANSAS County: LYKINS Township/Town, etc.: MIAMI Post Office: PAOLA Enumeration Date: JULY 1860 Census Film Number:

Page	1 Dwelling number	2 Family number	3 The Name of every person whose usual place of abode on the first day of June, 1860 was in this family.	4 Age	5 Sex	6 Color	7 Profession, Occupation or Trade	8 Real Estate	9 Personal Estate	10 Place of birth	11 Married within year	12 Attended school	13 Persons 20 or older who cannot read or write	14 Whether deaf and dumb, insane, idiotic pauper or convict
	671	671	WILLIAM HUFFMAN	45	M	W	UBN	600	500	OHIO				
			LEWVISA	19	F	W				IND				
			GABRIEL M.	17	M	W				IND				
			FRANKLIN H.	15	M	W				IND		/		
			ANGELINE	10	F	W				ILL		/		
			JONAS	6	M	W				IOWA		/		
			CHARLES L.	4	M	W				IOWA		/		
			ELAM S.	2	M	W				KANS TERR				
			SUSAN D.	1/12	F	W				KANS TERR				
			ALICE	44	F	W				NC				
	680	680	ANDREW J. HUFFMAN	24	M	W				IND				
			MARGARET I.	20	F	W				PA				
			MORTIMER G.	1/12	M	W				KANS TERR				

Figure 8:20. 1860 U.S. Census, Miami Township, Lykins County, Kansas.

2. Your own name in full, when born, where born; if born abroad, at what age you came to this country; located where; how many brothers and sisters.

Gabriel M. Huffman, born Park Co., Indiana Feb 27th, 1843.

3. If married, when and to whom; wife living or dead; if latter, died when; if married again, person and date; how many children have you had; how many are living.

Married 1867 to Sue Neidig, wife living, four sons, two daughters, all living.

4. General Remarks:

Was Presiding Elder for ten years, Member of Gen. Conference 1889, 1893, 1897. Trustee of Lane University 25 years, Pres., Board of Trustees 13 years. My father, still living, has been a UB minister for fifty years. I have two sons and one son-in-law in the ministry; all members of Kansas Conference. Served three years in the Rebellion in Co. H, 22nd Iowa Infantry. Was a prisoner of war six months at Tyler, Texas. Was in the Campaign at Vicksburg under Grant and the Virginia Campaign under Sheridan. Was honorably discharged as 3rd Sergeant of Co H. August 1865.

Analysis: Gabriel's biographical sketch provided information not found in any other records. He stated his mother's birthplace as Randolph County, North Carolina and the fact that she was of English Quaker heritage, two valuable clues to follow. His mother's maiden name was also given as Davis, a fact that would surface when her marriage record was obtained, but to locate that record required knowing where she married William Huffman. At this point their county residence in Indiana was unknown. Gabriel Huffman stated that he was born in Parke County, Indiana, providing the first place to check for his parent's marriage record.

Gabriel also offered the name of his wife and mentioned his Civil War service. The *Civil War Pension Application File Index* was immediately checked to see if he or any of his brothers applied for a pension. He and Franklin H. Huffman were listed in the index and their application files were requested from the National Archives. The contents of those records will be discussed later.

William Huffman's obituary appeared in the 10 October 1900 edition of *The Religious Telescope,* a publication of the United Brethren Church:

Rev. William Huffman was born in Butler County, Ohio and died at his home in New Lancaster, Kansas, Sept. 16, 1900; aged 85 years, 2 months, and 16 days. In 1831 he with his father moved to Indiana, in 1845 to Illinois, thence to Iowa in 1851, and in 1857 he moved to Miami County, Kan. His home, has been in this county for forty-three years.

No._____ Folio_____   (Form A.)

☞ TEAR OFF THIS HALF SHEET AND RETURN, WITH QUESTIONS ANSWERED, IN ENCLOSED ENVELOPE. ☜

Biographical Sketch.

Please give the information asked for below as fully as you can. If there is not room enough use an additional sheet. Write names and dates very plainly. Answer and return at once in enclosed envelope, so it will not be forgotten. To make the book complete we will need every name. If there have been incidents in your life of *special interest*, give them, even if not included in list of questions. Use the other side of this sheet if necessary.

1. Give names of your parents, with their nationality, date and place of birth.

William Huffman Born 1815 Butler Co Ohio. Mother Alice Lewis
English Quaker stock Randolp Co North Carolina 1815

2. Your own name in full; when born; where born; if born abroad, at what age did you come to this country; located where; how many brothers and sisters.

Gabriel M Huffman Born Parke co Ind. Feb 27th 1843

3. Your common school education; if graduate of college, when and where; of theological seminary, when and where; of any other department, when and where; if recipient of any degrees, conferred when and by whom; your literary work, if any.

All told about five terms common school. One year in Western College. D.D. 1894 Lane University.

4. When converted; at what age; circumstances leading thereto; when licensed; what conference did you join and when; of what others have you been a member; when ordained and by whom; how many years an itinerant; what positions have you held in the Church; what in state, county, and municipal affairs; name anything of interest in connection with your religious life or ministry.

Converted Feb 1859. Age 16 years. Quarterly Con licence 1865. Joined Kans Con 1869. Ordained 1873. JJ Glossbrenner. 29 years an itinerant.

5. If married, when and to whom; if latter, died when; if married again, person and date; how many children have you had; how many are living.

Married 1867. To Sue Neidig wife living, four sons two daughters all living.

GENERAL REMARKS:

Was Presiding Elder for ten years. Member of Gen Conference 1889-1893-1897. Trustee of Lane University 25 years. Pres Board Trus. 13 y. My Father still living has been a U.B minister for fifty years. I have two sons and one son in law in the ministry, all member of Kans Con. Served three years in the war of the Rebellion in Co H. 22d Iowa Infantry - was a prisoner of war six months at Tyler Japan. Was in the Campaign Vicksburg under Grant and the Virginia Campaign under Sheridan was honorably discharged as 3rd seargent of Co H. Aug 1865

I will most likely want a copy of the above mentioned "*Cyclopedia*" when published.*

Name *G M Huffman*
Date *Sept 30th 1898.* P. O. *Leavenworth Kansas.*

*This is not a subscription, but an indication to the publishers, what demand they may expect for the work when properly completed.

Figure 8:21. Biographical Sketch, Gabriel M. Huffman, United Brethren Minister, dated 30 September 1898.

In 1843, in the State of Indiana, he entered upon the Christian life, and soon after his conversion took up the work of the ministry, preaching continuously as health would permit. He preached his last sermon on the fifth Sunday of last April. He was the first to preach the gospel in this community, and organized the first Sunday School in 1859. He was a member of the Kansas State legislature in 1867 and 1868. There is no means at hand for ascertaining the number of persons he received into the United Brethren Church, but undoubtedly it will reach into the thousands. His life was an open book, nothing hidden or dark; his light continually shone. Even when suffering great bodily affliction he could rejoice. He was loved and respected by all that knew him. He was married to Alice Davis in Indiana in 1835, and to them were born ten sons (one of whom is Rev. G. M. Huffman, D. D., of the Kansas Conference) and six daughters. There are fifty-seven living grandchildren, one of whom is Rev. N. H. Huffman, our missionary at Ponce, Puerto Rico. He buried the wife of his youth in June, 1860. He was married in 1863 to Mrs. Lucy Nichols, who survives him. Serving faithfully in the gospel ministry for more than fifty-five years, fell asleep in Jesus, and well may it be said of him, "Blessed are the dead which die in the Lord from henceforth; Yea saith the Spirit, that they may rest from their labors and their works do follow him."

Analysis: William's obituary provides a number of valuable facts and many new clues to follow in future research. William's birthplace is again given as Butler County, Ohio, supporting Gabriel's statement in the biographical sketch. His birthdate is not stated but it can be arrived at through calculation. He died 16 September 1900 at age 85 years, 2 mos, 16 days:

1900	09	16	Death date
−85	02	16	Minus age at time of death
1815	07	01	Equals birth date (There is no 0 July 1815, thus he would have to have been born on the first of the month)

The obituary also provides more specific migration dates which will assist in pinpointing birthplaces for his children: Butler County, Ohio, 1815-1831; Indiana, 1831-1845; Fulton County, Illinois, 1845-1851; Iowa, 1851-1857; and Miami County, Kansas, 1857-1900. Of greater importance, however, is the part which states that William Huffman was the father of ten sons and six daughters. At this point in research only seven sons and five daughters have been identified. Assuming that the information is correct, four of William's children appear to have died in infancy and remain to be identified.

A second obituary notice appeared in *The Miami Republican* and offered the following additional information:

1. William Rollen Huffman died at five o'clock Sunday evening, 16 September 1900 at his home in New Lancaster.

2. He was born in Butler County, Ohio, 5 July 1815.

3. He was one of the first United Brethren ministers in Kansas and his early circuit extended to every settlement in the state. He organized the first Sunday School held in Miami Township at the home of his son, A. J. Huffman, in 1859. He was largely responsible for the building of the first schoolhouse in New Lancaster and preached his first sermon there soon after its completion also in 1859.

4. Rev. Huffman and his son, A. J., came to Miami County from Iowa in the trying times of the early settlement of the state. They located on claims in north Richland Township where the large Wellhouse orchard now stands. They did not preempt their claims, choosing instead to relocate at Miami Township where they homesteaded.

5. Politically Rev. Huffman was a Democrat prior to 1856. His first Republican vote was cast for John C. Fremont in 1856 when he left the Democrats over the slavery question. He was an ardent Republican thereafter. He was a member of the state legislature in 1867 and 1868 and filled the offices of justice of the peace and treasurer of Miami Township on numerous occasions.

6. Rev. Huffman was married to Alice Davis in Indiana in 1835. They were the parents of ten sons and seven daughters. Seven sons and two daughters were still living in 1900: A. J. Huffman at Lyndon, Kansas; G. M. Huffman at Lecompton, Kansas; Frank H. Huffman at Mont Ida, Kansas; J. D. Huffman at Liberty, Missouri; D. S. Huffman at Paola, Kansas; C. L. Huffman in Oklahoma; E. S. Huffman at New Lancaster, Kansas; Mrs. Louisa Tracy at New Lancaster, Kansas; and Mrs. Rebecca Ann Walley at Osawatomie, Kansas.

Analysis: There are two major discrepancies between the two obituaries. First, William's birthdate is reported as 1 July 1815 and then as 5 July 1815. The first calculation is supported by facts on his tombstone. The second mentions that William was the father of ten sons and seven daughters and the first gives only ten sons and six daughters. This discrepancy may never be resolved because not all of the children are identifiable since they died in infancy. In all probability William Huffman kept a record of his family in his Bible, but it has not been located in seventeen years of searching.

The list of his living children is very useful in locating them in the 1900 census. There were no other references to their whereabouts after leaving Miami County. If you are attempting to identify all of the living descendants of an ancestor, an obituary notice is usually quite helpful. While it may not list each living descendant by name, it often gives the number of living grandchildren and great-grandchildren, thereby telling you the number of people you need to locate.

Correspondence was sent to Parke County, Indiana as soon as that location was noted as Gabriel M. Huffman's birthplace. The results of that request disclosed that the marriage of William Houghman [sic] and Alice Davis took place in Rockville, Indiana on 15 January 1835 and is recorded in *Marriage Record Book A*, page 19. They were married by Matthew Noel.

Analysis: This record is a perfect example of how names can be recorded as they are heard pronounced. You should always consider all the possible ways of spelling a surname. One simple surname was spelled fifty-three different ways in the 1790 U.S. Census. When Ambrose Karr and Martha P. Huffman's marriage record was first requested, the clerk wrote back saying there was no record. When a second request was made indicating the surname may be listed as Carr, the appropriate record was located. Remember that record clerks are neither skilled genealogists nor record searchers. If you feel there may be a problem identifying an ancestor or relative in a record, explain the problem and list all possible spellings to help them conduct a thorough search in your behalf. As recordkeepers usually charge for the search whether it's positive or negative, you'll also save money if you instruct them properly the first time.

Most ancestors who held public office are going to be mentioned in county histories or state historical publications if they served on that level. There are several references to William Huffman's public offices, and these clues need to be followed. However, most of the information found in the *Annals of Kansas*, *Kansas* by A.T. Andreas, and *Kansas Historical Collections* only repeated the information found in William's obituaries, and their contents will not be reproduced here. Such repetition is not always the case and you should check each source of information carefully, regardless of how much you already know. Each of those records was searched in hope of finding some mention of William Rollen Huffman's parents. Additionally, if you are preparing a family history, the historical information found in printed sources lends color to your ancestor's life.

It's time to update the working family group record for William Huffman's family to get an idea of what has surfaced thus far and what remains to be done to complete the charts. There are some incomplete birthdates which may never be extended beyond the birth year without locating William Huffman's family Bible. His descendants in the Miami County, Kansas area have no idea where it went after his death.

William Huffman's family group record is fairly complete as far as birth, marriage, and death information for him and his wife. The children should be the main focus of research at this point. The field trip to Kansas dicussed earlier included many searches for the Huffman family and a considerable amount of information surfaced there. Miami County marriage records contained numerous entries for the Huffman family:

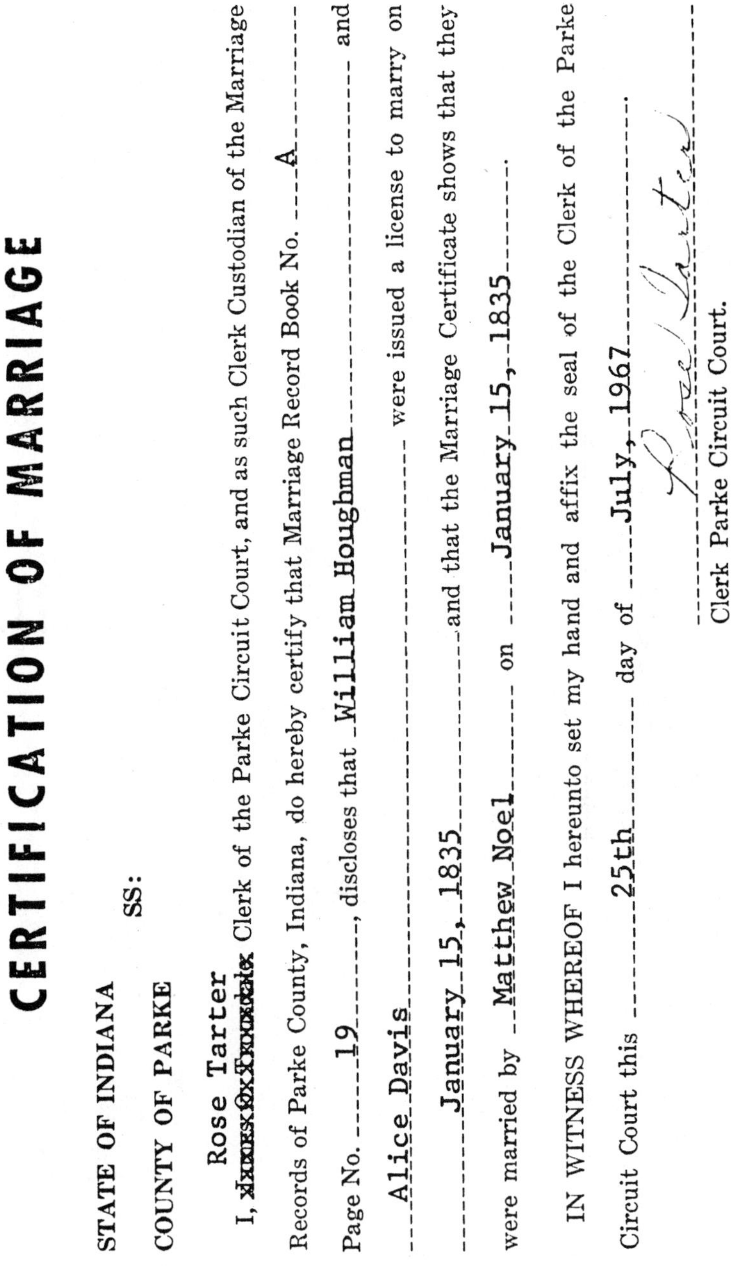

CERTIFICATION OF MARRIAGE

STATE OF INDIANA   SS:

COUNTY OF PARKE

I, ~~Rose Tarter~~ Clerk of the Parke Circuit Court, and as such Clerk Custodian of the Marriage

Records of Parke County, Indiana, do hereby certify that Marriage Record Book No. ---- A ----

Page No. ---- 19 ----, discloses that __William Houghman__-------------------------- were issued a license to marry on

---- __Alice Davis__----------------------------

-------- __January 15, 1835__------------------and that the Marriage Certificate shows that they

were married by __Matthew Noel__-------- on ---- __January 15, 1835__----.

IN WITNESS WHEREOF I hereunto set my hand and affix the seal of the Clerk of the Parke

Circuit Court this ----- __25th__--------- day of ---- __July, 1967__---------.

Clerk Parke Circuit Court.

Figure 8:22. Certification of Marriage, William Houghman [sic] and Alice Davis, 15 January 1835, Parke County, Indiana.

FAMILY GROUP SHEET

CONTINUED ON SHEET #2

HUS. WILLIAM ROLLEN HUFFMAN   OCCUPATION(S)

BORN	1 JUL 1815	PLACE Butler County, Ohio
CHR.		PLACE
MARR.	15 JAN 1835	PLACE Parke County, Indiana
DIED	16 SEP 1900	PLACE New Lancaster, Miami, Kansas
BUR.	20 SEP 1900	PLACE New Lancaster, Miami, Kansas
FATHER		
MOTHER		

OTHER WIVES: MRS. LUCY NICHOLS 1863

WIFE ALICE DAVIS

BORN	15 MAR 1816	PLACE Randolph County, North Carolina
CHR.		PLACE
DIED	28 JUN 1860	PLACE New Lancaster, Miami, Kansas
BUR.		PLACE New Lancaster Cemetery, New Lancaster, Miami, Kansas
FATHER		
MOTHER		

OTHER HUSBANDS

SEX	CHILDREN	DATE BORN / PLACE BORN	DATE MARRIED / TO	PLACE	DATE DIED / PLACE DIED
1 M	ANDREW J. HUFFMAN	CAL 1836 / Parke County, Indiana	MARGARET		
2 x F	MARTHA P. HUFFMAN	1829 / Parke County, Indiana	26 MAY 1859	New Lancaster, Miami, KS	15 JUN 1877 / New Lancaster, Miami, Kansas
3 F	LEWVISA WARD HUFFMAN	JAN 1841 / Parke County, Indiana	AMBROSE N. KARR		1935 / New Lancaster, Miami, Kansas
4 M	GABRIEL MILTON HUFFMAN	21 FEB 1843 / Parke County, Indiana	C. F. TRACY 1867		
5 M	FRANKLIN HAYDEN HUFFMAN	1844 / Fulton County, Illinois	SUE NEIDIG		
6 F	REBECCA ANN HUFFMAN	CAL 1848 / Fulton County, Illinois	MARTHA P.		
7 F	ANGELINE HUFFMAN	CAL 1850 / Fulton County, Illinois			
8 M	JONAS D. HUFFMAN	MAY 1853 / Iowa	FRANCES		
9 M	DAVID S. HUFFMAN	MAY 1854 / Iowa	EMMA E.		1927 / New Lancaster, Miami, Kansas
10 M	CHARLES L. HUFFMAN	FEB 1856 / Iowa	MARTHA		

SOURCES OF INFORMATION

1. 1860 U.S. Census, Miami Twp., Lykins County, Kansas.
2. 1870 U.S. Census, Miami Twp., Miami County, Kansas.
3. 1880 U.S. Census, Miami Twp., Miami County, Kansas.
4. 1900 U.S. Census, Miami Twp., Miami County, Kansas.
5. 1860 U.S. Census, Fulton County, Illinois.
6. Tombstone Inscriptions, New Lancaster Cemetery, Miami County, Kansas.
7. 1865, 1875, 1885 Kansas State Census, Miami Twp., Miami County, Kansas.

Figure 8:23. Family Group Work Record, William Rollen Huffman and Alice Davis.

CONTINUED FROM SHEET #1

FAMILY GROUP SHEET

HUS. WILLIAM ROLLEN HUFFMAN

OCCUPATION(S)

BORN	1 JUL 1815	PLACE Butler County, Ohio
CHR.		PLACE
MARR.	15 JAN 1835	PLACE Parke County, Indiana
DIED	16 SEP 1900	PLACE New Lancaster, Miami, Kansas
BUR.	20 SEP 1900	PLACE New Lancaster Cemetery, New Lancaster, Miami, Kansas
FATHER		
MOTHER		OTHER WIVES (2) MRS. MARGARET ABBOGAST 1863

WIFE ALICE DAVIS

BORN	15 MAR 1816	PLACE Randolph County, North Carolina
CHR.		PLACE
DIED	28 JUN 1860	PLACE New Lancaster, Miami, Kansas
BUR.		PLACE New Lancaster Cemetery, New Lancaster, Miami, Kansas
FATHER		
MOTHER		OTHER HUSBANDS

SEX	CHILDREN	DATE BORN / PLACE BORN	DATE MARRIED / TO	PLACE	DATE DIED / PLACE DIED
1 M	ELAM S. HUFFMAN	JUL 1856 / New Lancaster, Miami, Kansas	FRANCES		
2 F	SUSAN D. HUFFMAN	JUN 1860 / New Lancaster, Miami, Kansas			
3					
4					
5					
6					
7					
8					
9					
10					

OTHER MARRIAGES

SOURCES OF INFORMATION
8. Obituary Notice, The Religious Telegraph, October 14, 1900, William Rollen Huffman
9. Marriage Record, Parke County, Indiana, Book A, Page 19.
RESEARCH NOTES

Marriage Book A		Page
Huffman, Patsie and Ambrose Carr [sic]	26 May 1859	16
Huffman, William and Mrs. Lucy E. Nichols	27 Sep 1863	74
Huffman, Rebecca and Alvin G. Walley	15 Sep 1866	146
Huffman, Franklin H. and Martha P. Ellis	1 Mar 1866	160
Huffman, Angeline and William G. Meyers	5 Apr 1866	163
Huffman, Lewvisa W. and Calvin F. Tracy	8 May 1866	164

Marriage Book B		Page
Huffman, Jonas D. and Florence Campbell	30 Aug 1873	184
Huffman, Adam R. and Dell White	8 Jun 1874	288
Huffman, David S. and Elva J. Rhodes	2 Nov 1876	—

Marriage Book C		Page
Huffman, Charles L. and Susan Long	30 Jun 1878	—
Huffman, Elam S. and Fannie Harrison	23 Mar 1883	—

Analysis: There was only one Huffman family in Miami County, Kansas between 1860 and 1900 and none of the records searched mentioned Adam R. Huffman as a member of that family. Adam was a common name in Alice Davis's family and members of her family intermarried with other members of the Huffman family. Adam R. Huffman may have been one of William's nephews who visited his family and married someone he met in New Lancaster.

U.S. Census enumerations between 1860 and 1900 and Kansas State Census records between 1865 and 1885 contain dozens of entries for William Huffman's children, too many to list individually. These entries are excellent sources for identifying William's descendants and compiling family group records for his children. The following list of descendants was compiled from all of the census enumerations in which his family appeared:

Andrew J. Huffman			Martha P. Huffman		
Margaret I. Humphrey—wife			Ambrose N. Karr—husband		
Mortimer G. Huffman	b. 1860		James Marion Karr	b. 1862	
Mary L. Huffman	b. 1862		Mary Alice Karr	b. 1864	
Clara J. Huffman	b. 1864		Sarah Jane Karr	b. 1866	
Clyde S. Huffman	b. 1879				

Lewvisa Ward Huffman			Gabriel Milton Huffman		
Calvin F. Tracy—husband			Susan Neidig—wife		
Lucy Tracy	b. 1867		William M. Huffman	b. 1868	
William Tracy	b. 1873		Eda A. Huffman	b. 1870	
John Tracy	b. 1876		Nathan H. Huffman	b. 1872	
Franklin Haden Tracy	b. 1878		Leroy B. Huffman	b. 1875	
Blancy Tracy (twin)	b. 1881		Leonora Huffman	b. 1878	
Bertha Tracy (twin)	b. 1881		Howard H. Huffman	b. 1881	

Franklin Haden Huffman
Martha Phebe Ellis – wife

Lorenzo Huffman	b. 1867
Mary Etta Huffman	b. 1869
Elpha Huffman	b. 1873
Ora Huffman (m twin)	b. 1875
Lora Huffman (f twin)	b. 1875

Jonas Davis Huffman
Florence Campbell – wife

C. E. Huffman (m)	b. 1875
Ely Huffman	b. 1878
Frank Huffman	b. 1881
Halley Huffman (f)	b. 1883
one unidentified child	

David S. Huffman
Elva Jane Rhodes – 1st wife

Louis Huffman	b. 1878
Elfie Huffman	b. 1884

Emma E. Thompson – 2nd wife

Grace Huffman	b. 1897
one or more unidentified children	

Charles L. Huffman
Susan Long – 1st wife

Guy Huffman	b. 1884
Ray C. Huffman	b. 1886
Zora M. Huffman	b. 1890
Reuben A. Huffman	b. 1892

Martha C. – 2nd wife

Myron C. Huffman	b. 1900

Elam S. Huffman
Francis Harrison – wife

Alice Huffman	b. 1884
Jessie Huffman (f)	b. 1886
Otto Huffman (m twin)	b. 1891
Ollie Huffman (f twin)	b. 1891
two unidentified children	

Analysis: Forty-two of William Huffman's fifty-seven grandchildren were identified in the census records. Rebecca and Angeline Huffman left the Miami County area after they married. Their families have not been located and most likely include the remaining fifteen grandchildren who were living when William Huffman died.

Civil War pension application files are excellent sources for exact birthdates and birthplaces of veterans. They sometimes include names of spouses and children and their birth and death dates. Gabriel M. Huffman and Franklin H. Huffman applied for and received pensions for their Civil War service. Pension files often contain physician's examinations taken periodically after a pension was granted. These examinations always state the date and place of the exam as well as information that will help to trace the movement of an ancestor after the war. Space does not permit illustrations of a complete pension file and only the two documents containing the most genealogical information are discussed. The following summary of the key facts found in each pension file is given below:

Gabriel M. Huffman's File

1. Gabriel M. Huffman enlisted in Company H, 22nd Regiment, Iowa Infantry on 6 August 1862 at Iowa City as a private and was honorably

discharged at Savanah, Georgia on 25 July 1865.

2. He was born 27 February 1843 in Parke County, Indiana and married Susan Neidig in Muscatine, Iowa on 19 May 1865.

3. Gabriel and Susan Huffman were the parents of the following children: William N. Huffman, born: 28 Jul 1868, died: 21 Mar 1902; Eda A. Huffman, born: 27 Sep 1870; Nathan H. Huffman, born: 30 Nov 1872; Leroy B. Huffman, born: 14 Jun 1875; Leonora Huffman, born: 17 Feb 1878; and Howard H. Huffman, born: 4 Dec 1881.

4. When Gabriel enlisted, his physical description was recorded on his muster roll: Height: 5 feet 9 ¾ inches; Eyes: Blue; Hair: Brown; Complexion: Fair.

5. He was taken prisoner of war at Lavacca, Calhoun County, Texas on 22 January 1864 while on a scouting mission. He was imprisoned at Tyler, Texas until his release on 31 August 1864. Gabriel took part in the siege of Vicksburg under Grant and the Virginia campaign under Sheridan. He was discharged as a sergeant.

Analysis: Gabriel's pension file provides additional evidence of his Parke County, Indiana birthplace. It also offers information not available in Miami County records, stating that he married Susan Neidig at Muscatine, Iowa on 19 May 1867. No other record located gave his marriage date and place, and there were no clues to suggest that he had returned to Iowa after the family moved to Kansas. While locating his children's birthdates could have been achieved through other sources, finding them listed in the pension file saves time and effort. Their birthdates are circumstantial evidence and are further supported through census records. Further proof in support of those birthdates could be obtained in their death records once death dates were established.

Franklin H. Huffman's File

1. Franklin Haden Huffman enlisted in Company D, 15th Kansas Cavalry at New Lancaster on 10 August 1863 as a private.

2. He was born 10 September 1844 at Parke County, Indiana and married Martha Phebe Ellis on 1 November 1866 at New Lancaster.

3. Franklin and Martha Huffman were the parents of the following children according to a document dated 7 August 1915: Lorenzo Huffman, born: 3 Sep 1867 (deceased); Mary Etta Huffman, born: 1 Jul 1869; Elpha Huffman, born: 10 Feb 1873; Ora Huffman (m twin), born: 15 Feb 1875 (deceased); and Lora Huffman (f twin), born: 15 Feb 1875 (deceased). Mary Etta Huffman's married surname was Studebaker and Elpha Huffman's was Garrison.

4. Franklin H. Huffman died 23 January 1923 at Salina, Kansas, and his wife received a widow's pension after his death. She was born at Green County, Ohio on 11 March 1848. Witnesses to her application were

C. M. Garrison of Salina, Kansas and Lucy Tracy of LaCygne, Kansas (Lucy Tracy was Franklin's niece and daughter of Lewvisa Ward Huffman).

Analysis: Franklin Haden Huffman's birthdate and birthplace were not previously known. His pension file is circumstantial evidence and his birth information required additional support. His death certificate was requested to obtain a second piece of evidence. As in the case of Gabriel Huffman's family, the pension lists all of his children, their birthdates, and whether they were living or deceased at the time a document was completed. Record of his marriage to Martha Phebe Ellis further supports the original marriage record obtained at the Miami County Courthouse.

Death records were requested for Lewvisa, Gabriel, Franklin, and David Huffman from the State of Kansas. Record clerks were only able to locate the death records of Lewvisa and Franklin. A study of those records follows:

	Lewvisa Ward Tracy	Franklin Haden Huffman
Full Name:	Lewvisa Ward Tracy	Franklin Haden Huffman
Place of Death:	Miami County, Kansas	Salina, Kansas
Date of Death:	18 July 1939	23 January 1923
Usual Residence:	————	Salina, Kansas
Sex:	Female	Male
Race:	White	White
Marital Status:	Widowed	Married
Name of Spouse:	C. F. Tracy	Martha Huffman
Date of Birth:	14 January 1841	10 September 1844
Age:	98 yrs, 6 mos, 4 days	77 yrs, 4 mos, 13 days
Occupation:	Household Duties	Retired Farmer
Birthplace:	Parke County, Indiana	Indiana
Father:	Wm. Huffman	Wm. Huffman
Father's Birthplace:	Not Known	Pennsylvania
Mother:	Alice Davis	Alice Davis
Mother's Birthplace:	South Carolina	South Carolina
Informant:	Miss Lucy Tracy	Wm. Garrison
Informant's Address:	Fontana, Kansas	Salina, Kansas
Cause of Death:	Arteriosclerosis	Asthma and Bronchitis
Date of Burial:	19 July 1939	25 January 1923
Place of Burial:	New Lancaster, Kansas	Gypsum Hill, Salina, Kansas
Undertaker:	J. B. Hays, Drexel, Missouri	Rush Smith, Salina, Kansas

Analysis: Most of the information in these death certificates supports previously known facts about their lives and their parentage. The most important discrepancy to be noted is in Alice Davis's birthplace incorrectly stated as South Carolina instead of North Carolina in each record. Lewvisa's death record provides her birthdate and place of birth, previously unknown information.

A search of the biographical sketches included in *History of the State of Kansas* (Chicago: A. T. Andreas, 1883) was conducted to find more information on William Huffman's children. Only Andrew and his father were mentioned in the history:

> Andrew J. Huffman, farmer, Section 13, Township 18, Range 24, P.O. New Lancaster. Mr. Huffman was born in Parke County, Indiana, November 2, 1836; moved to Illinois with his parents when ten years of age; eight years later to Iowa, and in the fall of 1865 to Kansas. He located on his present farm of 186 acres in 1869. He was married in Benton County, Iowa in 1858 to Margaret I., daughter of Joseph and Margaret Humphrey. Mrs. Huffman was born in Pennsylvania. They have four children, two sons and two daughters — Mortimer G., Mary L., wife of C. Bodenhammer, of Miami Township, Clara J., wife of John Woldridge of Cass County, Missouri, and Clyde Sherman.

Analysis: Once again, this is a source that offers information not found anywhere else. There is little doubt that Andrew J. Huffman was born in Parke County, Indiana because every other piece of evidence states clearly that the Huffman family was there from 1831 until they moved to Illinois in 1845. Andrew's birthdate is circumstantially accepted and subject to further evidence. This sketch is the only evidence of the Huffman family's possible Iowa residence. There is also information attesting to Margaret Humphrey's parentage which should be followed up in Benton County, Iowa records. The only known discrepancy is in the date Andrew settled in Kansas. He arrived with his father in 1857 and was enumerated in the 1860 census of Miami County.

Looking again at William Huffman's family group record, you will note that his and Alice Davis's parents have not been identified. No clues were given to their identities in any of the dozens of records searched. Some clues to William Huffman's early origins exist and suggest that research should continue in those known locations, namely Butler County, Ohio and Parke County, Indiana.

When you have no clues to the identity of an ancestor's parents you must determine who lived in the area where that ancestor was born, either at the time of, immediately before, or just after his or her birth. William Huffman was born in 1815 at Butler County, Ohio. There was no census for that county in 1810, leaving only the 1820 census. Four Huffman families were found living in St. Clair Township, Butler County, Ohio with a male zero to five years old:

Sampson Huffman, Gabriel Huffman, Jacob Huffman, and John Huffman. Since William Huffman would have been five years old in 1820 and was known to have lived there until 1831, he would have to be the son of one of those four men.

A study of Parke County, Indiana land records and census enumerations shows that Sampson and Jacob Huffman never resided there. Gabriel Huffman moved to Parke County, Indiana in 1829 and in 1830 he had no males in his household between fifteen and twenty years old, suggesting that his son died between 1820 and 1830. A Henry Huffman, yet a fifth possibility, was listed in the 1830 census of Parke County, Indiana and had a male between fifteen and twenty years old in his household; however, property records show that he moved to Parke County, Indiana in 1824, seven years before William Huffman came with his father. Based on that early arrival, Henry Huffman was eliminated as William's father. That left only John Huffman.

John Huffman first purchased property in Parke County, Indiana in September 1828 while still a resident of Butler County, Ohio. His second purchase took place in September 1832, with Parke County, Indiana given as his residence. William Huffman was already married when the 1840 census of Parke County, Indiana was taken. He was living near the following individuals listed on page 294: John Huffman, 60-70 years old; Miller Davis, 50-60 years old; Warner Davis, 50-60 years old; and Edmond Davis, 20-30 years old.

Analysis: Proximity alone does not prove relationship and should be used only as the suggestion of possible relation between two or more individuals. The presence of John Huffman in Butler County, Ohio in 1820 and his move to Parke County, Indiana between 1830 and 1832 fits William Huffman's account of his movements with his father. John had a male child in his household in 1820 who fit the age group William would fall into and he was living next to William in the 1840 census of Parke County, Indiana. William Huffman married Alice Davis in Parke County, Indiana, suggesting that she was probably living there with her family. William and Alice Huffman were living in close proximity to Miller and Warner Davis, both men old enough to have been Alice's father. Their proximity suggests that research focus on them to determine whether she was related to either of them.

One approach in attempting to determine if William was John Huffman's son is to locate John's will or probate record. A request was sent to Parke County, Indiana asking for a copy of any estate records on file for John Huffman. No estate records were there, but property records showed that John sold his land in 1845 – the same year William sold his property and moved to Fulton County, Illinois.

William Huffman's residence in Illinois was not mentioned in any of the Kansas records searched. The Illinois State Archives maintains a card file index of the 1850 U.S. Census of Illinois, and in the absence of a printed census index in 1967, correspondence was sent to the Illinois State Archives asking for the 1850 census entry for William Huffman. It wasn't until several years

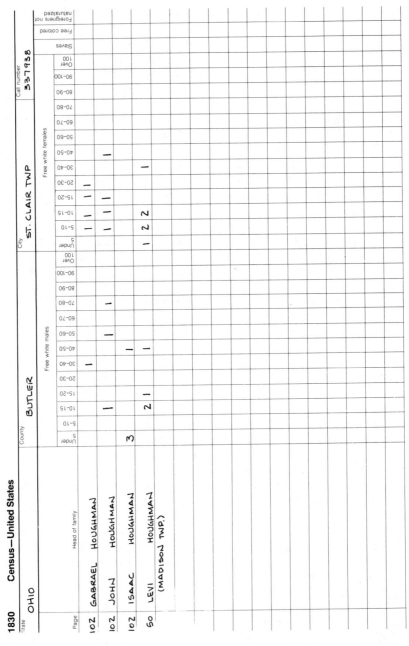

Figure 8:24. 1830 U.S. Census, St. Clair Township, Butler County, Ohio.

later that the entire Fulton County census became available. The following entries were extracted:

1850 U.S. Census, Fulton County, Illinois

Dwelling Number	Name	Age	Sex	Occupation	Birthplace
#42	John Huffman	75	M	Farmer	Virginia
	Mary Huffman	73	F		England
#56	Andrew Davis	29	M	Farmer	No. Carolina
	Catherine Davis	24	F		Ohio
	John Davis	8	M		Indiana
	Allen Davis	7/12	M		Illinois
#70	Isaac Huffman	67	M	Farmer	Virginia
	Sarah Huffman	53	F		Virginia
	Thomas Huffman	20	M		Ohio
	William Huffman	15	M		Ohio
	Elizabeth Huffman	15	F		Ohio
	Isaac Huffman	11	M		Illinois
	John Huffman	25	M	Laborer	Ohio
#77	William Huffman	34	M	Merchant	Ohio
	Alice Huffman	34	F		No. Carolina
	Andrew Huffman	14	M		Indiana
	Patsy Huffman	11	F		Illinois
	Lewvisa Huffman	9	F		Illinois
	Gabriel Huffman	7	M		Illinois
	Haden Huffman	5	M		Illinois
	Rebecca Huffman	2	F		Illinois
	Angeline Huffman	1/12	F		Illinois
#78	Edmond Davis	30	M	Tavern Keeper	No. Carolina
	Harriet Davis	28	F		Ohio
	Mary Davis	13	F		Indiana
	John Davis	10	M		Indiana
	Julia Davis	8	F		Indiana
	Ellen Davis	3	F		Indiana
	William Davis	3/12	M		Illinois

Analysis: This is a classic example of families moving west in groups. It appears that Isaac Huffman moved to Illinois first, bypassing Indiana completely.

His presence there may have drawn the other families to Fulton County. His age and Virginia birthplace suggest that he might be John Huffman's younger brother. Later research showed that Edmond Davis was Alice Davis's twin brother, his age incorrectly stated in the 1850 census. According to the Huffman family in Kansas, Edmond married William Huffman's younger sister, Harriet Huffman, and their marriage record was on file in Parke County, Indiana. A closer look at Edmond's census entry, shows that his oldest children were named Mary and John Davis, perhaps after their maternal grandparents? Naming patterns are significant clues to relationships that should be tested further in other records.

Still needing better evidence of a father-son relationship between John and William Huffman, a request was sent to Fulton County, Illinois asking for John's estate records. Unfortunately, no record was on file. John Huffman was not enumerated in the 1860 census of Fulton County and his whereabouts after 1850 are unknown. The preponderance of circumstantial evidence suggests that William Huffman was the son of John and Mary Huffman. John Huffman's relationship to Isaac Huffman was later established in deeds documenting the transfer of land from George and Elizabeth Huffman to their sons John, Isaac, Jacob, Sampson, and Abraham. No evidence shows that John Huffman moved to Benton County, Iowa with William's family.

As stated above, there were only two men listed in the 1840 census of Parke County, Indiana who were old enough to have been Alice Davis's father: Miller and Warner Davis. Before beginning in-depth research into the Davis family in Parke County, Indiana, the Family Group Records Archives (FGRA) was rechecked to see if anyone had submitted sheets for either Miller or Warner Davis. One was found for Miller Davis:

Miller Davis b. 1 Dec 1789 Center, Randolph Co., North Carolina m. 1 May 1811 d. 9 Nov 1865 Iowa Co., Iowa
son of Jesse Davis and Elizabeth Reynolds

Rachel Hoover b. 1 Sep 1793 Randolph Co., North Carolina d. 20 Mar 1871
dau of Jonas Hoover and Rachael Briles

Children:
1. Betsey Davis   b. abt 1812 Randolph Co., North Carolina
2. Polly Davis   b. abt 1813   "
3. Hannah   "   b. abt 1815   "
4. Alice   "   (twin)   b. 1816   "
5. Edmond " (twin)   b. 1816   "
6. Andrew "   b. 1820   "
7. Diana   "   b. 21 May 1822   "
8. Lucinda "   b. abt 1824   "

9. Caroline Davis	b. abt 1826	Randolph Co., North Carolina
10. Rebecca "	b. 1828	"
11. Susan "	b. 1831	"
12. Jonas "	b. 1 Feb 1833	Parke Co., Indiana
13. Rachel "	b. 1835	"
14. Martha "	b. 1839	"
15. William "	b. 1840	"

The source of the information submitted to the Genealogical Library of the LDS Church was the *Reynolds Family 1530-1959* by S. F. Tillman, page 49, Family #1106. The early generations discussed in the above family history are more reliable than later generations. Mr. Tillman received information from descendants of Christopher Reynolds and included it in his publication without verification.

Gabriel Huffman stated that his mother was of English Quaker heritage. The Society of Friends, the Quakers, kept some of the best records in America. William Wade Hinshaw published several volumes called the *Encyclopedia of American Quaker Genealogy*, including a volume of North Carolina Quaker records. Families are often listed in groups with birthdates and sometimes deathdates. A separate section follows family group listings and includes information such as disciplinary actions, receiving members from other monthly meetings and releasing members to other monthly meetings.

Miller Davis's family was not listed as a group in the *Encyclopedia of American Genealogy*, Volume 6. However, there was an entry showing that Miller Davis was disowned by the Marlborough Monthly Meeting in Randolph County, North Carolina on 8 March 1831. No reason was given for the action. Then there is an entry dated 1 December 1836 which states that Rachel Davis and daughters Mary, Alice, Dianna, Lucinda, Rebecca, Susannah, and Rachel had their memberships transferred to the Bloomfield Monthly Meeting at Parke County, Indiana.

Another entry found in the records of the Back Creek Monthly Meeting in Guilford County, North Carolina shows Miller Davis, son of Jesse and Elizabeth Davis of Randolph County, North Carolina, married Rachel Hoover on 1 May 1811. Their dates are entered as 1811, 5, 1—year, month, and day, and thus that notation represents 1 May 1811. (See the section on dates in Chapter 1 for an in-depth discussion of the Quaker dating system.)

The Quaker records supply the necessary proof to identify Miller Davis and Rachel Hoover as the parents of Alice Davis. Further research into the Davis family will be found in the study of the fifth generation. Just to make certain that Warner Davis wasn't Alice's father, his family was examined in the records of the Salem Monthly Meeting (Indiana):

Warner Davis	b. 28 December 1787 Bloomfield, Indiana
Milly (?)	

Children:

1. Alice Davis		b. 15 Dec 1814
2. Elizabeth	"	b. 22 Feb 1816
3. Jane	"	b. 17 Oct 1817
4. Joel	"	b. 24 Jul 1819
5. Carolina	"	b. 6 Jan 1821
6. Irena	"	b. 14 Jun 1822
7. Rumina	"	b. 14 Apr 1824
8. Ruhama	"	b. 14 Apr 1824
9. John	"	b. 24 Apr 1826
10. Jesse	"	b. 1 Oct 1828
11. Mary	"	b. 17 Feb 1830
12. David	"	b. 11 Feb 1833
13. Reuben	"	b. 11 Feb 1833

Analysis: Both Miller and Warner Davis had a daughter named Alice, not an uncommon occurrence in Quaker families who named their chidren after family members and friends. But Warner's daughter was two years older than William Huffman's wife, whose tombstone reads "Born 15 March 1816." There are cases showing as many as ten individuals sharing the same name, living in the same area, and born at approximately the same time. Each of them had to be properly identified and placed within his or her own family group. Always check to make sure that no one else living in the same area shares the name of your ancestor. If you don't, you may find you've established an incorrect relationship and built a faulty lineage upon that improper connection.

This concludes the identification of Bertha Ruth Smith's fourth generation maternal ancestors. The study of her fifth generation will be limited to only two families that take us into the 1700s. Only the Davis family will be taken beyond the fifth generation.

THE FIFTH GENERATION

MATTHEW KARR/KERR (6:2)
HANNAH PEES/PEAS (6:3)

American genealogical research prior to 1850 is more complicated due to the absence of vital records (outside of New England) and census enumerations listing each member of a household by name. It is important to gather as many clues as possible about each family's pre-1850 activities while identifying later generations. William Karr's biographical sketch offered the most significant details about his parent's early lives and movements. Let's review what is already known:

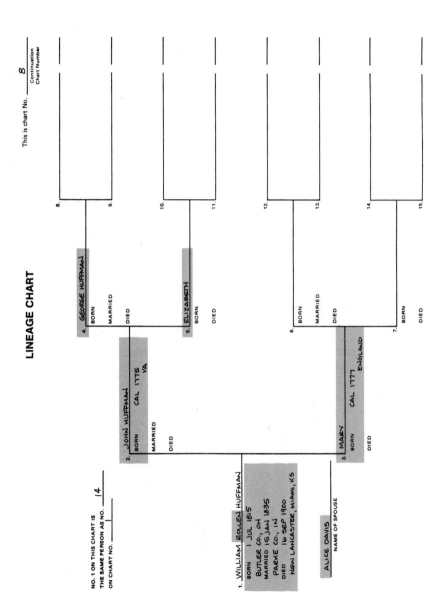

LINEAGE CHART

This is chart No. __8__

Continuation Chart Number

NO. 1 ON THIS CHART IS
THE SAME PERSON AS NO. __14__
ON CHART NO. _____

1. WILLIAM ROLLEN HUFFMAN
BORN 1 JUL 1815
BUTLER CO., OH
MARRIED 15 JAN 1835
PARKE CO., IN
DIED 16 SEP 1900
NEW LANCASTER, MIAMI, KS

ALICE DAVIS
NAME OF SPOUSE

2. JOHN HUFFMAN
BORN   CAL 1775
VA
MARRIED
DIED

3. MARY
BORN   CAL 1777
ENGLAND
DIED

4. GEORGE HUFFMAN
BORN
MARRIED
DIED

5. ELIZABETH
BORN
DIED

6.
BORN
MARRIED
DIED

7.
BORN
DIED

8.
9.
10.
11.
12.
13.
14.
15.

Figure 8:25. Lineage Work Chart 8, William Rollen Huffman.

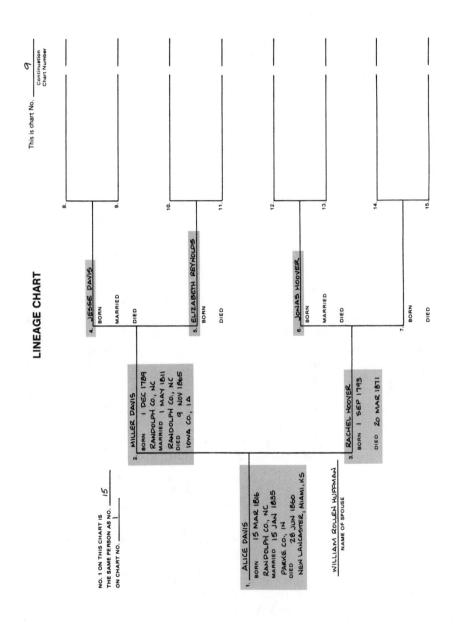

LINEAGE CHART

This is chart No. _9_

Continuation Chart Number

8. |

9. |

10. |

11. |

12. |

13. |

14. |

15. |

4. JESSE DAVIS
BORN
MARRIED
DIED

5. ELIZABETH REYNOLDS
BORN
DIED

6. JONAS HOOVER
BORN
MARRIED
DIED

7.
BORN
DIED

2. MILLER DAVIS
BORN   1 DEC 1789
RANDOLPH CO., NC
MARRIED 1 MAY 1811
RANDOLPH CO., NC
DIED   9 NOV 1865
IOWA CO., IA

3. RACHEL HOOVER
BORN 1 SEP 1793
DIED 20 MAR 1871

1. ALICE DAVIS
BORN   15 MAR 1816
RANDOLPH CO., NC
MARRIED 15 JAN 1835
PARKE CO., IN
DIED   28 JUN 1860
NEW LANCASTER, MIAMI, KS

WILLIAM ROLLEN HUFFMAN
NAME OF SPOUSE

NO. 1 ON THIS CHART IS
THE SAME PERSON AS NO. _15_
ON CHART NO. _1_

Figure 8:26. Lineage Work Chart 9, Alice Davis.

1. William Karr was the son of Matthew Karr and Hannah Pease/Pees. He was born 24 March 1813 at Washington County, Pennsylvania, his mother's birthplace.

2. Matthew Karr was born in northern Ireland and arrived in the United States with his family when eight years old.

3. Matthew moved his family to Franklin County, Indiana in 1814, where he remained until his death.

4. Hannah Pease/Pees died 9 May 1855 near Pulaski, Davis County, Iowa. Her father, Nicholas Pees, was a Revolutionary War soldier.

5. Hannah migrated to Iowa with her sons, James, George W., Andrew P., and William.

Before a research plan was devised, several letters arrived with additional details of Matthew Karr's family. One letter was written by Catherine Hopkins in 1920 to a niece who had inquired about Matthew and Hannah's family. Her letter is reproduced unedited to illustrate the difficulty you may encounter in sorting out information found in letters, diaries, and journals.

Stringtown, Iowa, Davis Co. was a little town with half dozen houses east of Bloomfield. Nine or ten miles out on the same road there was a town which was later moved to a farm adjoining the land of a man who bought the town. However, [your] Aunt Zillah Hopkins and I were born there before the town was moved. Our father [Andrew J. Hopkins] owned a tavern and the General Merchandise Store there. Uncle William Karr, with whom Grandmother Hannah Pease Karr made her home until she died, was a half mile or so from the cemetery where Grandma Pease Karr was buried. I do not remember her at all but Lizzie [her sister] does. [Lizzie] said she was lame and walked with a cane.

The way I figure it out if mother's father [Matthew] was 51 years old when he died and she was 21 months old that would make him born about 1776. Mother was born March 14, 1825. Her mother Hannah Pees Karr was a year or two older than her husband, Matthew. You could count out that she was born 1774-1775 and she died 1855. She was either 48 or 49 when mother [Martha Jane] was born, and I remember it as 49.

A man thought mother's sister was her mother and when he was told her mother's age he was astonished and made mother a little chair—as he was a cabinet maker—in honor of mother's age. So you see I am quite sure I have made no mistake as to the age of my [grandmother] Hannah Pees Karr.

My grandfather Matthew Karr and wife Hannah Pease Karr were married in Washington County, Pennsylvania. They moved to Mercer County, Penna sometime after they were married and lived about 75 miles from her father's place. She visited her parents twice a year, making the journey on horseback and taking the two youngest children with her. They

FAMILY GROUP SHEET

HUS. MATTHEW KARR — OCCUPATION(S)

BORN	PLACE	Northern Ireland
CHR	PLACE	
MARR	PLACE	
DIED	PLACE	Franklin County, Indiana
BUR	PLACE	
FATHER		
MOTHER		OTHER WIVES

WIFE HANNAH PEES

BORN	PLACE	Washington County, Pennsylvania
CHR	PLACE	
DIED 9 MAY 1855	PLACE near Pulaski, Davis, Iowa	
BUR	PLACE	
FATHER NICHOLAS PEES		
MOTHER		OTHER HUSBANDS

SEX	CHILDREN	DATE BORN / PLACE BORN	DATE MARRIED / TO	PLACE	DATE DIED / PLACE DIED
M	1 JAMES KARR				
M	2 GEORGE W. KARR				
M	3 ANDREW P. KARR				
x M	4 WILLIAM A. KARR	24 MAR 1814 / Washington County, Penn	19 FEB 1835 / Amanda Peace HOPKINS	Decatur County, Indiana	
	5				
	6				
	7				
	8				
	9				
	10				

OTHER MARRIAGES
4 md (2) MRS. MARGARET ABROGAST 21 SEP 1871

SOURCES OF INFORMATION
1. Portrait and Biographical Album of Sedgewick County, Kansas.

RESEARCH NOTES

Figure 8:27. Family Group Work Record, Matthew Karr and Hannah Pees.

returned to Washington County before leaving for Cincinnati, Ohio on a raft down the Ohio River. I do not know the date they landed there or in Indiana, only that it was spring in Indiana. My sisters think that Mother was the only child born in Indiana.

Catherine Karr Alley, Hannah's eldest daughter lived and died in Red Rock, Marion County, Iowa. She was married to Elihu Alley in Indiana and they had two children: Hannah the eldest and Elihu the son, called "Little Ike." If these children are living [in 1920] they might know something about the Pease family. I believe the daughter married a man named Dickey. There were George and John, brothers of Catherine Karr Alley who lived not far from Pella, Iowa. I do not know their wives names. Catherine's sister Eliza lived there too, but I don't know her married name. All lived in Marion County near Pella and Red Rock.

I am sure I told you that grandfather Matthew Karr came with his parents to this country when 7 years old from Northern Ireland as they were Protestants and Presbyterians, Scotch-Irish. How many children there were I do not know. I do remember that at the time of or soon after grandfather Karr's death, his two brothers came to visit grandmother—one named Archie. I do not remember the other but Lizzie said it was George—nor do I recall where they came from.

Father [Andrew J. Hopkins] and mother [Martha Jane Karr] were married March 29, 1845 and left Indiana the following month with William Karr's family, Grandmother Karr, and Elihu Alley's family.

Another letter was written by Mrs. W. E. Cole of Broken Bow, Nebraska to the *Hartford Times's* Genealogical Section on 23 January 1942.

In answer to #8980 part 2, I have a Matthew Karr mentioned as the brother of my ancestor Archibald Kerr whose father was Wm. Kerr and mother was Margaret. Archibald's brothers and sisters: (1) Archibald—b. 1775 d. 1846 md. Mary Huston 1798, (2) James, (3) Alexander, (4) Canada, (5) John, (6) William, (7) George, and (8) Matthew. Archibald lived in Washington and Greene, Pennsylvania and died in Virginia. I too am looking for Archibald's father who was William according to Bible records. There are so many Williams they are hard to locate.

A third letter included a page from the Clann Cearr Archives Section of the Kerr Family Association.

1. MATTHEW KERR, born about 1775 in Northern Ireland, came to America with his parents at the age of seven (1782). Said to have had a brother named William who later joined Matthew in Franklin County, Indiana. Married Hannah Pease (Pees) (Peas) daughter of Nicholas Pees, she died May 9, 1865, census of 1850 says she was 75 then, so must

have been born near 1775 also. Matthew spent some years in Pennsylvania where at least one of his children was born. Later moved west down the Ohio River to Cincinnati, where he spent one winter. Left there in the spring on a self-built raft with everything he owned he went to Franklin County, Indiana, later Bartholomew County. He died December 14, 1826 of pneumonia. Their children were:

1. CATHERINE KERR, born in Pennsylvania, married to Elihu Alley.
2. WILLIAM KERR, married first to Amanda Peace Hopkins, second to (?) Hyde.
3. ANDREW KERR, married Mary (?).
4. JAMES KERR
5. GEORGE KERR
6. JOHN KERR, born 1809 in Indiana. Married Caroline (?) (b. Virginia). Served in Mexican War and died in Mexico.
7. ISABELLE KERR, (Ibbie), married first to (?) Henderson, second to (?) Castile.
8. ELIZA KERR, born 1815 in Indiana, married John Dickey (b. 1815).
9. MARTHA JANE KERR, born March 15, 1825 in Franklin County, Indiana. Married Andrew J. Hopkins (b. September 1, 1825, Nicholas County, Kentucky–d. 25 Nov. 1912, New Brighton, Pa.) on March 30, 1845 in Bartholomew County, Indiana. She died September 20, 1913 in Topeka, Kansas. Their children were:
   1. Elizabeth Hopkins, born August 11, 1846, married William Young.
   2. Sarah Hopkins, born December 4, 1849, married George Ford, Jr. August 25, 1880, at least one child: Jeanette Ford, married John W. Woodruff.
   3. Catherine Hopkins, born May 31, 1853, married James Layton Wood.
   4. Zillah Hopkins, born in 1854, married Milton Pollard.
   5. William H. Hopkins, born March 24, 1856, married Hannah Nation.
   6. Amanda (Matty) Hopkins, born April 8, 1858, married Dr. J. W. Taylor.
   7. Hiram Ward Hopkins, born September 16, 1857, married Della.
   8. Joseph Houston Hopkins, born February 15, 1863, married first to Laura Bryan, second to Eva Erwin.
   9. Rachel (Ray) Hopkins, born in 1866, married R. Dietrich.
   10. Andrew Joslin Hopkins, born December 12, 1868, married Elizabeth Nation.
10. MARY KERR, may have married, but died as a young woman, buried near her father in Indiana.

Analysis: Each piece of correspondence offers hearsay and circumstantial evidence. Historical details, not found in public records, may or may not be proven accurate with further research. There are a number of discrepancies in each letter when compared to another and to other known facts.

The most valuable contribution of these letters is the naming of Matthew's ten children and enough information about a few of them to make research in Iowa and Indiana much easier in view of the large number of Karr/Kerr families and their propensity for naming their children after family members. Let's look at how Matthew's family is shaping up:

Matthew Karr/Kerr born about 1775 in Northern Ireland, died 14 December 1826 in Franklin County, Indiana.

Hannah Pease/Pees born about 1775 in Washington County, Pennsylvania, daughter of Nicholas Pees, died 9 May 1855 in Davis County, Iowa.

Children:
1. Catherine Karr—oldest daughter, married Elihu Alley.
2. James Karr
3. Andrew P. Karr—married a Miss Castile.
4. George W. Karr—married Eliza Dickey.
5. William A. Karr—born 24 March 1813 in Washington County, Pennsylvania. Married Amanda Peace Hopkins 19 February 1835 at Decatur County, Indiana.
6. Eliza Karr—born 1815, married John Dickey.
7. Isabel Karr—married Mr. Henderson and then Mr. Castile.
8. Mary Karr—died as a young woman and was buried near father.
9. John Karr—born 14 November 1818 in Franklin County, Indiana. Married Caroline Jones and then Anna Clark.
10. Martha Jane Karr—born 14 March 1825 in Franklin County, Indiana. Married Andrew J. Hopkins on 30 March 1845 at Bartholomew County, Indiana. Died 30 September 1913 at Topeka, Kansas.

RESEARCH PLAN
Research at this point should be designed toward compiling an accurate group record for Matthew Karr's family and to substantiate valid information in the letters provided by his descendants. Since there are so many families to sort out in Marion County, Iowa, the task would be easier if the spouse of each of Matthew's children was identified before a census study was initiated.

1. Marriage Records—search the records of Franklin, Bartholomew, Decatur, and Shelby counties, Indiana and Marion County, Iowa. Pennsylvania

did not require registration of marriages until 1885, thus any record of Matthew's marriage to Hannah Pease/Pees would be found in Washington County church records, if any exist.

2. Census Records—search the 1850 through 1900 U.S. Census records for Marion County, Iowa; the 1830 and 1840 U.S. Census records for Bartholomew County, Indiana; the 1820 U.S. Census for Franklin County, Indiana, and the 1790 through 1810 U.S. Census records for Washington County, Pennsylvania.

3. Probate Records—search the Franklin County, Indiana probate records for mention of Matthew's estate and Washington County, Pennsylvania records for mention of Matthew as an heir to his father's estate.

4. Cemetery Records—search Marion County, Iowa cemetery records for tombstone inscriptions that give death dates for Matthew's children and then request death records for those who died after registration began.

There are nearly 250 census entries for Matthew Karr's descendants in Iowa and Kansas between 1850 and 1880, obviously too many to review individually. The following represents a summary of those enumerations used to construct his family group and those of his children. Dates of birth are calculated from ages given in census enumerations.

Catherine Karr Alley	(1800)	John Karr	(1804)
Elihu Alley—husband	(1804)	Hesther Doty—1st wife	
Hannah Alley	b. 1828	Maria(h) Karr	b. 1829
Dodridge Alley	b. 1829	Mary Karr	b. 1831
Cyrus Alley	b. 1831	John Karr	b. 1832
Matthew Alley	b. 1834	Andrew Karr	b. 1834
John Alley	b. 1840	Hesther Karr	b. 1836
Elihu Alley	b. 1841	Clarissa Karr	b. 1838
		Direxey Karr	b. 1839
Mary Karr	(1802)	James Karr	b. 1841
no known children		Jane Crosby—2nd wife	
		George Karr	b. 1845
		William Karr	b. 1848
Andrew P. Karr	(1808)	Geneva Karr	b. 1850
Mary Doty—1st wife		Harriet Karr	b. 1852
Eliza D. Karr	b. 1838	Hannah Wise—3rd wife	
George W. Karr	b. 1841	no known children	
Hannah Karr	b. 1845	Elizabeth Richards—4th wife	
Alexander Karr	b. 1848	no known children	
Louisa A. Karr	b. 1850		
Ruth Robinson—2nd wife		Isabel Karr	(1810)
no known children		William Henderson—1st husband	
		Caleb Casteel—2nd husband	
		families not traced	

George W. Karr	(1812)
Eliza Dickey—wife	
John M. Karr	b. 1837
Mary Jane Karr	b. 1838
Minerva Karr	b. 1840
Cynthia A. Karr	b. 1845
Matthew Karr	b. 1846
Edward Karr	b. 1847
Martha Jane Karr	b. 1849
Thomas P. Karr	b. 1851
Andrew Karr	b. 1854
William Karr	b. 1857
George Karr	b. 1859
Elihu Karr	b. 1860
James Karr	b. 1861
Francis R. Karr	b. 1863

Eliza Karr	(1815)
John Dickey—husband	
Thomas Dickey	b. 1837
Francis Dickey	b. 1840
Catherine Dickey	b. 1843
Mary Dickey	b. 1845
William H. Dickey	b. 1847
Rachel Dickey	b. 1850
Andrew P. Dickey	b. 1852
Amanda Dickey	b. 1855
Sanford Dickey	b. 1859

Martha Jane Karr	(1825)
Andrew J. Hopkins—husband	
Elizabeth Hopkins	b. 1846
Sarah Hopkins	b. 1849
Catherine Hopkins	b. 1853
Zillah Hopkins	b. 1854
William H. Hopkins	b. 1856
Hiram W. Hopkins	b. 1857
Amanda Hopkins	b. 1858
Joseph H. Hopkins	b. 1863
Rachel Hopkins	b. 1866
Andrew J. Hopkins	b. 1868

William A. Karr	(1813)
Amanda P. Hopkins—1st wife	
Ambrose N. Karr	b. 1838
Matthew Karr	b. 1839
James W. Karr	b. 1844
Elihu A. Karr	b. 1846
Sarah A. Karr	b. 1847
William H. Karr	b. 1850
Eldridge M. Karr	b. 1852
Elmyra J. Karr	b. 1854
Mrs. Margaret Abrogast—2nd wife	
no children	

John Karr	(1818)
Caroline Jones—1st wife	
Sarah Jane Karr	b. 1840
William E. Karr	b. 1842
Alexander Karr	b. 1844
George D. Karr	b. 1846
John W. Karr	b. 1848
Catherine Karr	b. 1849
Margaret E. Karr	b. 1852
Caroline Karr	b. 1854
Rebecca A. Karr	b. 1858
Anna Clark—2nd wife	
no children	
Mary E. Tilly—3rd wife	
no children	

Note the repeated use of the same given names in these families. This practice creates a research nightmare when determining which child belongs to which set of parents. The names appear in the following frequency:

William	6	Elihu	3
Andrew	4	James	3
Catherine	4	Matthew	3
George	4	Amanda	2
John	4	Eliza	2
Mary	4	Hannah	2

MARRIAGE RECORDS

The oldest child of each of Matthew's children (except Martha Jane's oldest), was born in Indiana according to census enumerations. Martha Jane reportedly married in Bartholomew County, Indiana before leaving for Iowa where her oldest child was born. Thus, based upon the birthplace of each first-born child, it is logical to assume that all of Matthew's children married their first wife or husband in Indiana. The following marriage records were found in Franklin, Bartholomew, Decatur, and Shelby counties, Indiana and in Marion County, Iowa:

Franklin County, Indiana

James Karr and Hesther Doty	11 Apr 1825
Isabel Karr and William Henderson	20 Feb 1830

Bartholomew County, Indiana

Andrew P. Karr and Mary Castell	14 Mar 1835
George W. Karr and Eliza Dickey	12 Dec 1834
James Karr and Jane Crosby	26 Sep 1844
Martha Jane Karr and Andrew J. Hopkins	30 Mar 1845
Isabel Henderson and Caleb Casteel	8 Sep 1835
Eliza Karr and John Dickey	8 Sep 1835

Decatur County, Indiana

Catherine Karr and Elihu Alley	29 Jun 1826
William Karr and Amanda P. Hopkins	19 Feb 1835

Marion County, Iowa

James Karr and Hannah Wise	4 Dec 1859
Andrew P. Karr and Ruth Robinson	21 Sep 1862
John Karr and Anna Clark	———

The only record not found was John Karr's third marriage to Mary E. Tilley mentioned by family members. James Karr, widowed three times, married Elizabeth Richards after moving to Kansas. Over seventy-five marriage records were on file for Matthew's grandchildren in Marion County, Iowa between 1846 and 1892.

PROBATE RECORDS

The only record of Matthew Karr's estate found in Franklin County, Indiana's circuit court records was the granting of letters of administration to his widow:

> Be it remembered that on the 2nd day of January 1827 Letters of administration were granted to Hannah Carr [sic] by Enoch McCarty clerk of the Franklin Circuit Court for the County aforesaid to enable her to administer on the goods and chattels & Credits of Matthew Carr [sic] deceased who gave Bond & was sworn according to law the day & year above written.
>
> S/Enoch McCarty Clerk

A search for record of the estate of William Karr, Matthew's brother, who reportedly lived in Franklin County, Indiana produced no results.

While the probate record did not give Matthew's exact deathdate, it suggests that he died shortly before 2 January 1827 when Hannah filed for administration. None of the records searched gave his exact deathdate to support the 14 December 1826 deathdate given by the Kerr Family Association.

CEMETERY RECORDS

Requests sent to Franklin County, Indiana failed to produce any record of Matthew Karr's tombstone inscription. He may have been buried on his farm without a stone being placed there. There is a Karr Family Cemetery about six miles northeast of Pulaski, Iowa (Davis County) on what was once William Karr's farm. The following tombstone inscriptions were copied from the monuments in that cemetery:

> Hannah Karr wife of Matthew Karr died 9 May 1855, age 70
> Matthew Karr son of William A. Karr died Feb. 11, 1857 age 17 years
> Elmyra J. Karr daughter of W. A. Karr died Nov. 28, 1856 age 2 years

A special marker was attached to Hannah Karr's stone by the Daughters of the American Revolution, indicating that she was the daughter of Nicholas Pees, a soldier in the Revolutionary War.

Marion County, Iowa cemetery records list hundreds of entries for descendants of Matthew Karr. The following tombstone inscriptions were found for his children:

> Red Rock Cemetery
> Elihu Alley d. 18 Feb 1871 67 years, 11 months, 10 days
> Katherine Alley, wife of Elihu, 25 Jan 1801–2 Jul 1881

> Koder Cemetery (Dunreath, Iowa)
> John Karr "Co 8, 3rd Inf in Mexican War" 14 Nov 1818–8 Aug 1902
> Caroline, wife of John, 13 Jan 1813–1 Jul 1877
> Ann, wife of John, d. 17 Jan 1893 age 82 years, 6 months

Karr Cemetery
Jane Karr, widow of James, 1808-1858
George W. Karr died 28 May 1898, age 87 years
Eliza, wife of George W. died 12 June 1911, age 95 years

After searching only four major record sources in each of the counties where the Karr family resided, eighty-five percent of Matthew Karr's family group record is complete. The most difficult task remains, that of identifying Matthew's and Hannah's parents. Continuing with the Washington County, Pennsylvania searches listed in the research plan, research focuses upon finding their parents.

Catherine Hopkins and the Kerr Family Association mention that Matthew had at least three brothers: Archie, George, and William. Their records also suggest that the family name was originally spelled Kerr. Family tradition also indicates that Matthew might have been the son of William and Margaret Kerr.

Washington County, Pennsylvania census records were examined first to determine the number and size of the Kerr/Karr families living there between 1790 and 1810. There were no listings for the surname spelled Karr in any of the census schedules. The Pease/Pees/Peas family was also checked in each of the above census years.

The Kerr surname was quite common in Washington County, twelve entries for that surname listed in the 1790 census of that county.

1790 U.S. Census, Washington County, Pennsylvania

Head of Household	Males Over 16 Years	Males Under 16 Years	Females
Wm. Kerr	1	2	3
Dan'l Kerr	1	2	2
Mary Kerr	0	2	1
Thomas Kerr	2	0	2
Jno. Kerr	3	1	1
James Kerr	5	1	4
David Kerr	1	1	2
Jas. Kerr	1	0	2
Jno. Kerr	1	1	2
William Kerr	2	1	3
Robert Kerr	2	2	3
Moses Kerr	1	1	1

If Matthew had at least three brothers—Archibald, George, and William— they were all still living at home in 1790, except perhaps William, who might be one of the men listed by that name. This means that Matthew would be found in a family with at least four males in it (three sons and a father). Only three households have that many males listed: Jno. Kerr, James Kerr, and Robert Kerr. If Matthew had a sister named Canada, as the *Hartford Times* letter suggests, the family may also consist of a minimum of two females, providing his sister wasn't married in 1790. Only James and Robert Kerr had more than two females in addition to the required number of males.

There were also two Peas families listed in that census, including Andrew Peas and Nicholas Peas. Andrew lived next door to Nicholas and may have been his son. Nicholas had two males under sixteen, one over sixteen, and four females in his household, one of which is presumed to have been Hannah.

By 1800, nineteen Kerr households were found in Washington County, including two headed by a Matthew Kerr. One lived in Nottingham Township and had no females under ten years of age. The other, a resident of Strabane Township, listed one male between sixteen and twenty-six years old, one female under ten years old, and one female between sixteen and twenty-six years old. Those ages exactly match the ages of Matthew, Hannah, and Catherine Karr in 1800. They are living a short distance from Nicholas and Andrew Pees. There are two other Kerr entries in Strabane Township in 1800: James Kerr and Thomas Kerr.

James Kerr – 2 males under 10 years	1 female under 10 years
3 males 16-26 years	1 female 10-16 years
2 males 26-45 years	1 female 16-26 years
	1 female 26-45 years
Thomas Kerr – 1 male over 45 years	1 female 26-45 years
	1 female over 45 years

Thomas Kerr is old enough to have been the father of both James and Matthew Kerr, and James is old enough to have been Matthew's father. Archibald Kerr, the brother who reportedly visited the family after Matthew's death, was living in Donegal Township next door to a William Kerr, who was old enough to have been his father. William Kerr had four males in his household under twenty-six years old. By 1810, there were thirty-two Kerr listings in Washington County. Matthew was not among them because he was living in Mercer County, Pennsylvania during that census year. Checking Strabane Township where Matthew lived in 1800, two heads of households are noted.

James Kerr – 1 male under 10 years	2 females under 10 years
1 male 10-16 years	1 female 10-16 years
1 male 16-26 years	1 female 26-45 years
1 male 26-45 years	1 female over 45 years
1 male over 45 years	

In view of the young children in the household, it appears that two families are represented.

Margaret Kerr—1 female 16-45 years
1 female over 45 years

The other Matthew Kerr listed in the 1800 census was not living in Washington County in 1810.

A plat map of Washington County's North Strabane Township shows that a John Kerr owned a plantation called "Happy Loft" less than two miles from "Amsterdam" plantation which was owned by Nicholas Pees. John Kerr obtained a warrant for the land 16 March 1786 and a final patent for the same land 9 September 1786. This was the earliest land entry in Strabane Township for anyone named Kerr.

At this point it is time to look into the estate records. One of the early Kerr wills on file in Washington County was that of John Kerr of Strabane Township. His will names his wife Rachel, children Polly and John, and brother William Kerr as his heirs. The will, dated 2 June 1794, provided one family group which matches an entry in the 1790 census.

Another will disposed of the estate of Alexander Kerr. This indicates he was a single man because he left all of his property to relatives in Ireland. He mentions a brother named Thomas Kerr "living in the County Down and town land of Shanhannon, Ireland." He also mentions Alexander Kerr as Thomas's son. His will was written in 1783, very near the date Matthew Kerr arrived in Pennsylvania from Ireland—if he came to America at eight years of age.

A second John Kerr left a will dated 14 May 1788. He was of Nottingham Township and left the following children as heirs: James, John, Joseph, Rebeckah, Matthew, William, Robert, Mary, and Margaret. No wife was listed. Sons Matthew and William were minors when he died.

Thomas Kerr, listed in Strabane Township in the 1800 census with James and Matthew Kerr, left a will dated 2 August 1800. He states that he is of Strabane Township and a yeoman (farmer). His will lists the following heirs: Margaret Kerr—wife, Agness Mellone—daughter, Alexander Kerr—son, and Jean Kerr—daughter. His will was proven in court on 1 June 1819; however, he was not listed in the 1810 census of Strabane Township. His wife was listed with a daughter twenty-six to forty-five years old, presumed to have been Jean Kerr.

Analysis: Based on the census data and the evidence in the estate records of Washington County, the following conclusions are drawn. The Matthew Kerr listed in Nottingham Township was the son of John Kerr of that township who died in 1788 and was not the husband of Hannah Pees who lived in Strabane Township. Land records indicate that Matthew Kerr lived and owned property only in Strabane Township, in Washington County.

Figure 8:28. Plat Map of North Strabane Township, Washington County, Pennsylvania.

Thomas Kerr arrived in Strabane Township in 1783, just after inheriting land there from his brother Alexander. Thomas named only three children in his will; however, he may have had other children. Thomas Kerr's 1790 household lists only two males over sixteen years old and two females, suggesting it contained Thomas, Alexander, Margaret, and Jean Kerr. Thus, Matthew Karr was not a part of his household.

John Kerr of Strabane Township left a will dated 1794. He was listed in the 1790 census with one male under sixteen years old and two females, representing John, Polly, and his wife Rachel, eliminating him as Matthew's father.

Only James Kerr of Strabane Township remains a candidate as Matthew's father. James left a will that was proven in court 25 September 1834 and named the following heirs: an unnamed stepmother of his children, John Kerr—son, William Kerr—son, Polly Moore—daughter, Jean Vance—daughter, James P. Kerr—son, and Betsey Scott—daughter. Again, Matthew Karr is not mentioned in the will, and although it was proven nearly eight years after his death in Indiana, it was written the January before he died in 1826.

It is still to be proven that Archibald Kerr was Matthew's brother. Biographical sketches in the *History of Greene County, Pennsylvania* and *The Horn Papers* (focusing on Washington County, Pennsylvania) discuss the ancestry of Archibald Kerr and his brother William. Their father, William Kerr, of Irish descent, was born in New Jersey in 1747. His children were James, Archibald, William, and John. Since Matthew's parents came from Ireland to America, he could not have been the son of William and Margaret Kerr or the brother of Archibald Kerr. There were no other Archibald Kerrs in Washington County, Pennsylvania between 1790 and 1820.

Since none of the sources included in the initial research plan produced information about Matthew's parentage or his place of birth in northern Ireland, additional searches had to be added to the research plan:

1. Search all printed histories and biographies of Washington County, Pennsylvania.

2. Examine Washington County land records to see if Matthew was sold or given property by his father.

3. Check Washington County probate and court records to see whether Matthew is mentioned in the administration of his father's estate.

The only Kerr family discussed in printed histories of Washington County was that of William Kerr born in New Jersey and the father of Archibald Kerr. References to the presence of early Kerr families were found throughout the publications, but none were related to Matthew.

Based on family tradition and printed biographical information, Matthew arrived in America when he was about seven or eight years old. He was fifty-one when he died in 1826; thus his birth year is calculated as 1775 and his arrival in America calculated between 1782 and 1783. Land records were searched to determine which Kerr families acquired property after 1782. It is already proven that Alexander Kerr had land in 1783 when he bequeathed it to his brother, Thomas, in Ireland. The following warrants were on file among Washington County land records:

James Kerr—20 acres on Ten Mile Creek adjoining land Robert Benham and others on 1 Jul 1775.

John Kerr—300 acres on Shirtees [sic] Creek adjoining the land of Dorsey Penticost and others on 1 Mar 1785.

Alexander Kerr—313 acres on Chartiers Creek assigned to his brother Thomas Kerr on 4 Jun 1783.

Joseph Kerr—400 acres along the Ohio River at the upper side of Raccoon Creek adjoining the land of Jacob Bowman on 1 Mar 1776.

William Kerr—400 acres adjoining land of Jacob Huff and David Williamson, and others on Buffalo Creek on 12 May 1794.

Only one deed mentioning Matthew Kerr was dated 4 September 1797 when Matthew purchased property in the town of Williamsport in Washington County, Pennsylvania. This appears to involve the other Matthew Kerr because the land consisted of only 12,000 square feet—too small an area to farm.

The only other deed on file of any interest is one dated 13 May 1811 recording the sale of twenty-nine acres to Andrew Pees by James Kerr and his wife Elizabeth.

Matthew did not appear in the Washington County probate records either. Research was conducted at the Genealogical Library of the LDS Church, and while their Washington County collection is excellent, not all of that county's records were filmed. Before assuming that Matthew's parentage and birthplace cannot be identified, records in the county's possession and in local historical and genealogical societies must be searched and that requires either hiring a professional record searcher or genealogist in the area or going there to conduct the research personally. Research will be completed in the future when time allows a trip to Washington County.

Based on what was found, it appears that Matthew may be the son of James Kerr of North Strabane Township. James was old enough to have been Matthew's father; he lived on land adjacent to Nicholas and Andrew Pees, served as executor of Nicholas's will, and acquired his land from Robert Crouch on 5 July 1796, after the date Matthew's family arrived in the United States. There is no reason to believe that his family moved directly to Washington County after their arrival unless they followed family members who arrived earlier. There were four Kerr property owners in Strabane Township: John, Alexander, Thomas, and James Kerr. Thomas Kerr was from Shanhannon, County Down, Ireland and a search of that town's records may show that all four individuals were related. Thus, research can actually continue on two fronts simultaneously by hiring an Irish research specialist in County Down.

Turning to the Pease/Pees/Peas family in Washington County, research focused upon Nicholas Pees, who was named as Hannah's father and as a Revolutionary War soldier on her tombstone. A letter from one of her descendants provided the following information:

> The first Pease of which we have authentic history is Nicholas, father of Andrew Pease Sr. who was married to Hannah (?) and both were Germans and talked the German language. They lived in Maryland on the Potomac River and moved to Washington Co. Pa., in 1773 with his wife and eight children, a then unbroken wilderness. Nicholas Pease came from Germany at the age of 16. Was placed in the care of his uncle to whom the father gave the passage money which he kept and the boy was sold for his passage. Two years after his removal to Pa. an Indian War broke out which lasted nine years. In the summer time the women and children were kept in the forts. For eight yrs they pounded all the grain they ate in the top of a hollowed stump. They built the first grist mill in that county about the year 1781. His son Andrew Pease, Sen. was a soldier in the War of the Revolution. In "Pennsylvania Archives of the Revolution," vol. 14 in *History of the Sandusky Expedition,* beginning May 24, 1782, under Col. William Crawford. His name appears in "Miscellaneous List who received vouchers for pay" but whose company was not there designated. He was among those who escaped when Col. Crawford was captured by the Indians and burned on the Sandusky Plains, near Wyandotte, Ohio. He was married first to Mary Engle and second to Mary Blakeney. By first marriage they had sons, John, Nicholas, George, and Andrew; daughters Linnie, Margaret, Elizabeth, Mary, Hannah, and Rebecca. By the 2nd marriage three sons, James B., Boyd E., and Jonathan L.

Crumrine's *History of Washington County, Pennsylvania* includes the following about Nicholas Pees:

> Nicholas Pees — a German, came here prior to 1780, bringing his wife, his oldest son Andrew, born 1763, his daughter Molly and his son George, four years old. He built a cabin on Chartier's Creek, just above the present mill of John Berry. Afterwards he built a log mill and distillery.
>
> His daughter Molly married John McGlumpy, who settled on land owned by James Coney. George Pees bought one hundred acres of land from his father. He lived on the homestead and there his son Zachariah was born in 1798. George was born in 1765. (p. 874)
>
> Nicholas Pees, accompanied by an uncle, emigrated from Germany when he was 12 years old. He settled and married east of the mountains where three of his children were born, namely Mary, Andrew and George.

About 1769 Nicholas journeyed on foot to the backwood and located on what is now North Strabane Township, Washington County, Pennsylvania, building on Little Chartiers Creek where he owned 400 acres. He made the trip west with the aide of one horse which carried his worldly possessions and youngest child. He, his wife, and two children walked across the mountains. They lived in a small log hut where their younger children, Nicholas, Catherine, Betsey, Susan and Hannah, were born. All were married and raised families except Nicholas. Nicholas, the father, died at 105 years of age. He was over six feet tall, well proportioned, and capable of great physical endurance. His wife lived beyond 90 years of age. (p. 881)

Nicholas Pees left a will dated 13 January 1813 which was never proven in court.

In the name of God, Amen. I, Nicholas Pees, of Strabane Township, Washington Co., and Commonwealth of Pennsylvania being weak in body, but of sound mind and memory, blessed by God for same, do make this last will and testament, in way and manner following: First, I give my soul to God that gave it to me, and my body to be buried in a Christian like and decent manner at the direction of my executors, not doubting, but at the general resurrection I shall receive the same again by the power of God. And as to such worldly estate, as it hath pleased God to bless me with in this life, I give and dispose of the same in the following manner and form: First, I ordain all my lawful debts and funeral charges be paid out of my personal estate by my executors, and I give unto my well beloved wife, Hanna, the sum of sixty dollars for year during natural life. Forty dollars of it is to be paid to her by my son Andrew Pees, and twenty dollars of it is to be paid to her by my son, George Pees, each year. I give and bequeath unto my beloved son, Andrew Pees, and to his heirs and assigns forever, a part of my plantation on which he now dwells, on which the mill stands. The residue of my plantation that remains after that, I now bequeath unto my son, George Pees, that part of my plantation on which he now dwells, — beginning at the corner between me and James Thom, and thence running along the line of the plantation that was James Scott's line, as when turning off and running about a north course through the improvement about three perches and thence running about north west between my son Andrew Pees and my son George Pees files until keeping out field about four perches until it strikes James Herron, along said James Herron's line along the great road until it strikes McWhirters corner, nigh Herron's smith ship, line to place of beginning, taking in, by about thence running along McWhirter's line and James Thom aforesaid course as will contain one hundred and eighty seven acres with usual allowance for roads. Which I give and bequeath to my son, George Pees, then all the remainder of my lands I give and bequeath unto, Andrew Pees, together with all the Mills, and improvements therewith belonging to him and his heirs and assigns forever. But I will that part of the land and himself is subject to pay unto my daughter, Mary McGlumpy, two hundred dollars, and one hundred dollars to my daughter Hanna Kerr. To be paid to them by my son Andrew Pees, after my decease, but by him producing sufficient receipts of any part of it being paid, he is to be clear of all that he hath paid already. And I will that my son George Pees, and the land that I have willed and bequeathed to him be subject to two hundred dollars that I will to my daughter, Susanna Hutchison, after my decease, but him producing sufficient receipts of any part of it being paid before, he is to be clear of all that is paid before. Likewise I appoint James Kerr and James Roney, my trusty friends, executors of this, my last will and testament, and I hereby revoke and renounce all former wills and documents by me made, and I declare and pronounce this, and no other to be my last Will and Testament. In witness whereof, I Nicholas Pees, have hereunto set my hand and seal this thirteenth day of January, in the year of Our Lord, one thousand eight hundred and eighteen. Signed, Sealed and pronounced by the said Nicholas Pees as his last Will and Testament in the presence on one another.

Joseph Vaughn, William Herron, Moses McWhirter

N.B.—Before signing I will that my son, George Pees, pay to my daughter Betsey Lisk, the sum of two hundred dollars, and when he produceth sufficient receipts of payment being made to her, he is clear of her.

Nicholas Pees [seal]

Analysis: While the historical details in the biographical sketches and family records are circumstantial evidence of Hannah's relationship to Nicholas Pees, his will is direct evidence of their father-daughter relationship.

WILLIAM HOPKINS (7:2)
SARAH SMATHERS (7:3)

The last generation in this case study consists of research conducted into the William Hopkins family. Research has already proven that William and his wife Sarah Smathers were the parents of Amanda P. Hopkins Karr. Their family group record shown in Figure 8:29 illustrates what is known about William's family when research began.

RESEARCH PLAN

1. Obtain additional research notes from Jeanette Woodruff, a descendant of William Hopkins, who provided documentation of Amanda Karr's relationship to William Hopkins and Sarah Smathers.

FAMILY GROUP SHEET

HUS. WILLIAM HOPKINS, JR.   OCCUPATION(S)

BORN	1781	PLACE	Virginia
CHR		PLACE	
MARR		PLACE	
DIED	5 AUG 1856	PLACE near Bloomfield, Davis, Iowa
BUR		PLACE	
FATHER WILLIAM HOPKINS, SR.		OTHER WIVES
MOTHER		

WIFE SARAH SMATHERS

BORN	1788	PLACE	Virginia
CHR		PLACE	
DIED	9 MAY 1854	PLACE near Bloomfield, Davis, Iowa
BUR		PLACE	
FATHER		OTHER HUSBANDS
MOTHER		

SEX	CHILDREN	DATE BORN / PLACE BORN	DATE MARRIED / TO	PLACE	DATE DIED / PLACE DIED
1	M	JOSEPH S. HOPKINS	Kentucky	19 FEB 1836 / WILLIAM A. KARR	Decatur County, Indiana	22 NOV 1870 / New Lancaster, Miami, KS
2	M	AMANDA P. HOPKINS	1814 / Kentucky			
3	F	MARY ANN HOPKINS		MYERS		
4	M	ELDRIDGE HOPKINS	CAL 1823 / Kentucky			
5	M	WILLIAM W. HOPKINS				
6	M	AMBROSE J. HOPKINS				before 1856
7	F	ABIAH HOPKINS		HINER		before 1856
8	F	ELIZABETH HOPKINS				
9	M	ANDREW J. HOPKINS	1 SEP 1825 / Nicholas County, Kentucky	20 MAR 1845 / MARTHA JANE KARR	Bartholomew County, Indiana	25 NOV 1901
10						

OTHER MARRIAGES

SOURCES OF INFORMATION
1. Family Records
2. 1860 U.S. Census - Davis County, Iowa
3. Will of William Hopkins, Davis County, Iowa Probate Court
4. Tombstone Inscriptions - Davis County, Iowa

Figure 8:29. Family Group Work Record, William Hopkins Jr. and Sarah Smathers.

2. Since the Hopkins family is known to have lived in Bartholomew and Decatur counties, Indiana, attempts to locate marriage records for William's children should begin there and then move to Nicholas County, Kentucky where they lived prior to residing in Indiana, according to family tradition.

3. Conduct a census study of the family in Kentucky, Indiana, Iowa, and Kansas between 1800 and 1880 to estimate birthdates based on ages in census enumerations.

4. Check cemetery records for the areas in which the family lived to obtain birth and death dates.

5. Search Nicholas County, Kentucky estate records for wills and probate records that may mention William Hopkins as an heir to his father's estate.

Again, marriage records were searched first to identify the spouses of William's children so that census research would be less complicated. The first two counties searched were Decatur and Bartholomew counties, Indiana.

Decatur County, Indiana
Joseph Hopkins and Aseneath Morris	1 Sep 1835
Ambrose Hopkins and Permelia Robbins	6 Aug 1840
Elizabeth Hopkins and Hiram W. Shelton	27 Jul 1830
Amanda P. Hopkins and William Carr [sic]	29 Feb 1835

Bartholomew County, Indiana
Eldridge Hopkins and Zillah Morris	31 Jan 1828
Ambrose Jones Hopkins and Lovina Robbins	2 Jul 1839
Polly Ann Hopkins and Anderson Meyers	22 Jan 1841
William W. Hopkins and Carolina P. Robbins	3 Mar 1843
Andrew J. Hopkins and Martha Jane Karr	30 Mar 1845

Nicholas County, Kentucky
Abiah Hopkins and Joseph Hiner	26 Nov 1824

Not all of William's children lived beyond 1850, complicating the calculation of their birthdates. William and Andrew Hopkins were already located in the 1850 census of Davis County, Iowa because they were living next to one another and their father. Joseph Hopkins was also living in Davis County in 1850:

Dwelling Number	Name	Age	Occupation	Birthplace
#62	Joseph Hopkins	34	Farmer	Kentucky
	Sarah Hopkins	26		Unknown
	Sarah Hopkins	16		Indiana
	Elizabeth Hopkins	13		Indiana
	Mary A. Hopkins	12		Indiana
	Abner M. Hopkins	7		Indiana

Joseph married Aseneath Morris in Decatur County, Indiana in 1835, but his wife in 1850 is named Sarah. A five-year span between Mary A. and Abner M. Hopkins suggests that his first wife died after Mary's birth. The mother in the 1850 family would have been only fourteen years old when Mary was born. While she could have borne a child at that age, it is highly unlikely.

Eldridge Hopkins remained in Indiana when the family moved west and was enumerated in the 1850 U.S. Census of Haw Creek Township, Bartholomew County, Indiana:

Dwelling Number	Name	Age	Occupation	Birthplace
#450	Eldridge Hopkins	44	Farmer	Kentucky
	Zillah Hopkins	35		Pennsylvania
	Asineth Hopkins	18		Indiana
	Henry C. Hopkins	7		Indiana
	Cirena Morris	7		Indiana

Since pre-1850 census records do not list every person in a household by name, ages must be roughly calculated based on age groupings. The following early census records contributed information that permitted those calculations:

1810 U.S. Census, Floyd County, Kentucky

William Hopkins Jr.	1 male	26-45 years	[William Jr.]
	1 male	0-10 years	[Eldridge]
	1 female	16-26 years	[Sarah]
	1 female	0-10 years	[Abiah]

1820 U.S. Census, Nicholas County, Kentucky

William Hopkins	1 male	26-45 years	[William]
	1 male	10-16 years	[Eldridge]
	2 males	0-10 years	[Joseph and Ambrose]
	1 female	26-45 years	[Sarah]
	1 female	16-26 years	[Abiah]
	3 females	0-10 years	[Elizabeth, Amanda, and Mary Ann]

1830 U.S. Census, Decatur County, Indiana

William Hopkins	1 male	40-50 years	[William Sr.]
	2 males	10-15 years	[Joseph and Ambrose]
	1 male	5-10 years	[William W.]
	1 male	0-5 years	[Andrew J.]

	1 female	40-50 years [Sarah]
	1 female	15-20 years [Elizabeth]
	2 females	10-15 years [Amanda and Mary Ann]
Joseph Hiner	1 male	20-30 years [Joseph]
	2 males	0-5 years
	1 female	20-30 years [Abiah]

Analysis: Estimates of the children's birthdates also required analysis of their marriage dates. The average age at which young men and women in the North married during the nineteenth century was between eighteen and twenty-two years. Census and family records already established calculated birthdates for Eldridge, Amanda, William W., Joseph, and Andrew J. Hopkins. Family tradition states that Elizabeth was born after her mother miscarried twice. There is a nine-year span between Eldridge and Amanda that suggests the loss of children. Elizabeth's birth is estimated as 1812 since there was a fifteen to twenty year old daughter in the 1830 census, presumably Elizabeth. The next span of years occurs between Joseph, who was born in 1816 and William W., who was born in 1823. Ambrose Jones Hopkins married for the first time in 1839, thus his birthdate is estimated as 1818. That leaves Mary Ann, whose birthdate is estimated as 1820 based on her 1841 marriage date, her age in the 1830 census, and family tradition.

Now that the names and approximate birthdates of William's children have been determined, their birthplaces must be identified. Since there are no birth records for Kentucky at the time they were born, William Hopkins's movements must be pinpointed by other means. At this point we know some of his residences and when he lived there: 1810 Floyd County, Kentucky; 1820 Nicholas County, Kentucky; and 1830 Decatur County, Indiana. Did he live other places in between the census enumerations? When did he arrive at and leave a particular residence? These questions can only be answered by searching land and tax records which were not included in the original research plan and must be added at this point. Family tradition states that William started his tenure in Kentucky in Montgomery County and then moved to Floyd, Bath, and Nicholas counties.

William Hopkins Jr. appeared on the 1802 Montgomery County, Kentucky tax list. His presence there indicates that he was twenty-one years old. Just how long he remained in that county is unknown, but he was definitely in Floyd County, Kentucky on 26 August 1809 when he witnessed a deed. His arrival in Floyd County was probably noted in that county's land and tax records; however, the courthouse and its records burned in 1808. He was still in Floyd County in 1812 when he and his wife joined the Baptist church.

The name William Hopkins first appeared in Nicholas County, Kentucky tax lists in 1813 and last appeared there in 1831:

1813	Wm Hopkins—no land, 8 slaves, and 4 horses
1814-1816	Wm Hopkins—150 acres on Cassidy Creek
1817	Wm Hopkins—155 acres on Cassidy
	George Hopkins—115 acres
	John Hopkins—183 acres
	Joslin Hopkins
	Robert Hopkins—46 acres
1818-1819	Tax Lists Destroyed
1820	Moses Hopkins
	John Hopkins—183 acres on Taylors Creek
	Joslin Hopkins—100 acres on Cassidy
	Robert Hopkins—100¾ acres on Somerset Creek
	Joseph A. Hopkins—103 acres on Somerset Creek
	Josiah Hopkins—58 acres on Cassidy
	William Hopkins Sr.—100 acres on Cassidy
	William Hopkins Jr.—50 acres on Little Flat
1824	William Hopkins—100 acres on Cassidy
	Josiah Hopkins—28 acres on Cassidy
	Joslin Hopkins—202 acres on Cassidy
	Isaac Hopkins—80 acres on Somerset
	Eldridge Hopkins—50 acres on Cassidy
	Wm. Hopkins—100 acres on Somerset
1826	Wm. Hopkins—100 acres
	Moses Hopkins—6 horses
	Eldridge Hopkins—50 acres
	Isaac Hopkins—74½ acres
	Josiah Hopkins—4 horses
	Joslin Hopkins—123¾ acres
1827	William Hopkins Sr.—100 acres on Cassidy
1830	Wm. Hopkins—165 acres on Cassidy
	Joslin Hopkins—290 acres on Cassidy
1831	Wm. Hopkins—165 acres on Cassidy
1833	Elizabeth Hopkins—165 acres on Cassidy Creek
1839	Elizabeth Hopkins—Cassidy
	Joslin J. Hopkins—584 acres on Cassidy

Analysis: Based on the tax lists, William Hopkins Sr. arrived in Nicholas County first. He is the only Hopkins listed between 1813 and 1817. William Jr. arrived between 1818 and 1820. The missing tax lists for 1818 and 1819 prevent our knowing exactly when he was there. William Sr. is listed consistently from 1813 to 1831, and then Elizabeth Hopkins appears in 1833 with exactly the same number of acres on Cassidy Creek as William listed in 1831. This suggests that William Sr. died between 1831 and 1833 and that probate records should be searched to verify that supposition.

William Hopkins Sr. left a will dated 4 October 1831 and it was proven in the county court of Nicholas County, Kentucky on 1 July 1832. His will was quoted as follows:

In the name of God, Amen. I, William Hopkins of the County of Nicholas and State of Kentucky, being aged and infirm and of course, must shortly be removed from this world, do make this and ordain this my last will and testament in the manner and form following, to-wit:

After my decease, let my body be decently buried, after the usual manner, and I recommend my soul to God who gave it, and, as it respects what property I shall leave, it is my will and desire that my family remain on the farm, which I now occupy, under the care and direction of my beloved wife, Elizabeth, and it is my will that she shall live on the farm, and enjoy all the benefits and profits thereof, together with my slaves and all my personal estate for the purpose of enabling her to school and raise my children now living with me and under the age of twenty-one years, until my youngest child arrives at the age of fourteen years, provided, however, that, if in the opinion of my Executors, there should be more stock on the farm than is necessary, such surplus shall be sold and the money arising from the sale appropriated towards schooling my children or should there be more land than can be well cultivated by the hands, under the direction of my wife, Elizabeth, in that case, my Executors may rent it out but not to any person who may wish to keep a family or stock on the farm, and the money arising from the rents may be put at interest or appropriated to schooling my children and providing for them, if found necessary, or put at interest as above; should any of my children, at any time, after they arrive at the age of twenty-one years wish to separate from the rest of the family, and do for themselves, they may call upon my Executors for a division and equal share of my estate, provided in such a division, care shall be taken, not to injure the rest of the family in keeping house or working the farm.

After my youngest child, Caroline, arrives at the age of fourteen years, it is my will and desire that after my beloved wife Elizabeth should she be then living, has her thirds laid off and divided, the remainder of my estate, including her dower in land, shall be equally divided amongst my seven youngest children, to-wit: David, Peace, John, Joseph, Walter, Phebe, and Caroline, each to have an equal share. Should any of my children above named die before they may be of lawful age, their part, provided they have no lawful heirs, shall become common stock and be divided among the survivors of my above named children, provided, however, that if my beloved wife, Elizabeth, should marry at any time, previous to the time my youngest child shall arrive at the age of fourteen, then and in that case, my Executors, after assigning to her her dower, according to law, shall proceed to sell all my personal estate and put the money at interest, and rent out the farm for the benefit of my above named children, as they may come of age, and so soon as any one of them may be entitled thereto my Executors shall pay it over to them or their Guardians as the case may be, provided that none of my slaves or their increase should be sold out of family, if they behave well, and I will and bequeath to my daughter, Polly Owings, and my grandson, David Hopkins, twenty dollars each, and I do hereby constitute and appoint my son, Joslin Hopkins, and Hugh Wiley, Executors of this my last will and testament, hereby revoking and annulling all former wills.

In Witness Whereof, I have hereunto set my hand and seal, this 4th day of October 1831.

Wm. Hopkins (Seal)

Analysis: Even though the will does not name William Hopkins Jr. as an heir, it is a valuable document. William Jr. was born in 1781 in Virginia, approximately fifty years prior to his father's death. Estimating that William Sr. was at least twenty years old when his namesake was born, it is reasonable to assume that William Sr. was at least seventy years old when he died. (Research later revealed that he was born 15 November 1748 at Warwick, Rhode Island and thus he was eighty-three years old when he died in 1832.) Obviously, Elizabeth Hopkins was not William Jr.'s mother. An older group of children was born to his first wife.

Hopkins family tradition maintains that William Sr.'s first wife was named Peace (?). He married her before the Revolutionary War ended, presumably in Virginia where he was living and where William Jr. was born in 1781. They were living on the frontier in what is now Washington County, Virginia, where early records are sketchy. William and his father, Francis Hopkins, were Loyalists during the Revolution, and Francis was hung without trial in Washington County, Virginia in 1779. William was captured that same year and sentenced to death, but escaped and never returned to the area according to historians. Their loyalty to Great Britain is understandable when William's maternal ancestry is considered. Mary Joslin descended from Anglo-Saxon and Norman royal lines, and her more immediate ancestry included English nobility, many of whom were still living in England.

Only the Bath County, Kentucky records remained to be searched to verify family tradition stating William Hopkins lived there sometime between 1810 to 1820. Bath County records clearly state that William Hopkins purchased property there in 1815. This William is believed to be William Jr. because William Sr. was living on Cassidy Creek in Nicholas County, Kentucky in 1815. The older William may have lived there earlier. He definitely returned to Bath County on 9 September 1815 to marry Betsy Brinson.

Among the Bath County records was the will of Andrew Smathers, dated 4 September 1824 and proven in court in May 1827:

In the name of God Amen. I, Andrew Smathers of Bath County and State of Kentucky, being very weak in body, but of a perfect understanding, and calling to mind, that it is appointed to all men to die.

I do make this my last Will and Testament; I commit my soul to God, and my body to the dust; to be buried in the discretion of my friend; And for such worldly goods as I am possessed of, after just payment of all my debts, I dispose of in the following manner, That is to say;

I leave to my Wife Elizabeth fifty acres of land, where I now live, so long as she lives a single life; But if she should marry, she is only to have her third of the place, and at her death it is to return to my children.

I also leave to my wife one-third part of all my Personal Estate; and leave the balance of My Estate to be divided among my Children equally; that is to say, Thomas Smathers, Joseph Smathers, Ann Jackson, Martha Fowler, Margaret Bristo, Sally Hopkins, Hugh Smathers; And I leave unto John Smathers, Elizabeth Fuget, and Susanna Gipson, one Dollar each; and I also name John McNabb, as my Executor in this my last Will and Testament; and I do hereby disannul all former Wills and Testaments; Allowing this to be my last Will and Testament. Given under my hand this the 4th day of September 1824.

his

Andrew X Smathers

mark

Whether Smathers was the true spelling of Andrew's surname is questionable. Joseph Smithers Hopkins was probably named after his uncle mentioned in Andrew's will. The surname was found spelled Smathers, Smithers, Smothers, Smuthers, Smeathers, and Smethers between 1750 and 1825.

This concludes a portion of Bertha Ruth Smith's fifth generation. Research is still being conducted on many lines and once completed will appear in several volumes to be published as time permits. If you have material on the following surnames and would like to contribute it for possible inclusion in one of the family histories, forward your material and a statement releasing it for possible publication to Johni Cerny, P.O. Box 2607, Salt Lake City, Utah 84115.

West	Huffman	Robinson	Welsh
Easton	Stewart	Carter	Andrews
Miller (Eng)	Wilhoit	Doty	Davis
Wilhite	Davenport	Carroll	Casteel
Briles	Reynolds	Pledger	Wells
Dickey	Hiner	Parker	Wood
Dickson	Hopkins	Morris	Clayton
Karr/Kerr	Ethington	Smathers	Robbins
Sittner	Marlowe	Lanier	

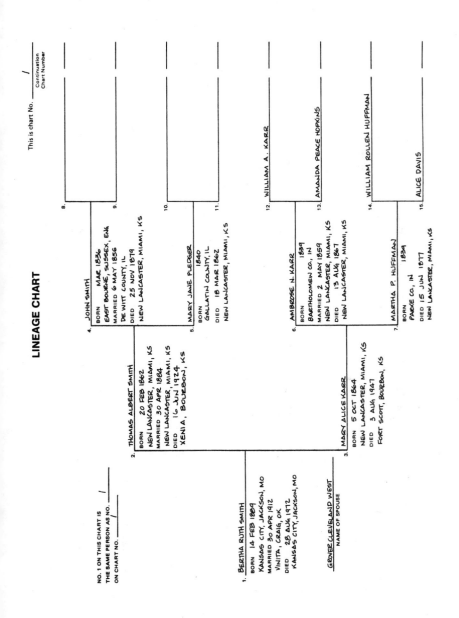

LINEAGE CHART

This is chart No. ___ / Continuation Chart Number

NO. 1 ON THIS CHART IS THE SAME PERSON AS NO. ___ / ON CHART NO. ___

1. **BERTHA RUTH SMITH**
BORN 14 FEB 1889 KANSAS CITY, JACKSON, MO
MARRIED 30 APR 1912 VINITA, CRAIG, OK
DIED 28 AUG 1972 KANSAS CITY, JACKSON, MO

GROVER CLEVELAND WEST
NAME OF SPOUSE

2. **THOMAS ALBERT SMITH**
BORN 20 FEB 1862 NEW LANCASTER, MIAMI, KS
MARRIED 30 APR 1884 NEW LANCASTER, MIAMI, KS
DIED 16 JUN 1924 XENIA, BOURBON, KS

3. **MARY ALICE KARR**
BORN 5 OCT 1864 NEW LANCASTER, MIAMI, KS
DIED 3 AUG 1947 FORT SCOTT, BOURBON, KS

4. **JOHN SMITH**
BORN MAR 1856 EAST BOURNE, SUSSEX, ENG
MARRIED 6 MAY 1856 DE WITT COUNTY, IL
DIED 25 NOV 1879 NEW LANCASTER, MIAMI, KS

5. **MARY JANE PLEDGER**
BORN 1840 GALLATIN COUNTY, IL
DIED 18 MAR 1862 NEW LANCASTER, MIAMI, KS

6. **AMBROSE N. KARR**
BORN 1839 BARTHOLOMEW CO., IN
MARRIED 2 MAY 1859 NEW LANCASTER, MIAMI, KS
DIED 13 AUG 1867 NEW LANCASTER, MIAMI, KS

7. **MARTHA P. HUFFMAN**
BORN 1839 PARKE CO., IN
DIED 15 JUN 1877 NEW LANCASTER, MIAMI, KS

8. ___

9. ___

10. ___

11. ___

12. WILLIAM A. KARR

13. AMANDA PEACE HOPKINS

14. WILLIAM ROLLEN HUFFMAN

15. ALICE DAVIS

Figure 8:30. Final Lineage Chart 1, Bertha Ruth Smith.

LINEAGE CHART

This is chart No. _____ 6

Continuation Chart Number

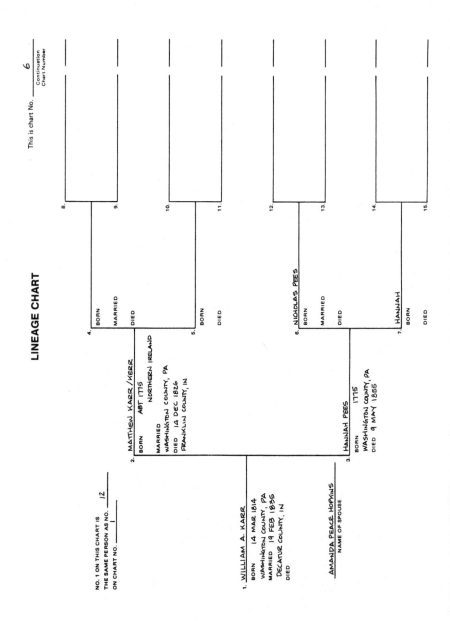

NO. 1 ON THIS CHART IS
THE SAME PERSON AS NO. _____ 12
ON CHART NO. _____ 1

4.
BORN
MARRIED
DIED

5.
BORN
DIED

6. NICHOLAS PEES
BORN
MARRIED
DIED

7. HANNAH
BORN
DIED

8.
9.
10.
11.
12.
13.
14.
15.

2. MATTHEW KARR/KERR
BORN   ABT 1715
         NORTHERN IRELAND
MARRIED
WASHINGTON COUNTY, PA
DIED   14 DEC 1826
FRANKLIN COUNTY, IN

3. HANNAH PEES
BORN   1775
WASHINGTON COUNTY, PA
DIED   9 MAY 1855

1. WILLIAM A. KARR
BORN   14 MAR 1814
WASHINGTON COUNTY, PA
MARRIED 14 FEB 1835
DECATUR COUNTY, IN
DIED

AMANDA PEACE HOPKINS
NAME OF SPOUSE

Figure 8:31. Final Lineage Chart 6, William A. Karr.

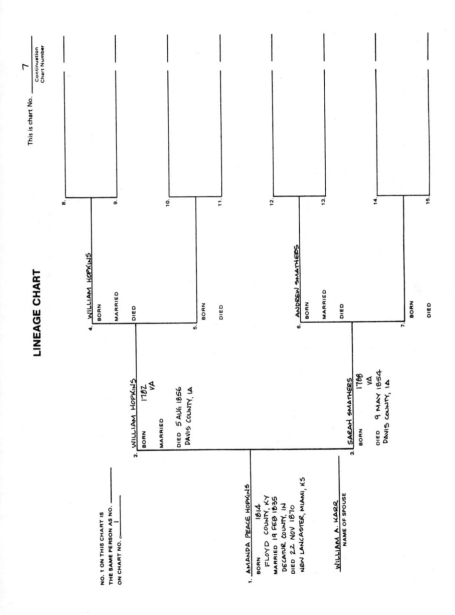

LINEAGE CHART

This is chart No. ___7___
Continuation Chart Number

NO. 1 ON THIS CHART IS
THE SAME PERSON AS NO.
ON CHART NO. ___1___

1. AMANDA PEACE HOPKINS
BORN 1814
FLOYD COUNTY, KY
MARRIED 19 FEB 1835
DECATUR COUNTY, IN
DIED 22 NOV 1870
NEW LANCASTER, MIAMI, KS

WILLIAM A. KARR
NAME OF SPOUSE

2. WILLIAM HOPKINS
BORN 1782 VA
MARRIED
DIED 5 AUG 1856
DAVIS COUNTY, IA

3. SARAH SMATHERS
BORN 1788 VA
DIED 9 MAY 1854
DAVIS COUNTY, IA

4. WILLIAM HOPKINS
BORN
MARRIED
DIED

5.
BORN
DIED

6. ANDREW SMATHERS
BORN
MARRIED
DIED

7.
BORN
DIED

8.

9.

10.

11.

12.

13.

14.

15.

Figure 8:32. Final Lineage Chart 7, Amanda Peace Hopkins.

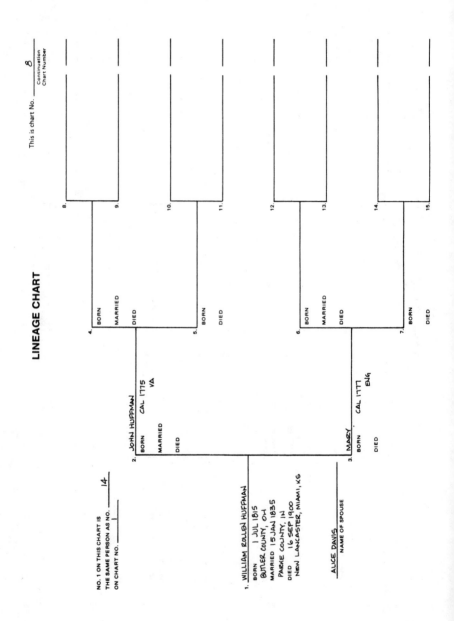

LINEAGE CHART

This is chart No. ___8___
Continuation
Chart Number

NO. 1 ON THIS CHART IS
THE SAME PERSON AS NO. ___14___
ON CHART NO. ___1___

1. WILLIAM ROLLEN HUFFMAN
   BORN   1 JUL 1815
   BUTLER COUNTY, OH
   MARRIED 15 JAN 1835
   PARKE COUNTY, IN
   DIED   16 SEP 1900
   NEW LANCASTER, MIAMI, KS

2. JOHN HUFFMAN
   BORN   CAL 1775   VA
   MARRIED
   DIED

3. MARY
   BORN   CAL 1777   ENG
   DIED

ALICE DAVIS
NAME OF SPOUSE

4.
BORN
MARRIED
DIED

5.
BORN
DIED

6.
BORN
MARRIED
DIED

7.
BORN
DIED

8.
9.
10.
11.
12.
13.
14.
15.

Figure 8:33. Final Lineage Chart 8, William Rollen Huffman.

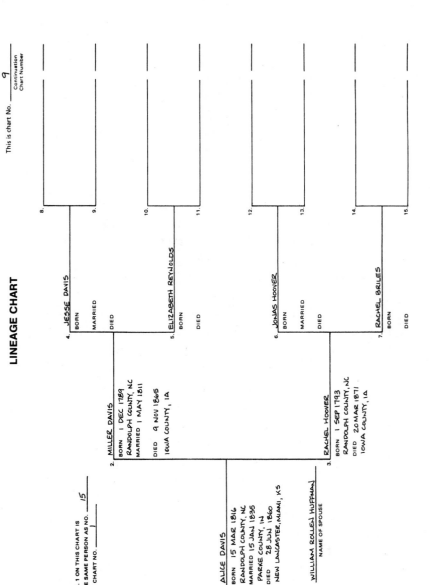

LINEAGE CHART

This is chart No. ___ 9
Continuation Chart Number

NO. 1 ON THIS CHART IS
THE SAME PERSON AS NO. ___ 15
ON CHART NO. ___ 1

1. *ALICE DAVIS*
BORN   15 MAR 1816
RANDOLPH COUNTY, NC
MARRIED 15 JAN 1835
PARKE COUNTY, IN
DIED   28 JUN 1860
NEW LANCASTER, MIAMI, KS

WILLIAM ROLLEA HUFFMAN
NAME OF SPOUSE

2. *MILLER DAVIS*
BORN   1 DEC 1789
RANDOLPH COUNTY, NC
MARRIED 1 MAY 1811
DIED   9 NOV 1865
IOWA COUNTY, IA

3. *RACHEL HOOVER*
BORN   1 SEP 1793
RANDOLPH COUNTY, NC
DIED   20 MAR 1871
IOWA COUNTY, IA

4. *JESSE DAVIS*
BORN
MARRIED
DIED

5. *ELIZABETH REYNOLDS*
BORN
DIED

6. *JONAS HOOVER*
BORN
MARRIED
DIED

7. *RACHEL BRILES*
BORN
DIED

8.

9.

10.

11.

12.

13.

14.

15.

Figure 8:34. Final Lineage Chart 9, Alice Davis.

FAMILY GROUP SHEET

HUS. GROVER CLEVELAND WEST   OCCUPATION(S) INTERIOR DECORATOR

	DATE	PLACE
BORN	18 FEB 1885	Moran, Allen, Kansas
CHR.		
MARR.	30 APR 1912	Vinita, Craig, Oklahoma
DIED	22 NOV 1953	Kansas City, Jackson, Missouri
BUR.	27 NOV 1953	Bronson Cemetery, Bronson, Bourbon, Kansas

FATHER WILLIAM ANDREW WEST   MOTHER LAURA STEWART   OTHER WIVES

WIFE BERTHA RUTH SMITH

	DATE	PLACE
BORN	14 FEB 1889	Kansas City, Jackson, Missouri
CHR.		
DIED	28 AUG 1972	Kansas City, Jackson, Missouri
BUR.	30 AUG 1972	Bronson Cemetery, Bronson, Bourbon, Kansas

FATHER THOMAS ALBERT SMITH   MOTHER MARY ALICE KARR   OTHER HUSBANDS

SEX	CHILDREN	DATE BORN / PLACE BORN	DATE MARRIED / TO	PLACE	DATE DIED / PLACE DIED
1 F	LAURA ALICE WEST	11 MAY 1913 / Nevada, Vernon, Missouri	20 FEB 1924 / (1) JOSEPH BRUCE WELSH	Kansas City, Jackson, MO	14 OCT 1983 / Kansas City, Jackson, MO
2 F	AVIS LORENE WEST	22 APR 1914 / Bronson, Bourbon, Kansas	24 JUL 1939 / RAYMOND JOHN SPENCER	Los Angeles, Los Angeles, CA	
3 F	GRETA CARROLL WEST	18 AUG 1915 / Bronson, Bourbon, Kansas	22 JUL 1956 / J. C. GARDNER	Los Angeles, Los Angeles, CA	JUL 1981 / Los Angeles, Los Angeles, CA
4 F	WILMA LOUISE WEST	7 DEC 1916 / Bronson, Bourbon, Kansas	17 MAR 1941 / CLARENCE MELVIN BROWN	Los Angeles, Los Angeles, CA	30 APR 1946 / Wichita, Sedgewick, KS
5 M	GROVER CLEVELAND WEST	26 Mar 1918 / La Harpe, Allen, Kansas			17 APR 1920 / Wichita, Sedgewick, KS
6 F	JUANITA BEA WEST	22 May 1920 / Bronson, Bourbon, Kansas	1941 / HARRY CARL SHEDRICK	Fullerton, Orange, CA	
7 F	LEAH CORRINE WEST	6 Nov 1921 / Bronson, Bourbon, Kansas	1941 / (1)ROBERT MICHAEL BUTLER	Kansas City, Jackson, MO	21 JUL 1967 / Kansas City, Jackson, MO
8 x F	VIVIAN ELAINE WEST	24 DEC 1922 / La Harpe, Allen, Kansas	20 MAR 1943 / JOHN STEVE CERNY	Kansas City, Jackson, MO	
9 F	VIROQUA JEAN WEST	11 DEC 1925 / Bronson, Bourbon, Kansas	23 JUN 1951 / JOHN DAVID GOLDSON	Los Angeles, Los Angeles, CA	2 DEC 1958 / Los Angeles, Los Angeles, CA
10 F	BEVERLY JOAN WEST	8 MAR 1930 / Bronson, Bourbon, Kansas	20 OCT 1956 / CARL VACCARO	Kansas City, Jackson, MO	

OTHER MARRIAGES

#1 Laura md (2) Max Westfall, (3) Robert Conley, (4) Robert Allen, (5) Ora Macaubrie

#7 Leah md (2) Edward Miller (3)Charles P. Ardayna, 25 Oct 1951

SOURCES OF INFORMATION
Birth, Marriage, and Death Records in possession of various family members.

RESEARCH NOTES

Figure 8:35. Final Family Group Record, Grover Cleveland West
and Bertha Ruth Smith.

FAMILY GROUP SHEET

HUS. GROVER CLEVELAND WEST | OCCUPATION(S)

BORN	18 FEB 1885	PLACE Moran, Allen, Kansas
CHR.		PLACE
MARR.	30 APR 1912	PLACE Vinita, Craig, Oklahoma
DIED	22 NOV 1953	PLACE Kansas City, Jackson, Missouri
BUR.	27 NOV 1953	PLACE Bronson Cemetery, Bronson, Bourbon, Kansas
FATHER	WILLIAM ANDREW WEST	OTHER WIVES
MOTHER	LAURA STEWART	

WIFE BERTHA RUTH SMITH

BORN	14 FEB 1889	PLACE Kansas City, Jackson, Missouri
CHR.		PLACE
DIED	28 AUG 1972	PLACE Kansas City, Jackson, Missouri
BUR.	30 AUG 1972	PLACE Bronson Cemetery, Bronson, Bourbon, Kansas
FATHER	THOMAS ALBERT SMITH	OTHER HUSBANDS
MOTHER	MARY ALICE KARR	

SEX	CHILDREN	DATE BORN / PLACE BORN	DATE MARRIED / TO	PLACE	DATE DIED / PLACE DIED
M	11 JAMES EVERETTE WEST	2 MAR 1933 / Bronson, Bourbon, Kansas	20 SEP 1958 / ETHEL MARIAN GASMAN	Madison, Dane, Wisconsin	
	2				
	3				
	4				
	5				
	6				
	7				
	8				
	9				
	10				

OTHER MARRIAGES

SOURCES OF INFORMATION

RESEARCH NOTES

FAMILY GROUP SHEET

HUS. THOMAS ALBERT SMITH

BORN	20 FEB 1862	PLACE New Lancaster, Miami, Kansas
CHR.		PLACE
MARR	30 APR 1884	PLACE New Lancaster, Miami, Kansas
DIED	16 JUN 1924	PLACE Xenia, Bourbon, Kansas
BUR.	18 JUN 1924	PLACE Bronson Cemetery, Bronson, Bourbon, Kansas
FATHER	JOHN SMITH	
MOTHER	MARY JANE PLEDGER	OTHER WIVES

OCCUPATION(S)

WIFE MARY ALICE KARR

BORN	5 OCT 1864	PLACE New Lancaster, Miami, Kansas
CHR.		PLACE
DIED	3 AUG 1947	PLACE Fort Scott, Bourbon, Kansas
BUR.	6 AUG 1947	PLACE Bronson Cemetery, Bronson, Bourbon, Kansas
FATHER	AMBROSE KARR	
MOTHER	MARTHA P. HUFFMAN	OTHER HUSBANDS

SEX	CHILDREN	DATE BORN / PLACE BORN	DATE MARRIED / TO	PLACE	DATE DIED / PLACE DIED
X F	1 BERTHA RUTH SMITH	14 FEB 1889 / Kansas City, Jackson, Missouri	30 APR 1912 / GROVER CLEVELAND WEST	Vinita, Craig, Oklahoma	28 AUG 1972 / Kansas City, Jackson, Mo
	2				
	3				
	4				
	5				
	6				
	7				
	8				
	9				
	10				

OTHER MARRIAGES

SOURCES OF INFORMATION
1. Death Certificates for Husband, wife, and child
2. Marriage License of Husband and wife,

Figure 8:36. Final Family Group Record, Thomas Albert Smith and Mary Alice Karr.

FAMILY GROUP SHEET

HUS. AMBROSE N. KARR   OCCUPATION(S) FARMER

BORN	1838	PLACE Bartholomew County, Indiana
CHR.		PLACE
MARR	26 MAY 1859	PLACE New Lancaster, Miami, Kansas
DIED	13 AUG 1867	PLACE New Lancaster, Miami, Kansas
BUR.		PLACE New Lancaster Cemetery, New Lancaster, Miami, Kansas
FATHER	WILLIAM A. KARR	
MOTHER	AMANDA PEACE HOPKINS	OTHER WIVES

WIFE MARTHA P. HUFFMAN

BORN	1839	PLACE Parke County, Indiana
CHR.		PLACE
DIED	15 JUN 1817	PLACE New Lancaster, Miami, Kansas
BUR.		PLACE New Lancaster Cemetery, New Lancaster, Miami, Kansas
FATHER	WILLIAM ROLLEN HUFFMAN	OTHER HUSBANDS (2) William A. HOPKINS 4 Mar 1871
MOTHER	ALICE DAVIS	

SEX	CHILDREN	DATE BORN / PLACE BORN	DATE MARRIED / TO	PLACE	DATE DIED / PLACE DIED
M	1 JAMES MARION KARR	5 OCT 1862 / New Lancaster, Miami, Kansas	EMMA LANE SMITH	New Lancaster, Miami, KS	28 AUG 1942 / New Lancaster, Miami, KS
F	2 MARY ALICE KARR	5 OCT 1864 / New Lancaster, Miami, Kansas	30 APR 1884 THOMAS ALBERT SMITH	New Lancaster, Miami, KS	3 AUG 1947 / Fort Scott, Bourbon, KS
F	3 SARAH JANE KARR	31 DEC 1866 / New Lancaster, Miami, Kansas	24 APR 1888 ULYSSES S. GRANT PROWELL	New Lancaster, Miami, KS	12 MAR 1956 / Louisberg, Miami, KS
	4				
	5				
	6				
	7				
	8				
	9				
	10				

SOURCES OF INFORMATION
1. Death Records of children, State of Kansas.
2. Marriage Records, Miami County, Kansas.
3. Tombstone Inscriptions, New Lancaster Cemetery, Miami County, Kansas.
4. Probate Records of Ambrose N. Karr, Miami County, Kansas.
5. Guardianship Records, Probate Court, Miami County, Kansas.
6. Death Notice, Miami Republican, 22 June 1817.
7. 1860 U.S. Census, Miami and Osage Twps., Miami County, Kansas.
8. 1870 U.S. Census, Miami Twp., Miami County, Kansas.
9. 1860 U.S. Census, Miami County, Kansas.
10. 1865 Kansas State Census, Miami County, Kansas.
11. 1875 Kansas State Census, Miami County, Kansas.
11. 1850 U.S. Census, Marion County, Iowa.

Figure 8:37. Final Family Group Record, Ambrose N. Karr and Martha P. Huffman.

FAMILY GROUP SHEET

HUS. WILLIAM A. KARR — OCCUPATION(S) FARMER AND KANSAS STATE LEGISLATOR

BORN	24 MAR 1814	PLACE Washington County, Pennsylvania
CHR.		PLACE
MARR.	14 FEB 1835	PLACE Decatur County, Indiana
DIED		PLACE
BUR.		PLACE

FATHER MATHEW KARR / KERR
MOTHER HANNAH PEES / PEASE
OTHER WIVES (2) MRS. MARGARET ABROGAST   21 SEP 1871

WIFE AMANDA PEACE HOPKINS

BORN	1814	PLACE Floyd County, Kentucky
CHR.		PLACE
DIED	22 NOV 1870	PLACE New Lancaster, Miami, Kansas
BUR.		PLACE

FATHER WILLIAM HOPKINS
MOTHER SARAH SMATHERS
OTHER HUSBANDS

SEX	CHILDREN	DATE BORN / PLACE BORN	DATE MARRIED / TO	PLACE	DATE DIED / PLACE DIED
X M 1	AMBROSE N. KARR	1838 / Bartholomew County, Indiana	26 MAY 1859 / MARTHA P. HUFFMAN	New Lancaster, Miami, KS	13 AUG 1867 / New Lancaster, Miami, KS
M 2	MATTHEW KARR	21 SEP 1839 / Bartholomew County, Indiana			11 FEB 1867 / Davis County, IA
M 3	JAMES W. KARR	CAL 1844 / Bartholomew County, Indiana			1865 / New Lancaster, Miami, KS
M 4	ELIHU ALLEY KARR	16 May 1846 / Bartholomew County, Indiana	22 JAN 1867 / HANNAH JANE STEWART	New Lancaster, Miami, KS	15 JUN 1908 / Rolla, Phelps, MO
F 5	SARAH ANN KARR	CAL 1847 / Marion County, Iowa	H. BROWN		1930 / Wichita, Sedgewick, KS
M 6	WILLIAM HENRY KARR	CAL 1850 / Marion County, Iowa			
M 7	ELDRIDGE MILTON KARR	5 OCT 1852 / Marion County, Iowa			
F 8	ELMYRA J. KARR	10 OCT 1854 / Marion County, Iowa			28 NOV 1856 / Davis County, IA
9					
10					

SOURCES OF INFORMATION
1. 1860 U.S. Census - Lykins County, Kansas
2. 1870, 1880 U.S. Census - Miami County, Kansas
3. 1865, 1875 Kansas State Census - Miami County, Kansas
4. Marriage Records - Miami County, Kansas and Decatur County, Indiana
5. Tombstone Inscriptions - Karr Family cemetery, Davis County, Iowa
6. Portrait and Biographical Record of Sedgewick County, Kansas
7. 1860 U.S. Census - Marion County, Iowa

OTHER MARRIAGES
#4 md (2) ALMA POYNTER 15 NOV 1903

Figure 8:38. Final Family Group Record, William A. Karr and
Amanda Peace Hopkins.

FAMILY GROUP SHEET

HUS. WILLIAM ROLLEN HUFFMAN (CONT'ON SHEET #2) **OCCUPATION(S)** ~~BRETHREN~~ UNITED MINISTER - KANSAS STATE LEGISLATOR

BORN	1 JUL 1815	PLACE St. Clair Township, Butler, Ohio
CHR.		PLACE
MARR	15 JAN 1835	PLACE Parke County, Indiana
DIED	16 SEP 1900	PLACE New Lancaster, Miami, Kansas
BUR	20 SEP 1900	PLACE New Lancaster Cemetery, Miami, Kansas
FATHER	JOHN HUFFMAN	OTHER WIVES (2) MRS.
MOTHER	MARY	

WIFE ALICE DAVIS

BORN	15 MAR 1816	PLACE Randolph County, North Carolina
CHR.		PLACE
DIED	28 JUN 1860	PLACE New Lancaster, Miami, Kansas
BUR		PLACE New Lancaster Cemetery, Miami, Kansas
FATHER	MILLER DAVIS	OTHER HUSBANDS
MOTHER	RACHEL HOOVER	

SEX	CHILDREN	DATE BORN / PLACE BORN	DATE MARRIED / TO	PLACE	DATE DIED / PLACE DIED
1 M	ANDREW J. HUFFMAN	2 NOV 1836 / Parke County, Indiana	1858 / Margaret I. HUMPHREY	Benton County, IA	
2 X F	MARTHA P. HUFFMAN	1839 / Parke County, Indiana	26 MAY 1859 / (1) AMBROSE N. KARR	New Lancaster, Miami, KS	15 JUN 1877 / New Lancaster, Miami, KS
3 F	LENVISA WARD HUFFMAN	14 JAN 1841 / Parke County, Indiana	8 MAY 1866 / Calvin F. TRACY	New Lancaster, Miami, KS	18 JUL 1934 / New Lancaster, Miami, KS
4 M	GABRIEL MILTON HUFFMAN	27 FEB 1843 / Parke County, Indiana	14 MAY 1867 / SUSAN NEIDIG	Muscatine, Muscatine, IA	
5 M	FRANKLIN HAYDEN HUFFMAN	10 SEP 1844 / Fulton County, Illinois	1 NOV 1866 / MARTHA P. ELLIS	New Lancaster, Miami, KS	23 JAN 1923 / Salina, Saline, KS
6 F	REBECCA ANN HUFFMAN	CAL 1846 / Fulton County, Illinois	15 SEP 1866 / ALVIN G. WALLY	New Lancaster, Miami, KS	
7 F	ANGELINE HUFFMAN	Oct 1850 / Fulton County, Illinois	5 APR 1866 / WILLIAM G. MEYERS	New Lancaster, Miami, KS	
8 M	JONAS DAVIS HUFFMAN	23 MAY 1852 / Benton County, Iowa	30 AUG 1873 / FLORENCE D. CAMPBELL	New Lancaster, Miami, KS	
9 M	DAVID SMITH HUFFMAN	1853 / Benton County, Iowa	2 NOV 1876 / (1) ELVA JANE RHODES	New Lancaster, Miami, KS	
10 M	CHARLES L. HUFFMAN	1856 / Benton County, Iowa	30 JUN 1878 / SUSAN LONG	New Lancaster, Miami, KS	

SOURCES OF INFORMATION
1. 1860 U.S. Census - Lykins County, Kansas
2. 1870, 1880, 1900 U.S. Census - Miami County, Kansas
3. 1865, 1875, 1885 U.S. Census - Miami County, Kansas
4. Marriage Records - Miami County, Kansas and Parke County, Indiana
5. Tombstone Inscriptions - New Lancaster Cemetery, Miami County, Kansas
6. Civil War Pension Application Files of Gabriel M. and Franklin H. Huffman
7. Death Certificates of Lenvisa W. Tracy and Franklin H. Huffman

OTHER MARRIAGES
#2 md (2) William A. Hopkins 4 Mar 1871

Figure 8:39. Final Family Group Record, Matthew Karr and Hannah Pees.

FAMILY GROUP SHEET

HUS. MATTHEW KARR /KERR		OCCUPATION(S) FARMER
BORN ABT 1775	PLACE Northern Ireland	
CHR.	PLACE	
MARR ABT 1799	PLACE Washington County, Pennsylvania	
DIED 14 DEC 1826	PLACE Franklin County, Indiana	
BUR.	PLACE	
FATHER		
MOTHER		OTHER WIVES

WIFE HANNAH PEES/PEASE	
BORN 1775	PLACE Strabane Township, Washington, Pennsylvania
CHR.	PLACE
DIED 9 MAY 1855	PLACE near Pulaski, Davis, Iowa
BUR.	PLACE Karr Family Cemetery, near Pulaski, Davis, Iowa
FATHER NICHOLAS PEES/PEASE	OTHER HUSBANDS
MOTHER HANNAH	

SEX	CHILDREN	DATE BORN / PLACE BORN	DATE MARRIED / TO	PLACE	DATE DIED / PLACE DIED
1 F	CATHERINE KARR	25 JAN 1800 / Washington County, Pennsylvania	24 JUN 1826 / ELIHU ALLEY	Decatur County, Indiana	4 JUL 1861 / Red Rock, Marion, Iowa
2 F	MARY KARR	CAL 1802 / Washington County, Pennsylvania			before 1850
3 M	JAMES KARR	CAL 1804 / Washington County, Pennsylvania	11 APR 1825 / (1) HESTHER DOTY	Franklin County, Indiana	4 OCT 1890 / Franklin County, Indiana
4 M	ANDREW P. KARR	CAL 1808 / Washington County, Pennsylvania	15 MAR 1825 / (1) MARY CASTEEL	Bartholomew County, Indiana	Miami County, Kansas
5 F	ISABEL KARR	CAL 1810 / Mercer County, Pennsylvania	20 FEB 1830 / (1) WILLIAM HENDERSON	Franklin County, Indiana	
6 M	GEORGE WASHINGTON KARR	2 SEP 1812 / Mercer County, Pennsylvania	12 DEC 1834 / ELIZA DICKEY	Bartholomew County, Indiana	28 MAY 1898 / Duneath, Marion, Iowa
7 M	WILLIAM A. KARR	24 MAR 1814 / Washington County, Pennsylvania	19 FEB 1835 / (1) AMANDA PEACE HOPKINS	Decatur County, Indiana	
8 F	ELIZA KARR	CAL 1815 / Franklin County, Indiana	8 DEC 1825 / JOHN DICKEY	Bartholomew County, Indiana	
9 M	JOHN KARR	14 NOV 1818 / Franklin County, Indiana	28 NOV 1839 / (1) CAROLINE JONES	Shelby County, Indiana	8 AUG 1902 / Marion County, Indiana
10 F	MARY JANE KARR	14 MAR 1824 / Franklin County, Indiana	30 MAR 1845 / ANDREW J. HOPKINS	Bartholomew County, Indiana	20 SEP 1913 / Topeka,

SOURCES OF INFORMATION:
1. 1850 U.S. Census - Marion County, Iowa
2. Marriage Records - Franklin, Bartholomew, Decatur, Shelby Counties, Indiana
3. Marriage Records - Marion County, Iowa and Miami County, Kansas
4. 1830, 1840 U.S. Census - Bartholomew County, Indiana
5. Tombstone Inscriptions - Karr Family Cemetery, Marion County, Iowa
6. 1820 U.S. Census - Franklin County, Indiana
7. Tombstone Inscriptions - Marion County, Iowa

OTHER MARRIAGES
#3 md (2) JANE CROSBY 26 SEP 1844
　　　 (3) HANNAH WISE 4 DEC 1859
　　　 (4) ELIZABETH RICHARDS
#4 md (2) RUTH ROBINSON 21 SEP 1862
#5 md (2) CALEB CASTEEL 8 SEP 1835
#7 md (2) MARGARET ABZOGAST 21 SEP 1871

Figure 8:40. Final Family Group Record, William Rollen Huffman and Alice Davis.

FAMILY GROUP SHEET

HUS. WILLIAM ROLLEN HUFFMAN   (CON'T FROM SHEET #1)   OCCUPATION(S) UNITED BRETHREN MINISTER - KANSAS STATE LEGISLATOR

BORN	1 JUL 1815	PLACE St. Clair Township, Butler, Ohio
CHR		PLACE
MARR	15 JAN 1835	PLACE Parke County, Indiana
DIED	16 SEP 1900	PLACE New Lancaster, Miami, Kansas
BUR	20 SEP 1900	PLACE New Lancaster Cemetery, Miami, Kansas
FATHER	JOHN HUFFMAN	OTHER WIVES
MOTHER	MARY	

WIFE ALICE DAVIS

BORN	15 MAR 1816	PLACE Randolph County, North Carolina
CHR		PLACE
DIED	28 JUN 1860	PLACE New Lancaster, Miami, Kansas
BUR		PLACE New Lancaster Cemetery, Miami, Kansas
FATHER	MILLER DAVIS	OTHER HUSBANDS
MOTHER	RACHEL HOOVER	

SEX	CHILDREN	DATE BORN / PLACE BORN	DATE MARRIED / TO	PLACE	DATE DIED / PLACE DIED
M	1 ELAM L. HUFFMAN	JUL 1858 / New Lancaster, Miami, Kansas	23 MAR 1883 / FRANCES HARRISON	New Lancaster, Miami, KS	
F	2 SUSAN D. HUFFMAN	JUN 1860 / New Lancaster, Miami, Kansas			1860 / New Lancaster, Miami, KS
	3				
	4				
	5				
	6				
	7				
	8				
	9				
	10				

OTHER MARRIAGES

SOURCES OF INFORMATION:
8. Historical Collections, United Brethren Church
9. History of Kansas by A. T. Andreas
10. 1850 Census - Fulton County, Illinois
11. Will of William Rollen Huffman, Miami County, Kansas Probate Court
12. Kansas Historical Collections, Kansas State Historical Society, Vol. X, 1907-8

FAMILY GROUP SHEET

HUS. WILLIAM HOPKINS, JR.		OCCUPATION(S)
BORN	30 MAR 1781	PLACE
CHR.		PLACE
MARR.	CAL 1802	PLACE
DIED	5 AUG 1856	PLACE near Pulaski, Davis, Iowa
BUR.		PLACE
FATHER WILLIAM HOPKINS, SR.		
MOTHER PEACE	OTHER WIVES (2) TEMPERANCE	Virginia

WIFE SARAH SMATHERS		
BORN	1788	PLACE Virginia
CHR.		PLACE
DIED	9 MAY 1864	PLACE near Pulaski, Davis, Iowa
BUR.		PLACE
FATHER ANDREW SMATHERS		
MOTHER SARAH	OTHER HUSBANDS	

SEX	CHILDREN	DATE BORN	PLACE BORN	DATE MARRIED TO	PLACE	DATE DIED	PLACE DIED
1 F	ABIAH HOPKINS	CAL 1804	Floyd County, Kentucky	26 NOV 1824 JOSEPH HINER	Nicholas County, Kentucky		
				31 JAN 1828	Bartholomew County, Indiana		
2 M	ELDRIDGE HOPKINS	CAL 1806	Floyd County, Kentucky	27 JUL 1830 ZILLAH MORRIS	Decatur County, Indiana		
3 F	ELIZABETH HOPKINS	CAL 1812	Floyd County, Kentucky	19 FEB 1835 HIRAM W. SHELTON	Decatur County, Indiana		
4 F	AMANDA PEACE HOPKINS	CAL 1814	Floyd County, Kentucky	1 SEP 1835 WILLIAM A. KARR	Decatur County, Indiana	22 NOV 1870	New Lancaster, Miami, KS
5 M	JOSEPH SMATHERS HOPKINS	CAL 1816	Floyd County, Kentucky	2 JUL 1839 ASENATH MORRIS	Bartholomew County, Indiana		
6 M	AMBROSE JONES HOPKINS	CAL 1818	Nicholas County, Kentucky	(1) LOVINA ROBBINS	Bartholomew County, Indiana		
7 F	MARY ANN HOPKINS	CAL 1819	Nicholas County, Kentucky	22 JAN 1841 ANDERSON MEYERS	Bartholomew County, Indiana		
8 M	WILLIAM WARD HOPKINS	1823	Nicholas County, Kentucky	3 MAR 1843 CAROLINE P. ROBBINS	Bartholomew County, Indiana		
9 M	ANDREW J. HOPKINS	1 SEP 1825	Nicholas County, Kentucky	30 MAR 1846 MARTHA JANE KARR	Bartholomew County, Indiana	25 NOV 1901	
10							

OTHER MARRIAGES

SOURCES OF INFORMATION:
1. 1850 U.S. Census - Davis County, Iowa
2. Tombstone Inscriptions - Davis County, Iowa
3. Will of William Hopkins, Davis County, Iowa Probate Court
4. Marriage Records - Bartholomew and Decatur Counties, Indiana
5. Tax Lists - Floyd and Nicholas Counties, Kentucky
6. Family Records

Figure 8:41. Final Family Group Record, William Hopkins Jr. and Sarah Smathers.

CHAPTER 9

Tracing Ancestors with Common Surnames

I f you have a common surname to trace such as Smith, Brown, Williams, or Green, traditional research approaches may have filled your files with too many candidates for your own ancestor. Culling through extensive files can prove very discouraging. Your task will be easier if you select from the search strategies presented in this chapter, plans that cross-reference the variety of records that have survived.

Approach research on a common surname as you would an intricate jigsaw puzzle. Complete the borders, creating a frame that will give your research focus and direction. Items that will define your search are the names of key ancestors, their relationships to others, places of residence, and the time period they lived there. From here, you must design search strategies to (1) eliminate the noncandidates, those who could not possibly belong to your family because they were born in the wrong places, are too old or too young, or lack any characteristics which fit, and (2) identify all potential candidates, those who seem to fit within the set dimensions. You will focus the rest of your searches on these individuals.

Eliminating noncandidates and identifying potential ones means that you must not form preconceived notions as to who your ancestor is. Rather, you should examine a selected body of data that provides enough details to distinguish one from two or more persons of the same name. Using known information, select the persons most likely to fit for closer scrutiny. Rather than molding the data to fit your common surnamed ancestor, examine the data for fit.

SEARCH STRATEGIES

Several search strategies for common surnames will enable you to separate potential candidates for your ancestor from all the others. What follows are examples of how to search certain types of records for common surnames, methods easily applied to other genealogical resources. Note that each depends upon certain identifying or qualifying characteristics you will already have discovered from your searches in family records and through contacting cousins.

FAMILY SOURCES AND TRADITION

Family data is especially valuable when tracking a common surname, as sometimes small details passed generation to generation are the pieces of the puzzle needed to fit the other pieces into place. Knowledge of places of residence, of religious affiliation, of important persons you are related to, of cemeteries where family members are buried, and many other facts come from your family. Try not to censor what your relatives tell you. Write it all down and keep it for comparison with facts taken from public records.

Look for family sources among private collections and family papers in archives and libraries. This can prove frustrating, as you have no way of knowing in advance where your family's records will end up. Letters substantiating research on Nancy Hanks Lincoln, mother of Abraham Lincoln, for example, are deposited in the Seattle Public Library because the person who researched her ancestry moved to Washington state and took the records with him. You should examine the *National Union Catalog of Manuscript Collections*, affectionately called NUCMC ("nuckmuck"), for various locations of collections pertaining to your common surname.

One client of mine was sure that no one in her family had been prominent enough to have papers deposited anywhere. With encouragement, however, she examined NUCMC, and to her surprise found that West Virginia University had registered a collection belonging to her family. The collection included original land grants, surveys, tax records, receipts for six of the persons on her search name list, including William Parsons, a name high among the 2,000 most common surnames in 1790.

NUCMC is published by the Library of Congress, with annual volumes from 1958 through 1981 listing manuscripts in libraries and archives throughout the United States. Each volume is carefully indexed by place and subject, and every person named in any description is separately indexed. Begin searching for family papers by drafting a list of family surnames, names of sons-in-law, and close family associates. Then pay a visit to your local public library or university library and search for the names in NUCMC.

After checking NUCMC, search archive inventories for the principal depositories in the area where your ancestor lived and where the members of your family now reside. You have probably considered libraries and archives for printed census indexes and even microfilm copies of the censuses themselves. They usually do not come to mind when you think of family papers; yet the most likely spot to safeguard the personal papers would be in a local library or archive.

The public library may also have some vertical file folders on your person with newspaper clippings, correspondence from cousins unknown to you asking for information, index references to county or town histories, obituaries, land holdings, public service records, and other items. The library may also have a card index of burials in local cemeteries which will tell you precisely where your John Smith or William Johnston is located.

Duke University's William R. Perkins Library has 626 separate items and seven volumes of the personal papers of Zachariah Johnston and his son Thomas, 1717-1858. These materials include bills and receipts for taxes, Zachariah's original will with probate notations on it, his journals compiled during a trip into Kentucky in 1794, telling where he stayed each night and whom he saw, and an account book for his father, William Johnston, begun in 1709 in Ireland that shows the money he loaned to family and friends in Ireland, in Nottingham, Pennsylvania, and Augusta County, Virginia.

These records help to qualify your William Johnston from others of the same name before you begin actual research in public records. Knowing that your William is Irish, that he lived in Nottingham, Pennsylvania and Augusta County, Virginia are useful facts; but the names of his family members and close friends in that account book are invaluable in identifying your Johnston family (third on the list of the 2,000 most common surnames in 1790) from all the others.

INTERNATIONAL GENEALOGICAL INDEX

The IGI is a quick reference to a large body of source materials when searching for a common surname. For example, if you are researching Smith in Pennsylvania, you can expect to identify a substantial portion of the German Smiths recorded in the Pennsylvania German churches without checking the unindexed church records. If you are researching Foster in Massachusetts, you can identify about half the Fosters in the state through the town vital records indexed in the IGI without reading the difficult handwriting of the originals.

The IGI includes broad sections of material for consecutive years and these sources are carefully recorded in the *Parish and Vital Records Listings* for control. The IGI is also a source for information that can help you block out geographical areas. For example, a search of the 1900 census soundex was made for William Black Thom. While the Thom surname is not common in New York, it is in Scotland. For William Black Thom, born in Scotland 28 February 1889, the IGI yielded only one possible fit. A search of the vital records of New York for William's sister, the only one in the family born in the U.S., was next, and the birth return filed in 1895 matched the census.

The birth records named her father, David S. Thom, allowing a second IGI search that produced detailed information about him. These three sources—the 1900 U.S. Census, birth records, and the IGI—matched the family data sufficiently to block out a portion of the lineage geographically for in-depth searches into local sources in both Scotland and America.

The result of these preliminary searches is not a proven lineage, but a *work* lineage. From this you can make the necessary searches to prove or disprove the information. We have focused on one segment of the Thom surname to see if it really fits.

FAMILY GROUP SHEET

HUS. DAVID SHARPE THOM   OCCUPATION(S)

BORN 16 NOV 1860	PLACE Brechin, Angus, Scotland	
CHR.	PLACE	
MARR.	PLACE	
DIED	PLACE	
BUR.	PLACE	

FATHER GEORGE THOM
MOTHER CATHERINE CRABB

OTHER WIVES (2) CATHERINE BURGESS

WIFE (1)   [BLACK] ?

BORN	PLACE
CHR.	PLACE
DIED	PLACE
BUR.	PLACE

FATHER [WILLIAM BLACK] ?
MOTHER

OTHER HUSBANDS

SEX	CHILDREN	DATE BORN / PLACE BORN	DATE MARRIED / TO	PLACE	DATE DIED / PLACE DIED
1 M	WILLIAM BLACK THOM	28 FEB 1869 or JUN 1867 / Anstertool, Fife, Scotland			
2					
3					
4					
5					
6					
7					
8					
9					

OTHER MARRIAGES

SOURCES OF INFORMATION
Family Records and IGI (1981) Scotland
1900 U.S. Census, NY, Vol. 165, Ed. 749, Sheet 16.

RESEARCH NOTES
Names in brackets [ ] assumed from child's name.

Figure 9:1. Family Group Record, David S. Thom and first wife.

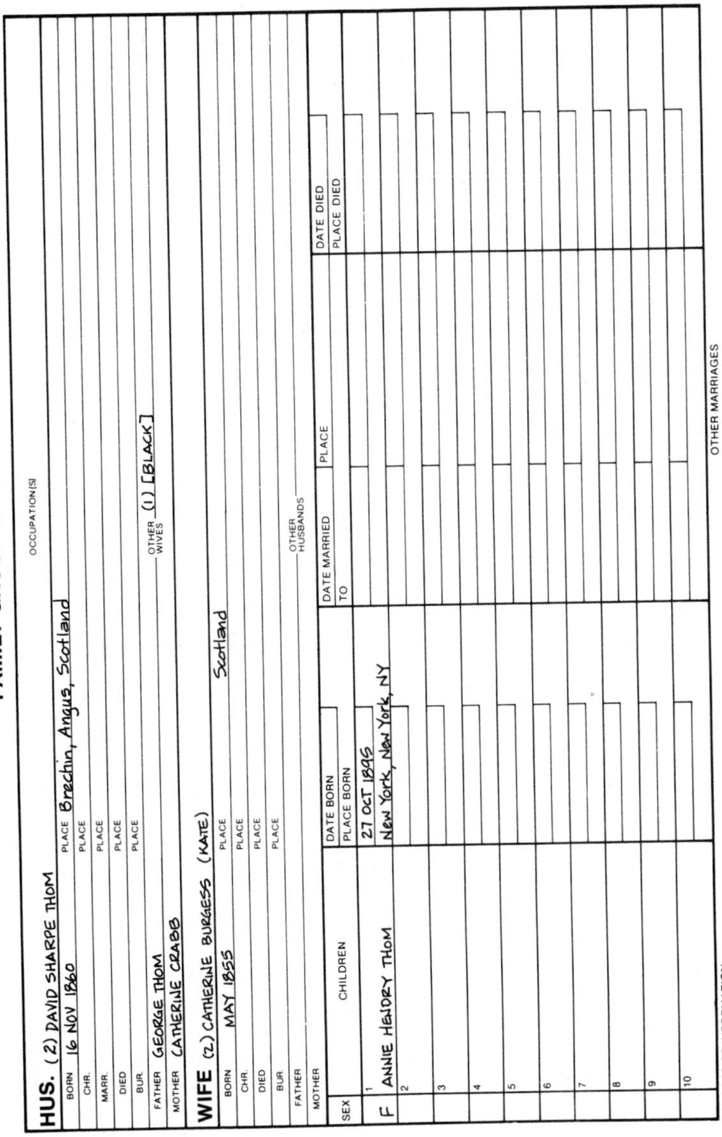

FAMILY GROUP SHEET

HUS. (2) DAVID SHARPE THOM   OCCUPATION(S)

BORN	16 NOV 1860
CHR.	PLACE Brechin, Angus, Scotland
MARR	PLACE
DIED	PLACE
BUR.	PLACE

FATHER GEORGE THOM
MOTHER CATHERINE CRABB

OTHER WIVES   (1) [BLACK]

WIFE (2) CATHERINE BURGESS (KATE)

BORN	MAY 1855 PLACE Scotland
CHR.	PLACE
DIED	PLACE
BUR.	PLACE

FATHER
MOTHER

OTHER HUSBANDS

SEX	CHILDREN	DATE BORN / PLACE BORN	DATE MARRIED / TO	PLACE	DATE DIED / PLACE DIED
1 F	ANNIE HENDRY THOM	27 OCT 1896 / New York, New York, NY			
2					
3					
4					
5					
6					
7					
8					
9					
10					

OTHER MARRIAGES

SOURCES OF INFORMATION
Family Records and IGI (1981) Scotland
1900 US. Census - New York, Vol. 165, Ed. 749, Sheet 16
Birth Certificate #45631, New York, NY
RESEARCH NOTES

Figure 9:2. Family Group Record, David S. Thom and Catherine
Burgess.

FAMILY GROUP SHEET

HUS. GEORGE THOM

OCCUPATION(S)

	PLACE
BORN	
CHR	PLACE
MARR	PLACE
DIED	PLACE
BUR	PLACE
FATHER	
MOTHER	

OTHER WIVES _____

WIFE CATHERINE CRABB

	PLACE
BORN	
CHR	PLACE
DIED	PLACE
BUR	PLACE
FATHER	
MOTHER	

OTHER HUSBANDS _____

SEX	CHILDREN	DATE BORN / PLACE BORN	DATE MARRIED / TO	PLACE	DATE DIED / PLACE DIED
F	1 ISABELLA ANN SMITH THOM	5 AUG 1856 / Brechin, Angus, Scotland		(c. 112751-053I)	
M	2 JAMES CRABB THOM	15 OCT 1858 / Brechin, Angus, Scotland		(c. 112751-1257)	
M	3 DAVID SHARPE THOM	16 Nov 1860 / Brechin, Angus, Scotland		(c. 112751-2241)	
M	4 GEORGE CHARLES MULLIG THOM	14 JUN 1864 / Brechin, Angus, Scotland		(c. 112751-3359)	
F	5 CATHERINE ANN DUTHIE THOM	15 JUN 1868 / Montrose, Angus, Scotland		(c. 113413-027)	
	6				
	7				
	8				
	9				
	10				

OTHER MARRIAGES

SOURCES OF INFORMATION

IGI, Scotland (1981 edition)

RESEARCH NOTES

Figure 9:3. Family Group Record, George Thom and Catherine Crabb.

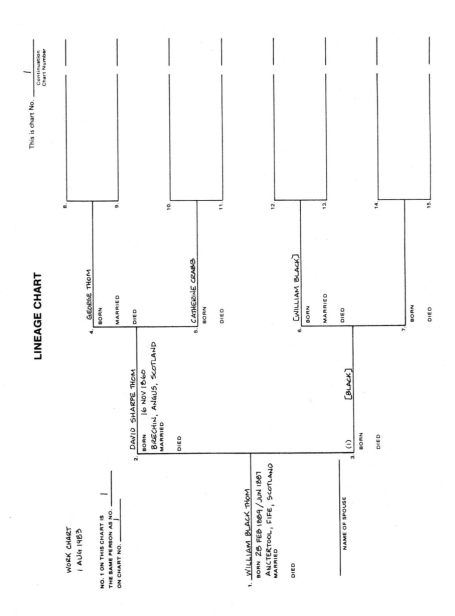

LINEAGE CHART

This is chart No. _____
Continuation Chart Number

WORK CHART
1 AUG 1983

NO. 1 ON THIS CHART IS
THE SAME PERSON AS NO. _____
ON CHART NO. _____ 1

1. WILLIAM BLACK THOM
BORN 25 FEB 1889 / JUN 1889
ANCTERTOOL, FIFE, SCOTLAND
MARRIED
DIED

NAME OF SPOUSE

2. DAVID SHARPE THOM
BORN 16 NOV 1860
BRECHIN, ANGUS, SCOTLAND
MARRIED
DIED

3. [BLACK]
BORN (1)
DIED

4. GEORGE THOM
BORN
MARRIED
DIED

5. CATHERINE CRABB
BORN
DIED

6. [WILLIAM BLACK]
BORN
MARRIED
DIED

7.
BORN
DIED

8.

9.

10.

11.

12.

13.

14.

15.

Figure 9:4. Lineage Work Chart, William Black Thom.

MARRIAGE INDEXES

From marriage indexes, extract or photocopy every entry for your common surname. If there is only a groom index, check the alpha sections for your surname, then search name by name each bride through the whole index. This will identify potential sons-in-law of your ancestor. Be sure to get all of the information in the record, including witnesses and identification of the officiator (MG, minister of the gospel, JP, justice of the peace, etc.). Arrange them in chronological order to coincide with census years. Watch for all those married before a given year in the next census.

Now match marriage and census entries together. If the name is Smith and the county is average in size, you could end up with 500 or more matches. Make extracts on family group records or census extracts from the beginning. This speeds analysis and matching of information from one source to another. Though tedious, it is much quicker and you are less likely to overlook or forget a potentially significant entry than if you write the information down in a notebook.

At this point eliminate all of those who could not be in your ancestral family: those born in the wrong place, those who were immigrants when your family had been in the U.S. for several generations, those who were the wrong ages, those whose children do not match your ancestor's, and those who didn't live in the area long enough. Don't destroy this information. Set it aside in case you need it again.

From the matched entries, draft a name list for searches in deeds, wills, tax rolls, and court records. List your surname and then the names of all those heads of household in the census, including grooms who married women of your surname, potential sons-in-law of your ancestor. Use sources that are easy to search either because they are indexed or because they contain enough information to identify potential family members. In this way you narrow down the number of Smiths you will have to examine.

CENSUS RECORDS

Censuses, even those taken between 1790 and 1840, are excellent finding tools. They can identify potential fathers and mothers for ancestors, especially important for those with common surnames. To make this search strategy effective, you must first extract all of the data from the census. When looking for the parents of William Thomas Smith, you will need all households with a William, a Thomas, a W.T., a W., a T., and a T. W. Smith. Then you can lay your extractions out on a table and mix and match them to fit. You will need these entries for all census years the family is suspected of living in the area. If you are lucky, you might have a clue or two on how long your ancestor lived there to guide your analysis.

Known Information:

William Thomas Smith b. 1849 m. 16 Jan 1868, Frances Bernettie

Scoggins d. 19 Aug 1879, Franklin County, GA. A daughter was born posthumously and named for her father, *Thomas* Lula Jane Smith.

William Thomas Smith died during the twelve months prior to the census, so the first place to search is the 1880 Mortality Schedule. It tells how long he lived in Franklin County and will give us a time frame in which to evaluate the census data.

Mortality Schedule:
    William F. Smith, age 33; married; male; white; born GA, father born SC, mother born GA; died August, disease of the liver. How long a resident of the county? 33 years. Dr. A. W. Banner.

Each qualifying search you make will contribute to your overall research. Be meticulous in recording exactly what you have done, noting the source you searched, how you searched it, and what you found. A research calendar is suggested so you can follow up any notes you make as the search progresses.

William Thomas Smith lived his whole life in Franklin County, Georgia beginning about 1847. His father was born in South Carolina and his mother in Georgia. Let's see who of the possible candidates living in that county most closely fits the information known about William Thomas's parents.

On a large sheet of paper, line up all the facts for comparison. Only two candidates qualify—if William Thomas "lived in the county 33 years": (1) W. or William, son of James and Rebecca, and (2) William T., son of Ezekiel and Nancy. Previous research placed Ezekiel and Nancy on the lineage chart, but they were eliminated because William T. had a wife, Mary, not Frances, and he lived next door to Nancy in the 1880 census when we know William Thomas was dead.

Analysis: The only census entry between 1850 and 1880 that had bearing on the research problem was that of James and Rebecca Smith who had two sons named William in 1860, one probably having another given name to avoid confusion in the household. And William was often called Thomas, a name given to his daughter, born posthumously, Thomas Lula Jane. James and Rebecca did not stay in the area, thus accounting for the lack of family tradition as to who the parents were.

All of these are risky speculations. Nowhere does the census say that this William is the one being sought or that James and Rebecca were his parents. Additional research is necessary. With a surname like Smith, however, knowing that James and Rebecca are the best potential candidates for parents, it is well worth the time it has taken to extract and digest the data carefully.

Using a process of elimination, it is possible to identify a candidate for parents using censuses from 1790 to 1840. That they do not name all members of the household makes the analysis hazardous and requires careful corroboration from other sources to prove conclusions. Family tradition, while subject to distortion and error, always contains some kernel of truth. The generation to which the tradition refers could be different, the place where the event occurred could be different, and the relationships may be mixed up, but the surnames are usually accurate and the given names valuable clues. Shattuck is a fairly common name in New England, and identifying the parents of Sarah Ann Shattuck required examining early census enumerations as shown below.

Known information:
    Sarah Ann Shattuck b. 19 May 1826, Nashua, Hillsboro County, NH
m. 16 Mar 1844, Groton, Middlesex County, MA to George Foster.

First we extract all Shattuck entries from the census records from 1810 to 1850 for Nashua, New Hampshire and for Dunstable, Massachusetts, just on the other side of the border, as they were originally one jurisdiction. Four candidates old enough to have a daughter born in 1826 were located:

    1. Nathan Shattuck, son of Zachariah, listed in 1830 only, no female child in household.
    2. Sarah Shattuck, widow of Edmund, listed in 1830 and 1840, no females in household young enough to be Sarah Ann.
    3. Daniel Shattuck, listed in 1840 with no female child young enough to be Sarah Ann.
    4. Andrew Shattuck, son of Jeremiah Shattuck, listed from 1820 to 1850:

1820, 1 female under 5	
1830, 2 females 5-10	[Sarah Ann, age 4-5]
1840, 1 female 15-20	[Sarah Ann, age 14-15]
1850, 1 female 18	[Emeline J.]
1 female 10	[Helen M.]
	[Sarah Ann married 1844]

As usual, the data does not fit precisely. Additional research is needed to prove the conclusion that Andrew is the best candidate for Sarah Ann's father. We have allowed the census to give us a potential ancestor; now searches can prove or disprove that candidate.

DEED INDEXES
    If you are researching Smith surnames, you will never live long enough to collect them all. What you want to do is eliminate candidates so you don't have to extract documents on them, too. Spend your time only on those who could be your ancestors, but control the process and carefully evaluate the results.

First, copy every entry for your surname in the deed indexes. Be sure you check both grantee (buyer) and grantor (seller). Then evaluate what you have found. You will need to extract or copy each document where:

1. Buyer and seller have the same surname.
2. Estate divisions are suggested. Watch for triggers like et al. (and others), exrs. (executors), admrs. (administrators), heirs of, est. (estate), or where there are several transactions involving your surname on the same day or within a short period of time. Sometimes it is possible to identify who the et al. is from the index alone by comparing volume and page references.
3. Transactions involve a substantial amount of property and little consideration: 200 acres for $50, an inner city lot for $5, etc. Some indexes list the consideration as well as the property description.
4. Several transactions have occurred in a short period for the same property.
5. Obvious relationship is indicated: "for $1 and other valuable considerations," or "for the affection I hold. . . . "

Evaluating that many documents requires copying the index entry, not only the name and page of interest. Don't rush and compromise your ability to evaluate the data. Extract or photocopy documents for each entry marked and read them carefully. The following checklist will guide you in extracting property records so all significant facts are listed.

_____ All names, including neighbors, witnesses, clerks, and bondsmen.
_____ All places.
_____ All dates.
_____ All relationships.
_____ All references to other documents.
_____ All property descriptions, including land, personal property, chattels, and shares.
_____ All considerations, including money, affection, produce, exchanges, agreements, and contracts.
_____ All signatures or marks exactly as they appear.
_____ All historical information that may serve as clues to other sources, such as occupation, religion, military service, nationality, membership in organizations, involvement in migrations, and acts of God.
_____ All biographical descriptions.

Figure 9:5. Extracting Checklist. Courtesy of the Genealogical Institute, Salt Lake City.

Neal ranks among the 2,000 most common surnames in 1790. The entries listed in Figure 9:6 represent all the Neals under various spellings in the deed indexes for Talbot County, Maryland before 1800. Those marked with a check will be copied or extracted for analysis.

Grantee/Grantor Index for Deeds, Talbot County, MD

Date	Neal/Neale/Neall		Other Party	Inst.	V	Pg
1693	✓Neale, Charles et al	to	Simon Trumball	Deed	7	59
1693	✓Neale, Elizabeth et al	from	Simon Trumbull	Deed	7	59
1704	Neale, Elizabeth	to	Robert Gould	Deed	9	233
1721	✓Neale, Elizabeth etrix	to	Thomas Wiles	Deed	13	8
1727	✓Same	to	Francis Neale	Deed	13	448
1728	✓Same	to	Dominick Caravan	Deed	13	461
1734	✓Neale, Elizabeth etrix	from	Thomas Wilds	Deed	14	49
1736	✓Same et al	from	Arthur Rigby	Deed	14	183
1742	Neall, Edward	from	Grace Woodward	Deed	15	262
1745	✓Same et wife	from	Richard Ragan et wife	Deed	16	239
1754	✓Neal, Elizabeth etrix	to	Peter Denny	Deed	18	251
1757	✓Neal, Edward	from	Levin Stacy	Deed	18	422
1761	✓Neall, Edward	from	Richard Ragain et wife	Deed	19	89
▪	✓Same	from	Levin Stacy	Deed	19	91
1799	✓Neale, Elizabeth etrix	from	John Troth	Deed	28	365
1788	Neall, Joseph	from	Peter Denny et wife	Deed	23	314
▪	Same	to	Peter Denny	Deed	23	316
1795	✓Neale, Joseph	from	Robins Chamberlain	Deed	26	275
1797	✓Neale, Joseph	from	Robins Chamberlain	Lease	27	367
▪	Same	to	Samuel, Henry Nicols	Lease	27	369
1793	✓Neale, Joseph	from	Robins Chamberlain	Deed	28	30
1799	Neale, Joseph	to	Joshua Taggart	Lease	28	396
1721	✓Neale, Jeremiah et wife	to	Thomas Wiles	Deed	13	8
1724	✓Neale, Jonathan, Hannah	from	Francis Neal	Deed	13	169
1727	✓Neale, Jonathan et wife	to	Francis Neale	Deed	13	448
1728	Same	to	Dominick Caravan	Deed	13	461
1733	✓Neale, Jeremiah	to	Francis Neal	Deed	13	772
1734	✓Same et wife	to	Thomas Wilds	Deed	14	49
1736	✓Same	from	Robert Smith	Deed	14	182
Same	✓Same et al	from	Arthur Rigby	Deed	14	183
1754	Neal, Jonathan	from	William Barman	Deed	18	224
1755	Same	from	Joseph Falkner et wife	Deed	18	265
1768	✓Neal, Jonathan et al	to	William Hayward	Deed	19	524
1747	✓Neal, Martha	to	Certificate of Valuation		17	32
1773	✓Neale, Mary etrix	to	Samuel Neal	Deed	20	271
Same	✓Same	to	Thomas Wilson	Deed	20	293
1773	✓Neale, Robert et wife	to	Samuel Neale	Deed	20	271
Same	Same	to	Thomas Wilson	Deed	20	293
1799	✓Neale, Robert et al	from	Samuel Dickinson	Lease	28	180
Same	Same et wife	to	John Troth	Deed	28	365
1773	✓Neale, Samuel	from	Robert Neale et wife	Deed	20	271
1775	✓Neale, Solomon et al	to	William Merrick	Deed	20	441
1799	✓Noel, Sarah etrix	to	Rev Joseph Telford	Deed	28	284
1678	Neale, Thomas	from	John Edmonson et wife	Deed	3	3
1753	Neal, Thomas	from	Thomas Neighbores wf	Deed	18	---

Figure 9:6. Neal entries in Grantee/Grantor Index for Deeds, Talbot County, Maryland.

Photocopies of documents are preferable to hand-copied extracts because they contain a full property description (that may be needed later to plat the land holdings), abbreviations exactly as the clerk made them, and signatures of the parties and witnesses.

Unlike an uncommon name, all those named Smith or Brown or Neal are usually not related; however, there will be exceptions. An important trigger indicating that everyone could be related is finding one small cluster of that name in the midst of many names usually uncommon. For example, you discover ten entries for Smith in a valley full of Cookseys. This reversal of the numbers will alert you to check on possible relationships among them all. If the area is a small, backwoods, rural place, even Smiths not originally related will end up related through intermarriage.

ORPHANS' COURT RECORDS

Other indexes can lead to important distinctions too. This example with the common surname of Brown combines the Orphans' Court Index for Monmouth County, New Jersey with entries from probate records and deeds to find the parents of William Saxton Brown.

Research began with the examination of William Carlisle Brown's journal, which stated:

My father, William Saxton Brown, was born 22 March 1800 near Manahawkin, Monmouth County, New Jersey. At age 18 he went to Bordentown on the Delaware River to apprentice as shoemaker with a Mr. Pettit. At age 21, he set out for "far west" with Abram Platt, Allen Cornelius, wife Marian, Samuel Reynolds, and others in a wagon train.

The Orphans' Court Records Index was searched, then compared with probate entries.

These two sources enabled identification of potential fathers for the orphaned children. Then property records were searched to distinguish from the numerous Samuel Browns the most likely candidate for William's father.

#1	Samuel Brown, died before 28 Jan 1814
	wife: Mary
1807	of New Hanover, Burlington County, NJ
1807	moves to Stafford, Monmouth County, NJ
1814	died in Stafford
	Others in Burlington County: Preserve Brown, 1753;
	Benajah, John, John Jr., and Thomas.

#2	Samuel Brown, died before 4 Feb 1794
1801	children: Jeremiah and Sarah
1793	military list, Shrewsbury, NJ

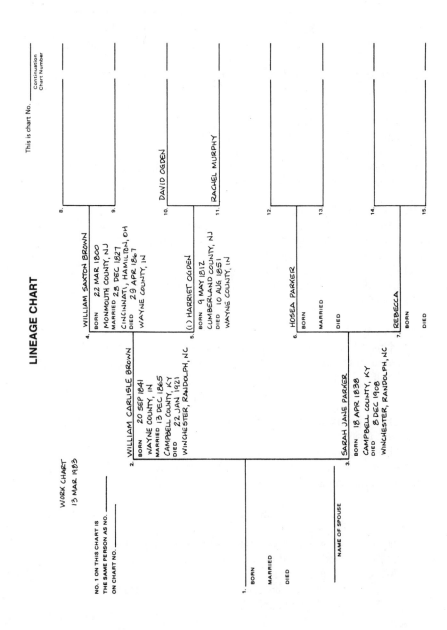

Figure 9:7. Lineage Work Chart, William C. Brown and Sarah J. Parker.

SUMMARY OF WILLS/ADMINISTRATIONS

Date	Name	Locale	Wife	Children	
13 Jul 1688	Nicholas Browne	Shrewsbury			
21 Feb 1711/12 1712	Nicholas Brown	Shrewsbury	Mary	Mary	
3 Jan 1723/ 1724	Nicholas Brown	Manahockin	Elizabeth	Abraham Joseph Elizabeth Daughter	
4 Apr 1749	William Brown	Monmouth Co	Ann		
13 Mar 1757	Arthur Brown	Monmouth Co	unnamed	Cabes Jane	Mary Isabel
17 Sep 1771	John Brown	Middletown	Jemimy	William Ephraim Jemimy Mehitibel	Desire Hannah Daniel Mary
26 Jul 1775	Abraham Brown	Stafford		Richard Abraham	
26 Jul 1781	Joseph Brown	Monmouth Co		Joseph (Admr)	
24 Apr 1787	Jeremiah Brown	Monmouth Co	Rachel	Samuel John	
4 Feb 1794	Samuel Brown	Monmouth Co		Jeremiah Sarah	
6 Apr 1799	Joseph Brown	Monmouth Co		William (Admr)	
27 Aug 1804	Samuel Brown	Stafford	Eleanor	Mary Crane Ellen Crane Elizabeth Bennett Sarah Kent Theodocia Letts William Clayton Samuel, Jr. Catherine Thomas	
25 Nov 1806	Mary Brown		unmarried		
30 Nov 1811	William Brown	Shrewsbury	Sary		
28 Jan 1814	Samuel Brown	Stafford	Mary	William Rebecca John	
9 Jan 1816	Joseph Brown	Stafford	(Southard)	Stephen David Moses Joseph Jesse Hannah	Elizabeth Edith Sybel Sarah Phebe Mary

Figure 9:8. Summary of Wills/Administrations, Monmouth County, New Jersey.

ORPHANS' COURT RECORD INDEX

Date	Name	Vol.	Document	Page	Comparison with Probate Entries
1794	Brown, Samuel	Book B	Decree for maintenance	32	⎤
1797	"	"	Settlement accounts	95	⎬ 1
"	"	"	Decree to invest money	83	
1799	"	"	Settlement accounts	125	⎦
1801	Brown, Jeremiah	Book C	Guardianship	4	⎬ 2 f. Samuel
"	Brown, Sarah	"	"	4	d. 1794
"	Brown, Samuel	"	Order to sell land	4	⎤
"	"	"	"	34	⎬ 3
1803	"	"	Settlement of accounts	45	⎦
1804	Brown, Abigail	"	Guardianship	113	⎤
"	Brown, Sarah	"	"	113	⎬ 4 f. Joseph
"	Brown, William	"	"	113	d. 1799
"	Brown, Abigail	"	Rule to show cause	114	
"	Brown, Sarah	"	"	114	
"	Brown, William	"	"	114	
"	Brown, Joseph	"	Rule to show cause	115	⎬ 5
"	"	"	Order to sell land	124	
"	Brown, Abigail	"	Application dismissed	125	
"	Brown, Sarah	"	"	125	
"	Brown, William	"	"	125	
"	Brown, Sarah	"	Report of Guardian	136	
"	Brown, Abigail	"	"	136	
"	Brown, William	"	"	136	
1805	Brown, Joseph	"	Confirmation of sale	138	
"	Brown, Sarah	"	Settlement accounts	142, 164, 172	
"	Brown, Abigail	"	"	142, 164, 172	
"	Brown, William	"	"	142, 164, 172	
"	Brown, John	"	Order to sell lands	173	⎬ 6 f. Jeremiah
1806	Brown, Samuel	"	Settlement accounts	187	d. 1787 ⎬ 7
"	"	"	Trustee's bond approval	214	

Figure 9:9. Orphans' Court Index, Monmouth County, New Jersey.

Date	Name	Vol.	Document	Page	Comparison with Probate Entries
1808	Brown, Joseph	Book D	Settlement accounts	34	8 Unmarried
"	Brown, Mary	"	"	40	
"	"	"	"	52	
1812	Brown, William	"	Rules to bar/limit creditors	236	9 William d.1811
1814	Brown, William	Book E	Guardianship	21	10 f. Samuel d. 1814
"	Brown, Rebecca	"	"	21	
"	Brown, John	"	"	21	
"	Brown, Joseph	"	Settlement accounts	95, 122	
1816	"	"	Citations	208, 209	
"	"	"	Subpoena	209	
"	"	"	Proceeding discontinued	211	

Record goes to 1867. No further Brown entries to 1829.

#3   Samuel Brown Sr., died 27 Aug 1804
wife: Eleanor Cutler
served Revolutionary War
blacksmith
1793   moves into Stafford, Monmouth County, NJ
1804   died in Stafford

#4   Samuel Brown Jr., son of Samuel Brown Sr.
wife: Rachel
1809   buys land from Thomas Letts, Stafford, Monmouth County, NJ
1815   "late of Stafford County" no mention where he went

#5   Samuel Brown
wife: Betsey Forrester
cooper, Upper Freehold Township, Monmouth County, NJ
1802   buys and sells land in New Egypt, NJ

A possible relationship exists between #1, #3, and #4. Samuel Sr. (#3) has a son Clayton Brown who migrated to Clermont County, Ohio, where (#1) Samuel's son John Lloyd Brown was located for awhile. Further research may show the exact relationship.

The solution to identifying William Carlisle's parents was found in the marriage of William Saxton Brown's son, William Carlisle, to Sarah Parker in Campbell County, Kentucky. She was the daughter of Hosea and Rebecca Parker. But nowhere in his journal did William Carlisle Brown tell us that Sarah was his cousin—a common occurrence. Family tradition left no clues stating that the Parkers and Browns were related except through the marriage of Sarah and William Carlisle.

Monmouth County, New Jersey deeds, corroborated by the Orphans' Court Index and the probate records shown in Figures 9:8 and 9:9, provided the proof that Rebecca Brown Parker was William Saxton Brown's sister and that they were Samuel and Mary Brown's children.

As the search moves into a new county (for Samuel Brown, that will be Burlington County, New Jersey), new qualifying searches must be made to distinguish Samuel and his potential parents from all the other Browns. A qualifying search is not the answer for all periods nor all locations in the history of this Brown family. But with each new period and locality, there are a variety of qualifying searches to choose from.

The key to successfully linking ancestors with common surnames lies in the analysis of *every* available record to eliminate those who do not fit known descriptive facts. Common surname research is demanding and time consuming —but not impossible.

CHAPTER 10

Ancestry by Occupation

W hat an ancestor did for a living creates specific record sources unique to that occupation, as one's occupation determines the resources left to be drawn upon. Tracing an ancestor with a known occupation requires two types of research—historical and genealogical. First, what exactly did your ancestor do? How does this determine where you look for information? Second, what information is produced by occupation sources? How does this information match what you know, and how does it lead to additional facts?

As you interview relatives and search basic sources such as census records, city directories, newspapers, or county histories, make note of the occupation your ancestor pursued. Then subject that occupation to analysis. This will enable you to determine which sources can be checked with reasonable expectations of finding information, such as where your ancestor was most likely to meet a future spouse and the potential identity of parents and in-laws.

Several different types of occupations and types of records you may need to search are discussed below.

CASE STUDIES

FRANKLIN E. HUNT, U.S. ARMY OFFICER

A career soldier such as Franklin E. Hunt, who served as a regular in the United States Army, was subject to a different set of jurisdictions than the volunteer soldier serving in his local militia, even if he was mustered into service in time of war. Tracing him requires searching many records, including military academy records, troop returns, muster and clothing rolls, enlistment papers, drill rolls and duty rosters, chaplain's records, morning reports, and a whole series of printed records. When beginning research, prepare a chronological list of the soldier's assignments, the years he was located at each post, and his rank.

It is easier to track a career soldier than it is a volunteer. A career soldier is clearly identified in the available records since those military sources are arranged in chronological order by command, by unit, and by post. Learn as much as possible about an army unit and the dates a career soldier served in it. A soldier's military personnel file will contain references to his dependents. Search local records near the posts to which a soldier was assigned — newspapers, church records, cemetery inscriptions, and others may offer details on this family.

Biographies of soldiers who attain the rank of major can usually be found in the standard biographical dictionaries. These biographies are invaluable if they provide lists of assignments and promotions. Histories of army installations usually include lists of officers, brief descriptions of their local contribution, and sometimes mention enlisted men.

Also check the general printed registers of U.S. Army officers and personnel. Each book will give bits of information not included in the others. Four sources and the information found on Franklin E. Hunt are given here:

1. *List of Officers, Army of the United States, 1779-1900.* Compiled by Col. William H. Powell. Reprinted. Detroit: Gale Research Company, 1967.

Hunt, Franklin E. Born N.J. appointed from N.J. Bvt. 2nd Lieut. 4th Art., 1 July 1829. 1st Lieut., 15 Aug 1836. Capt., 18 June 1846. Maj. P.M., 2 Mar 1855. Bvt. Lieut. Col. D.P.M. Gen., 3 Mar 1878. Retired 7 June 1879. Died 2 Feb 1881.

2. *Register of Officers and Graduates of the U.S. Military Academy at West Point, N.Y., 16 Mar 1802-1 Jan 1850.* Comp. by Capt. George W. Callum. New York: N.F. Trow, 1850.

1829. No. 560. Military Service. Franklin E. Hunt. Born N.J. Appointed from N.J. Rank 20. Artillery. Graduated 30 June 1829. Promoted Bvt. Second Lieut. 4th Artillery, 1 July 1829. Second Lieut., 1 July 1829. First Lieut., 15 Aug 1836. Capt., 18 June 1846.

3. *Official Army Register for 1860.* Washington, D.C.: Secretary of War, 1860.

Paymasters with the rank of Major. Franklin E. Hunt, commissioned 2 Mar 1855. Entered service Bvt. 2 lt. 4 art. 1 July 1829. Born N.J. Appointed from N.J.

4. *Register of Officers and Agents, Civil, Military, Naval in the Service to the United States, as of 30 Sep 1863.* Washington, D.C.: U.S. Government Printing Office, 1864.

Paymaster's Clerks, War Department, Franklin E. Hunt. Employed Kansas. Born Michigan. Appointed from Ohio. $700.00 compensation.

With the list of dates, promotions, etc., in-depth research in military records can begin. Records with direct relationship to Franklin E. Hunt include "Records of United States Army Commands, 1821-1920" (Record Group 393), "Records of United States Regular Army Mobile Units, 1821-1942"

(Record Group 391), "Records of the Office of Paymaster General" (Record Group 99), and "Records of the United States Military Academy" (Record Group 404). *Preliminary Inventory for the Records of the United States Military Academy,* published in 1976 by the General Services Administration, may also be useful. These records can only be searched at the National Archives in Washington D.C. in person or through a record agent.

JOB PINGREE, PUBLIC SERVANT

Early businessmen were an elite group within a city. They were mayors, aldermen, city or common councilmen, and held state and federal positions. The records to be searched if your ancestor was a public servant include voter polls, city council minutes, and quarterly and annual reports of city officials both elected and appointed.

Among the early files of the Ogden [Utah] City Council are several petitions dealing with the Weber River and its water supply that bear Job Pingree's signature. Job was an English immigrant with a keen interest in water access and flood control. His farmland bordered the river that provided water needed to grow crops.

Job hired himself and his team to reinforce the banks of the Ogden River against unnecessary flooding on several occasions in 1873. He also worked to drain spring run-off from the city's main street. When he was placed in charge of the water works, he became tireless in his efforts to develop a drainage system and a river-reinforced water storage program.

This was the beginning of Job Pingree's political career chronicled in detail in the Ogden City Council records, its minutes, petitions, quarterly and annual reports, and correspondence on file in the Utah State Archives. Selected segments of his public involvement are listed here.

Ogden City Council, February 1877-March 1882
Job was elected city councilman from the Second Ward Feb 1877, Feb 1879, Feb 1881. In 1877 he served with this slate: Mayor: Loren Farr. Aldermen: Walter Thompson, F. A. Brown, John Reeve, Frederick A. Miller. Councilmen: C. W. Penrose, Robert McQuarrie, Joseph Parry, Barnard White. In 1881, he served with this slate: Mayor: Lester J. Herrick. Aldermen: David M. Stuart, C. F. Middleton, Joseph Stanford, William B. Hutchins. Councilmen: N. C. Flygare, Winslow Farr, William C. Burton, S. H. Higginbotham.

Job was chair for the standing committee on licenses with S. H. Higginbotham and William B. Hutchins and the standing committee of public works with C. F. Middleton and S. H. Higginbotham.

Ogden School Board, 6 June 1881
Job was elected to the school board when the first district was consolidated into the Central School District of Ogden City. He served nine

years, part of the time as treasurer responsible "to pay all of the teachers."

On 21 April 1879 Job Pingree was present at a citizen's meeting in the central school (high school). Job was among those speaking in favor of a graded school. Again on 13 May 1879, when the previously appointed ad hoc committee presented its recommendations, Job spoke eloquently in favor of the project and suggested that a special tax be levied to cover the costs. Two years later, Job was elected to the board.

Waterworks Superintendent, October 1884

Early in the spring of 1881, water from the Ogden River was piped to the city reservoir on Tyler Avenue. This line brought water for culinary use and for sprinkling of gardens and yards. A system of fire hydrants, supplemented by hose carts and hooks and ladders, protected against fires. Job had helped to establish the system to begin with and he was now responsible to see that it worked correctly. About this time, the city established sprinkling districts and levied a special tax to pay for the upkeep of the system. Job was among the majority of citizens signing petitions against the districts. This is the only instance where Job opposed a program supporting itself by taxes.

DAVID EVANS, CARPENTER/JOINER

If your ancestor resided in a city or town, seek reference to an occupation as you search the basic sources — census, newspapers, marriage records, local histories, wills, city directories, etc. David Evans was a carpenter/joiner in Philadelphia. He kept an account book that listed commissions and payments, correspondence, and patterns for constructing coffins. Before licensed morticians and registrations of deaths, the carpenter's account book served as the community death register. His account book was discovered in the Pennsylvania Historical Society (1300 Locust St., Philadelphia, PA 19107) and contained some valuable information:

1793

July 12. Estate Joseph Shippen, making a Mahogany Coffin for deceased with Breastplate and Handles, 1793 £8.10.

Aug. 9. Bank of Pennsylvania, 6 Blinds for windows, £25.

Sept. 6. Estate of Dr. James Hutchinson, making a Mahogany Coffin for deceased, £7.10

Sept. 11. Estate of my brother Richard Gardner, a Walnut Coffin, £3. He died of Yellow fever. Was a clerk in the Bank of Pennsylvania and an admirable accountant. Buried in Friends Ground.

Oct. 12. My family, consisting of myself, my wife and five children, Anne, Sally, Rebecca, John, and Eleanor, (my son Evan went there a few weeks before), went to Dr. George DeBenneville's, near the city, where we were kindly received and remained three weeks, while the plague raged in the city.

David Evans also recorded information pertinent to his own family: the coffin he made for his brother Richard (no charge), removing his family (all named) from the city to the home of Dr. George DeBenneville, a possible relation. Note that Evans's business includes as a customer the Bank of Pennsylvania where his brother was employed at the time of his death.

GEORGE CROGHAN, INDIAN TRADER
George Croghan was an Indian trader in colonial Pennsylvania. Records for him include trading post and military fort daybooks, rosters, and post reports, claims against the U.S. Government, as well as account books, correspondence, petitions to colonial assemblies, land grants and sales, and other records.

Research on George Croghan offers a typical example of the importance of business associates which form the circle of contacts for an entrepreneur. Searches to prove his identity show that his circle of contacts covered most of the East: New York, his permanent residence where his will was filed and his estate settled, Pennsylvania, where his outfitting posts were located, Delaware, New Jersey, Ohio, Virginia (including the areas that became Kentucky and West Virginia), and possibly parts of New England.

A closer look at the evidence in George Croghan's records revealed that he was associated in business with several men. These associates all turned out to be close relatives. Besides William Croghan, his nephew, there were Edward Ward, his half-brother, Dr. John Connolly, his nephew, his cousins Thomas Smallmen, William Powell, and Daniel Clark, Lt. Augustine Prevost, Croghan's son-in-law, and William Trent, his brother-in-law. These family relationships yield additional evidence: the married surname of his mother (Ward), of his two sisters (Connolly, Trent), his daughter (Prevost), and three aunts — sisters of his mother and father (Smallmen, Powell, and Clark).

Relatives are frequently found among a person's business associates. Close family ties provide motivation for investment and support of the business effort.

PEARCE NOLAND AND NEEDHAM BURCH LANIER, PLANTATION OWNERS
Southern plantation owners were not only planters, they were highly skilled managers and businessmen who operated enormous quasifeudal estates. They managed field operations, provided food, shelter, and clothing for their families and slaves, negotiated the sale of crops at the highest possible price, and operated plantation support activities, such as blacksmithing, vegetable growing, weaving, and candlemaking. They also served as their own accountants, presided over the people who lived and worked on their plantation, and negotiated the purchase and sale of their slave labor force. The domain over which they ruled consisted of the manor house, fields, slave quarters, work houses, infirmary, produce gardens, barns, orchards, burial grounds, detention house, and a slave population that sometimes numbered in the hundreds.

By virtue of their wealth and social standing, plantation owners are mentioned in historical and biographical works more often than the average farmer in the North. As a result of diverse activities, plantation owners created far more records than their northern counterparts, yeoman farmers. Many helped build the area where they lived, some even holding public office. Such were the cases with a number of Warren County, Mississippi plantation owners, including Pearce Noland and Needham Burch Lanier.

A significant effort has been made in the South to preserve the past. Throughout the southern states one finds historical and genealogical societies, county museums, and an above average number of family historians. This exemplifies a propensity to preserve the past that isn't always found elsewhere.

Documenting the life and activities of a plantation owner is accomplished in much the same way any American research problem is approached. They are found in census, land, estate, church, military, and other often-used genealogical records. They also appear in other less frequently used records, such as plantation diaries and journals, slave bills of sale, slave schedules, and local histories.

Judge Pearce Noland presided over the Warren County Court for a number of years. A biography about his son states that the judge arrived in Mississippi in 1803 when he was thirteen years old. He was a Virginian who followed the path of many of Virginia's native sons and daughters to Mississippi during the early nineteenth century. He married Elizabeth Galtny of Adams County, Mississippi and lived in Jefferson County before relocating to Warren County. He also reportedly decended from a Revolutionary War soldier. When research focused on Judge Noland, he was found residing in Bovina Precinct, Warren County, Mississippi at the time of the 1850 census:

Dwelling Number	Name	Age	Occupation	Birthplace
#1132	Pearce Noland	60	Planter	Virginia
	Elizabeth Noland	52		Mississippi
	Pearce Noland	20	Overseer	Mississippi
	Elizabeth Noland	17		Mississippi
	Thomas V. Noland	14		Mississippi
	Henry Noland	8		Mississippi

His property was valued at $20,000, indicating that he was indeed a wealthy plantation owner.

Pearce Noland did not live to suffer the devastation Warren County experienced during the Civil War. His will, dated 31 January 1857 and proven in court the following year, clearly states that he owned "Sligo" plantation and a number of slaves. A petition was made in court on 28 January 1859 to have his estate divided among his heirs. It states that Mrs. Elizabeth Noland, widow of Pearce Noland, died in March 1858 and that her heirs were her children:

George D. Noland, Ellen D. Batchelor, Joseph Noland, Avery Noland, Pierce [sic] Noland, Elizabeth Norwood, Henry Noland, and T. Vaughan Noland.

Judge Noland's estate was inventoried and appraised on 27 April 1857, the bulk consisting of slaves valued in excess of $98,500. In 1837, his real estate consisted of an entire section of Township 15, Range 5 East. He sold a portion of that property in 1838 and then three more parcels to his son-in-law, Napoleon B. Batchelor, in 1841: 66 acres for $250; 10 acres for $50; and 320 acres for $6,000. Judge Noland's last deed, dated 1841, states that he purchased the land from the State of Mississippi in November 1833. He transferred 320 acres to George D. Noland for $6,000, that section being called "Gumwood" plantation. "Gumwood" was later purchased by Needham Burch Lanier. The remainder of the original section and 202 acres purchased from Michael Shawl in 1843 were divided between Thomas V. Noland and Henry P. Noland in 1862.

Most plantations have more than one burial ground. "Sligo" plantation had several: one for the Noland family, three for slaves, and others for subsequent property owners. Few plantations recovered after the Civil War, and many of the original burial grounds are overgrown by vegetation, a condition that makes finding them a challenge. Locating the Noland family tombstones required a guide who knew the area. Pearce Noland's tombstone consisted of a large slab that covered the top of his above ground crypt. The inscriptions were quite simple:

PEARCE NOLAND	ELIZABETH NOLAND	ELLEN D. BATCHELOR
died Feb. 11, 1857	born Jan. 31, 1801	born Dec. 10, 1826
aged 68 years	died March 13, 1858	died Dec. 16, 1893

As mentioned previously, few areas in this country have a greater devotion to preserving local history than does the South. The Old Museum Court House in Vicksburg, Mississippi is a classic example of this devotion. The museum contains original oil paintings of many plantation owners, including Judge and Elizabeth Noland. Though the mansion house at "Sligo" plantation burned earlier in this century and most of the plantation diaries, journals, and personal papers of Judge Noland were lost, the museum still has some of his letters and three slave bills of sale:

Know all men by these presents that I Willis W. Hundnall for the consideration of four hundred and thirty-five dollars to be paid by Pierce [sic] Noland, which is infull consideration for one Negroe girl Chany and the right and title of the said Negroe I do warrant and defend to the said Noland and his heirs forever free from the claim of all person or persons whatever and sound in body and mind Witness my hand and seal this 29th day of February 1828.

Teste Willis W. Hundnall (seal)

Rec'd of Jacob Lewis Two Thousand and fifty Dollars to me in hand paid the receipt whave of I acknowledge I bargain and sell the following Negroes: Charles, twenty-four years auld and Mariah, twenty-two years of age which Negroes I warrant helthy and sound in boddy and mind. I allso warrant the Rite and Title of said Negros to said Lewis his heirs and assigns forever. I allso warrant them slaves for life. I witness whave of I set my hand this 15th of April 1829.

Teste Pearce Noland

Jas. B. Crowder

Evidence of the valuable information found in the Old Court House Museum is better seen in its collection for the Lanier family. The following was taken from the museum's manuscript and newspaper collection:

Needham Burch Lanier was born in Brunswick County, Virginia on 24 November 1815. He moved west to settle in Warren County, Mississippi about 1830 and lived out his life there. He purchased land to establish two plantations, "Yucatan" and "Pleasant Hill," and became one of the wealthiest men in Mississippi, his homes centers of social activity during the antebellum years.

The Laniers in Mississippi by Mary Lanier Magruder, a manuscript compiled in 1976 after many years of research, states that Needham Burch Lanier married Elizabeth Ann Warnock Jordan on 25 March 1854. Widowed by Levi Jordan, she was the daughter of David Warnock and Catherine Adams of Adams County, Mississippi. Needham was the son of Thomas Lanier and Mary Katherine Peebles.

Needham was a Confederate spy during the Civil War who left his wife well provisioned while he was gone. An article appearing in the *Vicksburg Evening Post* 22 February 1933, contained a description of Elizabeth Warnock Lanier's experience during the siege of Vicksburg in her husband's absence. The words are her own.

My three oldest children remember when the Federals came in here. We all saw them take off with the meat and haul away the corn and fodder. They took my riding and carriage horses and the boy [Negro] too. The whole army camped about a mile and a half from our house. The next morning before breakfast it seemed the whole army was in my yard. They stripped my smoke house and storeroom of all provisions. We had four hogsheads of sugar and five barrels of molasses. They left a little sugar in a barrel. That is all my children had to eat for three days. One of the neighbors baked a pan of cornbread and sent it to us. Some of the soldiers would come every day. In ten days or less, there was not a hoof of anything left. I have an itemized list of what was taken. The account was made out when everything was fresh in our minds. We had a years supply for our family and eighty some-odd slaves. We hadn't bought any corn, bought a little meat sometimes. They destroyed our growing crop of corn. Foraged their horses on it. We paid a hundred dollars per barrel for flour. Paid fourteen dollars a pair for shoes for the colored people. I do not know the size of our cribs, but they were good sized. We had two on this place and two on our place near Big Black. We had a large barn, the loft was filled with fodder and we had some stacked.

The army moved nearer Vicksburg the next day after coming in here. General McClernand had charge of this road and about four and a half miles from us, afterwards General Ord had the place.

Most of the property was mine, inherited from my Father and Grandfather. I never did anything against the Union, would have done for the Federals in distress as well as for the Southern soldiers. I had no one in the army.

The value of the Lanier property stolen or destroyed during the siege of Vicksburg was $30,000, and claims filed after the war were never realized. General Grant signed papers to reimburse her for the carriage and two horses he personally took, but the order was never honored. The claim stated that 9,000 pounds of bacon and ham taken were valued at $900. When this article was written in 1933 those items were valued at $2,250; today, it would be worth well over $16,000.

The *Vicksburg Daily Herald* carried Needham Burch Lanier's obituary in its Tuesday, 6 February 1900 edition:

DEATH OF N.B. LANIER

Mr. N. B. Lanier, the revered and respected head of a well known Warren County family died at his home in the eastern part of the county on Sunday morning, in the eighty-fifth year of his age. Mr. Lanier had been an invalid for some years, and has long been confined to his home. He is survived by his wife and several children, several of the latter being well known in this city. The funeral was held at noon yesterday. Undertaker J.Q. Arnold having been sent for to prepare the remains for burial. The interment was in the family burying grounds at the well known Lanier homestead.

Details of a plantation owner's life and activities are found in greater abundance when visiting the area. Along with distant cousins still living in the area, local historians, libraries, archives, and museums are key information repositories.

CHAPTER 11

Tracing a Lineage Through Burned Records

T he courthouse burned," is one of the most disheartening things a county clerk can tell you. However, this statement is accepted without recognizing it for what it is. It is often an excuse for a clerk's inability to look for or find needed information. At other times, it is the easy way out for inexperienced and lackadaisical professional researchers who are unwilling to determine what records are available and where they are located.

Fires were a fact of life in a society accustomed to candles and inadequate storage areas for paper records. The South had the most fires resulting in significant record loss; however, the North has its share of lost or missing records, such as Hamilton County, Ohio, where records burned in three separate fires, and New York State's archives which burned when its capitol building caught fire in 1911. Sixty-six of the 120 courthouses in Kentucky have suffered floods, fires, and other disasters, mostly in the last century. Yet a county-by-county inventory of the records shows that only one county had lost all of its records. Woodford County lost most of its *original* records in a fire, but not before the Genealogical Library of the LDS Church microfilmed the deeds, wills, tax rolls, and marriage records. In all counties, only specific records were lost over the years, and in most, tax rolls survived intact regardless of other losses.

Union troops hit the South hard during the Civil War, destroying public buildings with resultant losses of records. Interestingly enough, South Carolina suffered greater losses from the advance of Sherman's Army than did Georgia. Sixty-eight Georgia courthouses had fires, some burning as many as four times; yet only *nine* burned during the Civil War despite Sherman's march to the sea.

ALTERNATIVE SOURCES TO BURNED RECORDS

If a county's records have been destroyed, there are a number of search strategies you can use to circumvent those missing records and obtain the information they were expected to supply. Using what records have survived, however, requires familiarity with a wide variety of sources beyond census records, vital records, and church registers. You will need to expand your record knowledge. If a land plat, an estray book, or a full set of tax rolls survived, you can search each for what information it may yield. But this assumes you know what information these records contain.

For missing deeds and mortgages, consult local title abstracting companies. Their fees are higher than genealogists charge, so ask for a cost estimate for supplying abstracts of specific documents. If the county indexes have survived, you can save a great deal of time by searching them first, selecting the land tracts you want documented (including the property description where recorded), and then ordering a search. Names and addresses of abstract companies in your place of research can be obtained from the national directory at any title firm.

For missing court records consult appeals courts where case summaries or complete transcripts are filed for cases on appeal. Completed federal courts case files (1790-1930), may be deposited in the Regional Federal Archives and Records Center. Indexes to these files are usually kept in the local courthouse where the court held jurisdiction. Legal briefs and files of local attorneys are deposited at historical societies or university libraries. The *Decennial Digests* indexing appeals cases in state and federal courts are located in most law libraries.

Surrounding counties, those created from a burned parent county, will have records useful to your research. Land holdings, business dealings, and estate settlements frequently crossed county lines. The parent county's records will sometimes give property descriptions, names of neighbors, relatives, and friends, heirs of estates, and many other useful pieces of information.

When Onondaga County, New York was created from Cayuga County in 1794, deed and mortgage transactions for those land sections which fell in the new county were recopied. This is a reason to check the parent county for land transfers unless you know for certain that an ancestor owned land prior to the county's division and no record appears in the copied volume. If the deed doesn't appear, then check the parent county deeds. The deeds for land which became Onondaga are listed as "Cayuga Filed Deeds and Records, 1794-1809" with a separate index. Instead of consulting all of the deeds for Cayuga, you only have to search those that apply to Onondaga territory prior to the establishment of Onondaga County.

POST-FIRE AND RERECORDED RECORDS

Be sure to check for any post-fire records. Deeds are often recorded many years after the original transaction, so that some recorded as late as the 1920s may describe transactions between people who died even a century earlier. Also watch for rerecorded records, as county business is dependent upon clear property titles. When records burn, the court will often ask residents to bring in their originals for rerecording and give them a time period during which the recording is free. At other times private groups and individuals have rerecorded records. Genealogists, DAR members, and self-appointed community historians have copied records to fill gaps. The DAR has transcribed courthouse documents including wills, tax rolls, deeds, marriages and divorces, land grants, voters' lists, naturalizations, and many other records.

Many DAR records are indexed and can save hundreds of hours of trying to reconstruct families from scattered or burned records. For example, the New York Committee on Records published a *Master Index to the New York State DAR Genealogical Records* in 1972. Copies of this index can be found in research libraries or on microfilm through the Genealogical Library of the LDS Church. A similar treatment for southern states is seen in E. Kay Kirkham's *An Index to Some of the Family Records of the Southern States* (Logan, Utah: Everton Publishers, 1979) which contains 35,000 microfilm references to the National Society of the Daughters of the American Revolution files. *An Index to Some of the Bibles and Family Records of the United States* (Logan, Utah: Everton Publishers, 1984) contains 45,000 useful references. Each volume lists call numbers for microfilm at the Genealogical Library.

Records are being compiled and published by genealogists in many states to fill gaps caused by burned counties. Publishers' catalogs as well as ads and book reviews in genealogical periodicals are places to look for these types of titles. An example is *Some Marriages in the Burned Records Counties of Virginia* (Easly, S.C.: Southern Historical Press, 1972) that rerecords nearly 1,500 marriages for Hanover, Dinwiddie, Charles City, Nansemond, Elizabeth City, Buckingham, Stafford, King and Queen, and Gloucester counties.

THE IMPORTANCE OF JURISDICTIONAL HISTORY

Tracing the jurisdictional history of your county when there is a suspicion of burned records is very important. Learn what counties, towns, states, colonial provinces, and national powers held jurisdiction in that area at what times. For county jurisdictions, check *The Handy Book for Genealogists*, 7th edition (Logan, Utah: Everton Publishers, 1981). Maps illustrating county boundaries during the 1790 to 1920 census years are available from Dollarhide Systems (Box 5282, Bellingham, WA 98227). Town and city jurisdictions can be determined by checking county histories. Clarence S. Peterson's *Bibliography of County Histories of the 3,111 Counties of the Forty-Eight States* (Baltimore: Genealogical Publishing Co., 1961) is the place to start. Watch for P. William Filby's new, annotated edition of Peterson's classic bibliography.

Consult a good history of the state in which your ancestors resided to determine whether the state or federal government kept the records for which you are looking. Public libraries or the history department of the principal state university can recommend titles you can order on interlibrary loan if they are not locally available.

NON-COURTHOUSE RECORDS

Non-courthouse records should be carefully searched. Twelve major genealogical sources deal with non-courthouse records: family and home sources, births, deaths, and cemetery records, census records, church records, military records, business and employment records, city directories, newspapers, finding aids and indexes, and compiled biographies. Some newspapers include court proceedings, such as legal notices of estate settlements, property sold for unpaid taxes or other fees, and lists of criminal convictions, marriages performed, and divorces granted. Specialty publications such as bar association newsletters offer synopses of court cases, decisions, and appeals.

Census records are another valuable non-courthouse tool. By carefully searching several census years, including both federal and state schedules, you can accumulate facts on families migrating in the same direction, families with similar origins, and names that match those you are seeking. You can also sort people into generations, aligning potential cousins, brothers, and sisters, and find evidence of second marriages.

Documents appropriating pensions for military service, granting name changes, and satisfying claims against the government can also supply information in lieu of court records. Most colonies before the American Revolution designated that certain typical county functions be taken care of at the provincial level rather than by county officials, like the collection of local taxes in Maryland before 1777 and probate estate settlements in North Carolina before 1760. The records for these functions have always been held in state archives, not county.

State archives often fall heir to other categories of records either by donation or purchase. Among those are pre-1900 prison records and registers of defunct mortuaries, orphanages, schools, and businesses. Personal papers, plantation diaries, and family portraits are frequently donated as well. Finally, most of the original thirteen states have transferred pre-Civil War records to state archives. Where this has been done and temperature-controlled, fireproof storage exists, the danger of record-destroying fires is past.

CASE STUDY: HARRIET OGDEN FINDS A HUSBAND IN CINCINNATI

According to family tradition, Harriet Ogden, the daughter of David Ogden, married in Cincinnati. While searching to determine who Harriet married and when, six different collections of marriage records for Hamilton County had to be consulted.

The Hamilton County courthouse burned 28-29 March 1884 during a riot when a jury returned a verdict of manslaughter and city residents believed the accused guilty of first-degree murder. By the time the fire was quenched, many records had gone up in flames. The county commission decided to reconstruct marriage records by calling in original documents and copying them at taxpayer expense. In addition to the official reconstruction, independent genealogists prepared their own records. These records are more reliable than the county recording since they include marriages originally documented only in ministers' diaries or justice of the peace dockets – sources not always included in county marriage registers.

The value of these reconstructed marriage records lies not only in the Cincinnati residents who can be documented. The city was a Gretna Green for couples who came from Kentucky, Indiana, and Illinois to be married quickly and without questions.

As research on Harriet Ogden began, a short sketch on the Ogden family was found in the *Dubois and Murphy Family* by A. B. Newkirk. This information was converted to a family group record (Figure 11:1) for analysis and comparison with new information discovered searching Hamilton County records. By searching all six versions of the marriage records, Harriet's marriage to William Saxton Brown on 23 December 1827 in Cincinnati was located. Other Brown and Ogden marriages were also extracted from the sources for later use in putting the whole family together.

Next the surviving records of Cincinnati and Hamilton County Ohio were searched to document David Ogden and his family to prove that the Harriet Ogden who married William Saxton Brown was his daughter.

David Ogden died in 1832 in Hamilton County, and his land holdings were distributed through a series of quitclaim deeds from the heirs in return for a money settlement. Every Ogden entry was copied from the indexes and each deed checked for relevant information. Between 13 November 1832 and 23 September 1834, David Ogden's land was transferred from his heirs to other buyers. The entry we specifically sought, however, was not listed in the index: no Harriet Brown was involved in any Ogden deeds. On a hunch that the index might be faulty, the deeds recorded several pages before and after the other transactions were searched. One record read "William S. Brown and Harriet his wife late Harriet Ogden one of the heirs of David G. Ogden deceased, late of Springfield township in Hamilton County and State of Ohio aforesaid. . . . " This extra bit of searching proved worthwhile.

Research began with a lot of information – the names and birthdates of David Ogden's children and some of their death dates. Despite the fire of 1884, searches in Hamilton County provided additional facts on some of David's children. More importantly, these searches proved that Harriet married William Saxton Brown in Cincinnati and that she was David Ogden's daughter. Bonus data included the fact that Harriet's two brothers, David Jr. and John Gilbert, lived in Butler County, Ohio when their father died and that David's wife, Rachel, married a second time.

The obstacles created by burned or missing records can be discouraging at first. Just keep in mind that alternative sources to the information you need most likely exist elsewhere. It may take a little extra thought and cleverness on your part, and the records you do find may provide only circumstantial clues. Nevertheless, burned or missing records need rarely prove the end of research.

FAMILY GROUP SHEET

HUS. DAVID OGDEN — OCCUPATION(S)

		PLACE
BORN	18 JUL 1775	PLACE
CHR		PLACE
MARR	1799	PLACE
DIED	28 AUG 1832	PLACE
BUR		
FATHER	JONATHAN OGDEN	
MOTHER		OTHER WIVES

WIFE RACHEL MURPHY

BORN	5 OCT 1780	PLACE
CHR		PLACE
DIED	18 SEP 1851	PLACE
BUR		PLACE
FATHER	WILLIAM MURPHY	
MOTHER	PHEBE SHERRY	OTHER HUSBANDS

SEX	CHILDREN	DATE BORN / PLACE BORN	DATE MARRIED / TO	PLACE	DATE DIED / PLACE DIED
1 M	WILLIAM OGDEN	4 FEB 1800			11 APR 1802
2 M	JOHN G. OGDEN	4 OCT 1801 / CUMBERLAND COUNTY NJ			
3 M	JAMES S. OGDEN	10 APR 1803			29 JUN 1811
4 M	DAVID OGDEN	4 MAY 1805 / CUMBERLAND COUNTY NJ			
5 F	SARAH OGDEN	11 MAY 1807			5 AUG 1809
6 F	NAOMI OGDEN	23 JAN 1810			25 JUL 1811
7 F	HARRIET OGDEN	4 APR 1812			
8 F	MARTHA OGDEN	23 JUL 1815	UNMARRIED		12 JUL 1881
9					

OTHER MARRIAGES

SOURCES OF INFORMATION

DUBOIS AND MURPHY FAMILIES by A.B. NEWKIRK

RESEARCH NOTES

Figure 11:1. Family Group Work Record, David Ogden.

FAMILY GROUP SHEET

OCCUPATION(S)

HUS. 1) DAVID OGDEN, SR.

		PLACE
BORN	18 JUL 1775	
CHR		
MARR	11 APR 1799	CUMBERLAND COUNTY, NJ
DIED	28 AUG 1832	SPRINGFIELD, HAMILTON, OH
BUR		
FATHER	JONATHAN OGDEN	
MOTHER		

OTHER WIVES

WIFE RACHEL MURPHY

		PLACE
BORN	5 OCT 1780	CUMBERLAND COUNTY, NJ
CHR		
DIED	18 SEP 1851	HAMILTON COUNTY, OH
BUR		
FATHER	WILLIAM MURPHY	
MOTHER	PHEBE SHERREY	

OTHER HUSBANDS

SEX	CHILDREN	DATE BORN / PLACE BORN	DATE MARRIED / TO	PLACE	DATE DIED / PLACE DIED
1 M	WILLIAM OGDEN	4 FEB 1800			11 APR 1802
2 M	JOHN GILBERT OGDEN	4 OCT 1801 CUMBERLAND COUNTY, NJ	3 JUN 1834 MARY TRENCHARD LOW	BUTLER COUNTY, OH	
3 M	JAMES S. OGDEN	10 APR 1803			24 JUN 1811
4 M	DAVID OGDEN	4 MAY 1805 CUMBERLAND COUNTY, NJ	4 JUL 1932 THEODOCIA LOWE	BUTLER COUNTY, OH	4 SEP 1836 will prob. HAMILTON COUNTY, OH
5 F	SARAH OGDEN	11 MAY 1807			5 AUG 1809
6 F	NAOMI OGDEN	23 JAN 1810			25 JUL 1811
7 F	HARRIET OGDEN	4 APR or 9 MAY 1812 CUMBERLAND COUNTY, NJ	23 DEC 1827 WILLIAM SAXTON BROWN	CINCINNATI, OH	10 AUG 1851 WAYNE COUNTY, IN
8 F	MARTHA OGDEN	23 JUL 1815 NJ	UNMARRIED		12 JUL 1881 WAYNE COUNTY, IN
9					

OTHER MARRIAGES

SOURCES OF INFORMATION
SUMMARY SHEET - 19 JAN 1983

RESEARCH NOTES
DAVID OGDEN, SR. BOUGHT LAND IN CINCINNATI IN 1825.

Figure 11:2. Family Group Record, David Ogden.

SUGGESTED READING

Mills, Elizabeth Shown. "Anderson of Buckingham: A Case Study in Family Reconstruction within a 'Burned County.' " *The Virginia Genealogist* 27 (1983):3-19.

_____."The Battle of the Burned Courthouse: Alternate Approaches to the South's Classic Genealogical Problem." *APG Newsletter* 4(December 1982):1-4.

CHAPTER 12

Tracing the Women in Your Family

S imply stated, identifying female ancestors is one of the greatest challenges a researcher faces. Until the twentieth century, women in the United States conducted few legal or business transactions on their own even though they, unlike blacks, were eligible to exercise such legal rights. Custom dictated that fathers and husbands act in behalf of their daughters and wives in legal and business matters. Therefore, women are only occasionally found in public records other than marriage records. Women do appear in estate, land, and tax records, but only after the death of the husband or father.

Early public records were not designed with the foresight employed in formatting records today. No one imagined that the role and position of women in society would change or that future generations would want to identify the females who were a part of their society. Tracing female ancestors in records of limited scope requires a thorough knowledge of sources most likely to document their existence and how to locate those records.

Female ancestors are recorded in some standard records, such as census, marriage, school, and birth and death records. The 1900 census is especially helpful in stating the number of children a woman had given birth to and the number still living when the census was taken. School census records list girls and sometimes their parents. Females appear in court, land, and probate records as wives and daughters. There are instances where a widow left a will further bequeathing the property left by her deceased husband. Minor female children appear in guardianship records when the court appointed a guardian to oversee their portion of their fathers' estates or when both parents were deceased. Courts in some areas appointed male guardians, even though the child's mother was still living, on the premise that women were unable to attend to matters themselves.

WOMEN IN THE WORK FORCE

Women who immigrated to the United States during the colonial period often became indentured servants or served apprenticeships, and those arrangements were frequently entered in county court records. Widowed and single women sometimes had to support themselves as teachers, milliners, dressmakers, and proprietors. They can be found advertising their products or services in local newspapers. Women who lived in industrial towns are found in factory employment records. In 1830, they comprised seventy percent of the work force between the ages of fifteen and twenty-nine years of age in Lowell, Massachusetts. Employment, personnel, and wage records for Lowell are located in the Baker Library of the Harvard Business School in Cambridge, Massachusetts and must be searched in person or by an agent.

Black females living in Illinois or Indiana at the turn of the century were employed in large numbers by the Pullman Company. They are listed in the nearly one million records of the Pullman Company located at the South Suburban Genealogical Society (161st and Louis Avenue, South Holland, IL 60473). Documents included in the files are birth certificates, photographs, addresses, and names of other family members employed by Pullman.

There were three to five midwives in the average nineteenth-century American community, with larger numbers present in metropolitan areas. While midwifery was an occupation, it is rarely found entered as such on census schedules because it was not formally recognized. Midwives were, however, licensed in some cities for tax purposes. Their names are recorded in special midwife ledgers and their journals list births they attended. Midwife journals are in great demand by medical schools, historical societies, and other repositories. The collection of midwife records at Northwestern University Hospital in Evanston, Illinois was microfilmed by the Genealogical Library of the LDS Church and is available through its branch libraries.

SPECIAL SOURCES
FOR TRACING WOMEN

TAX RECORDS

Women appear in tax rolls as widows and heirs. The Albemarle County, Virginia tax roll shown in Figure 12:1 contains entries noting the taxes paid on acreage owned by female heirs. While there is little direct genealogical information in these rolls, they are helpful when used in conjunction with other records. If marriage bonds fail to produce information about each daughter's marriage, the tax rolls can be searched forward to the year each daughter is no longer listed. A second search of the rolls is then made to see if a male owns property of the same description in that district.

CONGRESSIONAL RECORDS

The United States government sponsored a pilgrimage to the European gravesites of servicemen killed during World War I. Mothers and widows of those servicemen were eligible to participate in the pilgrimage and their names are listed in House Document No. 140, 71st Congress, 2nd Session (1930).

Albemarle Co., Virginia

Year	Name	Poll Tax		Property Tax										Servants	Negroes	Remarks
		Value	Assessment	Land (Acres)				Animals								
				Cleared	Uncleared	Sown-Grain	Acres-Value	Horses	Mares	Cattle	Sheep	Value				
1794–1807	Jean Hall Sally Hall Frankey Hall Nancy Hall						25 25 25 25									Part of a 100-Acre tract originally taxed to William Hall, dec'd
1808–1809	Sally Hall Frankey Hall Nancy Hall						25 25 25									Part of a 100-Acre tract on 3-Chopped Road
1810–1813	Sally Hall Nancy Hall						25 25									Part of a 100-Acre Tract from William Hall, dec'd
1814–1830	Sally Hall						25									On 3-notched Road to Charlottesville

Figure 12:1. Tax roll, Albemarle County, Virginia.

These records are available in public and university libraries with a U.S. Government Documents section or through the Library of Congress on interlibrary loan.

Women who contributed to or participated in a war effort petitioned Congress for pensions. Susanna D. Clark's petition is shown in Figure 12:2. Women's pension files are not found in Veteran's Administration records as are the files of their male counterparts. However, a library's government documents section will have a consolidated index to congressional records, and the contents of a file can be ordered from the National Archives once the reference number is known.

CEMETERIES

Cemeteries often hold the only tangible record of a woman outside of family sources. Tombstone inscriptions have been widely published and are valuable sources of birth and death information. Other evidence in a cemetery, such as a grave's location, can provide clues to follow. Since information of this type is rarely included in these alphabetically arranged volumes, it is worthwhile to search a cemetery. For example, Rachel Berry's grave is located on a slight hill at the north edge of the Old Augusta Stone Cemetery in Fort Defiance, Virginia. Her stone stands alone, although the cemetery is full. Some 100 feet to the south is the grave of her son, James S. W. Berry, who died when he was ten years old. Down the road about 200 feet and across a railroad track and state highway her husband, Thorton Berry, is buried with his second wife Nancy and daughter Mary. The alphabetized record for this cemetery does not reveal that James S. W. Berry's grave is surrounded by the graves of the Crawford family, suggesting that his mother may have been a Crawford. Research eventually proved that premise to be true.

WOMEN'S HISTORY ARCHIVES AND SPECIAL PROJECTS

The women's history movement on college campuses across the country has spurred the collection of sources dealing with women. A series of volumes about women includes biographies, letters, diaries, papers, petitions, etc. Specific collections are identified in Andrea Hinding's *Women's History Sources: A Guide to Archives and Manuscript Collections in the U.S.* (New York: R. R. Bowker, 1979).

Local and state projects to identify and chronicle women's contributions exist in many states. An example is "Women Who Were Born or Came to Ashtabula County, Ohio Before 1850." Thousands passed through Ashtabula County en route to another location and some remained there for as long as five years. The list cited above was compiled from a wide variety of sources and is helpful in determining whether a female ancestor left evidence of her life while in Ashtabula County. This interesting compilation is available on microfilm at the Genealogical Library of the LDS Church and its branches throughout the country. Similar records may exist in other locations.

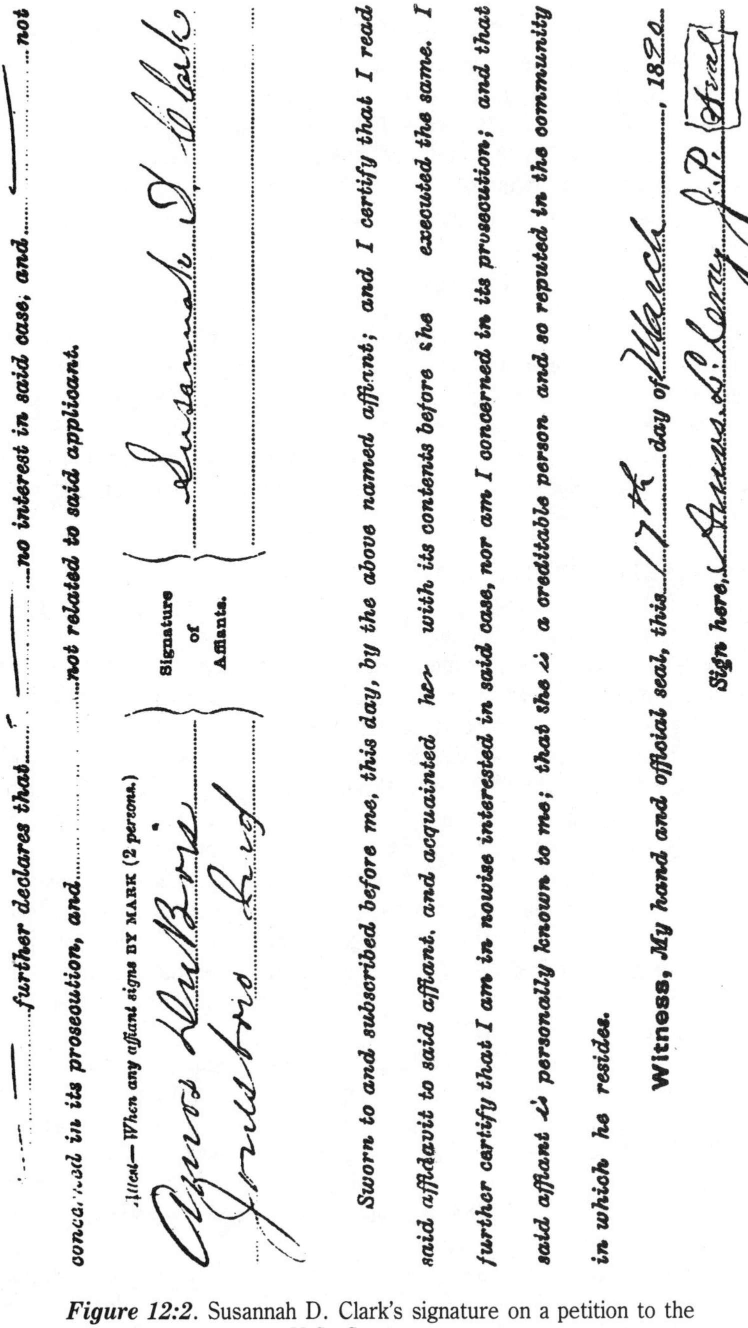

... ...further declares that...... ` ....no interest in said case; and...... ....not

concealed in its prosecution, and...... ....not related to said applicant.

Attest—When any affiant signs BY MARK (2 persons.)

Signature of Affiants.

Sworn to and subscribed before me, this day, by the above named affiant; and I certify that I read said affidavit to said affiant, and acquainted her with its contents before she executed the same. I further certify that I am in nowise interested in said case, nor am I concerned in its prosecution; and that said affiant is personally known to me; that she is a creditable person and so reputed in the community in which he resides.

Witness, *My hand and official seal, this* 17th *day of* March, 1820.

Sign here,

Figure 12:2. Susannah D. Clark's signature on a petition to the
U.S. Government.

Women can also be traced through lineage society records, such as those of the Daughters of the American Revolution, Colonial Dames of America, and many others. The DAR's "Index of Females Married to Revolutionary Patriots" found in the *DAR Patriot Index* is arranged alphabetically in four volumes. It is available at some local libraries, the National Society of the Daughters of the American Revolution Library in Washington, D.C., or on microfilm through the Genealogical Library of the LDS Church.

RESEARCH CAMEOS

Identifying maiden surnames and proving the parentage of female ancestors is a challenging genealogical problem. The following research cameos have been drawn from actual research cases. When each study began, the identity of a female ancestor was unknown. The identity of American women has always been closely tied to their fathers and husbands. Since few early records were produced exclusively by women, they are traced through the men with whom they were associated.

NANCY SHELTON ETHINGTON

The following information about Nancy Shelton Ethington surfaced while attempting to document Fielding Ethington's life. Research not only proved family tradition about his wife incorrect, it extended her ancestry two generations and moved her family from Kentucky to an exact county in Virginia, a difficult research task for that time period.

The identification of his wife's ancestry was an added benefit. Family members believed that Fielding's wife was Henrietta Shelton, but research definitely proved that her name was Nancy Shelton. Nancy was originally entered in family records as Fielding's third wife with whom he had no children. It was unusual to note that George W. Ethington, one of Fielding's sons, consented to payment of a bill when Nancy's estate was administered in court. Under normal circumstances, his consent would imply that he was Nancy's son. Moreover, James Ethington, a son of William Ethington, was the administrator of her estate, so there was no legal reason, beyond being an heir-at-law, for George to give his consent.

A printed volume of Owen County, Kentucky deeds produced evidence linking Fielding Ethington to the Sheltons. An 1824 marriage bond showed that Lewis Ethington (Fielding's nephew) married Sandereller Shelton, daughter of David Shelton, with Fielding Ethington as witness to the bond. A reference to a deed naming David Shelton and his wife, Henrietta, as grantors was entered immediately above the marriage bond. This suggests that Henrietta Shelton was Fielding's mother-in-law, not his wife.

David Shelton's will was proven in Owen County, Kentucky in 1839 and it mentions thirteen children, specifically: Austin, Nathaniel, Cinderella Ethington, and Nancy Ethington. He did not have a daughter named Henrietta Ethington, proving that Fielding was not married to a daughter of that name. Fielding was mentioned in a Shelton genealogy as the son of Peter Shelton and Frances Nichols of Louisa County, Virginia. David married Henrietta Thomason, daughter of Samuel Thomason in Louisa County in 1786. Peter Shelton married Frances Nichols in Louisa County in 1763 and served as a second lieutenant in the American Revolution.

MARY SLONE MADDEN

Making the best use of family sources is important in tracing female ancestors. That means getting in touch with as many descendants of an ancestor as possible. Visiting the places an ancestor lived is an excellent way to locate living descendants who are likely to have family records in their possession. Such was the case with the Arch D. Madden family.

Exhaustive research into census, land, probate, and tax records of several counties in Kentucky failed to produce the maiden name of Arch's wife Mary. A number of his grandchildren, all of whom were over eighty, were still living in Knott County, Kentucky when a professional genealogist went there in search of more information. One grandson owned a large photograph of Arch Madden and directed the researcher to other family members and local cemeteries where generations of the Madden family were buried.

After talking to several of Arch's descendants, one granddaughter recalled that Arch was married to Mary Slone. Early marriage records were destroyed and without a maiden name to pursue, it was doubtful that Arch's wife would have been found in existing records.

There were three Slone families living in Floyd County, Kentucky in 1850 and each had a daughter named Mary who was between nine and thirteen years old. Later census records permitted the calculation of Mary's birthdate as between 1836 and 1841. Thus, she could have been the daughter of any one of the three couples listed in the census. Reuben and Sarah Slone appeared the most likely candidates as Mary's parents because of naming patterns observed in Mary's children and grandchildren. The link to Reuben and Sarah was purely circumstantial, and further proof was needed to support their relationship to Mary Slone.

Reuben Slone left no will and there were no land records linking Mary to him. Other family members were contacted, one of whom had conducted excellent research into the Madden family. He stated that Mary Slone definitely had a brother named David who had worked for his family. He also said that Reuben and Sarah Slone were Mary's parents and that Sarah was the daughter of John W. Pigman. David Slone was born after births were registered in Floyd County and his birth record clearly stated that he was the son of Reuben Slone and Sarah Pigman. Reuben's death record disclosed that he was the son of Isham and Mary Slone. His father was born in Floyd County, Kentucky and his mother in Letcher County, Kentucky.

While much of the information was circumstantial and required further proof, Mary Slone Madden's maiden name would not have surfaced without the careful use of family and home sources. Her ancestry might have remained an unsolvable mystery.

SUSANNAH WRIGHT VINCENT

Not all research problems involving unknown female ancestors are as easy to solve as the preceding one. Some problems require exhaustive research in dozens of record sources. When massive amounts of information are gathered, each piece of evidence must be carefully evaluated to determine what applies to the missing woman.

The 1790 and 1800 Virginia census enumerations were destroyed and tax lists compiled between 1782 and 1787 have been published as substitutes. Those tax lists show a Charles Vincent living in Bedford County, and a William Vincent and Henry Vinson living in Henry County. Both Bedford and Henry counties adjoin Franklin County where Charles Vincent, the ancestor of interest, was living when he died. Charles left a wife named Susannah whose maiden name was unknown. There were also a Moses Vincent and two William Vincents living in nearby Pittsylvania County in 1785.

Pittsylvania, Henry, Franklin, and Bedford counties are closely related. Franklin was created in 1785 from Bedford and Henry counties, and Henry County was created in 1776 from Pittsylvania. Charles Vincent was living in Bedford County in 1782 and died in Franklin County in 1802. He probably never moved, but his county residence changed with the creation of new counties. Clusters of Vincent families lived in all four of these counties. They were also early residents of St. Paul's Parish in Hanover and Stafford counties, the area from which Bedford County was created. Other clusters of people of that surname lived in Halifax and Greenville counties, the area from which Pittsylvania was created. The records of each of these counties had to be considered in the research design to determine Susannah Vincent's maiden surname.

Initially, the best approach was to search the cluster of counties as a unit. Indexes and printed versions of basic sources such as marriage bonds, abstracts of wills and land records, and other major record sources were searched to determine if the Vincent surname appeared in the sources. Everyname indexes disclosed the names of others directly connected to the Vincent family, thus avoiding page-by-page searches. Using printed sources as a guide, specific originals were identified for further searching. The data found in original manuscript sources such as marriage bonds, wills, deeds, and court minutes is summarized on the following chronology chart. It is a useful device when analyzing large amounts of information. Facts pertaining to more than one person of the same name are quickly spotted.

CHARLES VINCENT/VINSON

Date	Event	Place	Comments
26 Oct 1776	Buys 50 acres on both sides of Maggotie Creek from Patrick Johnson for £20.	Bedford County	No witnesses. Johnson signs his mark.
Feb 1782	Buys 200 acres on a branch of Maggoty Creek from William Wright and Mary, his wife, adjoining William Wright, Abraham Abshire, and Richard Brown for £30.	Bedford County	Both Wright and wife Mary sign. Witnesses: Thos Arthur, Isaac Rentfro, Laughlin (x) O'Grady, Daniel French, John Talbot. Land later sold by Thomas and Charles Vinson to John Wilson, 3 Sep 1809. Witnesses include Abshire Sr. and Jr., John and George Wright, Thomas Macclewaine, and others.
1782	Tax list	Bedford County	No poll indicated.
28 Apr 1783	Sells 200 acres on Maggoty Creek to John Langdon for £110. Land adjoins William Wright Sr., tract purchased by John Langdon from William Wright Jr.	Bedford County	No witnesses. Vincent signs.
1786	Tax lists (personal property and real estate).	Franklin County	William Vincent also listed.
Nov 1786 May 1787 May 1788	John Hook vs. Charles Vincent and James Wright—land dispute listed as Doe vs. Roe in the court record.	Franklin County	

Date	Event	Place	Comments
6 Oct 1794	Buys 50 acres from William Wright adjoining Charles Vinson's, Samuel Houston's, John Kershaw's line, for £5.	Franklin County	£5 is less than usually paid for this much land.
7 Nov 1798	Son Thomas Francis marries Mary New.	Franklin County	Surety: John Vinson, brother.
2 Feb 1799	Son John marries Nancy McKlewain (daughter of John and Franky Kelly).	Franklin County	Surety: Wm. Kelly. Record is unclear —if Franky Kelly is the mother; the father's surname is not given again.
22 Apr 1799	Son Charles marries Sally McElwane (daughter of Nancy).	Franklin County	Surety: Wm. Kelly.
12 Oct 1799	Daughter Ruth marries Thos. McIlwain/ McLewain.	Franklin County	Surety: Charles Vinson.
14 Jan 1801	Daughter Susannah marries Abraham Abshire.	Franklin County	Surety: William Brown.
4 Oct 1802	Will: son Charles Vinson—land on south side of branch where he now lives.	Franklin County	Witnesses: Thomas Denniss, Samuel Houston, Thomas Houston.
	Son Thomas Vinson— land on north side of same branch . . . where I now live.		Executrix: Susannah Vinson; Bondsmen: Samuel Houston, James Wright, Charles Vinson.
	Son John Vinson—land below Spring Branch after mother's death.		

Date	Event	Place	Comments
	Daughter Martha Vinson −1 cow. Daughter Susannah Vinson −1 cow. Daughter Sarah Vinson −1 cow. Daughter Ruth Vinson −1 cow.		Inventory of estate includes only 2 cows, 7 Feb 1803. Appraised by John Wright, James Wray, Thomas Huston, William Brown Charles Vinson signs with mark.
2 Jan 1807	Daughter Martha marries Wm Lindsey.	Franklin County	Surety: Charles Vinson.

WILLIAM VINCENT

Date	Event	Place	Comments
1782	Tax list.	Pittsylvania County	4 white polls
1782	Tax list.	Henry County	1 poll
17 Jul 1779	Buys land on Snow Creek from Robert Boulton.	Henry County	
24 Feb 1779	Survey of Bucks Branch of Snow Creek.	Henry County	
22 Mar 1880	Sells land on Snow Creek to Philip Blassingame.	Henry County	William's wife is Mary.
24 Mar 1784	Buys land from Amos Richardson on south side of Snow Creek.	Henry County	
Apr 1786	William Vincent of Pittsylvania County sells to Anna Priddy of Franklin County.	Franklin County	Court orders*

*Copied deeds from deed books also. The property is on Snow Creek. William Vincent moved from Pittsylvania County to Franklin County where he already had land holdings. (It was Henry County from 1776 until Franklin was formed in 1785).

Date	Event	Place	Comments
Dec 1786	William Vincent deed to George Robertson.	Franklin County	Court orders*
Apr 1788	William Vinson deed to Harmon Cook.	Franklin County	Court orders*
1786	Tax lists (Personal property, Real estate).	Franklin County	

After evaluating the data, the following conclusions were drawn:

1. William Wright is a good candidate for Susannah's father, (her given name is from family sources). The Wright family lived next door; they served as witnesses on deeds and wills and as bondsmen, putting up their own resources to back the Vincent family. Susannah was the executrix for Charles's will and James Wright was one of her bondsmen—an indication of relationship.

2. William Wright Sr. sold 50 acres of land to Charles for £5—less than the going rate for land in the area and time. Such a favorable rate is evidence supporting the conclusion that William Wright is related to Charles Vincent.

3. There is no direct connection between William Vincent and Charles Vincent, but they live in the same county, and they represent two of only three families of Vincents in that general area. The most likely conclusion is that they, too, are related.

None of the above conclusions can stand alone without additional research to determine their correctness. The point of this cameo is to show the scope of research necessary to obtain sufficient evidence just to draw speculative conclusions that may prove accurate. This approach is particularly helpful in tracing colonial ancestry during a period when census and marriage records are not as extensive as in later periods.

SUGGESTED READING

Dublin, Thomas. "Women, Work, and the Family: Female Operations in the Lowell Mills, 1830-1860." *Feminist Studies* 3(1976):30-39.

Eakle, Arlene H. *Tax Records: A Common Source with an Uncommon Value.* Salt Lake City: Family History World, 1979.

CHAPTER 13

Military Ancestors

T here are few American families who are not interested in knowing if one of their ancestors served in the Revolutionary War. Professional genealogists will attest that finding a Revolutionary War ancestor ranks second only behind identifying an immigrant ancestor in the list of client priorities. There are hundreds of printed sources dealing with the Revolutionary War and some offer more genealogical information than others. Pension application files, however, usually contain the most valuable information and must be examined.

TRACING REVOLUTIONARY WAR ANCESTORS

A biographical sketch of one of Philip Thurman's descendants in the *History of Walker County, Georgia* states that Philip served in the Revolution. There are two quick sources to check to see if Philip's service has already been documented. The first is the *DAR Patriot Index*, compiled by the National Society of the Daughters of the American Revolution (Washington, D.C., 1966). The index lists the names of those patriots from whom members of the DAR descend. There are only five entries for the Thurman surname, including: Thurman, Philip b. 11-15-1757 d. 9-2-1840 m. Kesiah—Pvt SC. The second source to check is the *Index of Revolutionary War Pension Applications in the National Archives* (Washington, D.C.: National Genealogical Society, 1976). The index revealed that Philip Thurman, who served from South Carolina, received pension number R10584.

Revolutionary War pension application files have been microfilmed and are available at Regional Federal Archives and Records Centers and the Genealogical Library of the LDS Church. They are arranged in alphabetical order and can be easily photocopied.

Philip Thurman applied for his pension in Bledsoe County, Tennessee on 14 August 1832 at age seventy-four. He appeared in court to provide a statement concerning his service from which the following information was gathered:

Philip Thurman was living about twenty-five miles from Cheraw Hill in the Cheraw District of South Carolina when he enlisted to serve as private in the South Carolina Militia. He served in Captain Daniel Lundy's company in Colonel George Hick's regiment for three months and then he served one month in Captain Thomas Williamson's company in Colonel Stewart's regiment. Then in 1778, he served three months in Captain Benjamin Hendrick's company in Colonel Abel Culp's regiment. Late in 1779 he served three months in the same company and regiment. In 1780, Philip moved from Cheraw District to the Edisto River in South Carolina, and in 1781, he served about six weeks in Captain Benjamin Odom's company and was in the siege of Augusta. In the fall of 1781, he moved back to his old residence in Cheraw District, and from late in 1781 until 15 November 1782, he served a total of nine months at various times under captains Thomas Ellerbee, Maurice Murphy, and William Hendrick.

Philip was born 15 November 1757 in Anson County, North Carolina near the "Big Pee Dee." About nineteen years after the Revolution, he moved to Smith County, Tennessee and two or three years later to Anderson County, Tennessee. Two or three years following that move, he relocated to Bledsoe County. He married his wife, Kesiah, (maiden name not stated) on 10 July 1783. Though they lived in South Carolina, they were married in Anson County, North Carolina.

Pages from their son Eli's family Bible, published in 1817, were included in the file. The following genealogical information about Philip's children was listed exactly as follows:

> Eli Thurman was born the 22 April 1784
> Eli Thurman died the tenth day of March
> Eli Thurman 1842
> died March 10 1842
> Ephraim Thurman was born the 16 day of January
> 1797 and was married the 29 May 1817
> Lucinda Thurman was born 27 day June 1818.

Another document in Philip's file states that Ephraim Thurman, a resident of Marion County, Tennessee, appeared in court at Bledsoe County on 19 March 1852, stating that he was the seventh son of the late Philip Thurman and his wife Kesiah. His mother, prior to her death in May or June 1845 in Bledsoe County, applied for a widow's pension based on her husband's war service. At the time of her death she left the following children: Sarah Rogers, Elijah Thurman, Susan Bradfield, John Thurman, and Ephraim Thurman who was born in 1799. Ephraim applied to receive the pension funds due his mother at the time of her death.

Digging further into the pension file, Kesiah Thurman's application is found. She appeared in court on 6 November 1843 in Bledsoe County, stating that her husband died in that county on 2 September 1840. Other affidavits made in her behalf indicate that her son Eli's wife was named Sarah (maiden name not stated) and that they had at least one child, Elizabeth.

Philip Thurman's pension file, like those of many other veterans, is filled with valuable genealogical information that may not be found in any other records. Since Philip lived in South Carolina at the time he married, it is unlikely that Anson County, North Carolina records could be successfully searched for record of his marriage. South Carolina did not keep marriage records until late in the nineteenth century, and his wife's maiden name might only be found after considerable research in estate or land records produced by her father after her marriage. Anson County marriage bonds are available and should be searched. His pension file did not name his parents, but it did state that he lived in the Cheraw District of South Carolina. The search for his parents should begin there.

If you are faced with a difficult post-Revolution research problem involving someone whose father or uncles would have been between fifteen and forty years old when the war took place, always check the *DAR Patriot List* and the *Index of Revolutionary War Pension Applications in the National Archives*, looking for soldiers who served from the state or states where you believe your ancestor lived during or after the war. Then check the pension files for each person listed from those states for clues to earlier residences and relationships. Many difficult research problems have been solved using this approach.

There are many Revolutionary War soldiers who fought with considerable valor but did not live to apply for a pension. Evidence of their service can be found among the *Papers of the Continental Congress, 1774-1789*, available in two sections: (1) 9 rolls which include the printed journals of the Congress and (2) 204 rolls which are the original manuscripts arranged chronologically in groups according to the public official or military officer who sent the field reports or dispatches to Congress.

This collection is valuable not only because it has an everyname index published by the National Archives, but because it has so many references to men who fought in the Revolution and did not survive. Petitions from American POWs are found in this collection. There are lists of the wagoners who transported supplies and equipment for Washington's armies, including their complete birthdate and place and their physical description. War claims for officers and enlisted men who did not receive the wages or supplies promised them are also included in the collection, as well as casualty lists.

Copies of the indexes and microfilms are available in each Regional Federal Archives and Records Center and in many libraries. The Genealogical Library of the LDS Church has only the everyname index mentioned above.

If congressional records do not document Revolutionary War service for your ancestor, try state records. A valuable group of documents often overlooked are called indents. Indents, mostly small bits of paper, some being preprinted forms, were used by the soldiers as claims for payment. South Carolina lacked funds to pay for military services and provisions supplied to its troops and militia units, so its men were instructed to record all transactions, to have officers certify the time served and pay owed, to get receipts from commissary officers for all provisions supplied, and to record losses of equipment. All of these were indents used as claims against the government once the war was won. They now are a unique genealogical source.

Many of these indents have been abstracted and printed in a multivolume set available in research libraries. Note that the printed documents are selected and do not include all documents in a single file, since they represent ledger copies, not abstracts of the originals. Ledger volumes and individual case files, arranged alphabetically for each name, are located in the South Carolina Department of Archives and History.

These records are invaluable for identifying men who served, especially those of the same name. To make the identity, however, you must use copies of all the documents in the file and fit them together. The evidence in each varies enough to make the task an interesting challenge. The recording officer often made attempts to identify each person to whom he issued certification. Such details as "John Thompson, of Capt. Thompson," or "Mr. John Thompson," or "Capt. John Thompson" are listed. Many of the documents are signed and a comparison of the signatures distinguishes between the men. Obviously, the man who writes his own name is usually a different person from the man who makes his mark. Though many of the documents are undated, other items will provide the evidence needed to calculate dates: commanding officers, witnesses, proxies, and assignees whose names also appear on the documents can help distinguish between the men involved. Battle designations, regiments, and specific assignments are also identifiers.

What follows is a summary of the indents in the John Thompson file obtained from the South Carolina Department of Archives and History. The page numbers to the documents were arbitrarily assigned by clerks and do not run consecutively or chronologically. Selected from some eighty-six different items are those which distinguish between the John Thompsons in the file.

JOHN THOMPSON IN THE INDENTS OF SOUTH CAROLINA

1. *Capt. John Thompson.*

    p. 9, No. 2429 Book K (or H), 15 Apr 1786 John Thompson for 430 days duty as Captain of Horse from 10 Aug 1780 to the 27 Oct 1782 in Col Brandon's Regt, £215 sterling.

    p. 19, 29 June 85, John Thompson's pay bill in Col Brandon's Regt from 24 Nov 1779 to ye 8th Feb . . . pay for himself, Thomas Cook, Francis Satinwood (?), Joshua Sanders, £35.15.0.

    p. 27, 1642 K. John Thompson for 7 bushels corn for continental use, £1 Sterling (no date).

    p. 35, Recd 25 Apr 1786 full satisfaction for within indent No. 2429, K. John Henderson, "vide 1642 K".

    p. 83 Receipt signed by John Henderson.

2. *John Thompson, dec'd.*

    p. 4, (numbers in pencil in right corner of document) To John Thompson decd for militia duty in Brandon's Regt before the fall of Charleston.

Andersons Return . . . £54 . . . (no date).

p. 37, 26 June 86 John Thompson dec'd for militia duty in Brandon's Regt before the fall of Charleston. Anderson Return. £7.14.3 Sterling.

3. *John Thompson, Georgetown Dist. (Signature).*
   p. 51, 8 Apr 1785 warrant for £10.8.6.
   p. 52, reverse of p. 51 with receipt 26 June 1788 signed by John Thomson 417 N.
   p. 54, Summary of service of John Thompson 1780, 1781, 1782 under Capt Marian in Capt McCottrys, Capt Thornleys, Capt Greens companies, £265.0.0, Personally appeared John Thomson 6 Apr 1784 with signature.
   p. 58, 976 Y No 98, 26 Jan 86 John Thomson for 3 barrels of flour, £5.12.3 3/4.
   p. 59, 1779 to John Thomson 28 Feby to 3 barrels flour received by Col Elij. Kershaw for the use of the militia under his command. Certified by John Chesnutt 20th Sept 1785 Personally appeared before me John Thomson . . . never received any satisfaction for the same . . . signature of John Thomson.
   p. 60, reverse. acknowledge of receipt by John Thomson with signature.
   p. 61, Warrant for £5.12.3 26 Jan 1786.
   p. 62, Receipt of interest on money owed to John Thomson, 26 June 1788, 976 Y. (Also a receipt for payment of a piece of land Recd 10 Oct 88 one pound 4/10 by div on the within being ballance on 500 acres of land to Enos Tart . . . Jno Sanders. And "please discount this indent . . . 12 Feb 1789 Jno Sanders." Indent probably sold to Jno Sanders by Thomson).
   p. 63, Feby 1782 to John Thomson, To 10 bushels corn delivered to publick service in Washaw, Personally appeared before me John Thomson . . . 20th Sep 1785. Signature of John Thomson. (This is the same signature as p. 58-60 above).
   p. 78, Signature John Thomson (I believe the same as p. 58-60) receipt for one 3 year old steer (see p. 22).
   p. 226, also received 17 Sep 1781 of Mr. John Thomson a three year old steer for the use of my regiment. Peter Horry, 244-1.

4. *John Thomson, Davidson's Horse & Foot.*
   p. 53, 266 days duty as Davidsons Horse & Foot in the militia, 1780, 1781, 1782. £21.7.1 ½, N. 13.

5. *John Thompson, 5th Regt.*
   p. 24, John Thompson, for 16 months service as a soldier in the 5th Regt. £24.17.9.
   p. 25, To John Thompson to 16 months service as a soldier in the 5th Regt. £24.17.9 ½.
   p. 26, John Thompson being duly sworn made oath . . . 27 Sep 1785 Certified by Isaac Huger, 20 YY.

6. *Mr. Jno Thompson (signature).*

p. 10, No. 70 Book K 13 Sep 1784 warrant on SC Treasury for £41.15.8, 1 YY.

p. 11, Reverse of 10 Received 14 Sep 1784 £2.18.5 Signature of Jno Thompson.

7. *John A. Thompson, of Capt. Thompson (Signature).*

p. 12, Q 379 John Thompson his acct for sundries for militia use £21.18.2 ½ includes a rifle gun ⅝ £50. (no date).

p. 13, John Thompson for personal services under Capt Thompson, includes 99 days under Capt. McCullok and "to rifle gun lost at the Defeat Brunt Creek".

p. 17, These are to certify that I have received eight quarts of salt for the use of Col Briton's Regiment from John Thompson of Capt Jno Thompson.

Also on p. 17, 10 May 1783, Thos Kennedy and Wm Karr came before me . . . a certain rifle gun the property of John Thompson and lost at Brercreek defeat is worth £50.

p. 50, 232 L, 26 Mar 87 John Thompson for a horse lost in public service, 1781 £14.5.2 ½, 17 YY.

p. 68, No. 5/25 John Thomson £14.15.4, 17 May 1785, signature John A. Thompson ?

8. *John Thompson (his mark).*

p. 56, 57, Please deliver these indents to Capt. Jeremh Brown 16 Nov 1785, John Thomspon (his mark) Received So Carolina, Cheraws Dist.

9. *John Thompson (his mark).*

p. 39, Please deliver my indents to Mr. John Blossingame 2 Jan 1787, John Thompson (his mark) 9 YY.

10. *John Thompson (his mark).*

p. 32, 17 Jan 1786, 17 Jan 1785 Transfer of wages for 10 months to William Thompson. John (his mark) Thompson. Signature of William Thompson.

11. *John Thompson (his mark).*

p. 22 a, 16 Aug 1785 pleas to deliver my indents to John Hunter John (his mark) Thompson administrator, 2 YY.

There may be others included in the documents, or there may be multiple references to one or more of the men above. In all, there are nine different men based on identity and signature.

"John Thompson, dec'd" is the man we seek. He died in 1783 and his will names the same wife and children identified in earlier research periods. He may be the John Thompson of Capt. John Thompson who lost his rifle in battle. Since he served in Col. Brandon's regiment, he may also be the one who gave beef to the army and submitted a bill in 1779. He obviously cannot be the Capt. John Thompson who was issued his back pay in 1786 in person.

At present there is one man accepted as a DAR ancestor—Captain John Thompson. Finding nine different men opens the way for others to claim descent. All of them are documented in the indents of South Carolina.

CIVIL WAR ANCESTORS

The outcome of the Civil War was predictable considering the imbalance in manpower and resources between the industrial North and the agrarian South. The North had 4 million males between fifteen and forty years old who were eligible for military service. The South had a total population of 9 million, over one-third of which were black slaves. Only 1.5 million southerners were eligible for military service. By the time the war ended, the North enlisted 2.2 million men, slightly more than half their available manpower, while the South enlisted every eligible male.

Widows and minor heirs of Union Army soldiers were eligible for pensions as were soldiers permanently disabled by military service. The federal government paid pensions to them after approval of the Bureau of Pensions. Each individual state determined the Confederacy's pension policy, making payments from state funds.

Compiling a history of an ancestor's Civil War service can be accomplished by searching military service records, pension application files, and histories of military units. Military service records contain details of a soldier's enlistment, muster rolls, transfers from one unit to another, and records of imprisonment and desertion. They contain little direct genealogical information.

Civil War pension files of Union Army veterans contain a variety of documents, the number and type varying from file to file. If a pensioned veteran's wife outlived him, she became eligible to apply for a widow's pension by submitting proof of legal marriage. Both files may offer information about a veteran's movements after the war, his minor children, occupation, and relationships to others. The following research cameo illustrates the usefulness of a Civil War pension file in solving a tough research problem and how military histories provide insight into an ancestor's war experiences.

JESSE L. WOOD

Jesse L. Wood was first discussed in the family tradition section of Chapter 4. In review, Jesse was an Evangelical Methodist minister and a dentist who moved quite often in the performance of his ministerial duties. The absence of 1860 and 1870 census indexes makes tracking a frequent mover difficult, if not impossible, but if the head of a household received a Civil War pension the problem is minimized.

A family tradition said that Jesse was a friend of Abraham Lincoln, and because of that relationship, he chose to enlist in the Union Army. Tennessee, where Jesse lived at the outbreak of war, divided its loyalties and men between the Union and the Confederate armies. Brother fought against brother in many border states. In one document sent to the Governor of Kansas years later in a plea for clemency, Jesse noted that three of his brothers had been Confederate soldiers.

The Civil War Pension Application File Index listed two named Jesse L. Wood serving in Tennessee units; one was a sergeant, the other a private. Both files were requested from the National Archives and the sergeant's file was immediately forwarded. Information in that file proved he was not the Jesse of interest. Because the file of the Jesse we sought contained information about his imprisonment, it was placed in the custody of the Regional Veteran's Administration Center in Salt Lake City, as are the records of other veterans with negative information on file. A special request stating the intended use of the information was required to obtain a photocopy.

From his file, several things were learned. Jesse applied for a pension on 9 March 1868 at Carroll County, Tennessee. He enlisted in Company I, 7th Tennessee Cavalry Volunteers on 27 December 1863 at Huntingdon and was discharged on 1 July 1865 at Jeffersonville, Indiana. His commander was Lieutenant Colonel J. R. Hawkins, and while in the line of duty at Paducah, Kentucky, Jesse was wounded, sustaining partial loss of the use of his right leg. After discharge, Jesse did light work on a farm near McLemorsville in Carroll County, Tennessee.

The History of Carroll County, Tennessee, compiled by the Carroll County Historical Society, provided a history of Jesse L. Wood's regiment. Skirmishes between Union and Confederate troops were taking place in Huntingdon on the day Jesse enlisted. He joined for three years' service and was sent to Union City, a town thirty-five miles north of Huntingdon for training. Three months after his enlistment, a Confederate attack on Paducah captured Jesse's entire regiment. Only one Union soldier was killed and three others were wounded, including Jesse who was shot in the leg, this before Colonel Hawkins, his commanding officer, was bluffed into surrender. A federal force of 2,000 men was less than five miles away and would have averted the surrender if Hawkins had held out. The Confederates took 475 prisoners; only 75 escaped. The regiment had just been paid for the past year's service, and the Confederates confiscated $60,000 for purchasing needed supplies.

The Confederates took Jesse and the others south to Andersonville Prison near Americus, Georgia. Andersonville was the cruelest and most inhumane of Confederate prisons. Built in November 1863, Andersonville was designed to hold 10,000 prisoners. By May 1864, six weeks after Jesse's arrival, it housed 12,213. The prison's design was simple. Tall, straight pines were cut down, trimmed, and topped to form logs twenty feet long. Slaves trimmed them further to a thickness of ten inches before planting them five feet deep in a trench, making a wall fifteen feet high. The wall at Andersonville enclosed nearly seventeen acres.

Jesse was one of a few to escape from Andersonville. He traveled by night and foraged for food along the way. His gunshot wound had not been treated properly at Andersonville, and he further injured his leg during his long trek back to his regiment in Paducah, Kentucky. He reached there in September 1864. During November and December, he was treated at the post hospital at Paducah for rheumatism which had developed during his walk back to Kentucky. He developed a skin inflamation in February 1865 and was transferred to the Joe Holt Army Hospital at Jeffersonville, Indiana for continued treatment.

Jesse remained there until receiving a Surgeon's Certificate of Disability and a discharge on 1 July 1865, just five weeks before his regiment mustered out of service. He was twenty-six years old at the time of his discharge. The discharge states that he was born in Carroll County, Tennessee, had a dark complexion, dark hair, and black eyes, and stood seventy inches tall.

Once a veteran received a pension, he had to submit for periodic physical examinations to determine whether his condition had improved or worsened so the pension could be adjusted accordingly. Physical examination papers are dated and include the place where the exam took place. Jesse's postwar movements were fully documented in this pension file:

1868 – worked on farm in Dyer County, Tennessee.

1875 – semiannual exam at Shelby County, Iowa.

1876 – examined at Christian County, Missouri in June.

1876 – examined at Greene County, Missouri in October.

1877 – made statement of injuries in Christian County, Missouri.

1877 – examined at Christian County, Missouri.

1880 – statement filed at Christian County, Missouri.

1881 – examined at Dade County, Missouri.

1884 – applied for new pension certificate at Leavenworth County, Kansas. Stated that he left his papers in his library at Cherryvale, Montgomery County, Kansas when he was arrested. [He was sent to the Kansas State Prison on 24 September 1883.]

1886 – examined at Leavenworth County, Kansas.

1887 – applied for an increase in pension payments at Leavenworth, Kansas.

1888 – applied for increase in pension payments at Lansing, Leavenworth County, Kansas.

1889 – applied for increase in pension payments as resident of Lansing, Kansas.

1892 – examined at Lansing, Kansas.

1896 – pension terminated by death on 18 October 1896 in Oklahoma.

Shortly after Jesse's death, his wife, Mary Fuson Wood, applied for a widow's pension. She was living in Ashland, Oregon and noted that she was the sole support of his minor daughters, Bessie and Jessie. She had to prove that she was his lawful wife, a task that became formidable. She was unaware of Jesse's numerous marriages and at first stated that she had been his third wife. (She was actually his fourth). She married Jesse on 21 August 1887 at the Pritchet Hotel in Liberty, Tennessee. Previously married, her name at the time of her marriage to Jesse was Mrs. Mary Fuson. Her sister Maude E. Fuson (she and Mary married Fuson brothers) testified to Jesse's and Mary's marriage in a general affidavit.

In another affidavit, a resident of Jackson County, Oregon stated that he knew Jesse and Mary as residents of Ashland, Oregon. He testified that Jesse died in 1893 at Ardmore, Indian Territory, leaving two daughters, Jessie, about age eight, and Bessie, about age three.

A third affidavit came from Jesse's two sons from his second marriage, who lived in Ardmore. They stated that their mother, Nancy E. Wood, died near Huntingdon, Carroll County, Tennessee on 14 November 1880 and that she was the lawful wife of Jesse L. Wood at the time of her death.

By identifying Jesse's residences after the war, records of the counties where he lived could be thoroughly searched to locate additional genealogical information. His pension file provided a wealth of historical details that added color to the Wood family history. It also offered excellent clues to follow-up research in Tennessee, Iowa, Missouri, Kansas, the Indian Territory, and Oregon. Remember that each pension file contains differing amounts of information and documents, but almost every file will contain details of enlistment, physical characteristics, discharge, marriage, medical examinations, and termination of pension allowance—usually at the time of the veteran's death. If an ancestor was born between 1838 and 1845, there is every reason to believe that he served in the Civil War, and the *Civil War Pension Application File Index* should be checked to see if he applied for a pension. If you find an ancestor listed in the index, write to the National Archives for a copy of his complete military service record and pension file. Microfilm copies of the above-mentioned index are available at Regional Federal Archives and Records Centers and the Genealogical Library of the LDS Church and its branches.

CHAPTER 14

Colonial Ancestors

N ew England research appears to be easier than research in other localities, requiring the least amount of original research because so many family histories and genealogies have already been compiled. Naming patterns in New England are repeated each generation, and while these form a significant clue to relationships, they can also lead you astray unless you have enough evidence to distinguish between the generations. Many printed genealogies utilized mistake sons for uncles and tie husbands to mothers-in-law – easy errors to make.

Nearly all of the ancestors who lived in Massachusetts descend from some 30,000 persons who immigrated there between 1630 and 1642. This means a lot of people share the same New England roots. There are also some Scots-Irish and French Huguenots who settled in Massachusetts during the colonial period who carried the same surnames as the English settlers, thus adding to the confusion.

Of the compiled genealogies in print, many are available only in manuscript form in local libraries or at the New England Historic Genealogical Society in Boston, the Essex Institute in Salem, and in various New England state archives and libraries. Many manuscripts have been published, but the qualifying cautions written in the margins or attached on separate sheets have been omitted.

NEW ENGLAND ANCESTRY

Vital records – births, marriages, and deaths – for most Massachusetts towns before 1850 have been printed. These volumes are available in many research libraries across the country. Genealogists assume these volumes are complete and correct since vital records are registered by law and the volumes are printed with official endorsement. This is not the case. The original records preserve evidence of family connections since they are arranged in chronological order, some even in family units. The printed versions list the entries alphabetically with all births in one section, marriages in another, and deaths in a third section. Divided entries make it difficult to line up deaths with births for children who die young and for women who die in childbirth. Relationships drawn from the printed volumes are primarily guesses, while relationships suggested in the originals are quite reliable.

It is estimated that seventy to eighty percent of those born in Massachusetts prior to 1850 are mentioned in the printed vital records. Town vital records which were not printed are being converted to microfiche by the Holbrook Institute, and will be available in the same research libraries as the printed volumes.

There are no references to volume or page numbers where the original entry can be found, so the printed vital records are not a bypass source. They can serve as an index, but if an ancestor was known to live in a Massachusetts town and does not appear, check the originals. A second option is to use the International Genealogical Index for Massachusetts. The IGI functions as a statewide index to the Massachusetts vital records. Since some of the entries are extracted from the printed volumes, you will need to monitor the *Parish and Vital Records Listings* where the records included in the database are listed. If the extracts come from the originals (also on microfilm at the Genealogical Library of the LDS Church), the entries for these towns can be used as a bypass source. If they come from the printed volumes, check the originals.

Preliminary studies conducted by demographers on Massachusetts registration show that at least forty-five percent of all deaths occurring between 1845 and 1849 were unaccounted. A comparison of the 1850 census entries for children under five years of age with the registration of births during the five-year period shows that births too were underregistered—fifty-nine percent missed in 1842, forty-seven percent in 1845, and eighteen percent in 1850. By 1899, the degree of underregistration was less than two percent.

The population of New England was highly mobile, moving freely from one state to another and back again, as well as within state boundaries. Many moved west to New York, Canada, Ohio, the Midwest, and to the West Coast. Most families moved at least five to six times. Within city limits the maximum length of residence was seven to ten years depending upon age and economic circumstances. A recent study of Boston's population showed that forty-three percent of the population living there in 1850 moved away; thirty percent went to the suburbs, eight percent returned to their home towns or to farms in outlying areas, only two percent traveled to other cities. At least eighty-one percent died in Massachusetts, the majority staying within the same state.[1]

Where printed sources—genealogies and vital records—are available, use them to sketch the outlines of your ancestral family. Then verify the events where sources are given to see if the information has been copied correctly. Finally, document all other events from original manuscripts where possible and corroborate the facts where they are not. Careful analysis of the whole body of information will allow you to identify those facts that are accurate and to clarify where errors and discrepancies exist.

---

1. Peter R. Knights, "Facts of Lives: Or What Happened to 2,808 Nineteenth-Century Bostonians," *Genealogical Journal* 12 (Winter 1983-84):162-73.

The combination of high mobility, common surnames, and incomplete sources make a search of all available records essential if you are to compile an accurate record. Guard against the desire to link what has already been printed to your lineage without proving it belongs there.

Research to prove the ancestry of Benjamin Franklin Foster, born 17 December 1845, the son of Benjamin F. Foster and his wife Abigail Mills, began with a search of the printed literature and the discovery that Martha Anderson compiled an unpublished "Foster Genealogy." This manuscript traces the paternal lineage only, with reference to parents of women who married into the Foster family listed but not documented. For each date the source is given in parentheses. Earlier generations include references to court records, deeds, and other sources as well as vital records. Sources for the immediate generations are vital records and the printed *Foster Genealogy* by Frederick Pierce, published in 1899.

The generations, as they are given in the Foster manuscript, are summarized in Figure 14:1. Dates can be verified easily by checking them against the vital records of Carlisle, Massachusetts, the principal locality represented on the chart.

This exercise, however, merely proves that Ms. Anderson can copy correctly. While it is an important verification, it does not prove that Benjamin Franklin Foster is the son of Benjamin Foster – it merely links vital records. This is a significant distinction and represents one of the chief criticisms leveled at American genealogists by their British colleagues. What is needed is proof that Benjamin Franklin Foster is the son of Benjamin Foster.

The real proof of relationship comes from chains of evidence – sources corroborated by other records, name patterns repeated through generations, proximity of brothers and sisters to each other, and many other small details from a variety of sources and careful searching. If the records for Benjamin Franklin Foster, born 4 April 1814, are compared with the records for his brothers George and Aaron R., evidence surfaces that constitutes proof. No one piece of evidence stands alone; together they offer evidence suggesting additional searches which may establish a base for lineage extension into the colonial period.

Benjamin died intestate at thirty in Chelmsford, Middlesex County, Massachusetts. His heirs included his wife Martha, who was appointed the guardian of their children Martha Ann, Benjamin Franklin, George, and Aaron Robbins, all minors under fourteen on 5 October 1819. Martha Foster later made her will 24 September 1825, dividing her personal effects among these same four children. She died in 1832. Benjamin F. and George were over fourteen by then and chose Reuben Foster of Carlisle (the brother of Benjamin Foster) as their guardian. As Aaron was still under fourteen, Reuben was appointed his guardian as well.

Name patterns (Benjamin Franklin had sons George and Edwin; George had a son Edwin), proximity (Benjamin Franklin Foster appears in Lowell, Massachusetts in 1839 where he operates a piggery until his death in 1857. George

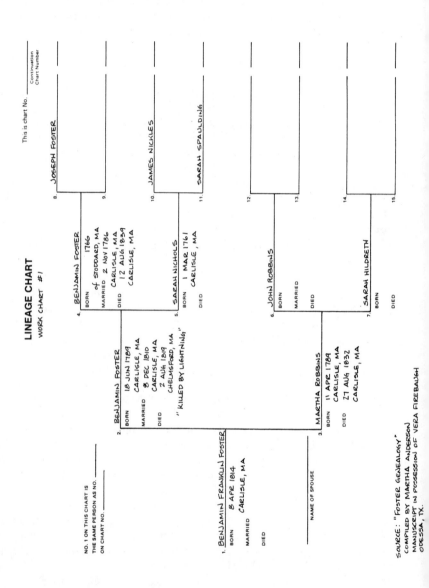

LINEAGE CHART
WORK CHART #1

This is chart No. _____

Continuation Chart Number

NO. 1 ON THIS CHART IS
THE SAME PERSON AS NO. _____
ON CHART NO. _____

1. BENJAMIN FRANKLIN FOSTER
BORN   8 APR 1814
       CARLISLE, MA
MARRIED
DIED

NAME OF SPOUSE

2. BENJAMIN FOSTER
BORN   18 JUN 1789
       CARLISLE, MA
MARRIED 8 DEC 1810
        CARLISLE, MA
DIED   2 AUG 1819
       CHELMSFORD, MA
       "KILLED BY LIGHTNING"

3. MARTHA ROBBINS
BORN   11 APR 1789
       CARLISLE, MA
DIED   27 AUG 1852
       CARLISLE, MA

4. BENJAMIN FOSTER
BORN   1766
       of STODDARD, MA
MARRIED 2 NOV 1786
        CARLISLE, MA
DIED   12 AUG 1859
       CARLISLE, MA

5. SARAH NICHOLS
BORN   1 MAR 1761
       CARLISLE, MA
DIED

6. JOHN ROBBINS
BORN
MARRIED
DIED

7. SARAH HILDRETH
BORN
DIED

8. JOSEPH FOSTER

9.

10. JAMES NICKLES

11. SARAH SPAULDING

12.

13.

14.

15.

SOURCE: "FOSTER GENEALOGY"
COMPILED BY MARTHA ANDERSON
MANUSCRIPT IN POSSESSION OF VERA FIREBAUGH
ODESSA, TX.

Figure 14:1. Lineage Chart, Benjamin Franklin Foster.

and Aaron R. reside in Lowell during the 1840s, though neither stays), dates, and generations align with vital records and probates in Carlisle.

Carlisle deeds include many transactions by Benjamin Foster Jr. or Lt. Benjamin Foster with Mary and Job Nickles[s]. Among them is the purchase of land on Foster Street in Chelmsford. This is the land mentioned in the probate of Benjamin Franklin Foster in 1860, land passed from Benjamin Foster to Benjamin Foster Jr. to Benjamin Franklin Foster—a three-generation link in proof of this lineage.

Family tradition forms another link: "Benjamin is right. I know because family tradition is that he had a new axe and was out in a storm, got under the tree, and put the axe under his coat to protect it. Lightning struck and killed him." Benjamin Foster's death was recorded officially as "struck by lightning."

Name patterns, proximity, and alignment of dates and places with no contradictory evidence are only circumstantial proofs that the right connection has been found. The transfer of land spans three generations and crosses town boundary lines. This is the real proof of relationship. Family tradition, which also spans generations and links them, supports the proof.

Many New England lineages are based only on information from printed vital records. Even where they can be verified as accurate, chances of placing the wrong Benjamin Foster on your lineage are high. Such evidence, easily obtained in printed volumes in libraries, is a guide only. Substantiate the information with actual proof of relationship.

COLONIAL VIRGINIA ANCESTRY

Virginia was the first permanent English settlement in America. It was organized and financed by the Virginia Company, a joint stock business enterprise similar in nature to the East India Company that had been successfully operated by other English business adventurers. Virginia was very different from English colonies in other parts of the world. It was unsettled, unproductive, of limited resources, and lacked the labor reserves found elsewhere. The Virginia Company was not well enough capitalized to see the venture to a successful end and it collapsed in 1624; however, its demise did not mean an end to the colony.

The Virginia Company's primary goal was to develop a prosperous tobacco export business to meet European demand for the product. The company's success depended upon its ability to cultivate the land and to create a strong labor force. Without a labor pool to tap, the Virginia Company began importing about 1,500 white indentured servants each year. Shiploads of servants arrived without adequate equipment or provisions, and the Virginia Company was too poorly capitalized to meet their needs. Thousands of importees died from malaria, starvation, and diseases caused by malnutrition. Once the king became aware of the needless waste of human life, the Virginia Company was dissolved. The English government took over the colony two years before the Puritans set sail from Holland to establish New England.

There was a vast difference between the civil organization of Virginia and New England. The latter was established for religious purposes and not primarily as a financial investment. The two fledgling colonies approached civil organization and recordkeeping quite differently. The Massachusetts settlers established themselves and their governments after English government and law, placing heavy emphasis on recreating towns and churches identical to those they left behind. They were accustomed to keeping excellent civil and church records and they began to do so immediately upon organizing themselves. Virginia, on the other hand, was less concerned about recreating English civil and ecclesiastical customs. They were totally occupied with survival and protecting their capital investment. The Virginians established laws requiring the church to maintain records of christenings, marriages, and burials and they required the maintenance of land grants, estate records, and other civil records, but they were not as devoted to recordkeeping as the New England colonists.

Virginia suffered greater record losses than the New England colonies, a fact that creates difficulty in tracing early Virginia genealogies. There are many more printed New England family histories and genealogies than there are for early Virginia settlers. Record losses and the differences in recordkeeping practices could explain the disparity. While research in the Tidewater area can be difficult during the earliest settlement period, it is much more difficult to trace ancestors who lived on the Virginia frontier prior to the Revolutionary War. The following case study shows how research can be accomplished for that period. Portions were adapted from an anonymous manuscript "Captain Samuel Stalnaker and His Descendants."

SAMUEL STALNAKER

Samuel Stalnaker, according to an unproven family tradition, was of German descent and arrived at Charleston, South Carolina from Holland with some of his brothers. Indian uprisings forced Samuel out of South Carolina into Virginia in 1732. An article in the *Baltimore American* of 25 August 1907 states, "There is no more interesting character in the history of pioneer Virginia than the brave old Indian fighter and explorer, Captain Samuel Stalnaker. Contemporary travelers as well as the official correspondence of Governor Dinwiddie prove him one of the most interesting and important men of his day."

Captain Stalnaker was living in Augusta County, Virginia in November 1746 when, according to court records, he and several others were ordered to build a road from Reedy Creek to Eagle Bottom and from there to the top of the ridge that parts the waters of the New River and the south fork of the Roanoke. This building party included Patrick Calhoun, the great-grandfather of John C. Calhoun.

Dr. Thomas Walker, a surveyor who had convinced the government to permit the exploration of the wilderness country for possible future settlement, met Samuel Stalnaker in 1748 and immediately recognized the tough frontiersman as the person with the most knowledge of the Virginia frontier. Walker asked Captain Stalnaker to accompany him on his exploration, but Stalnaker, on his way to settle some business with the Cherokee Indians, could not make the trip.

The *Virginia Magazine of History and Biography* states, "Samuel Stalnaker, probably one of the German emigrants from Pennsylvania to the western part of Virginia, was at one time the latter colony's most western inhabitant. Dr. Thomas Walker, in his journal states that in April, 1748, he met Stalnaker between Reedy Creek settlement and the Holston River, on the North side, a few miles above its juncture with the South Fork." Samuel had decided to settle on the frontier and Dr. Walker and his companions helped to build Stalnaker's house on 24 March 1750. It was the most western settlement in existence at that time. The location of Stalnaker's land is noted in James Patton's will which was proven 1 September 1750 in an Augusta County, Virginia court. The will states that Patton's land adjoined the land on which Samuel Stalnaker and others were living, known as Indian Fields, on the water of Holston's River, a branch of the Mississippi. The 1750 Augusta County tax list also states that Samuel Stalnaker lived on the Holston River. Samuel gave Dr. Thomas Walker directions to the Cumberland Gap, a discovery credited to Walker.

Samuel Stalnaker had been hunting and exploring in the wilderness for years. He undoubtedly foresaw the flood of population that would come through his settlement in the future. He petitioned the court to permit him to post a bond of 10,000 pounds of tobacco with King George II to maintain an inn at Indian Fields. The document is found in the early wills of the County Clerk of Augusta County, Virginia and reads:

Know all men by these presents that we Saml. Stalnaker and Alexander Sayers are held and firmly bound to our sovereign Lord, George the Second, in the sum of ten thousand pounds of tobacco to the which payment well and truly to be made we bind ourselves and every of us and every of our heirs, executors, administrators, jointly and severally, firmly by these presents sealed with our seals and dated this 7th day of Nov. 1752. The condition of this obligation is such that whereas the above bound Saml. Stalnaker hath ordained a license to keep an ordinary in this county; if therefore the said Stalnaker doth constantly find and provide in his ordinary good, wholesome and cleanly lodgings and diet for travelers and fodder and provender, or pasturage and provender as the season shall require for horses, for and during the term of one year from this seven day of Nov. and shall not suffer or permit any unlawful gaming in his house on the Sabbath day or suffer or permit any to tipple or drink more than is necessary, then this obligation to be void and of none effect or else to remain in full force and virtue.

Stalnaker's place was a stopping point for the militia, Indians, and explorers. Augusta County records disclose that in 1752 Samuel Stalnaker was appointed to a captaincy in the Virginia Militia. Later that year he signed as a surety on a bond made by John Smith as guardian of Catherine King. This document is also found in the Augusta County, Virginia court records. The fact that Samuel could post such bonds indicates that he was fairly well off. His reputation as an accomplished trader with the Indians further substantiates his economic status. Another document in Augusta County records dated 24 November 1753 orders that a road be built from Sam'l Stalnaker's to James Davis's. Samuel was appointed overseer of the road and more than twenty others, including his sons Jacob, George, and Adam, were appointed road builders.

Samuel testified in Augusta County in 1754 that Humberstone Lyon stole forty-three red deer skins belonging to James Conoly from the home of James Scagg. About two years later he served as captain in the militia during the French and Indian War under Colonel George Washington. *The History of Tazewell County, Virginia* states:

> In the summer of 1755, just about the time of the Indian attack upon Draper's Meadow, a scalping party of Shawnees made an incursion into the Middle Holston Valley. They attacked the more exposed settlements, killed several settlers and captured others. Captain Samuel Stalnaker who then had his cabin some four or five miles west of the present town of Marion, Smythe County, Virginia, was made a captive, and Mrs. Stalnaker and Adam Stalnaker were killed. Stalnaker and the other prisoners were taken through or across the Clinch Valley by the Indians on their return trip to their towns in Ohio. This is evidenced by the journal of Col. Andrew Lewis, on his expedition known as the 'Sandy Expedition,' which was made in the months of February and March, 1756.

How and when Samuel Stalnaker escaped from the Indians is unknown. The attack on his settlement took place in June 1755, and he did not appear at Governor Dinwiddie's in Williamsburg, Virginia until June 1756. He reportedly went directly there after his escape to report his experiences with the Shawnees and the size of their fighting force. Historians also claim that Mrs. Stalnaker was only wounded by the Indians. She reportedly made her way up a creek branching off the Holston River with one of her younger children. A rescue party found her body on the bank of the creek with her starving child nearby crying, "Hungry Mammy!" The creek was then called Hungry Mother Creek, and the entire area later became Hungry Mother State Park. The creek was originally called Stalnaker's Creek in land records.

Captain Stalnaker's activities after escaping the Shawnees are well documented in the Dinwiddie Papers, "The Official Records of Robert Dinwiddie" who was Lieutenant Governor of Virginia from 1751 to 1758. The governor considered the information Captain Stalnaker brought to him after his escape important enough to pass on to the governors of other colonies. He told them of the pending approach of a large force of French and Indians. One letter to Sir Charles Hardy of New York was written 1 July 1756:

Samuel Stalnaker, who was settled in Augusta County on our frontiers, was taken prisoner by the Shawneese [sic] about a year since, has made his escape and come here in the middle of June. He says that a little before he left the Shawneese towns there came 6 French Officers with 1,000 Indians from Oubatch and back of the Lakes; that they intended to invade out back settlements. Similar letters went to Governor Sharpe of Maryland, Governor Belcher of New Jersey, Governor Shirley of Massachusetts, and Lord Loudon in New York.

That large force of French and Indians routed the colonial militia under the leadership of General Braddock. Only George Washington was left uninjured and upon his return to Virginia he was appointed Commander-in-Chief of the Virginia forces. Samuel Stalnaker attended the Council of War on 27 July 1756 at the Augusta County courthouse. George Washington's papers in the Library of Congress include a "List of Militia Officers of Augusta County," which includes the name of Captain Samuel Stalnaker. He is mentioned extensively in Dinwiddie's Papers, in the "List of Colonial Soldiers of Virginia," and in the Washington Manuscripts.

After the French and Indian War, Samuel Stalnaker returned to his settlement and hosted a number of military officers on various expeditions against the Cherokee Indians. He was also visited by Daniel Boone who began an expedition into Kentucky from Stalnaker's settlement. When a treaty was made with the Cherokee Indians in 1768, Samuel Stalnaker carried the message from the Indians to the governor. His settlement continued to be a rendezvous spot for troops during the Revolutionary War, but that was after Samuel's death in 1769.

Court, land, and estate records, along with printed historical records and manuscripts are the keys to tracing early Virginia ancestry on the frontier. If ancestors lived closer to the coast, church and marriage records are also useful. Church records and family Bible entries may be the only sources of exact birth and death dates in colonial Virginia. There are relatively few church records in existence today; thus most birth dates will have to be estimated from other records. Approximate death dates will be found in estate records. Identifying the female children of colonial Virginians is sometimes impossible. For example, none of Stalnaker's daughters have been identified. Records only mention three of his sons, as noted when Jacob, George, and Adam Stalnaker were ordered to perform labor services in building roads. Daughters are most often identified in wills, probates, deeds showing the sale of land by the heirs of an estate, and marriage records that name the father of the bride. (See Chapter 12 for help in tracing female ancestors.)

Research in colonial Virginia should always include colonial papers, manuscripts, or journals and diaries. These records may not offer detailed genealogical information, but they will attest to the movements and activities of the individuals appearing in those sources. Remember that Americans have always been on the move and when they disappear from one area they should be searched for in the records of surrounding counties. Some colonial families owned land in different counties at the same time and moved freely between plantations in each. If an ancestor disappears in the records of one Virginia county about the time another area is being settled, check the records of the new county. The land they occupied earlier may have been redesignated as belonging to the new county.

Not all of Virginia's colonists were as adventuresome as Samuel Stalnaker, but they did participate in the everyday events of the young colony as road builders and overseers, property owners, soldiers in a local militia, jurymen, and witnesses to deeds, bonds, or court actions. Once every piece of available information is culled from the records, the life of a colonial ancestor begins to take shape.

FAMILIES ON THE MOVE

America is a transient society with family members spread across the country at great distances. Transience is not a twentieth-century phenomemon in this country. Americans have always been on the move, and tracking their movements is an important part of genealogical research. Historians, geographers, and genealogists have plotted migratory routes established during the frontier period; however, for unknown reasons, no comprehensive publication on internal migration designed specifically for use by genealogists exists.

Ancestors on the move are found in the same record sources used to trace the families in Chapter 8. Land and estate records often provide clues to a family's earlier residence. County histories, biographies, and military pensions provide that information with greater frequency. Rather than present a series of case studies to illustrate migration patterns, this section offers some insight into colonial and frontier migration routes.

The main centers of colonial settlement prior to 1675 were few in number. The Virginia Company established Jamestown in 1607 as a commercial venture. Growth was slow and there were years when its survival was doubtful, but by 1623 Virginia was beginning to thrive and it was accepted as a permanent settlement. The center of Virginia population during that early period was in the Tidewater area along the James, York, Rappahannock, and Nansemond rivers at the mouth of the Chesapeake Bay. Virginia colonists built forts out on the frontier and established settlements that extended in a one hundred mile radius from Jamestown.

The northern colony of Massachusetts began with the arrival of the Mayflower passengers in 1620. They settled at Plymouth to establish a place where they could worship as they pleased. They were followed by thousands of Puritans who founded Boston and the Massachusetts Bay Colony ten years later. Within a short time, industrious New Englanders had built towns throughout eastern Massachusetts. By 1639 they had established a string of towns along the Connecticut River. The new Puritan colony of Connecticut was founded, followed by Rhode Island, New Hampshire, and Maine.

The Dutch arrived on the heels of the Puritans and established the first settlement in New Netherlands along the Hudson River Valley in 1624. A substantial number of those early immigrants went up the Hudson River to settle what is now Albany, New York. New Amsterdam existed for forty years when it came under English rule and was renamed New York. Many Dutch families later moved into New Jersey and Pennsylvania.

By 1682, colonists were living in North and South Carolina, Maryland, and Pennsylvania. North Carolina was first settled by a group of Virginians who moved south to establish a settlement north of the Albemarle Sound in 1653. North Carolina's population increased slowly. The greatest growth took place when large numbers of Scots-Irish moved down the Shenandoah Valley to Virginia and then further south into North Carolina. Equally large numbers of Germans and English Quakers left Pennsylvania to relocate in North Carolina after 1750.

South Carolina saw its first permanent settlement in 1671 when two groups of immigrants from England and Barbados arrived at what they called Charles Town. They were followed by Dutch settlers who left New York when the English took over their settlement. Other Dutch groups from Holland, Quakers, and French Huguenots arrived later.

Pennsylvania was founded as a haven for those who suffered religious persecution. It is usually thought of as a Quaker colony, but William Penn opened its doors to people of any faith, and they came from England, Scotland, Ireland, Germany, Switzerland, and Wales. By 1740, Pennsylvania had become the nation's first melting pot.

Lord Baltimore obtained a land grant from the crown that became the Maryland colony. He sought to use the land as a refuge for Roman Catholics who were persecuted by the Church of England. The first group shipped to Maryland consisted of twenty Catholics and two hundred protestants. They were joined later by a number of Virginia colonists. Within the first century of Maryland's existence it became the home of English, Scotch-Irish, and German immigrants. Hundreds of Pennsylvania Germans migrated across the southern Pennsylvania border to settle in the Maryland Appalachians.

Virginia frontiersmen explored the interior by following footpaths and waterways used by the Indians for centuries. Dr. Thomas Walker is credited with discovering the Cumberland Gap, a passage through the Appalachians to the Cumberland River. His discovery provided pioneers a way into what later became Tennessee and Kentucky. Daniel Boone blazed a trail from Salisbury, North Carolina to the Cumberland Gap in 1774 by following old Indian trails and the Watauga River to Harrodsburg and Boonesboro. Harrodsburg became the first permanent white settlement in Kentucky in 1774 and was followed by Boonesboro in 1775.

The longest road in colonial America was the Post Road that extended from Portland, Maine to Boston and then south to Baltimore where it moved inland.

It passed through Richmond, Virginia, Raleigh, North Carolina, Charleston, South Carolina, Savannah, Georgia, and then St. Augustine, Florida. The road was built at British direction to link the colonies and provide a road for mail service.

Many roads that followed old Indian trails were built before and during the Revolution. There were three main routes west by 1812. One began in New England at Northampton, Massachusetts and extended northwest to Albany, New York, then over the Mohawk Turnpike to Lake Erie. The second road went from Philadelphia and Baltimore to Pittsburgh. The southern route west started with the Great Valley Road at Hagerstown, Maryland and extended southwest through the Appalachians to the Nashville and Wilderness Roads leading to central Tennessee and Kentucky. By 1818 the National Road between Cumberland, Maryland and Wheeling, Virginia was completed, affording access to the Ohio River to southern pioneers moving north.

A knowledge of migration routes and major migrations is important in genealogical research. Let's assume that a family left Pennsylvania to begin the trek west in 1835. They are in the 1850 census of Osage County, Missouri with children born in Pennsylvania, Indiana, Illinois, and Missouri. They began their migration from Washington County, Pennsylvania. How did they get to Missouri and where did they stop along the way? They could have taken two routes. The first route was the Cumberland Road that linked with the Indianapolis Turnpike that went through central Ohio to Indianapolis where it turned into the National Pike that extended west to Vandalia, Illinois. From Vandalia, pioneers went overland on smaller roads to St. Louis where they began river passage on the Missouri and Osage Rivers into the Missouri interior. The second route was water passage down the Ohio River from Pittsburgh or Wheeling along the southern borders of Ohio, Indiana, and Illinois to the Mississippi River. Pioneers then took the Mississippi north to St. Louis where it connects with the Missouri. From there they took the Missouri River to the Osage River to the interior of Missouri. It is likely that the family lived along the way in counties not too distant from the major routes west. Searches of county records in areas bordering those routes or slightly inland from them may locate an ancestor's prior residence.

There are dozens of migration routes west, too many to discuss in a single chapter. The following list includes the major routes and migrations used by most pioneers:

New England to Western New York

Major Migrations: Post-Revolutionary War period
        Routes: Migrants traveled from Northampton, Massachusetts to Albany, New York, then along the Mohawk Valley to Utica and west on the Genessee Road.

New England to New York to Upper Ohio, Michigan, and Wisconsin

Major Migrations: After 1820
Routes: Travelers went from Massachusetts to Buffalo, New York where water passage took them through the Erie Canal to Lake Erie. They could take water passage on the lake or the Seneca Road to Cleveland, Ohio. From there they took water passage on the lake to Toledo, Ohio and Detroit, Michigan. The Chicago Turnpike began outside of Detroit and ended at Chicago. From there wagon roads led north into southern Wisconsin and north to Green Bay.

Connecticut to New York to New Jersey to Pennsylvania

Major Migrations: Continuous migration from the colonial period
Routes: Migrants went along the Connecticut coast to New York and the Hudson River, then west and south into the Wyoming Valley to Pennsylvania and New Jersey along the Boston Post Road.

Pennsylvania to Kentucky and Tennessee

Major Migrations: After 1790
Routes: Immigrants who arrived at Philadelphia took one of several routes to the interior. The first was from Philadelphia to Hagerstown, Maryland, then south on the Great Valley Road to the Wilderness Road or the Nashville Road into Tennessee and Kentucky. They also took the Cumberland Road to Wheeling where they took water passage on the Ohio River to the Maysville Turnpike which led into the Kentucky interior.

Virginia to Ohio to Indiana to Illinois to Missouri to Iowa

Major Migrations: 1810-1850
Routes: Virginians generally moved west into Kentucky and then north to Ohio via the Maysville Turnpike. They also went north through Kentucky to reach the Ohio River which took them along the southern borders of Indiana and Illinois. They often followed the Ohio to the Mississippi River, taking the latter north to its juncture with the Missouri and Des Moines rivers. They took the Missouri River into the Missouri interior and the Des Moines River into the Iowa interior.

Virginia to North Carolina to South Carolina to Georgia to Alabama to Mississippi

Major Migrations: Post-Revolutionary War period and post-War of 1812 period

Routes: 1. Virginians picked up the Fall Line Road along its route through Virginia to central North and South Carolina. It proceeded south to Augusta, Georgia and then southwest to Columbus, Georgia and Montgomery, Alabama. The Upper Federal Road began at Montgomery and extended west to Natchez, Mississippi. Pioneers from North and South Carolina, Georgia, and Alabama to Mississippi joined the exodus along those roads leading to Mississippi.

2. The Upper Road from Washington, D.C. took travelers south through western North and South Carolina to Athens and Columbus, Georgia and then went south to Mobile, Alabama through Macon, Georgia and Montgomery, Alabama. The Fall Line Road connected with the Upper Road at Columbus, Georgia and led to Montgomery, Alabama.

3. Once in Natchez, travelers took the Mississippi River to other locations in the north, crossed the river into the interior of Louisiana or went down-river to New Orleans.

Virginia to Tennessee to Mississippi

Major Migrations: 1815 to 1840

Routes: Virginians took the Great Valley Road to Knoxville, Tennessee and then followed the Military Road south to Tuscumbia, Alabama, where the road split. One fork became the Natchez Trace and led to Jackson and Natchez, Mississippi. The Military Road continued south to Columbus, Mississippi and Madisonville, Louisiana.

North Carolina to South Carolina to Tennessee to Arkansas

Major Migrations: After 1830

Routes: Migrants left from Raleigh or Fayetteville, North Carolina and went through central South Carolina to Augusta, Georgia, then north on the Unity Road to Nashville, Tennessee. The road from Nashville to Little Rock was an unimproved connecting road that went south to Memphis on the Mississippi River and then west to Little Rock.

Pennsylvania to Ohio to Indiana to Illinois to Missouri

Major Migrations: Post-Revolutionary War period to 1850
Routes: The main overland route from Pennsylvania to the interior states began at Wheeling, Virginia with the Cumberland Road. It turned into the National Turnpike at Columbus, Ohio and extended west through central Indiana and Illinois, coming to an end at Vandalia, Illinois. Connecting roads took pioneers to St. Louis where river passage took them into the interior of Missouri. They also followed Boone's Lick Road to Franklin, Missouri.

New England to New York to Western Pennsylvania

Major Migrations: Post-Revolutionary War period
Route: Pioneers followed the Connecticut coast to New York and then went inland along the Post Road to Philadelphia where two roads led to Pittsburgh through southern Pennsylvania.

The maps in Figures 14:2-14:7 graphically illustrate the major roads and waterways used by those traveling west during major migration periods. Remember that pioneers were joined along the way by residents of the states through which they passed. Someone beginning in North Carolina would not travel to Washington, D.C. to pick up the Post Road.

It's important to remember that settlers moved in groups that included relatives, friends, and neighbors. Always take careful note of the families living near your ancestors to determine if they took the same migration routes. Their route is seen in the birthplaces of their children recorded in the later census enumerations. While there may be no clues to your ancestors' prior residences, there may be some reference to the origins of a neighboring family who traveled with them. Many difficult research problems have been solved using that approach.

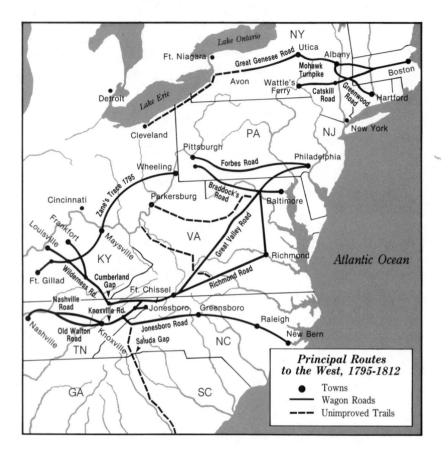

Figure 14:5. Principal Routes to the West, 1795-1812.

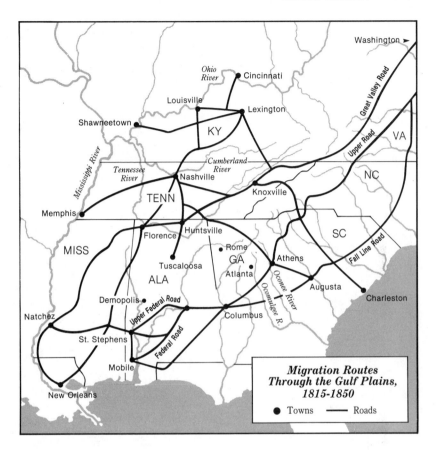

Figure 14:6. Migration Routes Through the Gulf Plains,
1815-1850.

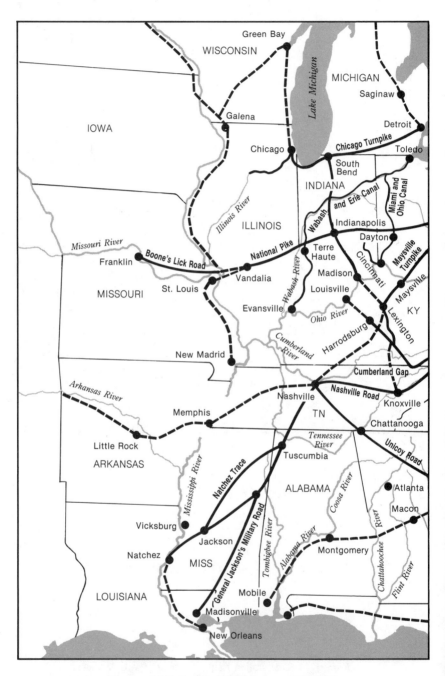

Figure 14:7. Canals and Highways, 1820-1850.

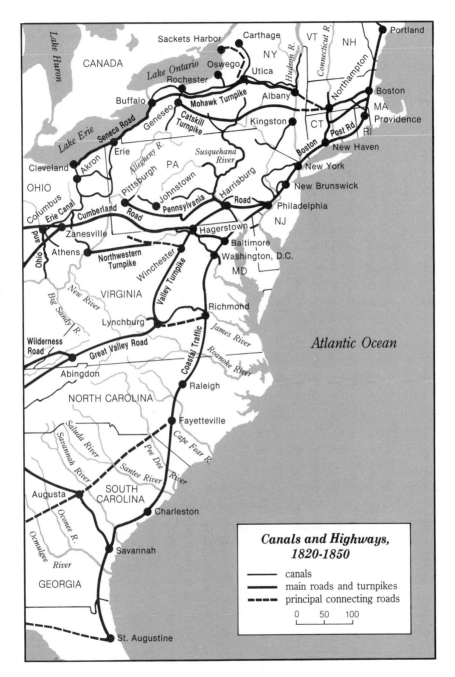

**Canals and Highways,
1820-1850**

——— canals
━━━ main roads and turnpikes
▬ ▬ ▬ principal connecting roads

0   50   100

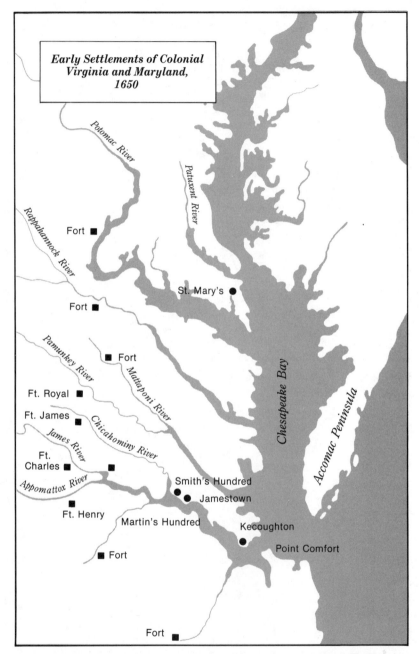

Figure 14:2. Early Settlements of Colonial Virginia and Maryland, 1650.

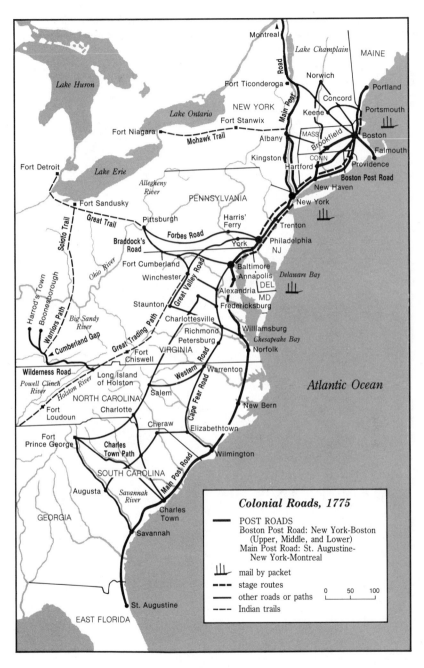

Figure 14:3. Colonial Roads, 1775.

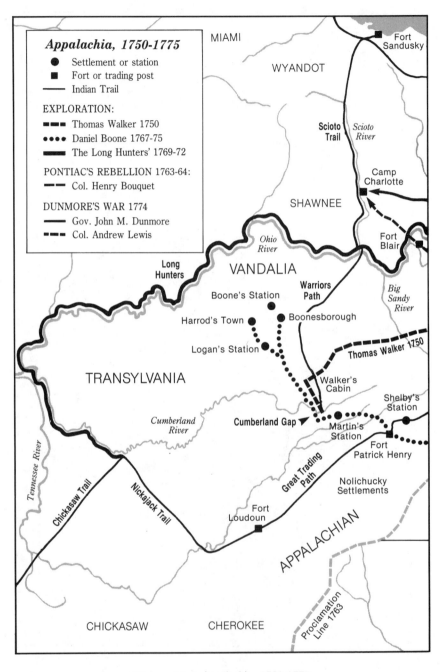

Figure 14:4. Appalachia, 1750-1775.

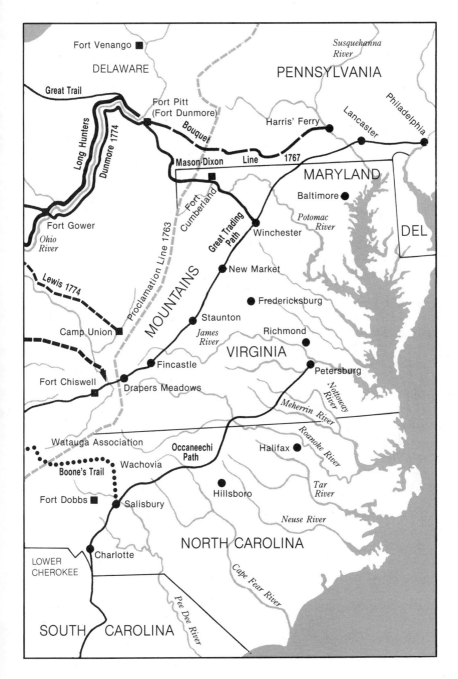

ON THE FRONTIER

Frontier research, particularly between the years following the Revolutionary War and 1850, requires considerable expertise. As new states developed, county boundaries changed, and research in one location often extends to a cluster of counties. Picking up the pieces of an ancestor's life when recordkeeping was unsophisticated necessitates using every available record, some of which take hours of tedious searching.

Genealogists run into a dead end on the frontier, research bogging down during the 1780 to 1840 time period. Members of the Ethington family began tracing their ancestry in 1920. There were few genealogical instructional manuals then and not much progress was made. The family believed that William and Fielding Ethington were brothers who moved to Kentucky around 1814 and settled in Henry County. Thirty years passed before a family researcher found a DAR pamphlet that listed Henry County deaths and noted William Ethington's entry with his father listed as J. Ethington, the first clue to the identity of their parent.

The thirty years following that discovery were spent searching every record available in the Genealogical Library of the LDS Church for J. Ethington's full identity, including census enumerations, marriage records, volumes of unindexed county court records, land records, and estate records. The Ethingtons moved around a section of Kentucky that included Henry, Shelby, Floyd, Owen, and Woodford counties.

Literally hundreds of references were found that documented the movements and families of William and Fielding Ethington. The will of William Williams, located in Woodford County records, mentioned his son-in-law, Fielding Ethington, the husband of his deceased daughter, Betsey, and his granddaughter, Polly. This was the first mention of any of Fielding's children and his first wife.

Many researchers are reluctant to take the time to read unindexed court records because entire volumes of tedious entries may not include a reference to the person for whom they are searching. Most difficult research problems are solved either directly or through substantive clues found in early court records. For example, the Ethington family believed that their ancestors did not arrive in Kentucky until about 1814 which was the date of the first document produced by the Ethingtons in Henry County. Their page-by-page search of *Woodford County Court Orders Book C* produced the following document:

> Ordered that the clerk of this court bind Feilding Edrington [sic] to Franklin Perry to learn the art and mystery of a stone mason to serve until he arrives at the age of 21 years . . . and then to receive a horse worth $50 a saddle and bridal and a suit of cloths [sic].

The most important information in the court order is the proof that Fielding Ethington was in Kentucky in 1805 as a fifteen-year-old boy, a fact that offered entirely new possibilities to study. The questions needing answers were: How did Fielding get to Kentucky and with whom did he arrive? Why was he being bound out? Who was Franklin Perry? Why did his older brother William remain in Virginia for several more years? Where were Fielding's parents?

The search continued focusing on Owen County, Kentucky records. Family members who were supposedly quite knowledgeable about Fielding's second marriage said that his second wife was Henrietta Shelton. Since Owen County marriage records for the period when that marriage took place were destroyed, the family tradition was accepted. A printed volume of deed abstracts for Owen County showed that Henrietta Shelton was the wife of David Shelton and that Fielding was married to their daughter Nancy. After sixty years of research, Fielding was recorded with his proper wife and not his mother-in-law.

Many genealogists who use the Genealogical Library of the LDS Church fail to realize that although that collection is by far the superior repository in the world, it does not include every record source in existence. Costs do not permit filming every volume of records in every county courthouse. There comes a point when some research problems cannot be solved in that library's collection. Such was the case in attempting to find the full identity of J. Ethington. Either a professional genealogist in the Woodford-Owen County area had to be hired or a professional genealogist familiar with the problem sent to the area to search the remaining county records. The latter is the preferable approach because it takes a considerable amount of time for another genealogist to become familiar with the research problem.

Once in Kentucky, research centered on circuit court records in Henry, Woodford, Owen, and Franklin counties. A number of significant facts surfaced. The first court case of interest involved James Ethington, the son of William, and the "Callender heirs" who were the relatives of James's mother Sarah Ann Callender. Located in the Owen County Circuit Court records, the case filed in 1805 involved a dispute that originated when the family was still in Virginia. William Ethington, Fielding's brother, was called as a witness in a Culpepper County, Virginia court. While the records provided a residence for William in Virginia, they did not shed new light on the identity of J. Ethington.

Many early Kentucky county records have been transferred to the Kentucky State Archives in Frankfort. Woodford County's early records are housed there, including county circuit court records. Among the list of packets in the circuit court records was an entry for Jeremiah Etherington vs. Johnston Malone. The packet itself had Jeremiah and Fielding Etherington vs. Johnstone Malone [sic] written on the outside. The 170-year-old record states:

> This indenture made this 21st day of April 1814 between Jeremiah Etherington infant son of Joseph Etherington, deceast [sic], and Fielding Etherington, guardian of said Jeremiah. . . .

Harold Ethington, who had been searching for J. Ethington for twenty years, found the entry. Although circumstantial in its linking of Fielding Ethington to young Jeremiah, it is a valuable clue to follow in searching for Joseph Ethington in Kentucky and Culpepper County, Virginia, to further support the circumstantial evidence in the court record.

The importance of giving close attention to those recorded in documents as witnesses and those who repeatedly appear in proximity to ancestors and their relatives cannot be emphasized enough. In this case the Ethingtons, Callenders, and Sheltons appear to have migrated together from Virginia, and while records attesting to the Ethington family may not reveal important clues, those produced by the other families may be helpful. Early frontier research requires dedication that ignores the path of least resistance and takes one into every available record source, regardless of the time and difficulty involved in conducting those searches.

CHAPTER 15

Ethnic Ancestors

There are hundreds of family traditions that include an obscure relationship to a Cherokee Indian, usually through a female line. Why Cherokee rather than Sioux, Comanche, or one of the many other tribes? One can only speculate that Cherokee ancestors were preferred because they were comparatively peaceful and much better known to midwestern frontier settlers. The Cherokee were resettled in an area that consisted of the Oklahoma and Indian Territories prior to Oklahoma statehood in 1908; however, they didn't live there alone. Thousands of whites lived on Indian land among the Cherokee, Choctaw, and Chickasaw nations. Such was rarely the case in the vast, desert reservations of New Mexico and Arizona.

Whatever the reasons, family traditions espousing Cherokee ancestry are considered true by those who reportedly possess Indian heritage. Like all other family traditions, those including an Indian ancestor must be put to the acid test of surviving documentation. Unfortunately, few prove valid. Cherokee research is interesting and there is an abundance of records to aid in sorting out the facts of family tradition. The following case study illustrates how to prove or disprove Cherokee ancestry.

RESEARCHING CHEROKEE ANCESTRY

When research began, the following information was provided by the family: Annie Lettie Bays was a full-blooded Cherokee who married an Irishman, Ephriam James Wilson, and died at age thirty-three of tuberculosis. Annie was the daughter of David Crockett Bays, the first cousin of Cherokee Chief Judge Mays. The Wilson and Bays families originated in the Carolinas and lived in Missouri and Arkansas before finally settling in Wagoner, Indian Territory. Ephriam Wilson moved his family to Texas for a short period in an effort to provide a better climate for Annie's lung condition. Annie was reportedly born in 1867.

Before rushing into Cherokee records, some preliminary census searches are necessary to get a picture of the families of interest. The 1900 U.S. Census schedules for the Oklahoma and Indian Territories were divided into two formats, one designed to enumerate the white population and another for the Indian population. Assuming that the family's information is accurate, Ephriam James Wilson's family would be found in the white population schedules and David Crocket Bays in the Indian schedules as a full-blooded Cherokee.

Ephriam J. Wilson was listed in the 1900 census soundex (phonetic index) of Texas, enumerated in the white population schedule of Montgomery County, Texas along with his seven children. The census listed him as widowed. Ephriam was born in Missouri, his father in Alabama, and his mother in Indiana. If he was an Irishman, his family had been in the United States for at least two generations. His migration pattern is outlined by the birthplaces of his children. He was in Arkansas between 1885 and 1889, then Texas between 1892 and 1894. His youngest child was born in Indian Territory in 1896.

David C. Bays was living in Wagoner, Indian Territory when the 1900 census was taken. He was enumerated with the white population, indicating that he was probably not a full-blooded Cherokee, and was living on land owned by the Creek Nation. According to the census, David C. Bays was born in March 1838 in Indiana to native Virginians. His wife, Precious Bays, was born in Illinois to natives of Kentucky and had been married to her husband for thirty-eight years. Their marriage date can be calculated as 1862.

David was born in 1838 and would have been of enlistment age during the Civil War. A search of the *Civil War Pension Application File Index* revealed that he applied for a pension in 1912 from Oklahoma. His pension declaration, obtained from the National Archives, stated that he was seventy-four when he applied on 20 May 1912 in Payne County, Oklahoma. He claimed that he enlisted in Company I, 59th Regiment, Indiana Infantry in January 1862 as a private, and that he was born 20 March 1838 in Greene County, Indiana. His physical description suggests that he had white ancestry: Height: 6 feet; Complexion: light; Eyes: blue; Hair: auburn. His postwar residences were in Illinois until 1870, Missouri until 1876, Arkansas until 1893, and Oklahoma thereafter.

His deposition to the Bureau of Pensions states that he lived in Logan County, Illinois in 1861 and returned to Greene County, Indiana about the first of December 1861 to conduct personal business. While in Indiana in January or February 1862, he went to Grosport, Owen County, Indiana to enlist in the Union Army. A few days after enlistment, he was exposed to the elements and developed pneumonia. He reportedly was granted permission to go home to be nursed by his mother in Greene County. As he never returned to his regiment, his pension application was denied.

The key information in his application is his birthplace and the fact that his mother remained there at least until 1863. The 1850 census of Greene County contains fifteen Bays families. David was living with his widowed mother in what appears to be her parents' home:

Name	Age	Sex	Occupation	Real Estate	Birthplace
Joseph Burch	70	M	Farmer	$300	North Carolina
Malinda Burch	66	F			North Carolina
Mitchell Burch	36	M	Laborer		North Carolina
Emily Bays	32	F	Widow	$400	Indiana
David Bays	13	M			Indiana
Newell Bays	11	M			Indiana
Josiah Bays	8	M			Indiana
Joshua Bays	6	M			Indiana
Tyre Bays	1	M			Indiana

A search of Greene County marriage records documents the marriage of Joshua Bays and Emily Burch on 12 May 1836 (*Marriage Book C*, page 25). Two of their children married there, including Newell Bays to Carrie Heaton on 18 September 1862 and Mitchell Bays to Anna Wilkerson on 11 July 1862.

The background information on David C. Bays and his parents was essential to research in Cherokee records. While information about David may not appear in these records, there may be something about his parents or siblings.

The Cherokee Indians originally occupied land in an area comprised of parts of what are now Kentucky, Virginia, North Carolina, South Carolina, Georgia, and Alabama, as shown in Figure 15:1. They were eventually relocated west of the Mississippi in an area designated as Indian Territory shown in Figure 15:2. The removal of the Indians was based on treaties that afforded compensation to the tribes for lands given over to the government. There were many treaty violations and claims were still unsettled in 1906, more than seventy years after the first treaty was negotiated.

An act of Congress approved on 1 July 1902 gave the U.S. Court of Claims jurisdiction over any claim arising from treaty stipulations that the Cherokee Indians had against the United States and vice versa. Three suits were brought before the Court of Claims and each was decided in favor of the Cherokees. The secretary of the interior was instructed to identify those persons of Cherokee descent entitled to a portion of the more than $1 million appropriated by Congress for use in payment of claims. Guion Miller, special agent of the Department of the Interior, was assigned to compile a roll of claimants eligible to receive compensation.

The court established that payment was to be made to all Eastern and Western Cherokees who were alive on 28 May 1906 and who could establish that they were members or descendants of members of the Eastern Cherokee Tribe at the time the treaties were made in 1835, 1836, and 1845. Claims were to be filed with Guion Miller on or before 31 August 1907. By that deadline nearly 46,000 applications were on file, representing about 90,000 individual claimants. Roughly one-third of these were entitled to a share. Miller used early

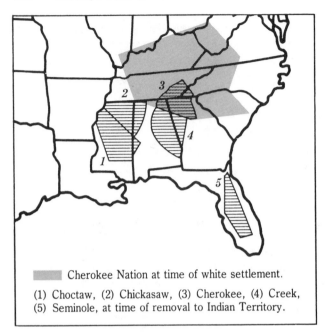

Cherokee Nation at time of white settlement.
(1) Choctaw, (2) Chickasaw, (3) Cherokee, (4) Creek, (5) Seminole, at time of removal to Indian Territory.

Figure 15:1. Locations of the Five Civilized Tribes in the South.

census lists and rolls compiled by other special agents between 1835 and 1884 to determine eligibility and create a new 1910 Eastern Cherokee Enrollment.

Congress authorized the allotment of land to the Five Civilized Tribes on 3 March 1893. Henry L. Dawes was appointed chairman of the commission organized to determine who was eligible to receive land. The Dawes Commission received over 200,000 applications for land selection. Cherokee allotments began in 1903. The applicants were required to submit documents and affidavits as proof of Cherokee citizenship.

It is important to search the Dawes Commission's Final Rolls of the Five Civilized Tribes *and* the "Guion Miller Rolls" when attempting to document Cherokee ancestry. Generally, any person of Cherokee descent will appear in both rolls, but because of the thousands of fraudulent applications received by Guion Miller, not everyone in the Guion Miller Rolls will be found in the Dawes Rolls.

David Crockett Bays applied for a share of the funds allocated by Congress to pay Cherokee claims, as did Joshua Bays, David Crockett Bays Jr., and Precious M. Turley (David Sr.'s granddaughter), and eleven other members of the Bays family. Regardless of whether an application was accepted, it contains exceptionally valuable genealogical information, and since nearly 60,000 fraudulent claims were filed, it is a good practice to check the Miller

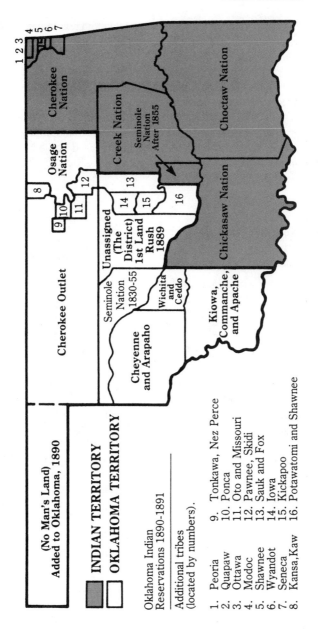

Figure 15:2. Oklahoma and Indian Territories. Based on Muriel Wright, *A Guide to the Indians of Oklahoma* (Norman: University of Oklahoma Press, l971) and John Morris, et al., *Historical Atlas of Oklahoma* (Norman: University of Oklahoma Press, 1976).

applications for any ancestor who lived in Oklahoma or Indian Territory. The following is a synopsis of the Eastern Cherokee Application #8223 filed 1 December 1906 by David Crockett Bays.

David Crockett Bays was born in 1836 in Greene County, Indiana and was seventy years old when he submitted his application as a resident of Wagoner, Indian Territory. His wife, Precious Bays, was sixty-seven years old. He stated that his father, Joshua Bays, was born in the "Virginia Cherokee District" and his mother, Emily Burch, in North Carolina. Joshua died in 1848 and Emily in 1886. His paternal grandparents were Joshua Bays and Lettie Mays. His maternal grandparents were Joseph and Mila Burch. He listed the following children of Joshua and Emily (Burch) Bays:

1. David Crockett Bays	b. 1836
2. Newell Bays	d. 1848
3. Tyre Bays	d. 1893
4. Josia Bays	d. about 1903
5. Joshua Bays	——

The children of Joshua and Lettie (Mays) Bays were:

1. Joshua	d. 1848	7. Alford	d. 1841
2. Walter	d. unknown	8. Joseph	d. 1848
3. Milly	d. 1848	9. Jackson	d. 1848
4. Clara	d. 1848	10. Polly	d. 1853
5. Betsey	d. unknown	11. James	d. 1852
6. Niecie	d. unknown		

David Crockett Bays Jr. filed two applications dated 1906 and 1907. He was born in Lamar, Barton County, Missouri. His mother was Precious Jones, the daughter of Samuel and Susan Jones. He gave a list of Samuel and Susan's children, all of whom were born in Logan County, Illinois: James, William, Precious, Anna, Elaine, Christian, Sada, and Amelia F.

Precious M. (Wilson) Turley's application was loaded with names and dates attesting to her ancestry:

Father: Ephriam James Wilson, born in Morgan County, Missouri and died 10 August 1902. Son of William R. and Margaret M. Wilson.

Mother: Anna Lettie Bays, born in Shelby County, Illinois and died 20 November 1899. Daughter of David C. and Precious Bays.

Children:
1. Ova A. Wilson	b. 1884
2. William R. Wilson	b. 1886
3. Precious M. Wilson	b. 18 Nov 1887
4. Martha A. Wilson	b. 1889

5. Anna L. Wilson	b. 1892
6. Ephriam J. Wilson	b. 1894
7. Joseph Wheeler Wilson	b. 1898

Children of David C. and Precious Bays:

1. Susan Bays	d. 1873
2. Emily Bays	d. 1864
3. Buckie J. Bays	——
4. Anna Lettie Bays	d. 1899
5. Docia M. Bays	d. 1890
6. David C. Bays Jr.	——

She stated that her grandmother [great-grandmother] Lettie Mays "was born in the Cherokee District of Virginia, she was ¼ Cherokee and our blood wasn't never denied by the Masters of Chancery Court of Muscogee, Indian Territory. Our papers were passed favorably and are now on file in Washington, D.C. Grandmother Bays' brother Samuel Mays name may be found on the roll of 1833 or 1835 or both in the State of Georgia."

There were similar applications on file with Guion Miller: Augusta Wilson, David Crockett Bays, and Bertha Tabor were each rejected because their common ancestors were not enrolled with the Cherokees in 1835, 1836, or 1845. There was no record of their having resided on Cherokee land.

The key to the Bays family's claim of Cherokee ancestry lies in the brother-sister relationship of Samuel and Lettie Mayes who were one-fourth Cherokee. Samuel is the cousin who the Bays family believed to have been a Cherokee tribal judge. Joshua Bays Jr. died in 1848. His wife Emily was thirty-two years old in 1850, placing her birth around 1818. Her husband's birth is estimated to have occurred about 1815 to 1818. Assuming that Joshua Bays Sr. and Lettie Mays were a minimum of eighteen years old when Joshua Jr. was born, their birthdates are calculated as between 1797 and 1800. These calculations are important in the analysis of the Mayes family.

The history of the Mayes family is well established. Samuel Houston Mayes was chief of the Cherokee Nation from 1885 to 1899. His older brother, Joel Bryan Mayes, was judge of the Cherokee Nation's Supreme Court and Chief of the Cherokees from 1887 to 1891.

Samuel and Joel are the sons of Samuel Mayes (b. 1803), a white man from Tennessee, and Nancy Adair, born 7 October 1808 in Georgia and died 18 March 1876 in Indian Territory. Nancy was part Cherokee, and when the tribe moved from Georgia to Indian Territory, she and her husband went with them. Based on Samuel Mayes's birthdate, he was born in the same generation as Lettie Mays. Additionally, he was a white man and the son of Joseph and Charlotte (Samuel) Mayes. Their ancestry is traced to William Mease who was born in

1574 in England. Lettie could not have been the daughter of Samuel and Nancy (Adair) Mayes because she was probably a few years older than Samuel. Lettie may have been born in what once was the Virginia Cherokee District, and she may have been related to Samuel Mayes whose ancestors were from Virginia, but she definitely was not his daughter. Samuel had only one daughter, named Rachel.

The original claim that David C. and Precious Bays were full-blooded Cherokees has no basis in fact. First, there is David's physical description in his pension file. His coloring, hair, and eyes did not reflect even a little influence of Indian blood. Then there is the fact that he was not enumerated in the Indian schedules of the 1900 census. Finally, his family, and that of his grandparents, were enumerated in the 1850 and 1860 U.S. Census schedules which did not include Indians.

There was no mention of David C. Bays or any of his ancestors in any Cherokee roll or census, nor did those records list any of Precious Jones's ancestors. Thus, it is concluded that this family tradition, like so many others, had no basis in fact.

SUGGESTED READING

Carpenter, Cecelia S. *How to Research American Indian Bloodlines: A Manual on Indian Genealogical Research*. South Prairie, Wash.: Meico Associates, 1984.

Clark, Dick. *Cherokee Ancestor Research*. Modesto, Calif.: Holland Printing Company, 1979.

Hill, Edward E. *Guide to Records in the National Archives Relating to American Indians*. Washington, D.C.: NARS, 1981.

TRACING SLAVE ANCESTRY

Whether ancestors were free or slave, black Americans should initially approach tracing their ancestry just as any other American research problem is begun. Discovering black ancestors back to the end of the Civil War can be accomplished without encountering an extraordinary number of obstacles. Chapter 8 should be consulted first, as the same types of record sources apply. If, however, the family descends from slaves (as ninety percent do), information predating 1865 becomes more difficult to find.

Slave research requires a broad understanding of black American history and the country's slave system. Slave families were considered the personal property of their owners and as such were without legal rights. They were prohibited from owning real or personal property and do not appear in land records except as named or unnamed slaves in records pertaining to their owners.

The most effective approach to identifying slave ancestors is to identify their owners and the plantations at which they worked. Research then focuses upon the owner's family and the records it produced, as well as the slave family itself. Since eighty-five percent of America's black population descends from at least one white ancestor, tracing the slave owner's family sometimes adds generations to a lineage. Slavery developed into a paternalistic system in which slaves often considered themselves an extension of the owner's family. Not all slave owners fit the stereotypical characters depicted in movies and novels. Many were caring individuals who adequately provided for the religious, cultural, and familial needs of their slaves as well as the necessities of food, clothing, and shelter. Evidence of their humane approach to slavery was seen at the end of the war when they deeded land to their slaves.

This system of paternalism eventually led to slavery's demise. Slaves began to regard themselves as people with rights, especially a right to be free. When the Civil War ended, many blacks experienced emotional upheaval because of bonds to their former owner's family on the one hand and a desire to take advantage of freedom on the other. Few left the area where they worked as slaves and many indentured themselves to their former owners. The Freedman's Bureau records include labor contracts specifying the terms of the indenture and the names of each person bound by the contract.

The following research cameo shows you how to identify the slave family's owner and the plantation where they worked.[1] The subjects of the study are ancestors of Quincy Jones. Though incomplete, this study was chosen because it is a classic example of how to identify a slave family's owner and the plantation where they lived and worked prior to and after Emancipation.

Henry Dickson and David Wells were among thousands of slaves freed in Warren County, Mississippi. They were both enumerated in the 1870 U.S. Census of Bovina Precinct, Warren County, Mississippi:

Name	Age	Occupation	Birthplace
Henry Dickson	60	Farm Hand	Maryland
Minerva Dickson	38	"	Mississippi
Priscilla Dickson	22	"	"
Betsy Dickson	20	"	"
Cordelia Dickson	12	"	"
Rebecca Ransabug	25	"	"
Minerva Ransabug	6		"
Victoria Ransabug	4		"
No Name Ransabug	5/12		"
Henry Stocking	5/12		"

1. Quincy Jones graciously agreed to sharing the research Lineages, Inc. conducted for him. Gordon L. Remington, Kendall H. Williams, and Johni Cerny worked on the early segments of the project and research still continues.

Name	Age	Occupation	Birthplace
David Wells	40	Farm Hand	Virginia
Dorcas Wells	47	"	Mississippi
Nelson Wells	18	"	"
Caroline Wells	16	"	"
Gabe Wells	10	"	"
Lucinda Wells	7		"
Samuel Wells	3		"
Wm. Wells	20	"	"
Sopha Wells	17	"	"

When research began, the source of their surnames was unknown. Some slaves took surnames before the Civil War ended, while others waited until they began establishing themselves as free citizens. Many slaves took the surname of their last owner or their father who might have been a white slave owner or overseer, a deceased slave, or a slave sold to another owner several years prior to the Emancipation. Hundreds of slave families took the name of a prominent American, a local political figure, or the given name of the father of the family. It wasn't uncommon for freed slaves to be known by several surnames, making a final choice years after the Emancipation.

The first step in determining the source of the Dickson and Wells family surnames was to assume that they took the name of their last slave owner and test that supposition. Most black families were too poor or too frightened to move away from the plantation where they worked as slaves. Assuming that Henry Dickson and Davy Wells were among those who remained in Bovina Precinct after the war, attempts were made to identify all the Dickson and Wells families in the area who owned slaves.

Slaves were not enumerated in the 1850 or 1860 U.S. censuses; however, special slave schedules were compiled during those census years, listing the slave owner and the sex, age, and color of each slave, but no name. Slave schedules were not indexed and must be searched page by page. Surprisingly, no Dickson or Wells slaveholders were found in the Bovina Precinct area in 1850 or 1860, thus casting doubt on the premise that Henry Dickson and Davy Wells took the surnames of their owners at war's end.

Because many families chose to stay on or near the plantations where they served as slaves, the 1870 census of Bovina Precinct was searched again to identify the major white landowners living closest to Henry Dickson and David Wells.

There were sixty-five major landowners (possessing land worth more than $1,000) living in the precinct. The owner closest to David Wells was Hal P. Noland who owned a plantation valued at $10,000. Hal's immediate neighbor was Ellen Batchelor who owned land valued at $4,000. Family tradition says the Wells family worked for the Batchelors after the Civil War; however, the

Noland family was investigated first due to closer proximity. Estate and land records produced by the Noland family were searched to see if there was mention of the Dickson or Wells family.

There were only two wills on record for the Noland family prior to the end of the war, a period when slaves would be listed as property of an estate. Only Pearce Noland's will, proven in court in 1857, listed any slaves:

> In the Name of Almighty God, Amen. I Pearce Noland Being weak in body but of sound mind and perfect memory make this my last will and Testament hereby revoking all others made by my hand before; *Item 1st,* I give and bequeath unto my Son George D. Noland the sum of one hundred Dollars in addition to what I have heretofore given him and his heirs forever. *Item 2nd,* I give and bequeath to my daughter Eliza [sic] D. Batchelor one hundred Dollars to her and her heirs forever, in addition to what I have heretofore given her. *Item 3rd,* I give and bequeath to my son [name illegible] one hundred Dollars to him and his heirs forever. *Item 4th,* I give and bequeath to my son Avery Noland the Sum of one hundred Dollars to him and his heirs forever in addition to what I have heretofore given him. *Item 5th,* I give and bequeath to my son Pearce Noland one hundred Dollars to him and his heirs forever in addition to what I have heretofore given him. *Item 6th,* I give and bequeath to my daughter Elizabeth Norwood eight thousand Dollars in cash to be paid by my executor, herein named. *Item 7th,* I will and bequeath that my Negroes and Stock of every description together with all my personal property on the place I now reside be kept together until all my lawful debts are paid and then I desire that there shall be a division of said property of every description both real and personal and that my wife Elizabeth Noland shall have her dower set apart in the land, Plantation known by the name of "Sligo," and that my said wife shall have twenty-five Negroes set apart by Families. *Item 8th,* I then give and bequeath unto my two sons, T. V. Noland and Henry Noland all the balance of said tract of land to be equally divided between them at the time herein before named. The said tract of land lying North of Whites Creek in the Robb Field until it strikes the sectional line between Sections 18 and 19 then West to Markham's line including all the land down in Warren County. *Item 9th,* I further give and bequeath unto T. V. Noland and Henry Noland my two sons all the balance of my Negroes on said place to be equally divided between them, and it is my desire that three Negroes (to wit): Warren, Sandy, and Jenny shall be allotted to my Son Henry Noland at their appraised value. *Item 10th,* I give and bequeath to my wife Elizabeth Noland my Riding Carriage and gear. *Item 11th,* I give and bequeath to my Son Henry Noland a Negro Boy named Lorenzo who is now learning the Blacksmith Trade. *Item 12th,* it is my will and desire that all the balance of my property of every description including stock of all Sorts, Farming utensils together with everything else be equally divided between my wife

Elizabeth Noland and my two sons T. V. Noland and Henry Noland. *Item 13th,* I hereby appoint my son T. V. Noland the Sole Executor of my last will and Testament. The 31st day of Jan'y 1857

Pearce Noland

Analysis: Pearce Noland doesn't mention all of his slaves by name but his will suggests that he owned a large number of slaves to be divided between his wife and two of his sons, T. V. and Henry Noland. He names "Sligo" as his plantation and Eliza D. Batchelor (actually Ellen D. Batchelor) as his daughter, thus linking the Nolands to the family David Wells worked for after the war. He provides a glimpse of his caring attitude toward his slaves when he specifies that they are to be "set apart by Families."

The will was only one of many estate documents and is followed in probate records by one or more entries attesting to how the estate was settled or divided. Pearce Noland's estate was not divided among his heirs until February 1862, more than a year after Mississippi left the Union and four years after Pearce Noland's wife died. The division of his property listed the following slaves in the first two lots:

Slave	Value
Davy Wells	$ 1,000
Dorcas	600
Curry	900
Davy Wells Jr.	750
Bill	700
Nelson	600
Carolina	350
John	200
Gabe	75
Jack	150

Analysis: A comparison of the names listed above with Davy Wells's family as it appeared in the 1870 census proves the same family is represented in both documents with several previously unidentified children noted in the estate division. It is highly unusual for a slave family to have a surname. Most slave owners forbade the use of surnames to prevent family unity, thus making the sale of one slave family member less troublesome. Judging by Pearce Noland's desire that his slave families be kept together and their use of surnames, he obviously was intelligent enough to know that a name had little to do with the effects of having a family member sold.

Pearce Noland's estate papers contained an unusual surprise when the second lot of slaves was found to contain Henry Dickson's family:

Slave	Value
Henry Dickson	$ 700
Minerva	500
Rebecca	900
Madison	800
Priscilla	700
Betsy	650
Cordelia	225
Robert	100
Sally	100

Analysis: Again a comparison was made to the 1870 census to make sure the same Dickson family was represented in both records, and again previously unidentified children were noted in the estate record. Rebecca Ransabug, who is listed in Henry's 1870 household, is presumed to be his daughter, Rebecca, who is also listed in the division of Pearce Noland's estate.

Knowing who owned the Dickson and Wells families, research concentrated on Pearce Noland's family to learn how Quincy Jones's ancestors lived and how Noland acquired them. According to the 1860 Slave Schedule of Warren County, Mississippi, the Noland and Batchelor families owned 240 slaves. They may have acquired them by purchase, deed, marriage, or inheritance. Thus far, research was accomplished by examining microfilm copies of Warren County records. Besides this count, they also provided a sketch of Henry P. (Hal) Noland which stated that Pearce Noland arrived in Mississippi when he was thirteen years old—about 1803. Pearce, who descended from a Revolutionary War soldier, first served as judge of the Jefferson County, Mississippi county court in the 1820s. Since he was a prominent man and accustomed to maintaining court records, it was assumed that he kept personal and financial records, including plantation records and diaries for "Sligo" that might still exist.

Such plantation records and personal diaries of plantation owners are not easy to locate. Some have been placed in local libraries, archives, or museums, while others remain in the custody of family members. They can be located through correspondence, by hiring a genealogist in the area to track them down, or by personal visit. Corresponding for information is least desirable because people will usually address your specific questions and not suggest where the records might be found. Hiring a genealogist is more acceptable providing his or her credentials are adequate for tracing black ancestry. The best approach is to visit the area in person. The one most familiar with the family and the research already accomplished will be sensitive to comments made during personal interviews that a person less familiar with the research problem will ignore.

While the principal goal of Quincy Jones's research was to extend his lineage, there was also the goal of compiling his family history. The only way to gather information about how his ancestors lived as slaves was to investigate thoroughly the Noland family in Warren County and hope clues to his ancestors' origins surfaced in the process. A professional genealogist went to Warren County to accomplish those goals by searching records not microfilmed by the Genealogical Library of the LDS Church and by interviewing descendants and neighbors of the Noland, Wells, and Dickson families still living in the area.

There were a few descendants of Judge Noland still living in Bovina Precinct. A great-grandson of Hal P. Noland reported that the mansion house at "Sligo" burned around the turn of the century and nearly all of the plantation diaries and records were destroyed. Portraits of Judge Noland and his wife were salvaged and now hang in the Old Court House Museum in Vicksburg, Mississippi. Two letters written by Judge Noland and a slave bill of sale are housed at the Smithsonian Institute in Washington, D.C. None of those documents mention the Wells or Dickson families.

Descendants of Henry Dickson reported that many of their family members were buried at "Sligo," and the burial grounds there were canvassed to locate their graves. "Sligo" no longer resembles its nineteenth-century layout. All of the original buildings are gone and the burial grounds are overgrown with vegetation. Grave markers for slaves were made of wood and were unreadable after being exposed to the elements for more than a century. Only stone markers placed there by family members after they had established themselves were legible. They were few in number and did not pertain to Quincy Jones's ancestors.

A history of St. Alban's Protestant Episcopal Church at Bovina disclosed that, " . . . three weeks after Secession Conference [4 February 1861] a large number of Negro slaves belonging to the Noland, Batchelor, and Downs families presented themselves at St. Alban's for confirmation by the Bishop." These slaves continued to attend church with white planters and their families and were listed in the parish register as regular communicants. They greatly outnumbered the white membership until St. Alban's became a segregated church at the end of the Civil War.

The Warren County Courthouse contained additional records attesting to the settlement of Judge Noland's estate. The inventory of his personal property listed his slaves in family groups, stating the age and appraised value of each. The aggregate value of Judge Noland's slaves was $98,650, a staggering sum when you know that a dollar in 1862 would be equal to about twenty dollars today.

	Name	Age	Value
Negro man	Dixon	40	$ 1,150
" woman	Manerva	35	500
" boy	Madison	10	700
" girl	Rebecca	13	700
" girl	Lucilla	8	500
" girl	Betsy	6	300

Negro	man	Davy	25	1,300
"	woman	Dorcas	30	1,150
		+ 5 mo. child		
"	girl	Creecy	15	1,000
"	boy	Davy Jr.	9	650
"	boy	Bill	6	450
"	boy	Nelson	5	350

Judge Noland owned 130 slaves at the time of his death. Those listed above were members of the Dickson and Wells families. There are age discrepancies between this document and the 1870 census; however, searches of later census enumerations indicate that the ages listed in the estate inventory are incorrect. Additionally, a number of each family's children are not listed in the inventory, indicating that it is incomplete or the family didn't follow Judge Noland's wishes and sold some of the slaves in incomplete family units.

With the destruction of "Sligo" plantation records, no clues remain to the exact origins of the Dickson and Wells families. Since his wife, Elizabeth Galtny, was from Adams County, Mississippi, Judge Noland possibly acquired the families from his father-in-law's estate. Two wills on file in Adams County for the Galtny family listed a total of seventy-seven slaves – but none have names resembling those of Pearce Noland's slaves.

Locating bills of sale for slaves is also difficult. Some are listed in county property records, yet most are not and will be noted in records kept by other plantation owners or in the logs of slave trade companies. Judge Noland only recorded three slave purchases in Warren County, Mississippi property records and none mentioned members of the Dickson or Wells family.

The question still remains how and where Judge Noland acquired the Dickson and Wells families. That they had surnames other than Noland suggests they were previously owned by Dickson and Wells families. The 1850 U.S. Census Index of Mississippi provided the following breakdown of entries for those surnames in the area close to Judge Noland's residence:

John Wells, Warren County	David Dixon, Warren County
Archibald Wells, Hinds County	Joseph M. Dixon, Warren County
Banister Wells, Hinds County	Alfred Dixon, Hinds County
Edward Wells, Hinds County	Church Dixon, Jefferson County
George Wells, Hinds County	Philip Dixon, Jefferson County
John J. Wells, Hinds County	Roger Dixon, Jefferson County
Miles Wells, Hinds County	
Thomas Wells, Hinds County	
Wm. M. Wells, Hinds County	

The probate records of each of the counties were carefully examined and only Roger Dixon's estate was located. He owned slaves but none was named Henry or Minerva.

Descendants of Pearce Noland have been contacted by historians at Rice University who are studying the judge's life. The judge is said to have founded Oakland College which later became Alcorn A & M, a black college. People in the Bovina area also knew of a Mr. Watson, the overseer of "Sligo" when it burned. They thought that he may have preserved the records and that his descendants might still have them.

Research Plan: Progress in tracing early slave generations is time consuming, requiring greater than usual devotion over a much longer period of time. Unlike records employed to trace white Americans, those used to trace slave ancestry are widely scattered and generally unindexed. Research now becomes a process of following up on existing clues and uncovering others. Records produced by each Wells and Dickson resident of Warren, Hinds, and Jefferson counties between 1820 and 1857 should be searched for mention of either family. This includes determining the names and locations of each plantation owned and the whereabouts of plantation records. Rice University and Alcorn A & M College should be contacted to determine the extent of their collection of Judge Noland's records. The Freedman's Bureau records should also be searched and efforts to locate commercial slave trade company records should begin.[2]

SUGGESTED READING

Rose, James and Eichholz, Alice. *Black Genesis*. Detroit: Gale Research Co., 1978.

---

2. Johni Cerny and Leonard Smith, manager of the musical group Earth, Wind and Fire, have cofounded the Registry of Black American Ancestry, a public charity designed to locate, computerize, and preserve records needed to trace slave ancestry. The Registry has the backing of blacks in entertainment, sports, business, and government. An index to the Freedman's Bureau records, the Registry's first major project, is due to be completed late in 1986. The public may contribute copies of their family histories and genealogies to the Registry of Black American Ancestry Library by mailing them to P.O. Box 417, Salt Lake City, Utah 84110.

CHAPTER 16

Immigrant Ancestors

G ermans began arriving in this country in large numbers midway through the eighteenth century when groups of immigrants from the Palatinate settled in Pennsylvania. The flow of German immigrants remained steady until late in the nineteenth century. Once fertile lands in Pennsylvania became scarce and expensive, German immigrants began settling in the central and northern Midwest. There were some sizeable German settlements in Texas, but most immigrants preferred to live in areas that most resembled the landscape they were accustomed to in Germany. Some came to America and formed groups that settled entire towns on property purchased from land companies.

Americans of German descent trace their ancestry back to the immigrant by searching the same record sources used to trace any American lineage. Once the German immigrant ancestor is identified, the real challenge begins. As Germany did not exist as a unified nation for most of the nineteenth century, births, marriages, and deaths were not registered on a national level. Records of those types were maintained by local towns and counties (*Kreise*) or by the Catholic and Lutheran parishes. There is no comprehensive index to the hundreds of civil and church records, thus the exact birthplace or residence of a German immigrant must be determined before research can begin in those records. German residence or birthplace is often determined by carefully searching records on this side of the Atlantic.

GERMAN IMMIGRANT ANCESTORS

The following study consists of a research report compiled for Richard P. Oelrich and Gwendolyn Oelrich Brimhall. Their paternal ancestors were German immigrants who arrived in the United States between 1865 and 1894 and settled in Custer County, Colorado. The research conducted illustrates only one approach to determining the ancestral home of immigrant German ancestors who arrived during that period.

PAUL CHRISTIAN OELRICH AND AUGUSTA THEEL, PATERNAL GREAT-GRANDPARENTS

When the 1900 U.S. Census was taken, Christian Oelrich was living in Custer County, Colorado on a farm adjacent to Fritz Erps's property:

Dwelling Number	Name		Mo	Year	Age	Birthplace
#293	Christian Oelrich	Head	May	1843	57	Germany
	Augusta Oelrich	Wife	Dec	1845	54	Germany
	Theodore Oelrich	Son	Mar	1880	20	Colorado
	Otto Oelrich	Son	Apr	1884	16	Colorado
	Laura Oelrich	Dau	Apr	1886	14	Colorado
	Minnie Oelrich	Dau	Jul	1888	11	Colorado

According to the census, Christian and Augusta were born in Germany. They had been married thirty-two years when the census was taken, placing their marriage date between 1867 and 1868. Augusta had given birth to ten children, all still living in 1900. Some of the older children were married and living in the Westcliffe, Colorado area:

#289	Herman Oelrich	Serv	Mar	1875	25	Colorado
#271	Richard Oelrich	Labr	Aug	1875	24	Colorado
#291	Fred Voss	Head	Jan	1861	39	Germany
	Emma Voss	Wife	Sept	1871	28	Colorado

The census also revealed that Christian Oelrich arrived in the United States in 1865 and Augusta in 1866, indicating they probably married in this country.

In 1880, the family was living in the West Mountain Valley area of Custer County when the census was taken:

Dwelling Number	Name	Relationship to Head	Age	Birthplace
#71	Christian Oelrich		37	Prussia
	Augusta Oelrich	Wife	34	Prussia
	Paul Oelrich	Son	11	Illinois
	Emma Oelrich	Dau	9	Colorado
	Richard Oelrich	Son	7	Colorado
	Harmand Oelrich	Son	6	Colorado
	Augusta Oelrich	Dau	4	Colorado
	Albertina Oelrich	Dau	2	Colorado
	Theodore Oelrich	Son	3/12	Colorado

This census presents a slightly different picture of the family's movements. Paul Oelrich's birthplace was listed as Colorado in 1900 and the above census gave his birthplace as Illinois, indicating that his parents did not go directly to Colorado upon entering the country. It appears that if Christian Oelrich entered the country in 1865, he may have lived in Illinois for four or five years.

Otto Paul Oelrich married Ella Sophia Erps, who stated after Otto's death that his father had come from "Holstein" as had her parents. "Holstein" is actually Schleswig-Holstein, a German principality bordering Denmark. Having knowledge of only the state or principality a German immigrant is from is insufficient, and research should focus on determining exactly where Christian Oelrich was born and raised in Schleswig-Holstein.

The first approach taken was to obtain Christian and Augusta Oelrich's death certificates from the State of Colorado, as well as those of their children. Death records were also obtained from Custer County. Christian Oelrich died 26 January 1913 at Westcliffe, Custer County, Colorado from internal hemorrhaging. His death certificate said that he was born 13 May 1844 in Germany, but his parents' names were not listed. Augusta Theel, his wife, provided the information recorded on the death certificate. While she did not know his parents' names, she did state that they were born in Germany.

Augusta Theel Oelrich died 11 January 1921 at Graves Hospital in Cañon City, Fremont County, Colorado from a heart attack. Her son Otto provided the information on her death record. He did not know her birthdate, birthplace, or parents' names. He stated that she and her parents were born in Germany. It is not unusual to find needed information about parents and birthplaces missing on death records of immigrants. Even though vital information is sometimes missing, death records must be obtained and checked on the chance that the information might be there.

Richard August Oelrich died 14 November 1946 at Westcliffe. Born 3 August 1873 in Custer County, Colorado, he apparently never married as he was listed as "single." The facts recorded on his death certificate were provided from Custer County welfare records. Only his father's name and country of birth were listed on the document—still no exact birth location.

When obituaries for Christian and Augusta were not found in local papers, research finally turned to the Hamburg Passenger Lists, lists containing the names of individuals recorded in the passenger lists of ships leaving Hamburg. Christian Oelrich was listed in the index for 1865 and the passenger list revealed that he sailed for New York on the ship *Oder*:

#211 Oelrich, Christian from Elpersbüttel, Holstein, age 22, farmer.

Christian apparently emigrated with a large group from Holstein but without any other family members, as none are mentioned in the passenger lists. There is no indication of how long Christian remained in New York, but he was in Chicago by 1869 when his son, Paul, was born. If Christian married in Chicago, record of it was destroyed in the great Chicago fire. Shortly after his son's birth, Christian's family joined a colony of Germans led by Carl Wulstein, Theodore Hanlein, and Rudolph Jeske to pioneer a settlement in Custer County, Colorado. The German colony of sixty-five families arrived in Custer County on 20 March 1870. County historians note that the group traveled by rail to Denver and then by mule train to Custer County. There were problems from the beginning. Some felt that the lack of social order, religious development, and financial regulation caused the demise of the colony. A government official confiscated the lumber and shingles being shipped to the pioneers creating hardships for everyone. The colony broke apart, carved out their own ranches, and lived in log houses until they could afford more lumber.

The colony wrote to the Lutheran Synod in 1871 to request a minister for the community. Rev. J. Hilgendorfer arrived by 17 November 1872 and started the Lutheran Church at a site near the Ogreske ranch. The Oelrichs contributed to the building of the Hope Evangelical Lutheran Church at Westcliffe in 1917, their involvement suggesting they were Evangelical Lutherans in Germany and that Christian Oelrich's birth and parentage could be recorded in Lutheran church records in Elpersbüttel.

The Genealogical Library of the LDS Church has microfilmed records in Germany extensively; however, Schleswig-Holstein has declined to have their civil and church records filmed. The only records available for Elpersbüttel in Salt Lake City were census enumerations for 1840 and 1845. Accordingly, Christian Oelrich, born 13 May 1843, would have been listed in the 1845 census. There were two Oelrich families with male children between one and two years living in Elpersbüttel and vicinity when the census was taken:

Elpersbüttel, Meldorf, Holstein, 1 February 1845

#46	Carl Oelrich	age 26 born Canzelei
	Wiebke Johannsen	age 26 born Elpersbüttel
	Paul Oelrich	age 2 born Elpersbüttel

Gudendorf, Meldorf, Holstein

	Paul Christian Oelrich	age 35 born Baskt
	Anna Catharina Oelrich	age 37 born Meldorf
	Elsse Maria Oelrich	age 6 born Gudendorf
	Margaretha Christine Oelrich	age 5 born Gudendorf
	An infant son Oelrich	age 1 born Gudendorf
	Julianne Christine Oelrich	age 20 sister-in-law
	Henrietta Margaretha Oelrich	age 14 sister-in-law

The only means of determining whether Christian Oelrich was related to one of these families was to write to the parish now serving Elpersbüttel located at Meldorf.

Carl Theodor Oelrich was born 6 August 1818. He was a carpenter in Elpersbüttel and married Anje Catharine Wiebje Jansen. Three children were born to the couple before Anje died:

1. Paul Christian, born 13 May 1840 – moved to America.

2. Anna, born 28 Jan 1843 – moved to America.
3. Gustav, born 26 March 1846 – moved to America.

Carl Theodor married a second time to Anna Elsbea Hennings and had four more children with her. The following record was compiled from earlier church records at the time of Carl Theodor's death on 8 April 1891:

1. Juliane Elsbea Margaretha, born 2 May 1855 – living in Elpersbüttel.
2. Auguste Magdalene, born 17 January 1852, married Heinrich Meyer and lives in Elpersbüttel.
3. Weilhelm Friedrich, born 29 April 1861, married Dora Reimers.
4. Otto Ferdinand, born 3 May 1867 – lives in Hamburg.

Going back over all of the material gathered then, discrepancies in Paul Christian Oelrich's birthdate are found:

1900 U.S. Census – May 1843
Death record and tombstone – 13 May 1844
1880 U.S. Census – 1843
1845 Census of Elpersbüttel – 1843
Meldorf Parish Register – 13 May 1840

The record given the most credibility is usually the parish register; however, in this instance, Paul Christian's birth entry was recorded at the time of Carl Theodor's death about fifty years afterwards. Correspondence has been sent to clarify the discrepancy, but remembering how discrepancies are handled (see Chapter 5), it is almost certain that the 1840 birthdate in the Meldorf Parish Register is incorrect. The preponderance of evidence suggests that he was born 13 May 1843.

JOHN JACOB ERPS AND ANNA KATHARINE TIMM, PATERNAL GREAT-GRANDPARENTS

According to Fritz Erps, he was named after his father's older brother who lived in Westcliffe with his large family. There was a Fritz Erps living on the ranch adjacent to Christian and Augusta Oelrich when the 1900 census was taken. That same Fritz and his wife, Katherine, were both born in 1848 in Germany. John Jacob Erps lived a short distance from Fritz and Christian at the time of the 1900 census:

Dwelling Number	Name		Mo	Year	Age	Birthplace
#305	John Erps	Head	Aug	1853	46	Germany
	Timm Erps	Wife	Jan	1861	39	Germany
	Albert Erps	Son	Jun	1884	15	Colorado

Louisa Erps	Dau	Feb	1886	14	Colorado
Ernest Erps	Son	Jan	1889	11	Colorado
John Erps	Son	Mar	1890	9	Colorado
Louis Erps	Son	May	1892	8	Colorado
Ella Erps	Dau	Aug	1894	3	Colorado
Emma Erps	Dau	Jul	1898	1	Colorado

John and Anna Timm Erps had been married sixteen years when the census was taken. Anna had given birth to nine children, seven of whom were still living in 1900. Both John and Anna arrived in the United States in 1883, indicating that they were probably married prior to emigrating.

According to John Jacob Erps's death record, he died 14 August 1931 from pneumonia. His birthdate was listed as 2 August 1853. His wife informed authorities that his father was John Erps and his mother a Menzer, both born in Germany. Anna Katharine Erps's death certificate stated that she died 24 September 1942 at Silver Cliff, Custer County, Colorado as did her husband. Her father was listed only as Tim. Fritz Erps stated that Anna's mother also lived in Custer County and had been married several times. She reportedly died as Louise Pankow in 1937 though no record of her death could be located.

John Jacob Erps's naturalization record indicated that he was born in Holstein. His will, dated 14 September 1941, named only a few of his children and his wife: Anna Erps, wife; Anna Blair, daughter; John Erps, son; Louis Erps, son; Emma Jagow, daughter; and Fritz Erps, son.

Neither John Jacob Erps nor his wife was listed in the Hamburg Passenger Lists, but his brother Fritz Erps and his family were listed. They sailed on the ship *Normannie* on 26 April 1894 from Hamburg to New York. This family was studied to facilitate research in German records.

1900 U.S. Census, Custer County				Ship *Normannie* Passenger List		
Erps, Fritz			1848	Erps, Fritz	age 46	(1848)
Erps, Katharine	Feb		1848	Erps, Catha	age 46	(1848)
Erps, Freda	Feb		1883	Erps, Johann	age 20	(1874)
Erps, Fritz	Jun		1884	Erps, Marie	age 19	(1875)
Erps, Wilhelm	Aug		1886	Erps, Margr.	age 17	(1878)
Erps, Emil	Mar		1887	Erps, Peter	age 14	(1880)
Erps, George	May		1888	Erps, Catha	age 13	(1881)
Erps, Rudolph	Oct		1889	Erps, Elfrieda	age 11	(1883)
Erps, Carl	Jul		1890	Erps, Fritz	age 10	(1884)
Erps, Heinrich	Dec		1891	Erps, Wilhelm	age 8	(1886)
				Erps, Emil	age 7	(1887)
				Erps, Georg	age 6	(1888)
				Erps, Rudolf	age 5	(1889)
				Erps, Carl	age 3	(1890)
				Erps, Wilm	age 4m	(1893)

These entries are obviously for the same family, and according to the Hamburg Passenger Lists they boarded in Löhe, Holstein, a town located a few kilometers north of Elpersbüttel in the Hemmingstedt District. The 1845 census of Löhe, Hemmingstedt, Holstein listed only one Johann Jacob Erps:

#1	Erps, Johann Jacob	age 29	born Reinsbüttel
			(Wesselburener)
	Seider, Christine	age 27	born Rickelshof
	Weibke Catharina		
	Erps, Anna Maria	age 3	born Rickelshof
	Erps, Johann Peter	age 2	born Löhe

The 1840 census of Rickelshof, Hemmingstedt, Holstein listed Christine Catharine Seider as a child in her parents' home:

#5	Seider, Peter	age 61
	Asmus, Anna Catharina	age 65
	Seider, Christine Catharina	age 22
	Seider, Antje	age 14

While these families were the only candidates for John Jacob Erps's parents, there is no linking evidence in American records except the name of John Jacob Erps Sr. on his namesake's death certificate. The only means of verifying the suggested relationship was through correspondence with the Evangelical Lutheran parish in Löhe. The link between John Jacob and Fritz Erps needed to be proven by writing to Löhe, Schleswig-Holstein and requesting searches of the Evangelical Lutheran Church registers. They forwarded the following information:

Johann Jacob Erps, day laborer in Löhe, illegitimate son of Anna Maria Eitter of Barlt and the estranged father Johann Erps of Norddrick (born in Kinsbüttel in 1816) and his bride Christiana Wiebke Catharina Seider, Konf. 33/18, age 23, the legitimate daughter of Peter Seider, laborer in Ridelshast and his wife Anna Catharina neé Ausmus, were married after banns were published on the 19th, 20th, and 21st Sundays after trinity in this church were proclaimed married this 28th Day of November 1841.

Johann Peter Friedrich, legitimate son of Johann Jacob Erps, day laborer, and his wife Christiana Wiebke Catharina neé Seider was born 27 September 1843 and baptized 26 December 1843. Godparents: Friedrich Danielsen of Heide, Peter Ehlers of Löhe, and Anna Hendrichs of Ridelshast, Hemmingstedt, 2 June 1844 by Schutt.

Anna Maria, legitimate daughter of Johann Jacob Erps, laborer, and his wife Christiana Wiebke Catharina, born Seider, was born 18 February 1845 in Ridelshast. Godparents: Anna Elsebea Drenssen, Anna Catharina Seider, Maria Catharina Dierds.

Johann Jacob, legitimate son of Johann Jacob Erps, laborer in Löhe, and Christiana Wiebke Catharina neé Seider, was born 2 August 1853 in Löhe. Godparents: Christofer Bartols, schoolmaster in Löhe, Johann Friedrich Fid, Peter Seider of Löhe.

Wiebke Catharina Margaretha, legitimate daughter of Johann Jacob Erps of Löhe and his wife Christiana Wiebke Catharina neé Seider, (thirty-eight years old) was born 2 May 1856 in Löhe. Godparents: Johanna Margaretha Bramner neé Hansen of Heide, Wiebke Drenssen neé Schröder in Löhe, Anna Kraus, born Melshirt.

Fritz Erps was not listed in the records sent by the parish in Löhe. He may have been born elsewhere or was overlooked when the register was searched. This is a classic example of one piece of family tradition leading to the extension of a lineage.

Not all German immigrant research problems are so easily solved. Most require years of digging into every conceivable record as is the case with the wives of Paul Christian Oelrich and John Jacob Erps. Research continues today, and with American sources exhausted, a search of census records is needed for the region in Schleswig-Holstein where their husbands were born. This search is suggested by the fact that all of the Custer County settlers from Germany married men or women from that region in Schleswig-Holstein.

If your ancestors arrived from Germany after 1900, consult naturalization and immigration records as shown in the study on eastern European immigrant ancestors. If they arrived during an early period, consult the many printed volumes on immigrant ancestors listed in *The Source*, pp. 502-04. Obituary notices are excellent sources of information about an immigrant ancestor's birthplace, as are biographical sections of county and local histories. Remember that German immigrants usually migrated together and formed colonies of settlement. If you cannot find the information you need about your ancestors look closely at their neighbors. They may produce the clues you need to bridge the Atlantic.

EASTERN EUROPEAN ANCESTORS

Nemšova, Trenčin, Czechoslovakia is a small village in the province of Slovakia not far from the village of Trenčianska Tepla. My paternal grandparents were born in those villages to poor peasant families. Ján Čierny and his wife Anna Solik were the parents of six children, including my grandfather who was named after his father. They owned a small parcel of farm land in Trenčianska Tepla just sufficient for supporting a family of eight. As their children grew toward adulthood, the Čiernys became painfully aware that their land would never provide enough to maintain the upcoming generation.

Anton and Maria, the oldest children, married in Trenčianska Tepla. Anton and his brother-in-law saw only a limited future there and moved to America, settling in Chicago. Anton's younger brother, Ján, followed them in 1910 when twenty-two. He married Theresa Záhorec in Chicago on 25 May 1913. Theresa, born in Nemšova to Josef Záhorec and Julia Papiérniková, arrived in America in 1905 when she was fifteen. She made the journey alone and settled with her older sister in the same neighborhood in which the Cernys lived. John and Theresa's first child was born 16 March 1914 in Chicago. She was named Aemilia but was called Emily. She filed a delayed birth certificate in 1969 that legalized her name change. Information cited on the delayed birth record included her baptismal record from St. Joseph's Catholic Church, dated 29 March 1914, and affidavits given by her father John P. Cerny and her sister Mary C. Cerny Clemens.

I became interested in tracing ancestry while my grandparents were still living. They were able to tell me where they were born and when they arrived in this country, as well as offer insight into their family histories in Czechoslovakia. Unfortunately, others develop an interest in ancestry long after their eastern European immigrant forebears have died. They have to go through the difficult process of determining the name of the town where the immigrants were born or lived prior to arriving in this country before research in Europe can begin. Such was the case when Emily Cerny's son and his wife became interested in tracing their ancestry.

Emily Cerny married John Joseph Wieruszewski on 23 May 1936 in Chicago. John Joseph Jr., their only child, was born on 22 March 1938 in Chicago and married Carol Ann Marszewski there on 18 July 1959. John's and Carol's paternal ancestors were from Poland and their maternal ancestors were from Czechoslovakia. Family members estimated that each immigrant ancestor arrived in the United States between 1900 and 1915.

John Joseph Wieruszewski Sr. died in Chicago on 8 August 1946 after a short illness. His death certificate states that he was born 27 January 1914 in Chicago and that his parents were James Wieruszewski and Agnes Zmarzlewski, natives of Poland. The only information that conflicted with family data was his father's name. Family members said that John's father was named Ignatius instead of James.

Chicago maintained birth records in 1914 and John Wieruszewski's was found under a variant spelling–"Vieruszewski." He was born 29 January in Chicago, the third child of Ignatz Wieruszewski and Agnes Zmarzlewski, both natives of Prussia. Ignatz, a machinist, was thirty-six and his wife thirty-two at the time of John's birth. They were living at 1015 Thirty-Second Street in Chicago.

Ignatz died in Chicago on 22 August 1962. His death record states that he was born in Poland on 24 July 1878 and that his parents' names were unknown. It is not unusual for death records to list only the country of birth, though some are more exact in listing the town, city, or province. When death records do not supply the needed information, searches must be made of church records, census enumerations, obituary notices, and naturalization records.

The 1900 U.S. Census revealed that Ignaz arrived in America in 1899. Immigrants had to meet certain residency requirements before naturalization.

After three years, a declaration of intent to become a citizen was filed with the court, and after five years residency, a petition for naturalization was submitted. If the immigrant met the requirements established by law, citizenship was granted. The earliest date Ignatz could have been naturalized was 1904. A card file of Cook County naturalizations listed the following for Ignac [sic] Wieruszewski:

> Ignac Wieruszewski 1015 W. 32nd St. Chicago, Illinois
> Certificate #P-12760 Superior Court, Cook Co., Ill.
> Country of Birth/Allegiance: Poland-Russia
> When Born: 7/25/76
> Date and Port of Arrival in U.S.: 1899
> Date of Naturalization: July 13, 1914
> Names and Addresses of Witnesses:
>> Stephen Ciesielski 1032 W. 32nd St., Chicago, Ill.
>> Martin Corski 914 W. 32nd St., Chicago, Ill.

Ignatz Wierusewski's naturalization papers contained his birthplace and residence prior to immigrating to the United States. He stated that he was born 25 July 1876 at Tesesaw, Russia and that he emigrated from Bremen on 1 May 1899, arriving at Baltimore on 14 May 1899 on the vessel *Bane*. His wife, Agnes, was born in Brzesie, Germany, and had given birth to the following children:

> Mary Wieruszewski born 1 Oct 1910 at Chicago, Illinois
> Frank Wieruszewski born 28 Nov 1912 at Chicago, Illinois
> John Wieruszewski born 29 Jan 1914 at Chicago, Illinois

Ignatz was described as 71 inches tall, caucasian, fair complexion, brown hair, blue eyes, and weighing 165 pounds. He resided at Wujein, Germany prior to immigration. He was naturalized 14 July 1914 in Chicago.

Carol Ann Marszewski's parents were Edward M. Marszewski and Anna Csicvara. Her mother was born 12 July 1915 in Chicago to John and Mary Csicvara. Mary's naturalization papers were on file in the Cook County Superior Court and included the following information:

Certificate of Arrival

U. S. Department of Justice Immigration and Naturalization Service
No. 11-341261

Know that the immigration records show that the alien named below arrived at the port, and in the manner shown, and was lawfully admitted to the United States of America:

Name: Ondyk, Marya
Port of Entry: New York, NY, August 16, 1913, SS Amerika.

Petition for Naturalization

Name: Mary Csicvara   Address: 5538 S. Rockwell St., Chicago, Ill.
Occupation: Housewife   Age: 48 years   Birthdate: 13 Dec 1894
Birthplace: Mlinarovic, Czechoslovakia   Sex: Female   Color: White
Complexion: Dark   Eyes: Brown   Hair: Black   Ht: 5'2"
Weight: 180   Race: White   Nationality: Czechoslovakian
Husband's Name: John   Marriage Date & Place: 25 Oct 1914, Chicago
Husband's Birthplace: Mlinarovic, Czechoslovakia
Husband's Birthdate: 26 Jan 1897
Husband's Date and Place of Arrival in U.S.: 8 Jan 1910, New York
Husband's Naturalization Date & Place: 27 Nov 1925, Chicago

Children:
Anna Csicvara	b. 12 Jul 1915	Chicago, Illinois
Mary Csicvara	b. 27 Jan 1917	Chicago, Illinois
John Csicvara	b. 01 Dec 1918	Chicago, Illinois
Sophia Csicvara	b. 08 Dec 1919	Chicago, Illinois
George Csicvara	b. 20 Feb 1924	Chicago, Illinois
Rose Csicvara	b. 18 Feb 1922	Chicago, Illinois
Margaret Csicvara	b. 10 Feb 1934	Chicago, Illinois

Residence Prior to Immigration: Mlinarovic, Czechoslovakia
Port of Emigration: Hamburg, Germany

RESEARCH IN EASTERN EUROPE

Research in Poland and Czechoslovakia cannot be accomplished without knowing the exact place of residence or birth of an immigrant ancestor. Once you know that information, Polish research can be conducted by searching records available in the United States or by correspondence. The Genealogical Library of the LDS Church in Salt Lake City has an extensive collection of vital records for most of Poland, including both church and civil records. Their record collection was microfilmed at the Polish State Archives and at other church and state archives outside of Poland. The collection does not include records for every location, nor does it include many vital records dated after 1870. If the location for which you are seeking records is not included in their collection, you can write to one of the Polish archives or the parish where your ancestors lived to request the information you need:

POLISH ARCHIVE ADDRESSES

1. Naczelna Dyrekcja Archiwow Panstwowych, ul. Dluga 6 skr. poczt. 1005, 00-950 Warszawa, Poland. The Polish State Archives has records for many locations that have not yet been filmed.

2. Archiwum Glowne Akt Dawnych, ul. Dluga 7, 00-950 Warszawa, Poland. The Main Archive of Ancient Documents has records from the former Polish territories ceded to the Soviet Union after World War II.

3. Urzad stanu cywilnego Prezydium, Dzielnicowej Rady Narodowej, Nowy Swiat 18-20, Warszaw-Srodmiescie, Poland. The presidium of the National Workers Council has records less than 100 years old in the Zabuzanski collection.

Czechoslovakian research cannot be accomplished in the United States. That country's records have not been microfilmed, and there is no indication that they will be in the near future. Research can be approached in only a few ways. If your family has maintained contact with relatives in Czechoslovakia, they may be willing and able to search records housed at local and regional archives for you, as well as local parishes and cemeteries. While their efforts in your behalf are surely appreciated, you must keep in mind that they are not professional record searchers or genealogists and may overlook important information.

Records attesting to birth, death, and marriage in Czechoslovakia have been removed from local record offices and placed in regional and local archives. Provisions have been made to permit searches of these records for genealogical purposes. Foreigners are allowed to search the records in person; however, since they are no longer in local records offices, it will take considerable time to track them down. Thus, the best approach is to go through the Consular Division of the Czechoslovak Embassy in Washington, D.C.

Two different services are offered. The first provides certificates of birth, marriage, or death for a particular ancestor. The second provides in-depth research at a rate of $12 per hour by a trained record searcher. Paid research is the best approach to take. Information is extracted and then checked by a supervisor. Copies of the records in which your ancestors were found recorded are not provided. Extracts of the genealogical information in each record are usually in Bohemian or Slovakian.

Before research can begin, you must provide some identifying information about the ancestor(s) of interest. The Czechoslovakian Embassy requests that application forms be used for clarity. The application currently used is shown below:

Application for Genealogical Research from Czechoslovakia in the Form
of Running Account
Žádost o Vyhledání Navazujících

Genealogických Inforaci Obsahujících Plné Výpisy z Matrik

Reference/File number of any previous correspondence with Czechoslovakian Embassy:

   1. Name and address of applicant:
   2. Name of person to be researched:
      Date of birth:

Place of birth (specific town or village):
Further identify the birthplace with the name of the county, the parish, or a larger town nearby:
Name of father:
Maiden name of mother:
Religion:

The most important items are name, date, and place. The date can be approximated.

3. Other information available about the person (such as date and place of death, if in Czechoslovakia, etc.):
4. Relatives of the person being researched. (This is optional but often very helpful.)
    a) Husband or Wife

Name:	Date of birth:	Place:
	Date of marriage:	Place:

    b) Children

Name:	Date of birth:	Place:

    c) Brothers and Sisters

Name:	Date of birth:	Place:

5. Sources:

[ ]   Please provide birth dates of all brothers and sisters of direct-line ancestors. Prosím, vyhledejte též narození všech souronzencu přímých předků.

[ ]   Please research direct-line ancestors only. Prosim, vyhledejte pouze předky přímých linek.

Deposit: $ Limit (if any): $ Date:
Additional Comments:

Research in the form of a running account requires a deposit of $30. If you have a limited budget you will want to set a limit on the amount of research you are willing to pay for. Before sending you the research results, the embassy will bill you for the difference between your deposit and the cost of the research performed. When they receive payment (cashier's check or money order) they will forward your research file. It usually takes about six months to receive a reply to your request. It is important to remember that you are paying for research hours and not specified results. If you provide faulty information and time is spent searching the wrong records, you will be charged for the time it took to do so. Do not attempt to put more than one ancestor on an application form; submit a separate form for each person you want them to work on. Send your completed application form to: Embassy of the Czechoslovak Socialist Republic, Consular Division, 3900 Linnean Avenue N.W., Washington, DC 20008.

IRISH IMMIGRANT ANCESTORS

There were only 44,000 persons of Irish descent in the United States when the first federal census was taken in 1790, mostly Scotch-Irish who arrived from Ulster after 1715. The number of Irish immigrants increased steadily until 1845 when the Great Irish Potato Famine began. Farmers began to harvest the 1845 potato crop and found that potatoes quickly decomposed into a black gelatin like substance. Animals died after eating the rotten potatoes and people became seriously ill. The famine lasted over ten years and caused the death of a million people. Another million left Ireland, most emigrating to the United States by taking advantage of low-cost steerage fares. They were packed into ships infested with typhus and other diseases. An estimated fifteen percent of those booking passage died before arriving at an American port. One commissioner for emigration wrote, "If crosses and tombs could be erected on water, the whole route of the emigrant vessels from Europe to America would long since have assumed the appearance of a crowded cemetery."[1]

Those who survived the voyage settled throughout the country. Irish population centers sprang up in Boston, New York, Albany, and Philadelphia, while thousands of families participated in settling the frontier. They arrived at a time when immigration and naturalization laws were more relaxed than those regulating the arrival of immigrants after 1905. The immigration and naturalization records produced during that earlier period contain fewer details of the immigrant's birthplace or residence prior to arriving in this country. For years it was practically impossible to identify an Irish ancestor in the passenger list of a ship arriving at New York because they were unindexed. Ira Glazier's and Michael Tepper's *The Famine Immigrants* (Baltimore: Genealogical Publishing Co., 1983) is a series of volumes listing Irish immigrants to this country during the famine by year of arrival. Not all of the famine years have been published; subsequent volumes will be released upon completion. But what about Irish ancestors who arrived before or after the famine?

It is much harder to determine the birthplace or residence of an Irish immigrant than for most other immigrant groups. They arrived much earlier than the eastern Europeans whose naturalization documents specify their date and place of birth and their residence at the time of emigration. Determining the origins of an Irish ancestor means digging deeply for clues.

James Connell was an Irish immigrant who was living in Greeley County, Nebraska when the 1900 census was taken. The census disclosed that he arrived in the United States in 1845, just prior to massive Irish famine immigration. Based on his children's birth data in the census, he lived in Illinois between 1859 and 1874. He would have been about nineteen years old when he came to America.

---

1. Peter Collier and David Horowitz, *The Kennedys: An American Drama* (New York: Summit Books, 1984), pp. 21-22.

James's death record stated that he was born in Ireland in 1826 to James Connell whose wife's maiden name was McNulty. He was naturalized in La Salle County, Illinois on 5 November 1860 after declaring his intention to become a citizen in the Court of Common Pleas for the City of New York on 8 December 1851. His naturalization records stated only his country of prior allegiance. The death records of James's children gave his birthplace as Ireland. Other Connell death records in Nebraska state that James had at least three sisters living in the United States: Catherine, Anna, and Margaret.

Every available record in the places James Connell's family lived in the United States was searched to gather as many facts as possible. Research trips were taken to the counties where they lived to locate records not available in library collections. Hundreds of details were logged, analyzed, and re-analyzed. In the end only one remote clue seemed promising. The 1925 Iowa State Census of Des Moines revealed that Julia Lynch, age fifty, born in Ireland, daughter of Patrick Lynch and Kitty Connell was a niece of James Connell.

Julia Lynch was born at a time when Ireland registered births, marriages, and deaths, and her birth may have taken place in the same town where her mother was born. An intense study of Ireland's birth and marriage indexes failed to produce a record of her birth or her parent's marriage. Assuming that she was not the oldest child born to Patrick and Catherine, every entry for a child with the Lynch surname was examined and an entry for the birth of Patrick Lynch, son of Patrick Lynch and Catherine Connell was found in the 1864 index. He was born in Pollakeel Township, Parish of Kilbride, Barony of Clanmahon, County Cavan.

The death records incorrectly stated that Catherine Connell lived in the United States. She was still in Ireland in 1901 when the census was taken. She was a widow and lived in the same place her son Patrick was born. Her age was listed as sixty-one and her birthplace County Meath. Catherine married Patrick Lynch in Old Castle Parish, County Meath on 19 May 1862. These facts provided a starting point for research in Ireland that will eventually lead to pinpointing James Connell's birthplace and parentage.

It is important to investigate every relative of an immigrant ancestor when records fail to give specific reference to that ancestor's origins. If that ancestor was not accompanied by relatives, look closely at neighbors and friends who might have come from the same place. The important things to remember are to search every available record source, not to give up until you have accomplished that end, and to analyze each piece of information for every possible clue.

Index

A

abstracts,
contents of, 102
importance of, 101-02
Accelerated Indexing Systems Index,
contents of, 55
errors in, 55, 137
uses of, 55
account books,
example of, 260
information in, 260
Act of Parliament of 1751, 17, 20
adoption records, 133
affidavits,
example of, 147
AIS, *See* Accelerated Indexing Systems
Index.
ancestor,
collateral, 22
common, 22
direct, 24
Ancestry, Inc., 85

B

batch numbers (International Genealogical Index),
explanation of, 52, 54
Bible records, 136
*Bibliography of County Histories of the
3,111 Counties of the Forty-Eight
States,* 269
bills of sale, 336
information in, 146
locating, 337
biographies,
analyzing, 163-64, 178, 180-81, 190, 196,
199
discrepancies in, 181
example of, 162-63, 178-79, 190
information in, 162, 164, 178, 180, 190,

196, 262
military, 258
using, 212
birth records, 108, 132, 281
compiling of, 135
errors in, 118-19
See also records, birth.
birthdates,
determining, 180
black ancestry,
researching, 330, 332, 334-38
See also slave ancestry.
book reviews,
research by, 59
boundary changes,
discrepancies in, 122
importance of, 57
See also gores.
Bureau of Pensions, 324
burned records,
alternative sources to, 267, 270

C

cemeteries,
researching, 175, 263, 278
cemetery records,
analyzing, 204, 207
example of, 207
obtaining, 113-14
researching, 145
using, 207, 218
women in, 278
census indexes,
information in, 137-38
census maps,
uses of, 57
census records,
analyzing, 143, 150, 156-57, 159-60, 166,
168, 172, 174, 187, 191, 193-94,
204-05, 208-09, 219-20
at the Genealogical Library of the LDS
Church, 110

at the Regional Federal Archives and
Records Center, 110
circumstantial evidence in, 136
common surnames in, 246, 248
contents of, 109-10
destruction of, 110
development of, 109
discrepancies in, 160, 175
errors in, 144, 157
evidence in, 144
example of, 186, 193, 208-09, 218-20
Germans in, 340
importance of, 119
information in, 137, 143, 156-57, 159,
166, 168, 172, 174, 186, 204
migration patterns in, 168-69
searching, 156
using, 159, 176, 218
census soundex, 141
censuses,
state, 160
certificates of marriage,
example of, 183
Cherokee ancestry,
documentation of, 323
proof of, 324-25, 328-30
researching, 323-25, 328-29
Cherokee Indians,
treaties with, 325
Cherokee records,
information in, 325
researching, 323, 326, 328
Chicago Manual of Style, 98
church records,
as a substitute for vital records, 109
biographical information in, 176
Colonial Virginia, 302, 305
contents of, 108-09
example of, 176
Germans in, 339, 342
slaves in, 336
using, 176
variety of, 108-09
circumstantial evidence, 133-34, 136,
144-45, 151, 175
See also indirect evidence.
citation, *See* documentation.
civil records,
Colonial Virginia, 302
Civil War,
ancestors in, 293-94, 296
record losses during, 262, 267
research in, 332
*Civil War Pension Application File In-
dex*, 166, 296
information in, 160
using, 294, 324
Civil War records,
analyzing, 188

information in, 187-88
using, 160
Cleveland Public Library,
periodicals at, 79
collateral ancestor,
definition of, 22
colonial papers,
researching, 306
colonial traders,
records left by, 261
Colonial Virginia,
ancestors in, 305-06
records losses in, 302
research in, 301-04
common ancestors,
definition of, 22
determining of, 23
common surnames,
family sources for, 240
in the International Genealogical Index,
241
library sources for, 240
research strategies for, 239, 247-49,
255-56
congressional records, 289
example of, 277
women in, 276, 278
correspondence,
analyzing, 165, 169, 199, 203, 214
contents of, 33
costs of, 36
discrepancies in, 203
example of, 33, 199, 201
field research, 47
information in, 169, 203, 214
with public officials, 33, 47, 145, 175,
182
with relatives, 32, 71, 157, 165, 199,
201, 214, 216
correspondence logs,
example of, 95
uses of, 93
corroboration,
importance of, 119
county histories,
analyzing, 163-65, 214
example of, 162
information in, 162-64, 182, 214
using, 212
county records, 321
court records,
contents of, 113
Colonial Virginia, 302, 304-05
Kentucky, 321
limitations of, 320
Czech ancestors,
researching, 346-47, 349-51
Czech records,
applying for, 350

researching, 350-51
DAR Patriot Index, 287, 289
women in, 280

D

DAR, *See* Daughters of the American
  Revolution.
dates,
  changes in, 17-19
  determining, 16-17
  double, 21
  errors in, 17
  estimating, 16-17
  from tombstones, 19
  importance of, 11
  Old Style/New Style explanation, 17
  rectifying of, 18-19
"Dates and the Calendar," 16
Daughters of the American Revolution,
  record transcription by, 268-69, 287
  women's records by, 280
Dawes Commission, 326
death certificates,
  example of, 135
  information in, 135
death records, 108
  analyzing, 176, 190
  compiling of, 135
  errors in, 119, 353
  example of, 135, 189
  information in, 136, 189, 344, 347
  researching, 341, 353
  See also records, death.
deception,
  discrepancies from, 123
deed indexes,
  common surnames in, 248-49
  search strategies for, 248-49
degree of relationship,
  definition of, 22
  determining of, 22-24
  See also relationship.
direct ancestors,
  determining of, 24
direct evidence, 66, 121, 124, 133,
  136-37, 166
  definition of, 117
*Directory of Genealogical Societies in the
  USA and Canada,* 41
discrepancies,
  charting of, 124
  evolution of, 121-22
  examples of, 122-23
  from deception, 123
documentation,
  examples of, 97
  importance of, 97, 99, 105

sources for, 98
style of, 98-99
thoroughness of, 98
double dates,
  analyzing, 196
  information in, 194
  recording of, 21
  use of, 21
  See also dates, double.

E

*Encyclopedia of American Quaker
  Genealogy,*
  using, 195
Enrollment of Soldiers Act of 1883, 160
Essex Institute, 297
estate records,
  analyzing, 146, 204, 210, 215-16, 222-24
  at the Genealogical Library of the LDS
    Church, 111
  Colonial Virginia, 305
  contents of, 110
  development of, 110
  example of, 222
  information in, 263
  using, 191, 210, 215, 222-24
evidence,
  circumstantial, 119-20, 133-34, 136,
    144-45, 151, 175
  compiling of, 115
  direct, 66, 116, 121, 124, 133, 136-37
  importance of, 115-16
  in census records, 119
  indirect, 66, 116, 119-20, 124
  preponderance of, 120-21
extract checklist, 249

F

family associations,
  activities of, 202
  example of, 202
  records by, 202, 208
family group records,
  completing, 87
  example of, 89
  uses of, 87
Family Group Records Archives
  (FGRA),
  contents of, 50
  example from, 194
  using, 156-57, 194
family records, 128
  as sources for occupation, 261
  errors in, 118

interpreting, 118
  See also records, family.
family sources, 61
  checklist of, 62-63
  searching, 66
family traditions,
  definition of, 117
  fallacies in, 79-80, 83-84
  importance of, 79
  verifying of, 79-82, 84
Famine Immigrants, The, 352
field research,
  correspondence for, 47-48
  guides to, 48
  planning for, 47
finding aids,
  examples of, 78
Five Civilized Tribes, 326
footnotes,
  research by, 59
footnoting, *See* documentation.
Freedman's Bureau,
  records of, 331, 338
French and Indian War,
  ancestors in, 304-05
frontier records,
  researching, 311, 320-22

G

genealogical correspondence, 61, 66
  queries in, 71
Genealogical Helper, 32, 49
  surname indexes in, 77
  vendors in, 42
Genealogical Library of the LDS
  Church, 150, 157, 296, 298
  census records at, 110
  estate records at, 111
  filming burned records, 267
  frontier records at, 320
  German records at, 342
  land records at, 111
  limitations of, 321
  midwife journals at, 276
  military records at, 112
  pension files at, 112
  Polish records at, 349
  probate records at, 111
  records at, 36, 129, 145, 195, 213, 336
  Revolutionary War records at, 287, 289
  women's records at, 278
genealogical materials,
  where to buy, 85
genealogical periodicals,
  indexes to, 78-79
genealogical publishing, 99
genealogical records,

types of, 117-18
  vendors of, 36-39
Genealogist, The, 98
genealogists, *See* professional genealogists.
Genealogy as Pastime and Profession,
  16
Genealogy Tomorrow,
  queries in, 71
generalities,
  discrepancies in, 122-23
geography,
  as a genealogical tool, 25, 27, 29-30
  importance of, 30, 306
German ancestry,
  researching, 339-40, 343, 345-46
gores,
  definition of, 58
  examples of, 58
guardianship papers,
  analyzing, 148
  example of, 149
  information in, 148
Guion Miller Rolls,
  documenting Cherokee ancestry with,
  326

H

half relationships,
  definition of, 25
Hamburg Passenger Lists, 341, 344
Handy Book for Genealogists, The, 57,
  269
historical preservation, 262
histories,
  county, 162-64, 182, 212, 214
history archives,
  women in, 278
Holbrook Institute, 298
home sources, 61
  checklist of, 61, 62-63
  searching, 66
homestead application files,
  analyzing, 152
  information in, 152
"How to Hire a Professional Genealogist," 43
how-to books,
  contents of, 58-59
  examples of, 59

I

IGI, *See* Internatonal Genealogical
  Index.
immigration records,
  information in, 347-48

indents,
  index to, 290
  information in, 289-92
  solutions in, 292-93
Index of Revolutionary War Pension Applications in the National Archives, 112, 287, 289
Index to Some of the Family Records of the Southern States, 269
indexes,
  census, 141
  county, 268
  deed, 248
  marriage, 246
  orphans' court, 251
  passenger list, 56
  statewide, 56
  surname, 77
  Work Projects Administration, 57
indirect evidence, 66, 105, 116, 119-20, 124
  in printed sources, 119
industrial records,
  women in, 276
interlibrary loan,
  how to use, 36
International Genealogical Index, 15, 132
  batch numbers, 52, 54
  common surnames in, 241
  contents of, 49, 52
  examples from, 51, 53
  guides to, 55
  organization of, 50, 52
  using, 50, 156-57
  vital records in, 298
interviews,
  family, 67
  family friends, 70
  guides to, 70-71
  importance of, 67, 70
  preparation for, 67
  questions for, 67-70
Irish ancestors,
  immigration of, 352
  researching, 352-53

J

Jacobus, Donald Lines, 16
jurisdictional history,
  importance of, 269

K

Kentucky,
  settlement of, 307, 320

L

land records,
  analyzing, 151, 191, 213
  at the Genealogical Library of the LDS Church, 111
  Colonial Virginia, 305
  types of, 111
  using, 213
legal briefs,
  as alternatives to burned records, 268
lineage charts,
  completing, 87
  example of, 86
  uses of, 87
Los Angeles Public Library,
  periodicals at, 79

M

Map Guide to the U.S. Federal Censuses, 1790-1920, 57
marriage indexes,
  common surnames in, 246
marriage records,
  analyzing, 150, 156, 160, 165, 186, 203-04
  discrepancies in, 182
  Colonial Virginia, 305
  example of, 182, 186, 206, 218
  information in, 189, 280
  researching, 325
  types of, 108
  using, 206, 218
marriage records, 133
Maryland,
  settlement of, 307
Master Index to the New York State DAR Genealogical Records, 269
middle names,
  development of, 13
midwifery,
  genealogical records of, 276
migration,
  clues to, 308, 311
  routes of, 306-08
  U.S. internal, 306-11, 341
  See also migration routes.
migration patterns,
  analyzing, 169
migration routes,
  examples of, 308-11
  maps illustrating, 312-19
military records, 258-59, 270
  at the Genealogical Library of the LDS Church, 112
  at the National Archives, 113
  compilations of, 258

contents of, 112
development of, 111-12
examples of, 258
research in, 257
variety of, 112
military service records,
information in, 293
See also pension application files.
mortality records, 143
mortality schedules,
common surnames in, 247

N

name changes,
clues in, 14-15
confusion from, 13
legal, 16
patterns of, 13-14
researching, 14
names,
changes in, 13-16
English, 12
importance of, 11
in the Middle Ages, 11
middle, 13
patterns of, 11, 13
naming patterns,
importance of, 11, 13
New England, 297, 299
National Archives, 152, 166, 324
Civil War records at, 294
military records at, 113
pension applications at, 289
records at, 36
women's records at, 278
National Genealogical Society, 112
National Genealogical Society Library,
periodicals at, 79
National Genealogical Society Quarterly,
98
National Society of the Daughters of
the American Revolution, *See*
Daughters of the American Revolution.
*National Union Catalog of Manuscript
Collections*,
contents of, 240
naturalization records,
example of, 348
information in, 344, 348
New England,
ancestors in, 306
researching in, 297, 299
New England Historic Genealogical Society, 297
*New England Historical and Genealogi-
cal Register*, 98
New Netherlands,
settlement of, 307

New Style dates,
explanation of, 17-18
New Year's Day, 20
rectifying of, 19
use of, 18
See also dates, changes in.
New Year's Day,
changes of, 19-20
determination of, 19-20
New York Public Library,
periodicals at, 79
newspaper records, 270
newspapers,
genealogical information in, 151
North Carolina,
settlement of, 307
notekeeping,
sources for, 96
systems of, 96-97
NUCMC, *See* National Union Catalog of
Manuscript Collections.

O

obituaries,
analyzing, 180-81
discrepancies in, 181
examples of, 265
information in, 178, 180, 265
researching, 341
occupation,
as a source to research on women, 275
research by, 60
search strategies for, 257, 261-62
sources for, 257, 259-61
Old Court House Museum (Vicksburg),
263-64, 336
Old Style dates,
explanation of, 17-18
New Year's Day, 20
rectifying of, 19
See also dates, changes in.
oral history, 128
development of, 67
problems with, 70
questions for, 67-69
organization,
importance of, 85, 102-03
original sources,
uses of, 105
Orphan Voyage,
names from, 32
orphans,
finding, 144
orphans' court records,
common surnames in, 251
example of, 251
ownership of research materials, 99

P

Parish and Vital Records Listings, 52,
241, 298
parish records,
Germans in, 342, 345
Passenger and Immigration Lists Index,
56
passenger list indexes,
contents of, 56
examples of, 56
passenger lists,
example of, 341, 344
researching, 341
patronymics,
use of, 12
Pennsylvania,
settlement of, 307
pension application files,
analyzing, 166, 188
information in, 166, 187-89, 288-89, 293
researching, 287, 293
solutions in, 294
See also military service records.
pension files,
at the Genealogical Library of the LDS
Church, 112
at the National Archives, 112-13
contents of, 112
importance of, 80
information in, 294-96, 324
periodicals,
genealogical, 78
personal papers,
common surnames in, 241
phonetic variations,
discrepancies from, 124
places,
definition of, 25
importance of, 11
places, 27, 29-30
plagiarism, 99
plantation owners,
records left by, 261
plantation records, 330-31
contents of, 66
information in, 261
slaves in, 335
Polish ancestors,
researching, 349
Polish records,
addresses for, 349
preponderance of evidence,
definition of, 120-21
primary sources, *See* direct evidence.
printed sources, 117
date changes in, 21
usefulness of, 298
See also sources, printed.

Privacy Act, 132
probate records,
analyzing, 146, 148, 166, 204, 207
at the Genealogical Library of the LDS
Church, 111
common surnames in, 251
contents of, 110
example of, 207, 251, 255
information in, 145-46
research strategies for, 251
slaves in, 334, 336-38
types of, 110
using, 191, 207
professional genealogists,
credentials of, 43
evaluation of, 47
grievances against, 47
guides to, 44-46
hiring, 42
sources of, 44-46
professional genealogy, 79-80, 141, 146
property records,
analyzing, 151
public records, 117
errors in, 118
examples of, 259
research in, 259
women in, 275
See also records, public.
public servants,
records left by, 259
Pullman Company,
records left by, 276

Q

Quaker dating system,
explanation of, 20-21
queries,
examples of, 76
in *Genealogical Helper*, 71
in *Genealogy Tomorrow*, 71
in *Tri-State Trader*, 71
through genealogy societies, 71
usefulness of, 71
quitclaim deeds, 271

R

record sources,
knowledge of, 101
recordkeeping,
development of, 105
records,
adoption, 133
analyzing, 176
Bible, 136

birth, 108, 118-19, 132, 135, 281
burned, 267-68, 270
cemetery, 113, 145, 204, 207, 218, 278
census, 109, 137, 141, 143-44, 150,
    156-57, 159, 166, 168, 172, 174, 176,
    186-87, 191, 193-94, 204-05, 208-09,
    218-20, 246, 248, 340
Cherokee, 323-24, 326, 328-29
church, 108-09, 176, 302, 306, 336,
    339, 342
Civil War, 160, 187-88, 264-65, 302
congressional, 276, 289
county, 321
court, 113, 268, 302, 304-05, 320-21
Czech, 350
death, 108, 119, 135-36, 189, 341, 344,
    347, 353
estate, 110, 146, 148, 191, 204, 210,
    215-16, 223-24, 263, 305-06
family, 118, 128, 261
family association, 202
frontier, 311, 320-22
immigration, 348
industrial, 276
land, 111, 151, 191, 213, 305-06
marriage, 108, 133, 150, 156, 160, 165,
    182, 186, 189, 203-04, 206, 218, 271,
    306, 325
military, 111, 112, 257-59, 270
mortality, 143
naturalization, 344, 248
newspaper, 270
non-courthouse, 269
orphans' court, 251
parish, 342, 345
plantation, 66, 261, 331, 335
Polish, 349
probate, 110, 145-46, 148, 166, 191, 204,
    207, 251, 334-38
property, 151
protection of, 270
public, 117-18, 259, 275
Quaker, 21
recopied, 268-69, 271
slaves, 331
tax, 221, 276
vendors of, 36-39
vital, 108, 297-98, 301
Regional Federal Archives and Records
    Center, 152, 296
    census records at, 110, 137
    federal court case files at, 268
    Revolutionary War records at, 287, 289
Regional Veteran's Administration
    Center,
    documents at, 294
registries,
    surname, 71
relationships,

determining, 21, 22-24, 116, 297-98
guide to, 26
half, 25
importance of, 11, 21, 116
in-law 25,
proof of, 169, 172, 176, 191, 194, 299,
    301
step, 25
research,
    documentation of, 97
    organization of, 85, 93, 102-03
    professional, 79-80
    success in, 100, 103
research calendar,
    for tracing common surnames, 247
research calendars,
    completing, 90, 92-93
    example of, 91
    uses of, 90
research extracts,
    example of, 94
    uses of, 93
research services,
    directories to, 40
    exchanging of, 40
    genealogical society, 41
    library, 41
    sources of, 40
research strategy,
    for finding women, 280-82, 286
    formulating, 156, 168, 190, 199, 203,
        212, 216
Revolutionary War,
    ancestors in, 287-88, 290-92

S

search services,
    availability of, 42
    professional, 42
    public agency, 42
    See also research services.
secondary sources, *See* indirect
    evidence.
slave ancestry,
    bills of sale for, 336-37
    clues to, 332-33
    enumerations of, 332
    researching, 330, 332-35, 337-38
slave bills of sale,
    examples of, 263
slave records, 331
*Some Marriages in the Burned Records
    Counties of Virginia,* 269
soundex, 141
source checklists,
    example of, 106-07
    uses of, 93
source guides,

contents of, 58
 using, 59
sources,
 family, 61, 66
 home, 61, 66
 original, 105
 printed, 21, 117, 119, 298
 secondary, 105
source guides,
 examples of, 58
Source: A Guidebook of American Genealogy, The, 98, 135, 151-52, 346
 record sources in, 59, 98, 101, 113
South Carolina,
 settlement of, 307
spelling variants,
 problems with, 13-14
 resolving, 15, 182
 See also name changes.
state archives,
 records available at, 270
state censuses,
 using, 160
state histories,
 analyzing, 190
 information in, 190
statewide indexes,
 examples of, 56
step relationships,
 definition of, 25
strategy,
 formulating, 156, 168, 190, 199, 203, 212, 216
surname indexes,
 examples of, 77-78
 in *Genealogical Helper*, 77
surname registries,
 table of, 72-76
surnames,
 characteristic, 12
 common, 239-41
 development of, 12
 occupational, 12
 place, 12

T

tax records,
 analyzing, 221
 example of, 221, 276
 women in, 276
telephone genealogy,
 domestic interviews, 32
 international interviews, 32
 sources for, 31
Tennessee,
 settlement of, 307

title companies,
 abstracts from, 268
 addresses of, 268
tombstones, 263
 analyzing, 176
 dates from, 19
 discrepancies with, 176
 information from, 145, 175, 336
 researching, 169
tombstones, 263
township map,
 example of, 211
"Tracing the Original Source of an IGI Batch Number," 52
tradesmen,
 records left by, 260
traditions,
 family, 79
Tri-State Trader,
 queries in, 71

U

Union List of Microfilms, 40
Union List of Newspapers, 40
Union List of Serials, 40

V

variant spelling, *See* spelling variants.
Virginia, Colonial, *See* Colonial Virginia.
Virginia Company, 301
Visiting Friends, 48
vital records, 298
 development of, 108
 information in, 297, 301

W

"What to Expect from Professional Research," 43
Where to Write for Vital Records: Births, Deaths, Marriages, and Deaths, 108, 135
wills,
 analyzing, 169, 216, 222-24
 examining, 210
 examples of, 222, 333
 information in, 169, 215
 using, 215-16, 222-24
women,
 in cemetery records, 278
 in congressional records, 278
 in history archives, 278
 in industrial records, 276
 in public records, 275
 in tax records, 276

maiden name research for, 281
occupations of, 276
research problems with, 275
research strategies for, 280-82, 286
Work Projects Administration Indexes,
    compiling of, 57
*WPA Historical Records Survey: A
Guide to the Unpublished Inventories,
Indexes, and Transcripts*, 57